LGBTQ+ History in High School Classes in the United States since 1990

Also available from Bloomsbury

Feminist Research for 21st-Century Childhoods: Common Worlds Methods
edited by B. Denise Hodgins
Feminists Researching Gendered Childhoods: Generative Entanglements edited
by Jayne Osgood and Kerry H. Robinson
Gender in an Era of Post-truth Populism edited by Penny Jane Burke, Rosalind
Gill, Akane Kanai, and Julia Coffey
Navigating Trans and Complex Gender Identities by Jamison Green, Rhea
Ashley Hoskin, Cris Mayo, and sj Miller
Progressive Education: A Critical Introduction by John Howlett
*Transnational Feminist Politics, Education, and Social Justice: Post Democracy
and Post Truth* edited by Silvia Edling and Sheila Macrine

LGBTQ+ History in High School Classes in the United States since 1990

Stacie Brensilver Berman

BLOOMSBURY ACADEMIC

LONDON • NEW YORK • OXFORD • NEW DELHI • SYDNEY

BLOOMSBURY ACADEMIC
Bloomsbury Publishing Plc
50 Bedford Square, London, WC1B 3DP, UK
1385 Broadway, New York, NY 10018, USA
29 Earlsfort Terrace, Dublin 2, Ireland

BLOOMSBURY, BLOOMSBURY ACADEMIC and the Diana logo are trademarks of
Bloomsbury Publishing Plc

First published in Great Britain 2022
This paperback edition published 2023

Cover design by Jade Barnett
Cover image © FatCamera/Getty Images

A catalogue record for this book is available from the British Library.

Library of Congress Cataloging-in-Publication Data
Names: Berman, Stacie Brensilver, author.
Title: LGBTQ+History in high school classes in the United States
since 1990 / Stacie Brensilver Berman.
Description: London; New York: Bloomsbury Academic, 2022. |
Includes bibliographical references and index.
Identifiers: LCCN 2021015209 (print) | LCCN 2021015210 (ebook) |
ISBN 9781350177321 (hardback) | ISBN 9781350177338 (pdf) |
ISBN 9781350177345 (epub)
Subjects: LCSH: Sexual minorities in education–United States. | Sexual
minorities–United States–History–20th century. | Sexual
minorities–United States–History–21st century. | History–Study and
teaching (Secondary)–United States. | Education,
Secondary–Curricula–United States. | Homosexuality and
education–United States. | Inclusive education–United States.
Classification: LCC LC2574.5.B47 2022 (print) |
LCC LC2574.5 (ebook) | DDC 371.826/60973–dc23
LC record available at https://lccn.loc.gov/2021015209
LC ebook record available at https://lccn.loc.gov/2021015210

ISBN: HB: 978-1-3501-7732-1
PB: 978-1-3502-2505-3
ePDF: 978-1-3501-7733-8
eBook: 978-1-3501-7734-5

Typeset by Newgen Knowledgeworks Pvt. Ltd., Chennai, India

To find out more about our authors and books visit
www.bloomsbury.com and sign up for our newsletters.

For my father, who wanted me to invest in my future.
And for my daughter, who will benefit from a future in which all children see
themselves in the history they learn.

Contents

Figures

Preface

This book discusses and evaluates organizational, bureaucratic, and pedagogical efforts to incorporate LGBTQ+ history in US history classes. The state of the field is different now than when I began my research in 2013. More teachers are aware of and include this history in their classes—and feel safe discussing their decisions to do so. Five more states have laws mandating LGBTQ+-inclusive curriculum in social studies and other academic subjects; additional counties and districts have similar requirements. Resistance to this inclusion persists; five states continue to have laws prohibiting positive representations of the LGBTQ+ community in public schools. On a national level, though, the absence of and need for LGBTQ+ history in our schools has become a part of the academic and public conversation.

Researching an evolving subject presents opportunities and challenges. I have a "front row" view of history in the making. I'm able to celebrate successes and triumphs with the teachers, scholars, and activists in my professional community as they see their work come to fruition. My research becomes part of the narrative in a topic of increasing importance and ever-present change. I have access to students who feel represented for the first time in their school experience and teachers who realize the necessity of a more complete version of US history. I also find myself constantly updating work that I think is finished and checking sources and facts to make sure that they are still accurate and relevant. For example, just prior to publication a sixth state—Nevada—passed a law requiring schools to include LGBTQ+ history. This book is the product of eight years of work and, therefore, significant and numerous revisions.

This book reflects the state of the field at the time of publication. Though it evaluates LGBTQ+-inclusive history from an historical perspective, it is not a historical subject. The information, ideas, and analysis in the following pages might change, requiring additional research and a new assessment of LGBTQ+ history's place and impact in the classroom. As someone committed to this practice and its benefits, I look forward to the future progress and accomplishments of this topic and its advocates, respectively.

Foreword

It has been many decades since we were high school students. And over the years, some memories from those early classroom experiences have faded. But one thing we both remember quite clearly is that in the history classes of our mid-twentieth-century high schools not a single moment was devoted to what we would today call LGBTQ+ history. And our high schools were not at all unusual in this regard. Back then no matter how "good" the school was, the history curriculum was heteronormative, and you could easily graduate from high school and then college, and even graduate school in history, as we did, without learning a thing about gays and lesbians. You would be led by the curriculum, in fact, to assume all Americans were heterosexual. Ignorance was part and parcel of the repressive world of Cold War America. History seeks to bury what it intends to reject.

Thankfully, the Long 1960s came along and with gay liberation came the beginning of the end of those dark ages, yielding a rich field of scholarship that explores the gay and lesbian experience in the American past. Of course, the break with the hetero-monopoly in the historical profession met with resistance. Lesbian denial was one of the manifestations of that resistance, with conventional historians so blinded by homophobia that no amount of empirical evidence could convince them that prominent women, among them Eleanor Roosevelt, had lesbian relationships.[1] By the end of the twentieth century, however, such resistance was starting to fade and great works were being done in LGBTQ+ history. So today most leading colleges and universities have courses, programs, and faculty focused on that history.

The key battle now, as Stacie Brensilver Berman's pathbreaking book *LGBTQ+ History In High School Classes in the United States since 1990* documents so powerfully, is at the high school level. Here a combination of institutional, political, and pedagogical conservatism has left the history curriculum far behind its university counterpart in exploring LGBTQ+ history. To this day in fact, New York, the state that has landmarked Stonewall, has yet to include a single LGBTQ+ history question on its Regents Exam in US History and Government. But as Berman's study shows, six states do require the teaching of LGBTQ+ history, and a small but dynamic group of inventive and intrepid teachers have been bringing LGBTQ+ history into their classrooms in states whose history standards do not require or even mention it. They do so out of respect for the past and out of hope for a future in which knowledge will replace ignorance and dignity will replace bigotry.[2]

We believe this book will assist teachers, students, and educational policy makers in their work to ensure that coming generations are educated in high school, as we were not, in ways that foster literacy in LGBTQ+ history. Such an education will provide young people with the historical sensibility that can lead to an America liberated from homophobia and committed to a new birth of freedom to explore history in all its sexual, class, and racial diversity and complexity.

Blanche Wiesen Cook and Robert Cohen

Acknowledgments

In 2013, I was a doctoral student at NYU-Steinhardt pondering dissertation topics. I wanted to write about something that would matter to and resonate with students and was not substantively included in the social studies curriculum. Robby Cohen, my mentor and advisor, pulled George Chauncey's *Why Marriage?* off his shelf. He told me to read it, think about the evolution of LGBTQ+ rights, and tell him what I thought. A day later, I knew I would write about the need for LGBTQ+ history in schools. Years later, that conversation evolved into this book. This work would not be possible without Robby's guidance, support, and encyclopedic knowledge. His insight and analysis helped me transform this research into a comprehensive piece of scholarship. This work is a product of the countless hours he spent reading drafts and helping me revise and refine it.

James Fraser is one of the greatest colleagues, teachers, and friends I have ever known. His work with me in the earliest stages helped me flesh out what I wanted to write and establish my thoughts and personal assessment of the state of LGBTQ+-inclusive education. He also consistently, and correctly, reminded me of the need to present a balanced narrative and the ways in which doing so would make this work richer.

Diana Turk has been a colleague, friend, collaborator, and sounding board for over twenty years. None of this work would have happened had she not urged me to apply for NYU's doctoral program and encouraged me to envision a professional life outside of my own classroom. Diana inspires me to reinvent my ideas about pedagogy and pushes me to use my experience and knowledge to help other teachers develop their practice. Our discussions about student agency and transforming the lens through which social studies is taught profoundly influenced this work.

I am fortunate to have an incredible editorial team at Bloomsbury. Mark Richardson, my editor, supported this book from the earliest proposal stages, offering sage advice and suggestions for strengthening the content and context. His enthusiasm, encouragement, and adaptability were invaluable as he guided me through the publication process. Evangeline Stanford answered innumerable questions with patience and grace. Her belief in this book and attention to detail helped in meaningful ways.

The teachers whom I interviewed gave generously of their time and never hesitated to respond when I asked for further clarifications or additional conversations. Courtney Anderson, Danny M. Cohen, Olivia Cole, Fred Fox, Christine Gentry, Mitchell James, Lauren Jensen, Hasmig Minassian, Felicia Perez, Dana Rosenberg, Lyndsey Schlax, Will Scott, Casey Sinclair, and Melanie Wells contributed valuable hours to participating in this research. Beyond that, and more significantly, all of them shared personal experiences, ideas, and history with me, some of which I know were difficult to relate and discuss. I can never thank them enough for the stories they shared and the way in which they trusted me to keep their confidences and do justice to their experiences.

The scholars and activists who helped along the way provided the foundation of my research and consistently offered firsthand, and sometimes cutting-edge, information that would not have been available in other sources. Several people offered their expertise and observations, but a few stand out. Don Romesburg walked me through every detail of developing and passing revisions to California's Framework on multiple occasions and offered to update me each time new advancements occurred. Kevin Jennings was one of the first people to volunteer to speak to me. Debra Fowler and Miriam Morgenstern gave me access to all of the trials and tribulations of starting an organization. Wendy Rouse and Emily Hobson shared their experiences establishing an LGBTQ+-focused teacher education program and teaching LGBTQ+ history, respectively, at the university level. Stephen Thornton shared his work and thoughts on this topic and remains a mentor. Rachel Reinhard, Kristi Rudelius Palmer, and Jinnie Spiegler provided important insights on curriculum development. Daniel Hurewitz brought an immersion in LGBTQ+ history and a commitment to seeing it included in high school curricula to his interaction with my work, offering a perspective that I greatly appreciated. Blanche Wiesen Cook has been an incredible cheerleader and, with Robby Cohen, graciously wrote the foreword to this book.

Olga Margolina created the charts and graphs in the latter chapters, transforming my ideas about conveying information into representative visuals.

I have an incredible personal support system that enables me to fulfill my academic and scholarly goals. My parents Vicki and Alvin Brensilver not only ensured that I could pursue anything and everything I ever wanted, but they also made sure I knew that I could be whatever I hoped to be. My mother's genuine curiosity about my work sustained me through this process; my father, to whom this book is dedicated, would have been so proud to see the finished product. Peter, Stephanie, Miles, and Scarlett are the best brother, sister-in-law, nephew, and niece I could imagine; they teach me new things about love, family, and connection every day. Steven, Adam, Noah, and Josh Berman make me laugh and challenge me to think deeper. My friends, especially those who listened to countless rants about my work and my feelings about it—Marina, Sarah, Jo, Jill, to name a few—are extraordinary. They indulged the times when I needed to work things out aloud and made themselves available whenever I needed moral support.

Lastly, none of this would be possible without Jeff and Mia. Over the past eight years they have been patient and understanding, and the best cheer section for which anyone could ever ask. They have listened to endless hours on the content, analysis, and sources in this study without complaint and looked past the stacks of paper and books that often crowd our apartment. Jeff and Mia literally and figuratively held my hand through every step of this process. This book is in many ways their accomplishment, as well. Their love, smiles, and unconditional support are on every page.

Abbreviations

AB	Assembly Bill
ACT UP	Aids Coalition to Unleash Power
ADL	Anti Defamation League
AHA	American Historical Association
CLAGS	Center for LGBTQ Studies
CLGBTH	Committee on Lesbian, Gay, Bisexual, and Transgender History
CTA	California Teachers' Association
CUNY	City University of New York
EQCA	Equality California
FAIR	Fair, Accurate, Inclusive, and Respectful
FLASH	Family Life and Sexual Health
GLAAD	Gay and Lesbian Alliance Against Defamation
GLF	Gay Liberation Front
GLSEN	Gay, Lesbian, Straight Education Network
GSA	Gay Straight Alliance/Gender Sexuality Alliance
GSAN	Gay Straight Alliance/Gender Sexuality Alliance Network
GSE	Garden State Equality
HB	House Bill
HRC	Human Rights Campaign
HRRC	Human Rights Resource Center
HUE	History Unerased
IQC	Instructional Quality Commission
LAUSD	Los Angeles Unified School District
LGBTQ+	Lesbian, Gay, Bisexual, Transgender, Queer, and beyond
NCSS	National Council for Social Studies
NCTE	National Council of Teachers of English
NEA	National Education Association
PFLAG	Parents and Friends of Lesbians and Gays
ReCAPP	Resource Center for Adolescent Pregnancy Prevention
SB	Senate Bill
UC	University of California

Introduction

In September 2012 *How to Survive a Plague*, David France's Academy Award–nominated documentary on the AIDS crisis and the rise and fracture of the AIDS Coalition to Unleash Power (ACT UP),[1] premiered in theaters. The film, which incorporates amateur video and television clips from the 1980s as well as interviews with key figures, comprehensively chronicles the AIDS epidemic and the government's response to it. It also illustrates the ways in which members of ACT UP implemented tactics used by activists in other social movements in their own struggle for acceptance, recognition, and to have their needs met. France hoped that educational institutions would use his work to instruct students on the history of the AIDS crisis, the activism it generated, and, more generally, the struggle for LGBTQ+[2] rights in the United States. Yet, almost everyone he consulted—including some of the most forward-thinking people in the field—insisted that high school history classes were the wrong place for such sensitive and controversial material and that none would consider his request.[3]

France, though, was persistent. As a filmmaker with no background in education, he stated honestly that he had "no idea" how teachers might use his film in their classrooms. He strongly believed that it was important to expose students to the history of the AIDS crisis, in general, and ACT UP, specifically, because though it accomplished major change it does not receive the same recognition as other movements.[4] Ultimately, in 2013, France approached Robert Cohen at New York University. Unlike other educators with whom France consulted, Cohen saw the possibilities inherent in using *How to Survive a Plague* in high school classes given the proper historical contextualization; he agreed that incorporating the AIDS crisis in the US history curriculum was imperative.[5] Cohen is an expert in social reform movements, especially those led by young people;[6] by 2013 he began advocating for greater attention to the gay rights movement, and LGBTQ+ history more generally, in high school classrooms. He proved a perfect ally for France at a time when France heard only a chorus of "no's."

France and Cohen, a filmmaker and a university professor, could not themselves defy convention and naysayers to bring *How to Survive a Plague* into high school classrooms. To do so they required a pedagogical partner with high school teaching experience. At that point, I entered the equation. As a researcher studying the challenges in incorporating LGBTQ+ history, I understood the obstacles France faced. Moreover, with ten years of high school teaching experience, I knew how to create a unit that could impart important information about the AIDS crisis, how the atmosphere in the United States in the 1980s contributed to the epidemic, and the need for activism around it. Students participating in this curriculum learned about the discovery and spread of AIDS as well as the origins and leading figures of ACT UP, including the way in which the lack of recognition and response on the part of the government, corporations, and the pharmaceutical community compelled people with AIDS to advocate on their own behalf for treatment options and anti-discrimination legislation.[7] Students also learned to identify how ACT UP built upon the strategies and tactics of other twentieth-century reform movements as well as the ways in which this organization was a product of its time; an essential part of this unit was eliciting these comparisons from students in a way that demonstrated the connection between various eras in US history. *How to Survive a Plague* was a major influence in the design and trajectory of the unit and its centerpiece; excerpts were used in conjunction with and to add context and significance to other sources and events. The students, seniors in high school, knew little about AIDS; most recalled discussing it briefly in a health class at some point in their schooling, if at all. Learning this history, then—as David France espoused from the start—was necessary and instructive.

France wanted high school students to see and learn from his film. Once that happened, he also wanted other teachers to learn about and from the curriculum I created and implemented so that more students might participate in that experience. Thus, after teaching and evaluating the lessons and the work students produced, I presented at the National Council for Social Studies (NCSS) Annual Conference. The NCSS presentation was only moderately attended; the majority of the audience saw the film previously and sought information on how they might use it in their classrooms. This supported France's idea that it had value for that purpose; these teachers believed the film was suitable but needed support to better grasp how to introduce it to their students. Other conference participants, though, questioned the film's appropriateness and whether there was actually a need to bring LGBTQ+ history into a US history class; a few made crude remarks when informed of my session topic. Though the unit and the film were well received by the students in the classes I taught and their final writing assignments demonstrated increased knowledge and understanding, it was not widely recognized or adopted as France hoped. In 2014 at one of the country's largest and most prominent conferences for social studies teachers, LGBTQ+-inclusive history curriculum was not yet widely or systemically supported.

The obstacles David France faced, the tenacity required to get his film into high school classrooms, and other teachers' lack of enthusiasm are indicative of the broader paradox surrounding the inclusion of LGBTQ+ history in high school US history classes. There are advocates, teachers, administrators, families, elected officials, and organizations that support and encourage this practice and work to ensure that LGBTQ+ history has a place in the taught curriculum. There is, however, also significant resistance to its inclusion, due to religious convictions, reticence to change, bureaucratic barriers, or apathy. Therefore, its consistent inclusion is rare relative to other topics and events. It is often by fortuitously happening upon a feasible scenario that this information is conveyed to students in a meaningful way. As France and others' experiences demonstrate, with institutional and/or systemic support LGBTQ+-inclusive history curriculum can succeed, but one has to first find and capitalize on that support for this possibility to exist.

How to Survive a Plague offers viewers a window on an essential moment in US history, but its controversial subject matter stymied its director's efforts to bring it to high school audiences. France's experience encapsulates the fraught climate that exists around introducing LGBTQ+ issues in US history classes, bundling the difficulties inherent to curriculum reform, the perpetually raging culture wars, and the profound concerns about embracing education as the next major issue in an increasingly successful LGBTQ+ rights movement. In an era when educators have started to reconsider the narrative that history classes convey, it is essential that LGBTQ+ history is part of that conversation.

LGBTQ+ Rights in the Twenty-First Century

In the 2015 case *Obergefell v. Hodges*, the Supreme Court ruled same-sex marriage constitutional, handing the gay rights movement a significant and hard-fought victory. That evening, rainbow lights illuminated the White House in honor of this landmark decision. Marriage rights were not among the gay rights movement's original goals. In his 2005 book *Why Marriage?*, historian George Chauncey asserted that demands for marriage emerged from "two searing experiences of the 1980s that forever impressed upon lesbians and gay men the importance of securing their relationships: the devastating impact of AIDS and the astonishingly rapid appearance of what everyone soon called the lesbian baby boom."[8] At first, the battle over same-sex marriage happened at the state level; Vermont's civil union law in 2000 and Massachusetts's law allowing same-sex marriages in 2004 touched off debates and advocacy in several other states, most notably California's battle over Proposition 8.[9] *Obergefell v. Hodges* (2015), which repealed state laws prohibiting same-sex marriage and the federal Defense of Marriage Act (1996), was thus a legal, moral, and personal victory for the LGBTQ+ community and its allies. In June 2015, the Supreme Court's decision seemed to represent a turning point for LGBTQ+ rights in the United States and corresponded with public opinion that supported this step toward equality for the nation's LGBTQ+ population: according to an ongoing Pew Research Center study, 55 percent of Americans supported same-sex marriage in 2015; 60 percent of Americans queried for a Gallup poll on the same topic responded favorably.[10]

Legalizing same-sex marriage was a significant accomplishment for the LGBTQ+ rights movement, but certainly not its only one. Since the start of the twenty-first century, the movement has achieved meaningful legal victories, with laws and statutes that limited and/or discriminated against the LGBTQ+ population overturned or deemed unconstitutional. In 2003, for example, the Supreme Court struck down Texas's anti-sodomy laws in *Lawrence v. Texas*, ruling, "The Texas statute furthers no legitimate state interest which can justify its intrusion into the personal and private life of the individual."[11] In 2010, meanwhile, Congress repealed Don't Ask, Don't Tell, a Clinton-era policy stating that gay and lesbian individuals could serve in the military provided they didn't reveal their sexuality; signing this repeal into law fulfilled a goal for which President Obama campaigned. Furthermore, Obama became the first president to reference the Stonewall riots in an inaugural address, declaring in 2013, "We, the people, declare today that the most evident of truths—that all of us are created equal—is the star that guides us still; just as it guided our forebears through Seneca Falls, and Selma, and Stonewall."[12] In later election cycles, Colorado elected the nation's first gay governor, Jared Polis, in 2018, and former South Bend, Indiana Mayor Pete Buttigieg became a significant player in the Democratic Party with his presidential run in 2020. The Supreme Court, meanwhile, ruled that Title VII of the Civil Rights Act protected LGBTQ+ individuals from discrimination in *Bostock v. Clayton County* (2020). Despite this political progress and, concurrently, emerging scholarship asserting the benefits of including LGBTQ+ history in social studies classes, history was being made but not taught outside the more liberal regions of the country.

Though many Americans celebrated these accomplishments, others opposed them. As the LGBTQ+ community became more prominent in the United States, new laws attempting to limit this population's rights—many targeting transgender individuals—began to emerge. In March 2016, North Carolina passed the Public Facilities Privacy & Security Act,[13] which immediately drew the ire of LGBTQ+ activists, human rights groups, politicians from other parts of the country, celebrities, and allies of the LGBTQ+ community. The law, which "ban[ned] individuals from using public bathrooms that d[id] not correspond to their biological sex," specifically targeted the transgender community and, opponents claimed, impeded individuals' ability to live authentically.[14] Similar bills were introduced, some successfully, in other parts of the country, and transgender bathrooms became an issue with which public facilities—including schools—across the nation contended. Moreover, the changing national atmosphere ushered in by the 2016 election led to a rise in public and political anti-LGBTQ+ sentiment. An increased number of Americans vocally advocated for the Supreme Court to overturn its decision in *Obergefell v. Hodges* (2015), a sentiment that gained momentum and legitimacy as the Court became more conservative; in June 2018, in fact, the Supreme Court ruled that Colorado's Masterpiece Cakeshop could, on First Amendment grounds, deny service to a same-sex couple.[15] In April 2019 the executive branch enacted a policy under which transgender military personnel "must use the uniforms, pronouns, and sleeping and bathroom facilities for their biological sex" and would be banned from service "if they have a diagnosis of gender dysphoria, a disorder in which a person's gender identity does not match their physical gender at birth";[16] in a 5–4 ruling the Supreme Court upheld this "transgender ban."[17] Idaho passed the Fairness in Women's Sports Act in April 2020, banning transgender girls and women from competing in interscholastic sports; a federal judge blocked the law four months later.[18] Several other states, including Tennessee, Arkansas, and Mississippi, likewise introduced and/or enacted laws banning transgender women from participating in sports.

Despite this increased attention and more frequent—and more virulent— debates about the LGBTQ+ community's rights, the struggle to bring the historical information that would help Americans contextualize these matters into classrooms continues.[19] Many Americans' opinions are informed by influential figures and sources in their personal lives rather than facts and evidence. Individuals coming of age in the twenty-first century know little of the extent to which this population was marginalized in prior decades or its efforts for recognition and equality. As LGBTQ+ rights and this population's societal status persist as one of several significant civil rights issues with which the United States grapples—Black Lives Matter protests in the spring and summer of 2020 called attention to the danger and violence Black transgender individuals, especially women, face—its absence from the majority of states' educational standards and resulting tenuous status in the social studies classroom leave students without the historical context to understand these political and cultural debates.

The Importance of LGBTQ+-inclusive Social Studies Classes

Several scholars argue that the purpose of social studies education is to create informed and engaged citizens who will participate in the democratic process.[20] Illustrating the many and varied ways in which national and international issues, past and present, relate to students' lives thus becomes central to the curriculum. As social studies scholar Stephen J. Thornton asserted, teachers are "gatekeepers" of information, making crucial determinations regarding the knowledge students receive.[21] In a culturally sustaining social studies environment, that knowledge revolves around the recipients and serves as a lens through which students learn about themselves and their society. In the twenty-first century, therefore, if students are learning relevant history in their social studies classes current events indicate that the curriculum should include LGBTQ+ history.[22]

The quest to create participatory citizens, an overarching goal of social studies education, focuses on teaching students how to apply information. Content is, therefore, a vital part of what happens in the classroom.[23] What students learn helps them come to terms with and hone their own notions and ideals; content is useful in that it offers students grounding and context for these thoughts and conceptions. Incorporating LGBTQ+ history, which has a direct bearing on the world in which students live, and instilling knowledge of that community's experiences and struggles can enable students to develop informed ideas and opinions about issues facing the LGBTQ+ population today so they can better participate in real world conversations.

It is impossible for students to understand the present when the version of history they learn is incomplete. Omitting entire groups from history curricula establishes and perpetuates those groups' invisibility, denies them proper representation in academic settings, and creates a situation in which students are unaware of the context for so much that happens around them. Moreover, presenting an incomplete historical picture ignores the complexities with which history is rife and contributes to students viewing history as much more simplistic and less nuanced than it actually is. Social studies classes that fail to include LGBTQ+ history, then, convey inaccurate accounts of the Harlem Renaissance, McCarthyism, the civil rights movements of the 1960s, and the conservatism of the 1980s, to name a few. While it is impossible to present US history in its entirety over the course of an academic year, failing to discuss LGBTQ+ Americans' roles in various eras or certain events' effect on this community does a disservice to students learning about the nation's past. Additionally, the absence of LGBTQ+ history indirectly perpetuates homophobia; it is difficult to overcome discrimination when classroom experience indicates that the LGBTQ+ community's past is less important than the events teachers, textbooks, resources, and curriculum designers choose to address.

One of the most pressing problems facing social studies education today is students' belief that events that happened hundreds of years ago have no bearing on their lives.[24] Unlike other subjects that are more obviously practical later in life, learning about events from hundreds of years ago has no such immediate resonance. Therefore, anchoring social studies education in students' personal lives and the world in which they live offers one means to convey historical information in a manner that piques and maintains student interest. Twenty-first-century high school students across the country have encountered someone who identifies as LGBTQ+, either personally or in the media products they consume; many students identify as LGBTQ+ or question their gender identity and/or sexuality in their teenage years. Moreover, controversies relating to transgender and gender-neutral bathrooms, and the more recent focus on Black Trans lives, directly impact students' lives. LGBTQ+ history is not simply a relic of the past but a topic to which students can relate. Its inclusion has the power to make history more honest and relatable and to illustrate that past events are not as removed from the present as high school students might believe. In an educational era emphasizing literacy and math, efforts to maintain history's importance in students' lives and school curricula are essential.

As historian John D'Emilio contended, in the late twentieth century the study of LGBTQ+ history evolved from a topic largely ignored in scholarly circles to one in which groundbreaking works received academic attention.[25] This increased attention led to the emergence of courses focused on LGBTQ+ issues in higher education;[26] later, scholars focused on social studies education began to consider the dearth of information on LGBTQ+ issues in K-12 education. Building on this trajectory, the following chapters evaluate the status of LGBTQ+ history instruction in high schools and resources pertaining to it, as well as resistance to that teaching, from 1990 to the present.

LGBTQ+-inclusive history education is a subject with increasing potential and momentum, but also, currently, a ceiling. Research and evidence indicate that a combination of grassroots efforts and top-down initiatives have contributed to progress in integrating LGBTQ+ history into high school US history classes that cannot and should not be ignored. More teachers incorporate LGBTQ+ figures, events, and issues in the curriculum they teach and the effort to do so receives greater media, legal, and educational attention than it did in the past. Six states and a growing number of counties and regions mandate its inclusion. There are also significant obstacles to widespread implementation of LGBTQ+-inclusive history, some of which may never be overcome. In many parts of the country this history's absence from state learning standards and a lack of institutional attention or support from both departments of education and LGBTQ+ advocacy groups impede fuller integration in US history classes. Meanwhile, in more conservative regions, deep-seeded resistance based on religious and political beliefs—some of which is codified in state law—stands in vehement opposition to discussions of LGBTQ+ history and issues in schools in any context. This is, therefore, a story of progress and possibility as well as opposition and tempered expectations.

Attempts to include LGBTQ+ information in classrooms often emphasize anti-bullying curricula and school safety initiatives, prioritizing this over inclusivity in academic subjects. Even the 2017 special issue of *Social Education*, a practitioner journal written for and read by social studies teachers, focused on school climate concerns and devoted one of its six articles to the way in which safety issues compel schools to implement inclusive curricula.[27] Social studies scholars have asserted the necessity of historically inclusive instruction, and there are and have been top-down, standards-focused attempts to push that agenda forward including California's FAIR Education Act and LGBTQ+ curriculum laws in New Jersey, Illinois, Oregon, Colorado, and Nevada. Despite these legislative and institutional mandates, though, LGBTQ+-inclusive history education receives neither the same widespread support nor financial resources nor manpower to turn scholars' contentions into reality in the same manner as anti-bullying and school climate initiatives. This lack of meaningful, widespread support undermines attempts to integrate this material and promote resources that might help teachers to do so.

There are myriad reasons for LGBTQ+ history's relative absence in social studies curricula. These reasons, though, have not squashed the motivation and attempts to incorporate LGBTQ+ issues and history in high school settings. Educators and advocates—like David France—who believe in and support this work consistently strive to find ways to turn their ideas into realities; their goals are hampered much more by a lack of institutional support than waning intentionality. In fact, the most significant obstacles to including LGBTQ+ history in high school US history classes—the lack of support from individuals and bodies that oversee education and policy, and the absence of this history from the standards that determine what students learn and the transmitted knowledge for which teachers are held accountable—can be reasonably overcome. Examining these multiple factors and perspectives, then, the following chapters highlight the ways in which they interact and impact upon attempts to include LGBTQ+ history in high school US history classes and the tenacity of and actions taken by educators and activists to ensure inclusivity despite these obstacles. It situates this struggle within the larger battle for LGBTQ+ rights and recognition and contextualizes it within the goals of social studies education.

The LGBTQ+ rights movement as a whole has made significant political and social progress, securing rights and access at a relatively rapid pace; advocates have and continue to devote resources and energy to workplace discrimination, AIDS, transgender rights, and marriage rights, among other legal efforts. Furthermore, the movement has long emphasized public education and awareness campaigns—the "coming out" process is a part of this effort—and promoted accurate media depictions of LGBTQ+ lifestyles and individuals. Schooling, however, was not a significant part of this educative process and, for several reasons, was not a priority for many gay rights activists in the second half of the twentieth century.[28] Though schooling has become more of a priority since 1990, most activists and organizations conceive of the need for LGBTQ+ inclusivity as it pertains to protecting and supporting queer and questioning teens; this corresponds with the movement's original agenda of ending harassment and recognizing differences.

Within schools, significant obstacles loom over any attempt to change social studies curriculum, especially where those revisions introduce information that any segment of the population might deem controversial. These hurdles, which have existed for years and intensified over time, challenge any real inclusion of LGBTQ+ history: a topic that must overcome both these general obstacles and people's fears and prejudices related to this material, in particular. Violence perpetrated against LGBTQ+ individuals, especially teens like Matthew Shepard, and the fatal impact of bullying, as in the case of Tyler Clementi, contextualized within the overall national anti-bullying agenda, created space within schools for lessons pertaining to the treatment and tolerance of LGBTQ+ students and classmates. This opening does not exist in the same way for history, despite scholars' contentions and survey data suggesting that the potential impact could fulfill a more expansive range of goals.

Existing resources available to teachers and schools seeking to make their curricula more LGBTQ+-inclusive reflect this trend and address social studies' civic goals by promoting safe spaces and focusing on the language students use and the behaviors they practice (Chapter 4). History, in many cases, simply serves as a springboard or entry point to tasks and activities that highlight why it's wrong to say "that's so gay" and emphasize the ways in which inclusive climates benefit all students. Organizations began developing lessons focusing on LGBTQ+ history for the straightforward purpose of conveying that content to the K–12 market later on; there are still fewer such resources available (Chapter 5). The need for more resources, coupled with the fact that many teachers never learned this history and are not conscious of what they omit, makes it difficult for this material to get into classrooms in a meaningful way; this is evident in California, for example, where the Fair, Accurate, Inclusive, and Respectful (FAIR) Education Act mandates including LGBTQ+ history, yet few teachers had a clear strategy for implementing this legislation in their classrooms (Chapters 6 and 7).

There are advocacy groups, educators, and individuals that champion change and assert the benefits of teaching an LGBTQ+-inclusive history curriculum. Gay, Lesbian, Straight Education Network (GLSEN), for example, promotes LGBTQ+ History Month, giving schools and administrators a yearly opportunity to highlight the LGBTQ+ population's contributions to American society (Chapter 1). California scholars whose efforts helped to secure the passage of the FAIR Act and revisions to the state Framework also conducted professional development seminars throughout the state to assist teachers and build the necessary skills to effectively teach this information.[29] Moreover, there are teachers who incorporate this history into their classes and discuss the transformative results (Chapters 8–10). They are a minority, but a dedicated one. These advocates are the seeds of a possible grassroots movement, whereby the work that they do has the potential to spread to other classrooms, schools, and states to create a change in the way that high school students learn history. They must also confront the reality, though, that prevailing ideas, laws, and attitudes in some regions in addition to conservativism and backlash to progressive advances make this effort more difficult, more pressing, and, possibly, even more relevant.

Social studies was established with the intention that young people's educational experiences should prepare them to participate in their communities and contribute to society. Though this is often conceived of in terms of political participation, acting as a member of one's community goes beyond voting or contacting one's representatives. Participation extends to understanding and being able to knowledgably and civilly converse about important issues, as well. Failing to integrate LGBTQ+ history, then, especially in the twenty-first century, undermines the cause and rationale behind social studies education because schools are not properly preparing students to participate in the world around them politically or socially. In this case, students not only receive an incomplete historical education, but they also leave school without the foundation necessary to support their opinions on significant issues in the present. In an era when the Supreme Court annually hears cases pertaining to LGBTQ+ rights, transgender individuals become more prominent and confront increased discrimination, and even the acronym used to refer to this group constantly evolves, the mission of social studies demands the inclusion of LGBTQ+ history.

There are compelling reasons to teach this history, as cited by scholars and advocates and witnessed in inclusive classrooms. Moreover, introducing this material in an academic subject offers students a greater number of perspectives from which to consider ideas with which they are presented elsewhere. As Stephen Thornton posited in 2014, teaching young people about LGBTQ+ history and issues can make a significant difference in how we discuss these matters and events as a nation.[30] Lyndsey Schlax, a San Francisco teacher who spearheaded an LGBTQ+ history elective, marveled at her students' ability to do just that, engaging in conversations they never could or would have prior to a semester immersed in this history. Her reaction, encapsulating the sentiments of others working for a similar goal, illustrates the determination of those who believe in inclusive curriculum and its place in social studies: "Be ready to fight, because it's worth it."[31]

1

Making History: The LGBTQ+ Movement's Evolving Struggle for Acknowledgment and Inclusivity

The idea of people coming together to defend rights is one that is long held in the United States, dating back centuries and, some might say, at the core of the nation's founding. Groups advocating for LGBTQ+ rights, then, join a long history of those who struggled to attain recognition, equality, and rights long denied to them. Similar to other movements, LGBTQ+ rights advocates have different priorities and tactics among them, and the proliferation of advocacy groups over time attests to this diversity of intent and agenda.

The Society for Human Rights was founded in 1924 and sought to educate legal authorities and legislators about gay rights.[1] Though it was short-lived, by the middle of the twentieth century other organizations were established with similar goals—to educate the public and change attitudes about the gay community and the people who comprised it.[2] For these groups and others that followed, education pertained more to raising awareness and changing public perception than to schooling. As the modern gay rights movement gained momentum after Stonewall, accumulating successes and appealing to Americans to open their minds, political and social change that would make history emerged as the movement's intention; teaching this history in classrooms was not a priority.

The Stonewall riots were motivated in large part by LGBTQ+ individuals' desire to be safe in the spaces that they created for themselves.[3] After years of harassment and arrests, LGBTQ+ people fought back against authority figures whose discriminatory practices derived from their targets' sexuality. The gay rights movement did not start with Stonewall, but it changed and became more prominent in the post-Stonewall era as new organizations, determined to secure political and civil rights for the LGBTQ+ community, were born. In 1972,

Jeanne Manford started Parents and Friends of Lesbians and Gays (PFLAG) after other young LGBTQ+ individuals asked her to speak to their parents when she marched with her son in New York's Christopher Street Liberation Day march.[4] After similar support groups began in other parts of the country, they united as a national organization dedicated to seeking equality and promoting legislation benefitting the LGBTQ+ community.[5] Within a decade, Lambda Legal Defense and Education Fund, the National Gay and Lesbian Task Force, the National Center for Lesbian Rights, and Human Rights Campaign (HRC) were founded with the goals of pursuing change through legislatures and courts, supporting pro-LGBTQ+ candidates, providing legal assistance to the LGBTQ+ population and ending discrimination.[6] These organizations sought, and continue to seek, equality, freedom, and justice; their efforts are in many ways responsible for ending discriminatory laws and increasing recognition and civil rights for the LGBTQ+ population.

Through these and other organizations' efforts, legislation and public opinion changed at a faster pace than other movements for social reform including the African American Civil Rights Movement.[7] In 1983, for example, Lambda Legal "won the nation's first HIV/AIDS discrimination case (*People v. West 12 Tenants Corp.*), helping establish that under disability laws it's illegal to discriminate against people who have HIV."[8] Working through the court system, Lambda Legal also secured Supreme Court decisions supporting government protection against discrimination for the LGBTQ+ population in *Romer v. Evans* (1996) and overturning previously upheld anti-sodomy laws in the landmark case *Lawrence v. Texas* (2003); moreover, Lambda Legal served as cocounsel on "one of the cases collectively known as *Obergefell v. Hodges*" (2015) affirming the right to same-sex marriage.[9] The National LGBTQ Task Force, an advocacy organization, "campaign[ed] to eliminate the sickness classification of homosexuality … worked to lift the prohibition on federal civil service employment for gays and lesbians … took the lead in the 1980s in national organizing against homophobic violence … [and] shaped the first serious efforts in Washington to address the [AIDS] epidemic," among other initiatives.[10] Furthermore, ACT UP was established in the late 1980s to advocate for government recognition of the AIDS epidemic and access to affordable HIV and AIDS medications; their work raised national awareness of the disease.[11] The gay rights movement and the organizations that encompass it, then, have experienced significant legislative and judicial success in the fifty years since the Stonewall riots. Unlike the accomplishments of other reform movements, whose advocates pushed for curricular inclusion,[12] incorporating these successes remains elusive.

The History of Education in the LGBTQ+ Rights Movement

LGBTQ+ rights organizations have and continue to emphasize education; their idea of education, though, historically applied more to raising societal awareness and acceptance of the LGBTQ+ community than school-based initiatives. The Gay Liberation Front (GLF), an organization founded in the wake of the Stonewall riots, encouraged gay and lesbian individuals to embrace their identity. The GLF's Manifesto declared, "The starting point of our liberation must be to rid ourselves of the oppression which lies in the head of every one of us. This means freeing our heads from self oppression ... The aim is to step outside the experience permitted by straight society, and to learn to love and trust one another."[13] The National LGBTQ Task Force, meanwhile, trains activists to work around the country to educate populations about and advocate for issues important to the LGBTQ+ community,[14] and the HRC Foundation works to "improve the lives of lesbian, gay, bisexual, transgender and queer (LGBTQ) people by working to increase understanding and encourage the adoption of LGBTQ-inclusive policies and practices."[15] It was and is undoubtedly important to address societal conceptions of LGBTQ+ individuals and lifestyles and, where possible, eradicate stereotypes and negative perceptions. Educating the public is also significantly less fraught than navigating state-monitored educational institutions responsible for minors. In thinking about the gay rights movement's relationship to education, then, it is imperative to distinguish between public education and schooling.

Statements and campaigns equating homosexual men, in particular, and the LGBTQ+ community, in general, with pedophilia made the connection between the gay rights movement and schooling especially contentious. The tension between the two garnered national attention in 1977 when Anita Bryant, a beauty queen and singer, launched the Save Our Children campaign in response to a Miami-Dade County law that prohibited discrimination in public accommodations and employment based on sexual preference. Though the scope of the law was broad, Bryant focused specifically on "homosexual teachers" whom she said "would 'sexually molest children,' serve as 'dangerous role models,' and 'encourage more homosexuality by inducing pupils into looking upon it as an acceptable life-style.'"[16] Ruth Shack, the commissioner who introduced the bill, called Bryant's charges "specious."[17] As the *Washington Post* reported at the time, "Save Our Children contends that passage of the law will enable homosexuals to 'recruit' youths."[18] Bryant declared, "What these people really want, hidden behind obscure legal phrases, is the legal right to propose to our children that theirs is an acceptable alternate life ... I will lead a crusade to stop it as this country has not seen before."[19] Bryant's emphasis on homosexual recruitment, coupled with her fame and national image, led directly to the Miami law's repeal and, according to law professor Clifford Rosky, indirectly to the rise of anti-gay curriculum laws in several states.[20] Save Our Children, born from opposition to a local law, had national reach.

Bryant's campaign, which began in Florida, captured the attention of like-minded individuals throughout the country including John Briggs, a California state senator who submitted Proposition 6, a ballot initiative—later known as the Briggs Initiative—that would have "allowed school districts to suspend, dismiss, and deny employment to 'any person who has engaged in public homosexual activity or public homosexual conduct'"; the latter included any statement or action that could be construed as supporting "homosexual activity."[21] Briggs, who proposed his initiative under the California Save Our Children initiative banner, closely aligned himself with and supported Bryant, echoing her pronouncements about the danger posed by homosexual teachers' influence over impressionable children. The Briggs Initiative aimed to eradicate that influence. As Rosky asserted,

> because the initiative prohibited "advocating," "encouraging," or "promoting" homosexual behavior it could be applied to heterosexual teachers, as well as gay teachers. And because the initiative prohibited speech that was "likely to come to the attention of schoolchildren and/or other employees," it could be applied to speech that occurred outside of the classroom, or even outside of school.[22]

The potential impact of the Briggs Initiative and the way in which it could be used against all teachers ultimately led to its failure in California, as even Ronald Reagan voiced opposition to it in the weeks leading up to the 1978 election.

Briggs was part of a larger push for anti-gay curriculum laws; his initiative was defeated, but similar laws, including one in Oklahoma, succeeded. Oklahoma's anti-gay curriculum law, adopted on April 6, 1978, passed the state legislature 42-0 and withstood judicial challenge two years later. Though it was "introduced by Mary Helm and John Monk, two of the state's most prominent conservative legislators ... in the popular press it was recognized as the work of Anita Bryant and John Briggs."[23] By the late 1980s, nine more states followed suit. Though the gay rights movement accumulated successes in other forums, the pervasiveness of Save Our Children made schooling a complicated arena to enter.

Adolescents were not well represented in the gay rights movement as it grew and became more prominent in the post-Stonewall era.[24] Activists in the mid to late twentieth century were more concerned, therefore, with issues important to gay and lesbian adults who suffered years of discrimination and lack of access to public life. The movement expanded, though, and young people in the twenty-first century are important advocates for LGBTQ+ equality. It was natural, then, for adolescents' plight to become more important to the movement as a whole. The way in which different organizations—founded for different purposes but united by a common philosophy—have addressed those struggles and worked to improve LGBTQ+ students' lives, as well as the obstacles they face, are thus relevant to schooling.

Where organizations do focus on schooling in the twenty-first century, their goals are similar to that of the Stonewall activists fifty years ago: creating and securing safe spaces for students who identify as LGBTQ+. The National Center for Lesbian Rights, for example, listed "Making Schools Safer" among its accomplishments for 2016–17, citing its work toward repealing a Utah law censoring LGBTQ+ content in schools.[25] PFLAG, as well, references "Safe and Welcoming Schools" as an organizational goal and maintains a program entitled "Cultivating Respect: Safe Schools for All" which "work[s] directly with schools and stakeholders in their communities, providing support, resources, training, creative programs, and even model policy to create an environment of respect."[26] HRC's Welcoming Schools program, established in 2006, "provid[es] training and resources to elementary school educators to welcome diverse families, create LGBTQ+ and gender inclusive schools, prevent bias-based bullying, and support transgender and non-binary students."[27] While these programs are designed to meet important needs and promote learning and tolerance for all students, they are merely one aspect of organizations' much larger agendas. Additionally, many school-based programs within these organizations were created years after they began accumulating political victories. It was essential, then, for organizations that were singularly focused on the school-based experience to emerge to fill that void.

The Movement Expands: Turning Toward Schools

In 1990, according to GLSEN founder Kevin Jennings, "there was simply no one" working to support LGBTQ+ educators and their allies; this was, after all, only thirteen years removed from Bryant founding Save Our Children and the wave of anti-gay curriculum proposals and laws that followed. Jennings, who started the first Gay Straight Alliance (GSA) at Concord Academy in Massachusetts, therefore adopted that mission.[28] Jennings stated, "The idea was to bring together people so that they can learn from one another and build from there. There was no vision at that point certainly of becoming this big national organization. It was more the idea that we would be stronger and more effective if we organized ourselves better and we're supporting each other and sharing ideas."[29] Over time, the network that Jennings started to assist and support LGBTQ+ and allied educators grew to encompass educators nationwide and evolved into an organization that supports and promotes improved school climates for both teachers and students. Eight years later, Carolyn Laub established GSA Network to unite and support the Gay Straight Alliances (now Gender Sexuality Alliances) that began to emerge in San Francisco schools; this organization, too, went national. GLSEN and GSA Network are therefore distinct from other LGBTQ+ advocacy organizations. Unlike those aiming to improve political and social conditions for the population as a whole, from their start GLSEN and GSA Network focused specifically on schools.

GLSEN, like other LGBTQ+ rights organizations, arose to fill an unmet need. In its original iteration, GLSEN, then the Gay and Lesbian Independent School Teachers Network (GLISTN), existed to personally and professionally support LGBTQ+ teachers and provide the resources they might need to present themselves authentically in the schools where they worked. As word of this work spread, the network grew to include public schools and people outside of education who supported the organization's cause; Jennings called GLSEN's growth "an opportunistic responding to people's expressed desire to get involved."[30] Moreover, as society changed GLSEN did, too. Though few high school students were "out" when GLSEN was established in 1990, many more were by the time Jennings left the organization in 2008; an organization whose programming was originally intended for teachers was, by that time, largely aimed at improving students' experiences. According to Jennings, regardless of this change, "the overall mission never evolved."[31]

As GLSEN grew, so did the number of schools with GSAs.[32] In 1998, Carolyn Laub began working with GSAs in the San Francisco area to encourage and support students attempting to establish these clubs at their schools. Within three years GSA Network, the organization she founded, went statewide, and by 2005 GSA Network went national.[33] Though GLSEN and GSA Network shared similar goals—creating safer, more welcoming environments for LGBTQ+ individuals—GSA Network began by focusing on the student experience, and

GLSEN, in its original incarnation, was a professional organization. Beginning with forty GSAs in San Francisco, Laub and her network trained and supported students hoping to start Gay Straight Alliances at their schools and worked with existing GSAs to strengthen students' leadership skills and help them grow their organizations. Moreover, in creating an interconnected network, Laub established a support system for all GSA members from which their activism could expand.[34] By the time GSA Network became a national organization in 2005, then, both organizations were positioned to improve the school experience for LGBTQ+ students and their teachers.

GLSEN and GSA Network employ multiple strategies to change school climate and make schools safer as a whole and for the LGBTQ+ population. Furthermore, in keeping with its original intention to support teachers, GLSEN offers an ever-changing array of resources, lesson plans, and professional development opportunities designed to "develop the knowledge and skills needed to create and sustain a safe, inclusive, respectful and healthful environment for all ... students."[35] While GLSEN provides schools with structured programs that students, teachers, and administrators can modify to meet their needs, GSA Network works more at the grassroots, "empower[ing students] to educate their schools and communities, advocat[ing] for just policies that protect LGBTQ+ youth from harassment and violence, and organiz[ing] in coalition with other youth groups across identity lines to address broader issues of oppression."[36] Together, GLSEN and GSA Network's strategies attempt to accomplish three goals: making schools safe for LGBTQ+ teachers; creating a welcoming, tolerant school environment for LGBTQ+ students; and amending curriculum to be more inclusive of the LGBTQ+ population and its issues. Fulfilling these goals would change culture and climate at a school-wide level and, in particular, help those who identify as LGBTQ+ whose school experience might be most adversely affected by a hostile environment.

GLSEN and GSA Network's larger goal—ensuring safe spaces for LGBTQ+ individuals—echoes that of the larger gay rights movement. That movement's focus on larger political goals rather than school-based concerns, however, both necessitated the emergence of organizations specifically focused on this demographic and contributed to early doubts about their ability to succeed. According to Kevin Jennings, the lack of attention to young LGBTQ+ people's situations and experiences was twofold. He recalled,

> There was the political sensitivity of it. I think secondly people tend to address things that affect them directly. Young people were not really represented in the

movement in significant numbers so their needs were not prioritized. ... Then there was a lot of nervousness among the adults about addressing these issues because of the fear of accusations that we were after kids.[37]

Young people who either identified as LGBTQ+ or struggled with their sexuality were therefore left closeted and/or in inhospitable situations. The gay rights movement, according to Jennings and others, shied away from addressing young people's issues for fear of being tainted with the pedophilia accusations long directed at gay men, as exemplified by Bryant's crusade. GLSEN, then, was much needed and, in its own way, a radical step within this movement for social justice. It opened the door to other organizations devoted to improving school climate; its approach and focus, which set a precedent for the organizations that followed, are the thing that differentiate it from the organizations that preceded it.

As Jennings posited, and the organizations' websites demonstrate, GLSEN and GSA Network are not presently alone in advocating for safe schools.[38] In the years since GLSEN's founding, significant societal changes have propelled the movement forward and revealed truths that were unacknowledged and unaccepted in 1990. GLSEN and GSA's work, as well as evolving public opinion and media depictions of LGBTQ+ people and lifestyles, put a spotlight on school-age LGBTQ+ individuals and their plight.

In the twenty-first century, organizations, especially those that concentrate on family life, devote efforts and resources to school-based content in addition to legal advocacy. PFLAG, along with other organizations like the Anti-Defamation League (ADL), Our Family Coalition, and HRC, develops and offers programs and resources for schools, teachers, and students aimed at making schools at every level safer and more inclusive for all. PFLAG's "Cultivating Respect: Safe Schools for All" offers a guide and training toolkit for adults in positions to change the school experience for LGBTQ+ youth and a scholarship program for high school seniors who self-identify as LGBTQ+ or as an ally. As part of its Welcoming and Inclusive Schools Program, Our Family Coalition "supports K–12 educators to implement lessons that include LGBTQ+ history, family diversity, challenging gender stereotypes, supporting transgender and gender non-binary identities, and anti-bullying strategies."[39] Meanwhile, HRC touts its Time to Thrive conference for educators and youth counselors as "the premier, national convening to build awareness and cultural competency, learn current and emerging best practices, and gather resources from leading experts and national organizations in the field."[40] It is imperative that teachers and school personnel understand the ramifications of a climate hostile to LGBTQ+ students and are able to effectively conduct lessons and workshops to reverse this behavior; professional development training, seminars, and guides to inclusivity are meant to build these skills. These programs are, in their own way, top-down; their attempts to create change are directed from those in positions of authority, similar to Lambda Legal, the American Civil Liberties Union (ACLU), and National Center for Lesbian Rights' legal efforts. They differ from legal advocacy meaningfully, though, because they focus primarily on the circumstances, atmosphere, and learning that happen inside the school building. They therefore have a more direct impact on students and their daily experiences.

Initiatives within larger organizations pursue similar goals. HRC's Welcoming Schools program and Southern Poverty Law Center's Learning for Justice,[41] for example, exist to develop and share school-based programs and resources in ways that their parent organizations do not and, in doing so, augment the extent to which they are able to help school populations at various levels. Welcoming Schools provides trainings to schools and districts around the country and "developed partnerships with national, regional and local education and safe school organizations and created a website to make resources accessible to elementary schools, educators and parents across the country."[42]

Learning for Justice, meanwhile, offers lessons and resources on a range of topics including African American civil rights, women's rights, immigration, and class in addition to its sixty-seven[43] lessons on gender and sexual identity. Many of these lessons examine gender and women's roles, with particular attention paid to gender stereotypes. Others explore LGBT rights and the intersection of the gay rights and civil rights movements.[44] Learning for Justice's lessons and resources require students at different grade levels of education to explore the social justice implications of the subject matter they learn.

Welcoming Schools and Learning for Justice illustrate the possibilities that exist when organizations prioritize schooling and education. The entire focus of both organizations is developing programs and materials that can be easily accessed and used in classrooms to improve students' learning and change the way they interact within their environment. This intentionality exists in both of these organizations because of their singular purpose. Thus, these organizations, subsidiaries of larger ones working for social justice, offer clear evidence of the need for LGBTQ+ rights organizations like GLSEN and GSA that are oriented entirely around schooling. They also indicate both the potential reach of organizations and initiatives that possess institutional support. Discussing the necessity of an organization like Welcoming Schools, former director of education and community engagement Kisha Webster contended that "schools

… homes … churches … are closed systems" that teachers need assistance in order to open effectively.[45] This significant change in the LGBTQ+ rights movement and the founding of more organizations dedicated to improving the school experience represent progress beyond what legally oriented organizations are equipped to pursue.

The History of Inclusivity: Attempts to Bring LGBTQ+ Topics into the Classroom

GLSEN's founding and the proliferation of GSAs did not happen in a vacuum. They occurred as the LGBTQ+ community and individuals gained more attention and media coverage and at a time when coming out was still a political statement with potentially significant life consequences. In some parts of the country, the idea that LGBTQ+ content might enter classroom discussions thus began to germinate among educators, specifically as it related to students' lives and communities; not everyone, though, was ready for this change. By the early 1990s, schools, and their students and faculty, became part of the struggle to live openly; in schools, as in society, such initiatives met a wide range of reactions and acceptance.

Developed a year after GLSEN's founding, New York City's Children of the Rainbow curriculum was created as a guide to teaching tolerance and acceptance of different cultures and family structures for first grade; it became a case study in the diverse reactions to and mobilization of forces for and against an attempt to include LGBT content in educational materials. The Rainbow Curriculum, as it came to be known, was released in 1992 as a 443-page guide, three of which "urge[d] teachers to include references to gay men and lesbians."[46] Efforts to make schooling more inclusive were in a nascent stage—GLSEN was founded two years earlier and had not yet achieved the national prominence it later would—and Children of the Rainbow was, at its foundation, an attempt to further the cause of multicultural, rather than LGBTQ+-inclusive, education. After struggling to have the LGBTQ+ community represented at all, Elissa Weindling, a gay teacher, joined the project and authored those sections. According to the *New York Times,*

> most of the curriculum offers such unexceptional lessons as pinning cutouts of exotic fruits and vegetables on a world map. While it includes no lessons about homosexuality, the curriculum's critics have focused on the few short passages

that urge teachers to tell their students that some people are gay and should be respected like anyone else.[47]

Those who opposed the curriculum also took umbrage with two books recommended in the bibliography: *Heather Has Two Mommies* and *Daddy's Roommate*. Opponents, led by District 24 leader Mary A. Cummins, labeled the Rainbow Curriculum "gay and lesbian propaganda" and refused to implement it in their schools;[48] Cummins, who claimed she had no personal bias against gays, declared, "5- and 6-year-olds don't know what homosexuality is. When a child is old enough to ask a question, you answer it, but that doesn't mean teaching that homosexuality is a morally valid alternative lifestyle."[49] This resistance touched off a battle between districts and schools chancellor Joseph Fernandez, and between the city's liberal and conservative blocs; the battle over Children of the Rainbow, and the media coverage that followed, blurred the lines between education and politics. While opponents on the right "denounced the curriculum as promoting sodomy,"[50] Richard Burns, the executive director of Manhattan's Lesbian and Gay Community Center, contended, "The basic lesson of this curriculum is to teach children to love thy neighbor—at the earliest possible age."[51] As Fernandez related in his memoir, "my supporting opinion was that if we're ever going to get this country together, we have to deal with such biases early, even in the first grade."[52] The fallout from the controversy led to school board defections and counterproductive division among those controlling education in New York City.

Ultimately, the curriculum guide was revised, substituting the potentially less offensive "same gender parents" for "lesbian and gay families"[53] and the chancellor was ousted, but the impact of the Rainbow Curriculum debacle was far more profound in city politics than it was in the classroom, where its implementation stalled. The controversy touched off a national conversation about morality in the classroom and the role of schools in imparting lifestyle information to young pupils at the same time as the 1992 presidential election juxtaposed Democrat Bill Clinton's support for gay rights against conservatives Patrick Buchanan and Pat Robertson's anti-gay stances. In December 1992 a nationally published article by *Washington Post* writer George Will commented, "I wonder: Are New York's sixth-graders as well-informed about history and geography and poetry as they are about it being (this from their AIDS curriculum) 'wise to use latex condoms with a contraceptive foam or cream containing a chemical, nonoxynol-9'?"[54] Politically, according to *Education Week*, "observers here say the Rainbow Curriculum is the central issue in about one-fifth of the local board races and a major issue in more than half of them."[55] Educationally, controversy over the Rainbow Curriculum—coupled with a concurrent battle over a proposed AIDS prevention curriculum—and its media coverage had a chilling effect on efforts to include LGBT individuals or experiences in the classroom.[56] Children of the Rainbow became a cautionary tale, rather than a groundbreaking effort to promote acceptance. Official attempts to create LGBT-inclusive curriculum, at a time when, as Kevin Jennings stated, there was little recognition that the LGBT population extended to adolescents,[57] were rendered dormant.

Children of the Rainbow was developed by the New York City Board of Education. It was, therefore, an officially sanctioned mandate rather than a matter of school, teacher, or district choice. Among the myriad reasons for the controversy surrounding this curriculum, then, was that it was delivered from on high, and schools, regardless of administrators' ideas or student population, were given no option other than to implement it. Moreover, Children of the Rainbow's target audience—elementary school children—contributed to the backlash against it. A 1993 *New York Times* article entitled "Schools Across U.S. Cautiously Adding Lessons on Gay Life" asserted that in other parts of the country lessons on homosexuality and family structure were integrated in middle and high schools and that, unlike in New York, districts worked in cooperation with parents, clergy, and community members on creating this material.[58] Thus, the factors that led to the demise of Children of the Rainbow did not apply to all attempts to integrate LGBTQ+ content. Programs established by outside organizations, though, which schools have the power to accept or refuse, offer a different set of opportunities and obstacles. LGBT History Month, created in 1994 by Rodney Wilson, followed the precedent set by Black History Month, established in 1976, and Women's History Month, which began in 1987. Like its predecessors, LGBT History Month carved out time in the academic year for students to focus on events, trends, and individuals often omitted from schools' history curricula. Though it was established in the same era as the Children of the Rainbow curriculum, its trajectory and staying power proved much different.

Rodney Wilson, a St. Louis teacher and graduate student at University of Missouri-St. Louis, founded LGBT History Month in 1994. He identified as gay but was not yet "out" and delved into this topic for himself through his graduate work in history. Wilson came out to his class while conducting a lesson on the Holocaust, stating that he likely would have been imprisoned in that era because of his sexuality; a "broader mission to teach young people about gay history" followed, culminating in his idea for a month commemorating LGBT history.[59]

In a 2015 article for *The Advocate* describing the inception of LGBT History Month, Wilson wrote, "LGBT history gave me self-confidence as a gay person and strengthened my resolve to live, as best I could, an honest, open, and integrated life. It gave me a deeper sense of place and potential. Could it do the same for others? I wondered."[60] Given the model established by other groups' "annual reminders that not all history is made by straight white men," Wilson posited, "I wanted the same for our community and in January 1994 proposed that October 1994 be recognized as the first annual LGBT History Month."[61] The way in which other groups like women and African Americans asserted their place in the canon of American history, then, was instructive for Wilson at a time when LGBTQ+ history was not often publicly discussed. Unlike Children of the Rainbow, which met with resistance within the community where it was launched, LGBT History Month was embraced within its community and the organizations that comprised it; Children of the Rainbow, after all, was aimed at elementary school children and introduced to an entire city while LGBT History Month, at its outset, existed within LGBTQ+ advocacy and liberal educational circles predisposed to support it.

According to Kevin Jennings, Wilson devised and began to seek support for LGBT History Month at the same time as GLSEN emerged as a national organization. A third party, therefore, connected these two men with aligned goals. Jennings and Kevin Boyer at Chicago's Gerber/Hart Library and Archive reacted favorably to Wilson's proposal and joined the first national coordinating committee; their participation gave LGBT History Month the institutional support it needed to gain scholarly and political attention.[62] Moreover, the governors of Connecticut, Massachusetts, and Oregon as well as historians Jonathan Ned Katz, William A. Percy, George Chauncey, and Martin Duberman officially endorsed Wilson's endeavor.[63] In October 1994 GLSEN hosted a national conference for historians and educators to launch LGBT History Month;[64] in 1995, according to the Library of Congress, "a resolution passed by the General Assembly of the National Education Association (NEA) included LGBT History Month within a list of commemorative months."[65] LGBT History did not immediately become a fixture in public education and many schools refused to participate,[66] but establishing LGBT History Month introduced the concept that this history had a place in schools and classrooms.

LGBT History Month was accepted and, in some cases, celebrated within scholarly and educational circles; like the Rainbow Curriculum, it also met with resistance in some schools, among parents, and from conservative groups like the Eagle Forum and Concerned Women for America. In an op-ed they wrote for *The Advocate*, Rodney Wilson, Kevin Boyer, Johnda Boyce, and Kevin Jennings recalled that these two organizations "bought full-page ads in newspapers condemning the NEA and scaring parents: 'It [LGBT History Month] may be celebrated at your school before the month is over. Please call now. This must be stopped.'"[67] The NEA, too, encountered backlash that led to it advocating for all of the commemorative months it supported in a more generic way; it did not falter, however, in its support for LGBT History Month.[68] LGBT History Month was not a product of a government agency, and its advent did not have the same political weight or mandate attached to it as the Rainbow Curriculum. It was able to exist and grow, then, despite this opposition as the schools and universities that adopted it at the outset continued to do so and acknowledgment and observation of this month spread.

Despite losing momentum in the early 2000s, in the second decade of the twenty-first century LGBT History Month has regained traction and receives support from major educational and advocacy organizations. HRC, Gay and Lesbian Alliance Against Defamation (GLAAD), GLSEN, and the NEA offer resources to schools and teachers looking to share this history with their students every October. Moreover, Equality Forum each year compiles a list of thirty-one LGBTQ+ icons about whom it recommends students learn as they commemorate this community's history and contributions. Leaders within the movement speak favorably of LGBT History Month and the opportunities it provides; Rodney Wilson wrote in 2015 that he was proud of the way his endeavor endured.[69] It established that space existed in schools in which this history could be conveyed and that there were educators willing and excited to disseminate it, but it also has its limitations. As Eliza Byard, GLSEN's then executive director, contended in 2015,

> as LGBT History Month begins today, it is astounding to see how much progress has been made. In recent years, individuals like Bayard Rustin and Harvey Milk have been celebrated officially as American heroes, and stories of LGBT lives and movements of the past are becoming more common in our culture.
>
> Very little of this has yet made it into the classroom, where it will have the most important impact on students' understanding of our shared past. ... Educators everywhere can take an important step forward by continuing this exploration of the reality of our past in their classrooms, this month and throughout the year.[70]

Byard made two salient points: first, that societal recognition of LGBTQ+ figures has not trickled down to classrooms, and second, LGBT History Month is not yet pervasive enough nor does it provide adequate time for students to learn this history in depth. The founding and continued existence of LGBT History Month is a positive step in the effort to teach LGBTQ+-inclusive history in K–12 schools, but also one upon which scholars and educators need to build for instruction to be truly inclusive.

Overcoming Obstacles?

The fallout from the Rainbow Curriculum is one of the most infamous examples of the risks inherent in incorporating LGBTQ+ content, or anything controversial, in classroom teaching. The political and parental reactions and pervasive public discussion of the curriculum and its implications proved to be significant obstacles to its implementation and affected the way the New York City school board designed curriculum around any topic related to the LGBT community for the immediate future.[71] This specific example, however, is not the only hindrance.

Conservative and religious groups object to LGBTQ+-inclusive curriculum in any subject on the grounds that homosexuality is a sin and a topic best discussed in the home. Laurie Higgins of the Illinois Family Institute, for example, an organization that "works ... to initiate, promote, encourage and coordinate activity designed to safeguard and advance public morality consistent with Biblical Christianity,"[72] declared in 2013,

> Email all your children's teachers now, telling them that under no circumstance is your child to be exposed to any resources or activities that address homosexuality or gender confusion. ... Tell them that you will be addressing those topics at home in a way that honors your beliefs and respects the dignity of all persons— which public school resources do not.[73]

Similarly, Barbara Anderson, the head of the Parents Action League—an organization the Southern Poverty Law Center designated as an anti-gay hate group—argued against the Safe and Supportive Minnesota Schools Act in 2014, stating, "The greatest threat to our freedom and the health and well-being of our children is from this radical homosexual agenda that is just so pervasive."[74] Focus on the Family, meanwhile, "provide[s] help and resources ... for parents to raise their children according to morals and values grounded in biblical principles."[75] Candi Cushman, the organization's Director of Education Issues, created True

Tolerance, an online resource that poses the following questions to parents concerned with their local schools' representations of LGBTQ+ lifestyles:

> Can we really afford to teach the next generation that there is nothing distinctive or particularly beneficial about having a mother and a father? That a family is nothing more than a group of individuals—no more unique than a herd of elephants in the jungle? Haven't we already reaped enough of the consequences of cheapening the value of the traditional family and of man-woman marriage in this society?[76]

These organizations and others with similar philosophies like the Family Research Council, which published a pamphlet entitled "Homosexuality in Your Child's School" advising parents on the ways in which schools endanger students by "promot[ing] the celebration of homosexual behavior and the silencing of any opposition,"[77] invoked religious beliefs to justify their opposition to LGBTQ+-inclusive curriculum. In doing so, they appealed to and garnered the support of the religious right in their attempts to prevent any mention of LGBTQ+ rights or history in school settings. As groups advocating for LGBTQ+-inclusive education accumulate successes, these organizations have, over time, increased the vehemence of their opposition.

From an instructional standpoint, scholars and educators argue that there are several more general reasons why LGBTQ+ content, particularly LGBTQ+ history, is not more widely included in the curriculum. Kevin Jennings, in fact, asserted that there are multiple impediments to integrating LGBTQ+ history. First, he stated, "history as a subject is less taught and less valued than it used to be" and, for that reason, "real estate in the history curriculum is very, very valuable." Jennings also posited, "The growth of the standards movement and the growth of more standardized curriculum has really put a damper on curricular innovation and curricular inclusion."[78] Historian John D'Emilio, echoing the arguments that surrounded the Children of the Rainbow curriculum, stated,

> Almost all adults in the U.S. had extremely unsatisfying and in some cases even horrifying experiences with sex education. Even though LGBT curriculum inclusion is not primarily about sexuality or sexual behavior, it brings up those worries and concerns—how do we talk about such things, how do we deal with questions that will make us uncomfortable … It's very much a "too hot to handle" subject and so it is easier to stay away from it, rather than figure out constructive courses of action.[79]

Furthermore, Kisha Webster argued that in order for any LGBTQ+-inclusive curriculum to succeed, historical or otherwise, schools and communities need proper training for teachers, excellent resources, and professional and financial investment in support of this endeavor. She said, "That's why it's so important that if school districts decide to do this, they have to have funds associated with it. To me, that's what community leaders, our voters, that's what they need to focus on … we need those who are really advocates for this to be the trailblazers and getting the necessary funds."[80] As Jennings, D'Emilio, and Webster elucidated, among those who promote LGBTQ+-inclusive education and advocate for incorporating LGBTQ+ history there is distinct awareness of the profound obstacles that have thus far prevented it from happening on a widespread basis; these obstacles, though, also point to opportunities. The reasons they discussed, combined with others—especially the fact that so many teachers are unfamiliar with this material[81]—illuminate why including LGBTQ+ history remains so difficult despite political and societal changes and the growing prominence of the LGBTQ+ community in the United States in the twenty-first century. Increased support for inclusive history curriculum within Departments of Education and LGBTQ+ advocacy organizations, though, could create the meaningful change necessary to make this goal a reality through increased awareness and revised standards.

* * *

The LGBTQ+ rights movement is more inclusive of adolescents and school communities in the twenty-first century than it was decades ago when Anita Bryant and her allies attempted to convince Americans that gay teachers posed a threat to children's safety. There is more conversation among activists and in society in general about the struggles that LGBTQ+ students face and ways in which to remedy these problems and transform the school experience for all students. This evolution resulted from growth and change in the larger movement as well as the intent and focus of individuals and organizations that saw schools as sites where the same struggles persisted. It also happened despite opposition and backlash that previously posed obstacles. In terms of schools, then, the LGBTQ+ rights movement, like others seeking social justice, expanded its mission over time and as organizations arose to meet the needs of additional members of the community.

Organizations specifically focused on schooling and promoting safe, inclusive educational environments for LGBTQ+ youth are powerful within the movement and visible within society. This is the result of grassroots efforts that gained enough support and attention to become a national movement. Greater attention and visibility, though, has not always translated to success. Attempts to integrate LGBTQ+ content met with resistance in the early 1990s and continue to encounter challenges in the twenty-first century, as evidenced by the controversy over Children of the Rainbow and the wavering fortunes of LGBT History Month; the latter faces an environment in which the emphasis remains on changing climate over teaching history. The movement has made meaningful strides in including young people in its purview since the days of Briggs and Bryant. Focusing on academic content is the next frontier.

2

Building a Model: LGBTQ+ History and Higher Education

Though K–12 schools have been slow to integrate LGBTQ+ topics, higher education institutions began to recognize the importance of the LGBTQ+ population in the United States as the gay rights movement progressed. Colleges and universities have long been sites of protest and progress, as evidenced by Civil Rights, Free Speech, and anti-war demonstrations on college campuses. Before Kevin Jennings created the network that became GLSEN, scholars and researchers at select institutions identified LGBT studies as a necessary academic discipline and worked to educate others on this interdisciplinary subject.[1] Unlike high school students in many parts of the country, college students today often have opportunities to explore LGBTQ+ lives and experiences through literature, anthropology, gender studies, and history.

Although many LGBTQ+ advocacy organizations focus more on school climate than historical content in K–12 settings, other institutions began and continue to provide instruction in LGBTQ+ and/or queer studies. Colleges and universities, free from the constraints facing public schools and the challenges that advocacy organizations target, were and are able to develop and teach information absent at other educational levels. According to the LGBTQ+ Studies page on the Hobart and William Smith Colleges website, "the discipline of LGBT Studies was founded by activists and nurtured in the visible social and political activism of the late sixties through the mid-seventies."[2] The first universities to offer courses in this discipline did so in the aftermath of the Stonewall riots that awakened the nation to an existing and, in some places, thriving gay rights movement. The University of California, Berkeley, introduced its first undergraduate LGBT studies course in the spring of 1970, with the University of Nebraska—despite attempts to ban discussions of homosexuality at a public institution of higher education—and Southern Illinois University following in the fall of that year.[3]

Though Stonewall was a catalyst for the earliest LGBT and queer studies classes, it did not lead to rapid or wholesale change. Through the 1980s and 1990s, in fact, few colleges and universities prioritized teaching LGBT history. When universities began to pay more attention to these issues, it was under the umbrella of LGBT studies—an interdisciplinary area often encompassing literature, sociology, anthropology, women's studies, psychology, and history— yet the vast majority of institutions began offering courses rather than establishing departments. The University of California, Los Angeles (UCLA), a university with deep connections to the LGBT community,[4] offered its first LGBT-related course, "Gay and Lesbian Literature," in 1976; it began offering other LGBT studies courses in 1992.[5] UCLA's Lesbian, Gay, Bisexual, Transgender, and Queer Studies Department elucidated the need to develop this line of research and education:

> As the political movement for lesbian and gay rights gained strength after 1969, the knowledge that had flourished underground for centuries found a public voice sufficiently strong to mount a sustained challenge to the official teachings concerning minority sexualities. ... This originally rather disparate work gradually coalesced into lesbian, gay, bisexual, transgender and queer studies, which, over the last two decades, has developed into an academic discipline of remarkable breadth and vitality.[6]

UCLA was a leader in the field, but other universities followed. Yale established its Lesbian and Gay Studies Center in 1986 and began hosting conferences on this topic in 1987; the department's website claims, "In ways the organizers could not have foreseen, these three conferences played a crucial role in constituting the field of LGBT Studies at a critical moment in its early development."[7] Yale established a research fund for Lesbian and Gay Studies in 1992, and course offerings in lesbian and gay studies began the same year. Historian Martin Duberman, meanwhile, established the Center for LGBTQ Studies (CLAGS) at City University of New York (CUNY) in 1991, a year before Yale established its research program, "as the first university-based research center dedicated to the study of historical, cultural, and political issues of vital concern to lesbian, gay, bisexual, transgender, and queer individuals and communities." In its current mission statement, CLAGS declares that it "provides a platform for intellectual leadership in addressing issues that affect lesbian, gay, bisexual, transgender and queer individuals and other sexual and gender minorities. ... and fosters network building among academics, artists, activists, policy makers, and community members."[8]

These early programs, which set the precedent for those established in the twenty-first century, continue to exist and thrive today. Though Yale's program, under the umbrella of the Women, Gender, and Sexuality Department, does not grant degrees, UCLA offers a minor in LGBTQ studies and CLAGS an interdisciplinary concentration in LGBTQ studies for CUNY doctoral students, in addition to supporting a minor at Brooklyn College, another CUNY institution. Each of these programs broke new ground in the academic exploration of LGBTQ+ lifestyles, experiences, influences, and history; the interdisciplinary nature of the programs gave now-prominent scholars a chance to develop their work. Students in LGBT studies programs weren't—and aren't—solely focused on history, but the course of study acknowledges its significance in students' learning and the country as a whole.

Colleges and universities, then, began to think about incorporating and disseminating LGBTQ+ content long before the vast majority of K–12 institutions acknowledged that such issues might need to be addressed. Many of the same obstacles that inhibit inclusion in primary and secondary education in the twenty-first century, including parental reaction and educational standards, would likely have impacted upon attempts to teach LGBTQ+-inclusive curricula to an even greater extent in the 1970s, 1980s, and 1990s when they were introduced at universities like UCLA, Yale, and CUNY, yet these obstacles are not the only thing that separates colleges and K–12 schools in this case. Faculty members at higher education institutions, many of whom specialize in specific fields, are more often attuned to cutting edge scholarship than K–12 teachers who, by and large, teach broad survey courses. Moreover, college and university departments, as evidenced by the work done at institutions that began to research and offer courses in LGBT studies in the 1970s, can react more rapidly to national and international events than public schools enmeshed in massive bureaucracies. Primary and secondary schools build skills and impart knowledge that children need in order to be prepared to enter, function, and participate in society; higher education provides students with the opportunity to explore and consider diverse topics in more profound ways. It therefore makes sense that colleges and universities preceded K–12 institutions in offering courses in LGBT-related fields. More than a decade into the twenty-first century, though, university faculty wish that students entered their LGBT studies and history classes with more foundational knowledge than their secondary schools offer.[9]

Multiple colleges and universities in the twenty-first century offer LGBTQ studies programs,[10] certificates, research clusters, and course options; some offer minors in this area.[11] These programs reflect collaboration and cooperation among academic disciplines, with scholars from several departments coming together to offer students a comprehensive, LGBTQ+-focused education. The University of Maryland's program was established in 2002 as "part of the institution's broad and deep effort to transform curricula ... and to ... convey some sense of the diversity of human cultures. The task of LGBT Studies is to highlight sex and gender variation as aspects of the diversity of the University community and of the knowledge generated by our faculty and students."[12] Maryland began offering courses in LGBT studies in the mid-1970s, beginning with "Homosexuality and Morality" and "Gay and Lesbian Philosophy"; the LGBT studies program's establishment was the result of years of work by university faculty to earn its approval.[13] Maryland's program, now an entrenched part of its academic life, currently offers courses including "Sexuality and Culture," "LGBT People and Communication," and "Constructions of Manhood and Womanhood in the Black Community," among several others;[14] it awarded eighty-nine certificates and forty-three minors as of December 2016. Hobart and William Smith Colleges—a small liberal arts institution as opposed to Maryland, a large public university—has a similar history with LGBT studies. Hobart and William Smith began offering a course entitled "Lesbian Cosmologies" in the 1970s and, in the 1980s, expanded to offer "Literature of Sexual Minorities," "Queer Film," and "Sexual Minorities in America." Like Maryland, the number of related courses and the emphasis on their importance grew throughout the 1990s with the establishment of a formal department in 2002.[15] Hobart and William Smith Colleges, which highlights the various methodologies incorporated in LGBT studies, also pays attention to the historical element of this program. According to the department website, "students in LGBT Studies explore the cultural and historical construction of sex, sexuality and gender in cross-cultural contexts. The program examines the lives of sexual and gender minorities throughout history, as well as the relation of gender and sexuality to the social body more generally." Moreover, Hobart and William Smith Colleges, corresponding with its statements on the importance of developing this field of study, offers a major as well as a minor in LGBT studies,[16] the first college in the nation to do so.

Other institutions, including but not limited to University of Colorado-Boulder, City College of San Francisco, DePaul University, San Diego State University, and UC Berkeley also offer students courses in LGBT studies. City College of San Francisco and San Diego State University, like Hobart and William Smith Colleges, offer a major in LGBT studies.[17] City College of San Francisco, which began offering LGBT studies classes in 1978, currently maintains a list of thirty-two available courses in LGBTQI+ Studies and related fields, all of which count toward the major.[18] San Diego State University's program began in 2009; it established the major three years later. DePaul University established its LGBT studies program, which "examines the history, politics, culture and psychologies of LGBTQ+ individuals and communities," in 2005 and offers a minor in this area;[19] DePaul, the largest Catholic university in the country, encountered resistance from some religious groups when it first announced its intentions.[20] University of Colorado-Boulder and UC Berkeley emphasize the inclusive and interdisciplinary nature of their programs. Boulder's program description states, "LGBTQ Studies involves the academic investigation of sexuality in established fields such as literature, history, theatre, law, medicine, economics, sociology, anthropology and political science. With its interdisciplinary approach, LGBTQ studies interweaves complex theories and analysis into the study of sexuality" and goes on to further reiterate, "By its very nature LGBTQ studies is interdisciplinary."[21] Berkeley, meanwhile, mentions its program's interdisciplinary nature and emphasizes its real world implications, asserting, "The field of [LGBT] Studies both addresses the particularities of the modern forms of sexuality we call lesbian, gay, bisexual, and transgender … and further addresses the phenomenon of sexuality itself in all its historical and cross-cultural diversity." Similar to other universities that explicitly state that their LGBT programs are open to students of all sexualities, Berkeley stresses the inclusive nature of its program and this course of study, contending, "LGBT Studies is not only by, about, or for lesbian, gay, bisexual, or transgender people—it includes all humanity in its purview."[22] At the college level, then, LGBT studies provides students with the opportunity to immerse themselves in LGBTQ+ lifestyles, culture, arts, issues, history, and discoveries. In a departure from K–12 education and the limitations it presents, college students are able to navigate the complexities presented by an interdisciplinary program that, by its nature, undertakes mature topics and discussions.

Though colleges and universities present students with greater opportunities to explore LGBTQ+ culture than secondary schools, similarities exist in the way in which this information is presented and conveyed. Where LGBTQ+-inclusive curriculum is present in high schools, the focus of the majority of this information is on improving school climate, encouraging acceptance, and decreasing the harassment and bullying LGBTQ+ students endure. In elementary schools, students learn about diverse family structures and lifestyles to reinforce the same message; the earliest attempts to convey this information, such as the Rainbow Curriculum, concentrated specifically on family life.[23] University-based LGBT studies programs, though more in-depth and culturally focused, employ similar tactics—albeit through academic disciplines like psychology, anthropology, and sociology as versus health classes, climate workshops, and GSAs. Lifestyles, then, are a prevailing theme of LGBTQ+-centric education at all levels. History, in higher education as in K–12 education, is merely one piece of the puzzle.[24] Nevertheless, its importance on its own merit is more widely acknowledged in a university setting and courses there are more pervasive than in high schools throughout the country.

University programs have different points of emphasis, yet they all include a historical evaluation of the LGBTQ+ community and its experiences to some extent. LGBTQ+ history instruction is present in schooling, therefore, even if it is not a significant presence in K–12 classrooms. The Committee on Lesbian, Gay, Bisexual, and Transgender History (CLGBTH), an affiliate of the American Historical Association, maintains a database of LGBTQ+ history course syllabi dating back to 1997, when Duke University offered "History of Sexuality in America" in its summer session. Similarly themed and titled courses have appeared at institutions around the country since, including Ohio State University, New York University, University of Chicago, and University of North Carolina at Chapel Hill, where David Palmer's "U.S. Lesbian, Gay, Bisexual, and Transgender History" examines "the formation of early LGBT communities from the colonial period through the mid-twentieth-century" and "aspirations for 'liberation' advanced by different LGBT-identified people since World War II."[25] Moreover, Notre Dame, a Catholic university, offered "History of Sex, Sexuality, and Gender in British North America and the U.S., to 1900" and "Historiography: The Histories of Women, Masculinities, Gender and Sexualities" in fall 2005. The list also includes universities in more conservative areas, like the University of Utah, which offered "The History and Psychology of the 'Gay' Family in America: Origins, Context, and Implications" and "Sexuality in 20th Century America" in spring 2011 and the University of North Texas, which offered "Gender and Sexuality in Early Modern Europe" in spring 2013. In all, CLGBTH's list—which does not hold syllabi from every course offered— includes more than eighty college and university syllabi from 1997–2018.[26]

Morehouse College, an all-male historically Black college, began offering "History and Culture of Black LGBT," a course taught via Skype by a Yale professor, in 2013 in response to anti-gay violence on campus.[27] Unlike K–12 schools that rely on anti-discrimination and anti-bullying programs to create a safer environment, Morehouse's response to threats to student safety was to teach history. It is a long-held axiom that those who ignore history are doomed to repeat it. It is reasonable, therefore, to deduce that history might also be instructive in the present and could serve similar purposes to school climate initiatives underway through LGBTQ+ advocacy organizations. Furthermore, the increasing availability of this information in higher education necessitates its presence in high schools to establish prior knowledge and indicates that, at educational institutions, the growth of this field is possible.

Quantity and variation in course offerings are greater at colleges and universities across the country than in the vast majority of elementary, middle, and high schools, where students enroll in a prescribed course of required classes. This difference is meaningful in explaining the rise of LGBTQ+ history at the higher education level despite its infrequent appearances in K–12 schools. It is inarguable that colleges and universities have made greater strides in LGBT studies and LGBTQ+ history, though Emily Hobson, who teaches courses in the history of sexuality, LGBTQ history, and queer studies at University of Nevada, Reno, asserted that "it's important to parse the difference between queer studies broadly and LGBT history" and cautioned against conflating the prevalence of these courses at selective universities and small liberal arts colleges with higher education writ large.[28] She stated,

> The history departments have been a little slower on the uptake, significantly slower, I would say. ... LGBT history is fairly still recent to many history departments. Certainly, in my own department, I am the first person specifically doing history of sexuality that my department has ever hired. ... And my department is not hostile or conservative.[29]

LGBTQ+ history in higher education, then, remains a work in progress. As history scholars at colleges and universities continue to promote this branch of history and its importance for students and the larger society, these advancements will likely continue. As Morehouse College decided, learning LGBTQ+ history is essential to changing the culture and climate. Therefore, in the same way that the rise of LGBT studies created space for students to learn LGBTQ+ history, the increased emphasis on school climate and creating safe spaces in K–12 institutions can provide a springboard, too.

Teacher Education

The clearest connection between colleges and universities and K–12 education are the teacher education programs housed in schools of education across the country. Though many preservice teachers in the twenty-first century seek out newer, more immersive paths to certification, education schools continue to offer programs through which undergraduates and graduate students learn and practice the tools of their trade. Within these institutions, individuals learn the methods, strategies, and subject matter they need to successfully run their own classrooms. LGBTQ+ history, though, is not a significant enough component of social studies teacher education programs, where it factors in at all, to prepare teachers to comfortably integrate this information into their lessons.

Wendy Rouse, a professor at San Jose State University, runs a teacher preparation program purposefully dedicated to training future teachers to incorporate LGBTQ+ history in their classrooms; she was motivated to create this program by the passage of the FAIR Education Act,[30] and it is now housed in the university's history department.[31] Rouse's program, which asks students to explore, evaluate, and apply the content they learn, does not provide teacher credentials; the undergraduates enrolled in the program transition into a credentialing program when they complete their undergraduate coursework. As Rouse described it, the program is a social science major for emerging teachers through which they become immersed in the content that they will teach in addition to the skills necessary to convey that information to students. LGBTQ+ individuals' contributions to US and California history are a through thread in all of the courses in which students enroll; they also have the opportunity to engage in a semester-long LGBTQ history class.[32] Given these circumstances, she has the space to concentrate on LGBTQ+ history in a way that more abbreviated or methodology-focused programs do not. Prospective teachers advance in their studies equipped with this knowledge in the hope that they impart it when they enter the classroom.[33] This is especially important in California, Rouse posited, where credentialing programs focus solely on pedagogy and undergraduate programs therefore must provide future teachers with the content and resources they will ultimately share with their students.[34]

Rouse reported that except for her own, she is unaware of any other teacher education program that focuses on LGBTQ+ history to a remarkable extent. Though faculty and instructors might choose to discuss this information in their classes and social studies education students at some colleges and universities have the option of enrolling in an LGBTQ+ or gender history class as part of their program—social studies students at Hunter College in New York regularly enroll in Professor Daniel Hurewitz's gender and sexuality history course in that institution's history department—few if any programs highlight LGBTQ+ history to the extent that San Jose State does. Incorporating this information into teacher education programs would allow the information conveyed at the university level to trickle down to K–12 schools, creating a wider circle of students and teachers with knowledge of LGBTQ+ history and preparing high school students for the courses to which they will have access at institutions of higher learning. It would also, in small part, alleviate one stated reason for this topic's omission in high school classes, as teachers would know and have experience with LGBTQ+ history; Lyndsey Schlax, in fact, insists it is necessary across the board in teacher education programs.[35] As colleges and universities progress toward embracing LGBTQ+ history, there are multiple ways that it might be beneficial for this information to find a place in schools of education, as well.

* * *

More than forty years after LGBT studies courses were first introduced, an increasing number of universities across the United States offer LGBTQ+ or queer history courses, with some institutions offering majors and minors in LGBTQ studies. These courses and the departments that offer them extend the possibility that, under the right circumstances, academic LGBTQ+ content can be part of a student's education.

Universities and K–12 schools adhere to different requirements and grapple with different sets of circumstances. The vast majority of elementary, middle, and high school students are minors whose schools act *in loco parentis* while children are in their care. Student age, therefore, imposes restrictions on the freedom schools have to impart information. Students at higher education institutions are mostly over eighteen and therefore legally adults; there are fewer limitations on what they consume. As John D'Emilio posited, inclusive curriculum is difficult in K–12 settings because "it also presses up against the discomfort that almost all adults experience when they think of sexuality in terms of the young."[36] Similarly, K–12 teachers risk parent reaction to controversial information to a far greater extent than college professors who often have more distance from their students' families. In addition, Emily Hobson, whose essay "Questions, Not Test Answers: Teaching LGBT History in Public Schools" explored the absence of LGBTQ+ history in high schools, contended that most high school teachers are not familiar with this material and therefore cannot teach it; colleges, meanwhile, are more likely to have faculty members who can.[37] Furthermore, Hobson asserted, standards and testing pose a significant hindrance to including LGBTQ+ history in K–12 education in ways that they do not in higher education. This dichotomy, in fact, clearly indicates the fine line between obstacle and opportunity in education: standards, which currently inhibit including LGBTQ+ history in the vast majority of states, could just as easily be the impetus for incorporating this material. Hobson stated,

Certainly, at the college level, those standardized tests from high school are now no longer really relevant and so you can really spend a lot of time talking about what is and isn't taught. ... You get to have conversations with students about what was included at the K–12 level and what wasn't and kind of all these various ways to talk about public memory and it opens up a lot of conversations.[38]

Thus, because it establishes what teachers must include and the way in which material is presented, testing stymies the introduction of and meaningful conversation about LGBTQ+ history in high schools. This, according to Hobson and her coauthor Felicia Perez, is the one of the most significant reasons that LGBTQ+ history is taught in college but not high school.[39] The removal of this retinue of obstacles on a college campus creates a more hospitable environment for LGBTQ+ content. If high schools followed the model established by higher education—greater openness to change and support from authority figures—efforts to teach LGBTQ+ history at the high school level could also be more pervasive.

3

Expanding Awareness: LGBTQ+ Content in Students' Lives

The LGBTQ+ community occupies a different space in the public consciousness than it did when advocates struggled for recognition and an end to harassment in the era after the Stonewall riots. This is, in large part, a result of those activists' work and the initiatives undertaken by organizations formed to fight for LGBTQ+ rights. Political activism, though, is not the sole reason for this change. In the half century since the Stonewall riots, societal norms and culture have changed, as well. Interactions that might have been uncommon or censored as recently as twenty years ago are now more commonplace; advertisers boycotted shows like *Thirtysomething* and *L.A. Law* that featured gay and lesbian characters in the 1990s,[1] yet shows like *Pose* and *Schitt's Creek* that regularly depicted LGBTQ+ characters interacting were among the most critically acclaimed in 2020. As the LGBTQ+ community became more prominent, some myths and stereotypes receded. To an extent, therefore, the gay rights movement accomplished one of its most intangible goals: removing the societal barriers that prevented LGBTQ+ people from safely and openly living public lives. This representation is educationally meaningful, as well. As young people are increasingly exposed to complex portrayals of LGBTQ+ individuals and themes in the media they consume, school-based discussions provide opportunities to talk about and contextualize the information and messages students receive elsewhere.

The LGBTQ+ Community in Popular Culture

GLAAD introduced its now annual *Where We Are on TV* report on LGBTQ+ representation on television in 2005. For the 2019–20 season, GLAAD found that "of the 879 regular characters expected to appear on broadcast scripted primetime programming this season, 90 (10.2%) were identified as gay, lesbian, bisexual, transgender, and/or queer"; according to the report this was the "highest percentage of LGBTQ series regulars GLAAD has found since beginning to gather data for all series regulars in the 2005–06 season."[2] In addition, cable shows featured 121 regular LGBTQ+ characters and streaming services featured 109. Moreover, nonbinary and transgender characters, as well as LGBTQ+ characters of color, populate television shows in greater numbers than in the past.[3] Though GLAAD also cites the ways in which television programming needs to continue improving—LGBTQ+ characters need to be better developed and LGBTQ+ representation on television does not truly reflect the full diversity of the LGBTQ+ community, to name two[4]—this increased representation, amid a trajectory of increasing representation, meets the goals GLAAD expressed in previous reports. President and CEO Sarah Kate Ellis concluded,

> GLAAD is calling on the industry to ensure that 20 percent of series regular characters on primetime scripted broadcast series are LGBTQ by 2025. Further, we would challenge all platforms to make sure that within the next two years, half of LGBTQ characters on every platform are people of color. While broadcast has actually hit this mark two years in a row, cable and streaming have yet to reach this goal. These two steps are key moves towards ensuring that entertainment reflects the world in which it is created and the audience who consumes it.[5]

Greater representation in the entertainment Americans consume contributed to increased social acceptance of the LGBTQ+ population in the twenty-first century.[6] Beyond television, films and music increasingly represent LGBTQ+ Americans. *Moonlight*, a film depicting the same-sex relationship between two Black men and its effect on their lives, won the 2017 Academy Award for Best Picture. An increasing number of chart-topping musicians—including Lil Nas X, whose "Old Town Road" spent seventeen weeks at number one in 2019— are openly LGBTQ+. Like social acceptance, though, accurate and fully diverse media representations are an uphill climb. While the media is more reflective of American society than it was in the past, resistance, economics, power dynamics, and public opinion slow the pace of change.

In addition to on screen entertainment products, children's and young adult (YA) books explore LGBTQ+ themes. Beginning in 1981 with *Jenny Lives with Eric and Martin* by Susanne Bosch, same-sex couples and diverse family structures emerged as a motif in books written for school-age children. The themes and availability of these books have proliferated over the years; an internet search for LGBTQ+-themed children's literature now yields hundreds of results. Among them are several different books entitled *Families*, or some variation thereof, all of which look at the vast number of family structures and cultures that exist in the United States and across the world.[7] There are also a wide variety that focus specifically on same-sex pairings; these books have become more mainstream and less controversial over the years. In 1989 Leslea Newman published *Heather Has Two Mommies*, a story with an inclusive message that was nevertheless derided by critics as inappropriate for its target audience.[8] Newman, a prolific author of LGBTQ+-themed literature and resources aimed at children and adolescents, later wrote *Daddy, Papa, and Me* (2009) and *Mommy, Mama, and Me* (2009), both aimed at toddlers, and for school age children, *Donovan's Big Day* (2011), about a boy's excitement as his two moms' wedding approaches; all caused less uproar in a changing world. Newman, who is gay, asserted, "I wrote these books because I think it is important for kids from all types of families to see themselves portrayed in books. It validates their experience, and teaches all of us that there are many different types of families and the most important thing about a family is that all the people in it love each other."[9]

LGBTQ+-themed picture books are, at their foundation, stories for children; in addition to the focus on family authors therefore write stories that resonate with their audience. Linda De Haan's *King and King*, for example, published in 2003, offers children a variation on the traditional fairytale—in this story, the prince chooses another prince as his betrothed. Moreover, in keeping with a classic children's literary device, some authors use animals to tell stories of same-sex relationships. In *And Tango Makes Three*, which proved as controversial when it was published in 2005 as *Heather Has Two Mommies* was in the 1990s, two male penguins "adopt" an egg, nurture it, and raise the baby penguin together. According to the New York Public Library, "*Tango* challenged some Americans' ideas and assumptions about homosexuality, age-appropriateness of the material, and raised the thorny question about what makes a family. ... *And Tango Makes Three* has topped the ALA's 10 Most Challenged Books List between 2006 and 2010."[10] *Worm Loves Worm*, published after the Supreme Court affirmed the right to same-sex marriage, explains that concept to young children as woodland creatures figure out how to conduct a wedding that does not reflect "how it's always been done."[11] LGBTQ+-themed children's books, like nearly all children's books, aim to convey a message. Often, as these stories reflect, the message is about love, more than traditions and cultural norms, binding families together. As the number of books available increased, children were and continue to be more exposed to these ideas—in regions where reading these books is socially accepted—than in the past.

Books about gender, and the bullying that often accompanies gender nonconformity, are more prominent on bookshelves, as well. *The Paper Bag Princess*, published in 1980, upended the traditional princess narrative when the titular princess saves the prince from a dragon, much to his dismay. *Jacob's New Dress* (2014) and *Morris Micklewhite and the Tangerine Dress* (2015) tell stories about children whose feelings, desires, and fashion choices don't fit into societally established norms and binaries. In *Introducing Teddy*, meanwhile, nothing substantively changes when Thomas, a teddy bear, realizes that he actually identifies as Tilly. All of these books, like those about same-sex families and relationships, share a message of acceptance and inclusivity. Children's literature, then, hues closely to ideas conveyed in schools where LGBTQ+ topics are included in the curriculum; they teach tolerance, open mindedness, and friendship. These books, perhaps, lay the groundwork for children and adolescents to internalize that particular message.

Middle grade and YA novels, written for upper elementary through high school students, also incorporate LGBTQ+ themes more frequently than in the past. *The Best Man*, published by Richard Peck in 2016, focuses on one child's experience finding out that two of his male role models, his revered uncle and his student teacher—who end up dating—are both gay. *George*, published by Alex Gino in 2015, tells the story of a transgender fourth grader who navigates the travails of sharing her secret, including bullying and family resistance. Gino followed with *Rick*, a 2020 book about a middle school student who explores his identity and surroundings in his school's "Rainbow Spectrum" club. *The Best Man*, *George*, and *Rick* were written for, and at the reading level of, fourth through sixth graders. *The Other Boy*, about the difficulties a transgender middle school student faces when his friends and teammates discover his identity, offers middle school students the opportunity to read about similar issues.[12]

Meanwhile, the number of YA novels with LGBTQ+ characters increased between 2003 and 2018. Author Malinda Lo, who compiles and evaluates statistics on LGBTQ+ representation in this genre, found that fewer than twenty YA books featured LGBTQ+ characters in 2003.[13] That number has increased significantly over time. In Lo's most recent report, evaluating books published through 2018, she found that LGBTQ protagonists and issues were prominent in 108 young adult books in multiple genres; that number represents a "300% increase over 2009," her baseline for the report, "when only 27 were published."[14]

Furthermore, a 2018 *Vulture* article asserted, "Just in the last few years, we seem to be entering a golden age of queer YA. We are seeing far more titles getting published than ever before, and a much broader array of stories being told. We still have a long way to go, however."[15] Some of these books, like Benjamin Alire Sáenz's *Aristotle and Dante Discover the Secrets of the Universe* and Becky Albertalli's *Simon v. the Homo Sapiens*—which became the motion picture *Love, Simon*—are widely read and part of teenagers' common consciousness. All of Albertalli's novels, in fact, feature LGBTQ+ characters and themes. Similarly, authors like Adam Silvera and Elizabeth Acevedo consistently write about LGBTQ+ young people from different cultures and backgrounds. Numerous options exist, then, for children at every age to immerse themselves in the LGBTQ+ experience through literature.

Children and young adults raised on these books came of age in an era of greater openness and, in some regions, tolerance about families and sexuality than prior generations. The continued, if decreasing, resistance to these books, though, as well as the minimal number of LGBTQ+-themed books published compared with other groups, indicates the need for further evolution. Moreover, because children are receiving this content in the books they read and entertainment products they consume, more widespread classroom learning could contextualize information that might otherwise exist in a vacuum.

LGBTQ+ Content in Schools

Though LGBTQ+ themes and content are not as pervasive in schools as they are in the media and other institutions, there are entry points for inclusion among several subjects. A recent GLSEN survey found that students are more likely to interact with LGBTQ+ content in their history, English, or health classes than other classes in which they are enrolled.[16] The information conveyed and resources considered in these subjects create space through which students can learn more about LGBTQ+ individuals and their lives, and, potentially, open their minds and become more aware and accepting. Thus, regardless of the discipline for which they were created, these materials echo LGBTQ+ advocacy organizations' calls and serve similar goals to social studies lessons.

High school English classes offer students opportunities to see worlds beyond their own through the literature they read and analyze, similar to the experience students may have reading LGBTQ+-themed YA novels. In an academic setting, as opposed to independently, teachers guide students through the process of learning more about the characters, their backgrounds and motivations, and the way in which events in a story influence and affect them. Topics relevant to gender and sexuality appear throughout literature, even in books that are not specifically noted as LGBTQ+- themed; teachers can introduce a queer lens through which to evaluate those themes more deeply than students might on their own.[17] Through this lens and these experiences, then, students learn more about LGBTQ+ lives over time.

In 2014, the National Council of Teachers of English (NCTE) issued a position statement entitled "Diverse Gender Expression and Gender Non-Conformity Curriculum in English Grades 7–12." In it, the organization asserted,

> it is imperative that English language arts educators develop a lens through which they can see and think critically about gender, gender expression, sexuality, and gender non-conformity. Through this lens, students would consider how gender and sexuality are represented in a range of texts; would gain awareness regarding gendered and heteronormative expectations; would work with texts featuring a diverse range of people (including those who are LGBTQ and/or gender non-conforming); and would express their own perspectives regarding these representations and expectations.[18]

The statement goes on to specifically recommend introducing books with LGBTQ+ characters, employing a "gendered or gender non-conforming lens" in text analysis, and providing students opportunities to incorporate personal and academic ideas about gender in writing assignments.[19] NCTE, an organization that works to support literacy, improve English education, and promote justice and equity in classrooms throughout the United States,[20] therefore claimed that making the discipline more inclusive was the way to do so.

Following NCTE's guidance, lessons and resources exist to promote inclusive English curriculum and push students to consider LGBTQ+ perspectives when they evaluate literature, verbally and in writing. Massachusetts, which amended its state framework in 2018 to promote inclusive education, developed lessons for English classes including "Is Nick Carraway Gay? A Hidden Gay Voice in an American Classic," which applies an LGBTQ+ lens to students' analysis of *The Great Gatsby*; "Jazz Poetry of Langston Hughes: A Reflection of African American and Queer Identity During the Harlem Renaissance"; and "Leslea Newman: An Influential American Voice and an Authentic Writer of the LGBTQ Experience in Literature."[21] Each of these lessons fulfills NCTE's goal of making the subject more representative and challenging students to think deeply about both the characters and ideas on the page and the authors who create them.

GLSEN, which creates resources for educators in addition to advocating for LGBTQ+ students and teachers, has two lessons available on its website: the interdisciplinary "He Continues to Make a Difference" and an English-language arts lesson focused on *Simon v. the Homo Sapiens Agenda* and the movie adaptation *Love, Simon*. "He Continues to Make a Difference," in which students learn about Matthew Shepard's life and murder, focuses on Leslea Newman's poem "The Fence" and asks students to engage in "text-text and text-self strategies" to analyze the poem, draw connections between Matthew Shepard and other LGBTQ+ individuals' experiences, and "create a work of fiction based on a real moment in LGBT history."[22] The *Love, Simon* lesson asks students to "compare identities and traits of main characters with a focus on 'invisible' identities'" and "reflect on their own identities around race, sexuality, gender, socioeconomic status, religion, and ability, in order to strengthen their capacity to empathize, connect, and collaborate with a diverse group of people." Students then write letters to discuss the characters' identities and share aspects of their own; one of the lesson's goals is for students to be able to better support peers struggling with revealing their gender or sexuality.[23] Both of these lessons build literacy skills by engaging students in reading and writing and asking them to apply information in new, thoughtful ways. They also promote tolerance for and understanding of LGBTQ+ lives, experiences, and struggles in ways that are indicative of the power of English education.

English teachers, through class discussions and writing assignments, gain insight into their students' thoughts and identities in ways other subject teachers don't often access. Furthermore, character analysis is, in itself, an identity study. Through curriculum and conversation, then, LGBTQ+ topics and content enter English classrooms. Christine Gentry, a former high school English teacher and current teacher educator, cited identity as a significant reason for instructing her students to critically evaluate literature through a queer lens that, she posited, is "very much attached to gender roles."[24] She personally identifies as queer and asserted that the absence of LGBTQ+ themes and information in her school experience hindered her from "embracing and accepting that side of [her]self";[25] she wanted her students to have opportunities that she did not. Gentry's classes read *The Color Purple*—the only Pulitzer Prize–winning novel with a lesbian protagonist written by a woman—because she "explicitly wanted to discuss" Shug Avery's relationships with men and women with her students. According to Gentry, "people who are queer who … have partners of both sexes or genders are often erased from both straight narratives and gay narratives." Highlighting these characters and individuals, she believes, contributed to meaningful conversations about "having trouble feeling included or truly part of a community when you're caught in between" that emphasized the queer lens and also resonated with her biracial students.[26]

Lauren Jensen, a Washington, DC, area teacher, focused on ensuring her students had access to this content despite its absence from state standards. She recalled, "While building my classroom library I devoted a section to LGBTQ+ literature, including daily book chats that highlighted said literature. It's not a mandated part of our curriculum, so I felt it necessary to build this in authentically in order to foster a community of acceptance in my classroom and provide texts through which students could see themselves."[27] Brooklyn teacher Rebecca McBride, meanwhile, uses photo stories from the *New York Times* and films like *Pariah* and *Moonlight* to convey LGBTQ+ content. She focuses on the impact of gender worldwide, using documentaries like *Period: End of Sentence* to provoke conversations about identity and its role in cultures beyond the United States.[28] According to Jensen,

> literature with LGBTQ+ content can act as a mirror for those LGBTQ+ students seeking narratives similar to their own. For non-LGBTQ+ students, literature can provide a window into the stories of others. Consequently, LGBTQ+ content and themes are not a luxury or privilege, they are VITAL to fostering students' authentic selves and understanding of others during a stage of their lives that is often burdened with questions about identity and fear of not being accepted.[29]

The analysis in which students engage in English classes offers meaningful opportunities to think critically about themselves, others, and the world in which they live. As Gentry recalled, "it's important to me that my humanity is a part of my teaching, and that my students see me and who I really am, and I see them, and all of them, and that that vulnerability is a two-way street."[30] McBride, Jensen, and Gentry's choices and inclusivity promoted that relationship building and authenticity in their English classes.

Health education, according to the New York City Department of Education, seeks to "teach students how to take care of their minds, their bodies, and their relationships with others."[31] Classes, depending on the grade level, encompass topics like puberty, mental health, nutrition, hygiene, and social emotional growth. Health classes are also the home to sex education in the schools and regions where this subject exists; students then learn about pregnancy, sexual health, and sexually transmitted diseases, among other topics. According to the Guttmacher Institute, in 2020 thirty-nine states and Washington, DC, required sex education and/or HIV education; of those thirty-nine, eleven states and the District of Columbia "require inclusive content with regard to sexual orientation."[32] There, and in classes in other parts of the country, students gain a better understanding of LGBTQ+ identity and matters and concerns important to their LGBTQ+ peers.

Washington state, which passed its Healthy Youth Act in 2007, mandates that sex education is "appropriate for students regardless of gender, race, disability status, or sexual orientation."[33] Its Family Life and Sexual Health (FLASH) curriculum aims to fulfill that edict, providing K–12 teachers statewide with targeted lessons that seek to "prevent teen pregnancy, STDs and sexual violence"[34] including two high school level lessons that address LGBTQ+ identities and stereotypes. In "Sexual Orientation and Gender Identity," students "differentiate between biological sex, sexual orientation, sexual behavior and gender identity" and discuss the ways in which heteronormativity and societal expectations can cause harm. "Undoing Gender Stereotypes," meanwhile, demonstrates the weight that accompanies preconceived notions about gender. Both lessons are inquiry and activity based: in the former students create advice columns, and in the latter, they participate in scenarios in which they consider how stereotypes impact upon behavior.[35] The ideas conveyed in these lessons provide students with science- and fact-based information that underscores and contextualizes what they glean from the media and other institutions of which they are a part. FLASH—which was used by 38.3 percent of the state's schools in 2019[36]— and Washington's laws provide a foundation from which students' ideas and acceptance can grow.

Outside of Washington, several organizations develop lessons and resources to increase students' awareness of LGBTQ+ students' plights and change school climate for the better. The Resource Center for Adolescent Pregnancy Prevention's (ReCAPP) "Toward Understanding … Some of Us Are Lesbian or Gay" aims to "sensitize participants to the difficulties society imposes on gay and lesbian youth and provides participants who have questions about sexual orientation with suggestions for finding support for themselves."[37] Students engage in an activity in which they learn what life is like for people who identify as LGBTQ+ and ponder how they might support this population. Advocates for Youth, an organization that supports young people's rights to sexual health information and proper care,[38] similarly provides students with the resources to learn about LGBTQ+ individuals, breakdown stereotypes, and promote acceptance and respect through discussion, introspection, and writing activities in "I Am Who I Am," a lesson that investigates identity in general and dispels myths related to sexual orientation and gender identity.[39] Other organizations, like the Safe Schools Coalition and Sex, Etc., focus more specifically on individuals' experiences in society and in schools, asking students to contemplate how they would feel if placed in situations that members of the LGBTQ+ population frequently confront.[40] Inspiring students to move past fears and preconceived notions and begin to consider and act upon new ideas accomplishes the goals of both the lessons and the organizations that develop them.

* * *

LGBTQ+-inclusive curriculum, regardless of the subject in which it is present, seeks to accomplish certain goals: overcome stereotypes, increase acceptance among students and faculty, and provide context and information beyond what students receive outside of school. It is also a necessity in an era when everyone from toddlers to adults has a window into LGBTQ+ lives, themes, and issues. There are myriad sources from which students can learn about LGBTQ+ individuals' experiences, many of which convey this information in ways that are relevant and relatable. Lessons in English and health classes provide a basis to understand what students read, watch, and consume across platforms, contextualize the information students receive elsewhere, and offer students the opportunity to evaluate this material in ways that they might not on their own. In this way, lessons in other subjects build the skills necessary to participate and involve oneself in society—the same skills that social studies classes, in general and through the LGBTQ+ information incorporated therein, seek to instill.

Creating Community: LGBTQ+ Content in Social Studies Classes

LGBTQ+ topics are a necessary aspect of students' education, a fact that is made clear in their proliferation in the content young people consume and their presence in the English and health class resources that students encounter. Moreover, students need to feel safe in their school environments in order to learn; climates in which students regularly confront bias, hatred, harassment, and bullying demand that attention be paid to the ideas and attitudes contributing to those dangers. Efforts and resources that integrate LGBTQ+ topics, then, serve a valuable purpose in addressing issues within the school community and enhancing students' lived and learning experiences.

The National Education Association's Committee on Social Studies established the subject in 1916 as a course of study to develop within students "an appreciation of the nature and laws of social life, a sense of responsibility of the individual as a member of social groups, and the intelligence and the will to participate effectively in the promotion of the social well-being." In the introduction to its report, in a section entitled "Aims of the Social Studies," the committee stated, "The social studies of the American high school should have for their conscious and constant purpose the cultivation of good citizenship."[1] The report recommended a comprehensive curriculum including civics, economics, and sociology in addition to history in its effort to fulfill these goals. This civically minded intention—creating participatory, contributing citizens— remains essential in twenty-first-century social studies education, as well. Resources that aim to build tolerance, bridge gaps, and create community and teach students the skills to do so, like those intended to enhance school climate, reflect social studies' foundational goals.

A change as potentially controversial as integrating LGBTQ+ history in students' academic content is a slow and arduous process. The controversy surrounding the Rainbow Curriculum attests to the resistance encountered mentioning something as simple as "families can have two mommies" as recently as thirty years ago. The pace of change around widespread anti-bullying curriculum, though, was more rapid. Because LGBTQ+ children and teens encounter harassment and violence more than most other groups, the efforts directed at curtailing bullying created an opportunity to integrate LGBTQ+ content in schools. The resources developed to meet those needs reference historical events, figures, and issues to varying degrees, but they consistently address the larger social studies-related intention of learning to live and work with others to create a well-functioning society and plant the seeds of historical learning upon which students can continue to build.

Battling Bullying

In the early part of the twenty-first century, amid changing ideas of how to teach and raise happy, thriving children, bullying became a national topic of conversation. In fact, in August 2010, the federal government held its first summit on bullying, after which Secretary of Education Arne Duncan said, "It is an absolute travesty of our educational system when students fear for their safety at school, worry about being bullied or suffer discrimination and taunts because of their ethnicity, religion, sexual orientation, disability or a host of other reasons. The fact is that no school can be a great school until it is a safe school first."[2] Moreover, in December 2011 the federal government released its "Analysis of State Bullying Laws and Policies" report; the Education Department stated,

> The report shows the prevalence of state efforts to combat bullying over the last several years. From 1999 to 2010, more than 120 bills were enacted by state legislatures from across the country to either introduce or amend statutes that address bullying and related behaviors in schools. Twenty-one new bills were enacted in 2010 and eight additional bills were signed into law through April 30, 2011.[3]

By 2010, then, the full weight of federal and state governments and the institutions under their purview—schools, for example—was behind eradicating bullying.

By September 2017 all fifty states had anti-bullying laws on the books; forty-two had additional policies in place in support of those laws.[4] Statistics showing that LGBTQ+ children and adolescents endured some of the most brutal bullying led to calls for programs and materials to specifically address bullying based on gender identity or sexuality. Additionally, the 2010 suicide of Rutgers student Tyler Clementi, who jumped from the George Washington Bridge after his roommate recorded his same-sex sexual encounters, gained national attention and fueled the conversation about addressing bullying as it pertained to LGBTQ+ youth. The It Gets Better project, founded in 2010 in the wake of Clementi's suicide, aimed to "reach out to lesbian, gay, transgender and bisexual youth who may be the victims of bullying"[5] and, according to the organization's website, hoped to connect and build community among LGBTQ+ youth to prevent the isolation and loneliness that can lead to suicide.[6] Organizations like GLSEN,[7] GSA, and Welcoming Schools, long at work on making schools safer for LGBTQ+ students, were part of the sea change wherein their efforts were more widely embraced and supported throughout the nation.

Since 2009–10, the government's, LGBTQ+ advocacy groups', and major educational organizations' dedication to LGBTQ-centric anti-bullying efforts have profoundly supported this mission. Bullying was—and remains—a crisis, and bullying based on gender identity or sexuality even more so. The National Gay and Lesbian Task Force advocated for more stringent laws and an end to LGBTQ+ bullying, criticizing a 2010 policy in Anoka-Hennepin, Minnesota—a school district where four LGBTQ+ students committed suicide that year—that promoted " 'neutrality' in regards [to] discussions of homosexuality"; this was meant to be an improvement over "their 2009 policy that prohibit[ed] teachers from discussing homosexuality as a 'normal, valid lifestyle.' " The Task Force argued, "All school staff need training on effective bullying prevention. Bullying and harassment because of sexual orientation and gender identity must be discussed with young people."[8] The federal government launched stopbullying.gov in 2012; the website has a page specifically devoted to LGBTQ youth that advises on the best ways to build a safe environment and recommends resources to assist in this process.[9] Furthermore, the George Lucas Educational Foundation, a national organization focused on developing and promoting innovative, engaging classroom experiences, published an article in favor of inclusive anti-bullying politics based on a 2013 GLSEN report. The article advocated for "ensur[ing] anti-bullying practices are inclusive. ... Rais[ing] awareness among the school community of both the policy in general and the specific LGBT inclusion. ... Provid[ing] professional development on bullying that includes knowledge and skills around LGBT-specific bullying and harassment."[10]

Anti-bullying and safe school programs, then, became valuable educational initiatives around which both LGBTQ+ activists and educators in general could rally support. Though scholars and educators published studies and journal articles earlier in the decade advocating for the inclusion of LGBTQ+ history in social studies classes, their ideas failed to gain similar traction.[11] This disparity illustrates the power of institutional support. Where it exists, change occurs; where it does not, attempts at reform remain at the grassroots. According to GLSEN, as of August 2020, twenty-one states and the District of Columbia have "enumerated anti-bullying laws protecting LGBTQ students."[12] National and local organizations that were already creating curriculum focused on improving school climate, and increasing tolerance, acceptance, and inclusivity for LGBTQ+ students thus increased in prominence as their work became more recognized and valuable amid changing societal ideas.

Bullying is an acknowledged problem with the infrastructure to support targeting it. Therefore, in terms of curriculum development it receives the bulk of advocates' attention. Many of the organizations developing LGBTQ+-inclusive curriculum are primarily focused on the struggles that these students endure in schools where they face insensitivity, discrimination, harassment, and, in the worst cases, violence. Studies indicate that the school environment, a bastion of pressure in general, is especially difficult to navigate for teens who identify as LGBTQ+.[13] These organizations work to educate all high school students, regardless of their sexuality or gender identity, of the dangerous impact that their actions, words, and attitudes might have on their classmates and the school climate as a whole. For organizations devoted to ameliorating the situation in which LGBTQ+ students find themselves on a daily basis and making school a positive, welcoming place, the majority of resources and curricula they develop focus on achieving that goal. Additionally, as LGBTQ+ students' plight—and the impact of bullying and environment on children and their learning in general—gained increasing national attention, a growing number of organizations and institutions recognized the need to create resources for schools to address these issues.

The Need for LGBTQ+-Inclusive Curriculum

In 1999, GLSEN began conducting what became its biannual student survey assessing students' perception of the school environment for LGBT youth. The results offer a glimpse of students' daily life and, in doing so, help determine the trajectory of its activism. As stated in the preface to the 2019 report,

> in this report, we see that the slowing of progress noted in 2017 has continued. Harassment and discrimination remain at unacceptable levels at the national

level. However, given the vicious attacks we have witnessed over the past four years, particularly on transgender youth, it is remarkable that dedicated educators and active student advocates have held the line as powerfully as they have. Despite the tenor of our times, we also find that more and more LGBTQ+ youth have access to the vital in-school supports that can change their lives for the better, particularly as GSA student clubs continue to emerge in more schools nationwide. Increasing presence of the supports can be a leading indicator for positive changes in school climate, making this another sign of hope for the future.[14]

The 2019 study, the most recent for which there are published results, revealed that 59.1 percent of the students surveyed felt unsafe at school because of their sexual orientation; 42.5 percent responded similarly regarding their gender expression.[15] Meanwhile, only 10.9 percent "reported that their school had official policies or guidelines to support transgender and gender nonconforming students."[16] It is widely acknowledged that inclusive curricula help, yet only 8.2 percent of students surveyed responded that they had access to sex education classes that covered LGBTQ+ topics, and less than 20 percent replied that they had opportunities to learn from LGBTQ+-inclusive textbooks and assigned readings.[17] Furthermore, although 33.2 percent of students said that LGBTQ+ topics were covered in their academic classes, 16.2 percent of the full sample claimed those representations were positive and 13.8 percent encountered negative depictions. Students reported that, when LGBTQ+ content was present, it was more likely to be in history (60.3 percent of those reporting positive representations/11.6 percent of full survey) and English (38 percent/7.3 percent) classes than other subjects.[18]

This study offers statistical proof that although nearly half of the LGBTQ+ students surveyed feel supported by the staff and administration,[19] inclusive curriculum is insufficient in many schools and subjects; its positive presence is necessary to making schools safer and more welcoming. There is a direct correlation between these statistics and the percentage of students who reported feeling unsafe. Moreover, though many of these statistics show decreased representation in academics from the 2017 survey, the number of students who reported receiving LGBTQ+ content in their history classes increased.[20] The results, therefore, offer a solution: history classes—those in which LGBTQ+ information and issues are already more prevalent and further integrating this material makes instruction more complete—offer an arena in which inclusive curriculum can grow and flourish.

Social Justice in Social Studies

Organizations focused on improving school climate for LGBTQ+ students, as well as others that work to eliminate bias and discrimination on a larger scale, develop and publish inclusive resources designed to accomplish these purposes and address the discomfort and danger made clear by the survey's results. Although these resources often include information on history and current events, it is frequently conveyed in the service of the more civics-oriented objectives of tolerance, discourse, and community building rather than in-depth historical exploration. These resources seek to raise awareness and break down stereotypes while making schools more inclusive environments for all students. History is, therefore, necessarily present, but the lessons address social studies goals more than specific historical objectives.

As a leader in its field and in keeping with its organizational goals, GLSEN offers resources designed to provide students with access to information about LGBTQ+ individuals and their struggles in an effort to have students see themselves in what they learn and enlighten students who do not identify as LGBTQ+ as to their classmates' plight. GLSEN's resources acknowledge and sometimes evolve from historical events and figures, but more often than not they provide the basis for discussions of inclusivity and changing the narrative, rather than in-depth analysis of historical events and circumstances.

Several other organizations focusing on social justice and human rights more generally also develop LGBTQ+-inclusive resources for use in high school classrooms. Similar to GLSEN, these lessons and units are meant to stimulate thought and discussion about both the information with which students are presented and the larger, more substantive ideas that the organizations hope students will grasp through that content. Project Look Sharp, an initiative at Ithaca College, was "designed to promote and support the integration of media literacy and critical thinking into curricula at all grade levels and across instructional areas, as well as to evaluate the effectiveness of media literacy education in the schools."[21] Therefore, according to curriculum writer Sox Sperry, its units, including one on the gay liberation movement, "focus on peace and nonviolence and social justice" using core content as the foundation from which students "think critically about, analyze, and produce media."[22] The ADL, established in 1913 "to stop the defamation of the Jewish people and to secure justice and fair treatment to all," now "speak[s] up for those whose voices are not always heard";[23] its lessons, thus, "focus on current events for which there is an anti-bias and social justice angle."[24] The Human Rights Resource Center, meanwhile, contextualizes its learning activities in the concepts elucidated in the Universal Declaration of Human Rights. It asserts, "One of the most powerful ways to promote the continued evolution of LGBT rights as human rights and to interrupt the cycle of abuses against sexual minorities is through human rights education. ... and learning how to respect others and support and defend their human rights." Schools, the Human Rights Resource Center contends, are vital to "creating a culture that supports the human rights of all, including lesbian, gay, bisexual, and transgender persons," but they must first undergo that transformation themselves.[25] For each of these organizations, LGBTQ+ history provides the springboard from which students learn about and internalize ideas about climate, culture, harassment, and social justice; this addresses social studies' mission, but often does not provide the depth of information to enable truly informed discussion. Similar to LGBTQ+ studies, historical learning is more often a piece of the puzzle than the ultimate goal; this piece, though, is a potential building block.

Climate Concerns

Organizations creating curriculum focus on changing school climate and increasing students' awareness of human rights and diversity with the goal of making schools safer, more welcoming, and more tolerant; these objectives are explicitly stated in many of the resources available to teachers. These materials seek to open students' minds to the impact of the words and phrases they use; they include studies of identity and self-reflection, the dangers accompanying stereotyping and bullying, and the effects of hatred with the idea that changing young people's thought process and worldview will compel them to reconsider the way they interact with peers and the communities of which they are a part. They align with anti-bullying objectives and are, therefore, institutionally supported and societally acceptable. Many ask students to look inward and consider their own notions and actions; the conversations they intend to spur are often personal and separate from learning the historical context of discussions present in society today. The goal of these resources is clear: improve the immediate environment for LGBTQ+ students as well as their interaction with students who do not identify as such.

GLSEN, following its mission to create safe schools for LGBTQ+ students, promotes that goal through programs entitled "No Name-Calling Week," launched in 2004, and "ThinkB4YouSpeak," established in 2008. Both address social interaction among teenagers and the language used in social situations.

"No Name Calling Week" was inspired by James Howe's *The Misfits*, a book about four best friends who, tired of being bullied, create a "no name calling" party and run on that platform in their school's student council elections.[26] The lessons, which examine cliques, popularity, labels, and bias, encourage students to examine these things in their own environment and think about how to build community and end harassment. The introduction to "ThinkB4YouSpeak" states, "The campaign aims to raise awareness among straight teens about the prevalence and consequences of anti-LGBT bias and behavior in America's schools. Ultimately, the goal is to reduce and prevent the use of homophobic language in an effort to create a more positive environment for LGBT teens."[27] These units, and other lessons created by GLSEN, address students' daily experiences and the habits they form, aiming to reverse trends that create unsafe school environments for LGBT students.

Learning for Justice publishes lessons highlighting the negative impact of homophobic language, actions, and representations in the media. Echoing GLSEN's "ThinkB4YouSpeak," Learning for Justice's lesson on controversial issues asks students to rethink their use of "that's so gay" using its "Disagree with Grace" activity, which it intends as a paradigm for debating sensitive topics in class.[28] "Challenging Gender Stereotyping and Homophobia in Sports," meanwhile, uses a prevalent activity and media event to foster discussion of the stereotypes students maintain and the ways in which they manifest themselves in a school setting.[29] In a 2018 paper on best practices, Learning for Justice espoused, "creating a supportive environment for LGBT students improves educational outcomes for all students, not just those who may identify as LGBT. And remember, it's not about politics—it's about supporting students. Any educator, regardless of his personal beliefs, can be a resource for LGBT students."[30] These lessons seek to position teachers and administrators in precisely that role.

The ADL, too, offers lessons on understanding homophobia, gender identity, and the impact of anti-LGBT slurs. Like GLSEN and Learning for Justice, students reflect on the phrase "that's so gay," as well as the derivation of the terms "gay, faggot, and dyke" in "The History and Impact of Anti-LGBT Slurs." In the ADL's version of this lesson, though, and in keeping with the ADL's more expansive view of past discrimination, students examine not only the words and their impact but also the "long history of judgment and hate behind these words."[31] In "Understanding Homophobia/Heterosexism and How to Be an Ally," students evaluate categories of bias and injustice including interpersonal, institutionalized, and internalized to better understand homophobia and its far-reaching effects and "identify ways that they can be an ally to LGBQ people in their school and community."[32] Meanwhile, "Transgender Identity and Issues" "provide[s] an opportunity for high school students to learn more about transgender identity and issues, the barriers faced by people who identify as transgender or are gender non-conforming and how we can make our schools safe and welcoming for transgender and gender non-conforming students."[33] As an organization, the ADL exists to bridge the gaps that divide different groups of people and eradicate discrimination. These lessons, all of which explicitly state the objective of creating allies, support that mission.

The Human Rights Resource Center and Project Look Sharp both created units devoted to enhancing students' understanding of the LGBTQ+ experience and the struggle that community has endured in the United States and abroad in the last fifty years. These units include lessons and activities that inform students and challenge them to think about this history, as well as featuring lessons focused on homophobia, language, and school climate seen through the organizations' respective lenses of human rights and media literacy. HRRC's "Words Really Matter," the first of nine activities in its unit, asks students to "examine the power of words," "challenge harmful connotations" conveyed by language, and rethink the way they use words that describe sexual orientation.[34] In "Gay Affirmative or Gay Negative?" Project Look Sharp uses documentaries and popular youth-oriented television series to "review intolerance directed at lesbian and gay people" and evaluate the influence of words and images on people's thoughts and ideas.[35] These lessons, like "ThinkB4YouSpeak" and others targeting phrases such as "that's so gay," alert students to behaviors and habits formed over the course of time and the negative impact these actions and statements intentionally and inadvertently have on their environment. Both organizations also include lessons on challenging homophobia, compelling students to consider creating environments absent of this bias. The HRRC provides students with testimony from teenagers who encountered homophobia while Project Look Sharp's lesson focuses on music and lyric analysis; both, though, ask students to analyze messages conveyed and how those messages might serve as catalysts for change. There are multiple angles, then, from which similar goals might be achieved.

Organizations focused specifically on developing and producing LGBTQ+-inclusive curriculum like GLSEN, Learning for Justice, and the Human Rights Resource Center are not alone in their mission to create environments in which students feel safe and accepted and in which learning, rather than resisting bias and harassment, can be the priority for all. This is the focus of the majority of LGBTQ+-inclusive curricula, regardless of content. Surveys, studies, scholarship, and common sense indicate that in order for learning to take place, students need to feel safe and secure in their environment, sentiments undermined by bullying and harassment. Attempts at improving school climate and changing the culture are essential for all students whether they identify as LGBTQ+ or not. Furthermore, these resources and the intentions supporting them echo the calls to end harassment that encompassed the *raison d'etre* of the Stonewall-era gay rights movement. These resources, then, make history in their own way. In an era where anti-bullying initiatives are a national educational focus, these lessons receive the institutional support and promotion that might allow more in-depth study of LGBTQ+ issues in their wake.

History as a Springboard

Resources that seek to create safe spaces also invoke historical events and figures to demonstrate the ways in which moments and individuals can be catalysts for change. These materials challenge students to navigate social justice issues and understand how identifying societal problems can lead to change. In 1916 the NEA asserted that it was more important for students to "be given experience and practice in the observation of social phenomena" and "understand that every social problem is many-sided and complex" than to focus exclusively on content knowledge.[36] Social justice–oriented LGBTQ+-inclusive resources aim to fulfill that goal and equip students with the skills they need to address homophobia, intolerance, and hatred.

Project Look Sharp's curriculum on Media Construction of Social Justice includes an overview lesson entitled "Out and Affirmed" that uses print and digital media sources to guide students through the gay liberation movement from 1960 to the present; this lesson is meant to provide students with background information that they need to explore the topics and themes in the aforementioned "Gay Affirmative or Gay Negative?" which asks students to consider media representations of LGBTQ+ people and communities and their ramifications on thoughts and behaviors. Project Look Sharp chose to build a unit on gay liberation specifically because it is often omitted from textbooks; LGBTQ+ issues, according to Sox Sperry, are "not just twenty-first century issues, these are historic issues throughout U.S. history. They're just not attended to."[37] "Out and Affirmed" and its broad sweep through history exist largely to provide information and fill gaps so that students are able to think deeply about the LGBTQ+ experience.

Matthew Shepard, whose torture and death because of his sexuality brought national attention to hate crimes, was a tragic catalyst for gay rights advocacy. He is the subject of lessons published by GLSEN and the ADL. In the introduction to GLSEN's "He Continues to Make a Difference," author Leslea Newman asserts, "When someone is reduced to a slur, he or she becomes, in the eyes of the tormentor, less than human. He or she becomes, in a tormentor's eyes, someone of no consequence, someone who doesn't matter, someone—or something—easy to destroy."[38] Like the majority of LGBTQ+-inclusive curriculum, the authors' goal here is to increase awareness and sensitivity and reduce incidents of bullying; the curriculum guide includes social studies questions contextualizing the events surrounding and implications of Matthew Shepard's murder. The ADL's "Current Events Classroom" lesson focused on the Matthew Shepard and James Byrd, Jr. Hate Crimes Prevention Act is more social studies oriented than interdisciplinary; it examines hate crimes, in general, and the circumstances surrounding Shepard's and Byrd's deaths, specifically.[39] Learning for Justice offers a similar lesson, reviewing this act and the circumstances that birthed it.[40] This lesson, like the ADL's, considers the nature of hate and the effectiveness of legislation meant to put an end to its violent effects. These lessons explore hatred in general, illustrating that, though Byrd and Shepard were different, hate is not defined by race or sexuality. This construct provides students with a valuable opportunity to discuss hate and ways to overcome it, but it needs more historical context for students to fully understand the legislation's passage and significance.

Unlike historical lessons that require in-depth examinations of cause and effect and ask students to synthesize new information with what they know of the past, these lessons acknowledge the history but look more closely at broader themes and skill building to accomplish their objectives. Hate, and its impact throughout history, is a recurrent theme in social studies classes where students learn the root of it in different groups, places, and times and develop a sense of its impact. Meaningful discussions on hatred and the crimes committed in its name also break down barriers between groups and, potentially, combat bias and discrimination in schools and societies, accomplishing the goals espoused by GLSEN, the ADL, and Learning for Justice. Though it is important to address and overcome hate as a concept, these lessons could be more impactful if they didn't remove hatred and its effects from their source. Here, a balance between skills and deeper content would be worthwhile.

Curriculum developers aiming to connect students with the LGBTQ+ experience on a personal level also create materials focused on individuals' struggles and/or contributions. LGBTQ+ history is rife with important individuals, be they leaders of the gay rights or other social movements or people whose circumstances or plights serve as a springboard to awareness and action. Similar to lessons focused on Matthew Shepard, examining these individuals' lives offers students the opportunity to gain a clearer understanding of history and its impact on the present. Advocates of LGBTQ+-inclusive history curriculum emphasize the importance of incorporating Bayard Rustin in discussions of US history.[41] Youth in Motion, an organization that provides LGBTQ+-themed films to GSAs and schools, offers students the opportunity to learn about Rustin in its curriculum guide to accompany *Brother Outsider: The Life of Bayard Rustin*, a documentary that emphasizes his civil rights work and the impact of his sexuality on his position in the movement. Youth in Motion's curriculum, in addition to its exploration of the civil rights movement of which Rustin was a significant part, includes guidelines on facilitating conversations on LGBT issues, encountering and responding to homophobia in schools and communities, and the use of art and media to create social change.[42]

The ADL, cognizant of the power of a recognizable figure as students grapple with difficult subject matter, published a lesson entitled "Caitlyn Jenner and the Power of Coming Out" following her appearance on *20/20* in 2015. This lesson, part of the ADL's "Current Events Classroom," identified a meaningful, teachable moment in the struggle and bravery of an internationally famous Olympic athlete and pop culture figure and used students' knowledge of Caitlyn Jenner and her family as an example. The lesson explores the coming out process and political and societal reactions to it as well as highlighting Jenner's coming out as transgender and the meaning behind that term.[43] The national fascination with Caitlyn Jenner and her journey brought transgender issues to the forefront of national consciousness and, more than other figures, began to reduce the stigma attached to it. This, then, was a wise lesson choice for an organization devoted to eliminating discrimination.

Historical context offers students a foundation from which to better understand lessons that focus on human rights and address the ways in which abridging LGBTQ+ rights violates human rights. The Human Rights Resource Center developed activities on the ways in which the Universal Declaration of Human Rights encompasses gay rights, issues of tolerance in democracy, equality, and rights abuses around the world. Its lessons rely upon this declaration and other laws and statutes created to eradicate discrimination and inequality and ask students to compare the promises in that document with LGBT rights as of 2000.[44] The ADL's "In-Group, Out-Group: The Exclusion of LGBT People from Societal Institutions" investigates the inclusion and exclusion of certain groups in public life and the role of fear and prejudice in this ostracism. The goal of the lesson, ultimately, is for students to "increase their awareness about the ways in which LGBT people are currently included/excluded from societal institutions."[45] In all of these lessons, information about the past and the impact of the past on the present is significant to the learning objectives. Ultimately, though, raising students' awareness and inspiring consideration of how to improve the present takes priority over in-depth studies of the past. Including current events in social studies classes is an essential aspect of student learning. Illustrating connections between the past and the present enables students to grasp the relevance of historical events, engages them in the subject in more meaningful ways, and enhances their ability to synthesize information. A strong foundation in events of the past, though, is necessary to these higher order learning goals. For students to join the conversation on LGBTQ+ issues and begin to address them they need social studies' citizenship-driven goals and a strong historical foundation.

Including history in lessons that serve civics-related objectives acknowledges the power of historical learning to create change. Organizations need to push that idea further and embrace history, and the social studies classes where it is taught, as the force for change it can be.

With studies continuing to find and evidence mounting to confirm that LGBTQ+ students face hostility, discrimination, and bullying on a daily basis, it is imperative to increase young people's awareness of the LGBTQ+ population, their contributions to society, and the struggles they endure in and outside of school buildings in addition to giving them the tools to create a better community. Moreover, with national issues pertaining to the treatment and status of LGBTQ+ individuals—and the violence that this group historically and currently suffers—consistently present across all forms of media, multiple opportunities for students to consider, discuss, and evaluate these issues are essential and timely. History, however, also remains important, and the fact that resources position history as a conversation starter rather than offering students more profound opportunities to study LGBTQ+ history diminishes their chance to understand the issues and circumstances that these materials attempt to address. Positioning history in the service of seemingly larger goals suppresses its importance, both in terms of students' knowledge of LGBTQ+ history and regarding the status of the subject matter in general.

Harassment, bullying, and violence need to be addressed and eradicated, but this does not preclude the need for, or make these issues exclusive from, historical learning that can serve the same objectives and yield the same results for LGBTQ+ students and their classmates. Social studies teaches skills essential for academic success and twenty-first-century citizenship: critical thinking, evaluating sources, argumentation, analyzing multiple perspectives, and civic participation, to name a few. Building students' competency in these areas can ameliorate hostile situations and improve the climate and atmosphere for marginalized groups, in this case, a school's LGBTQ+ population. Social studies is vital to achieving anti-bullying goals, as is the historical education that comprises a significant part of students' experience with this subject. History provides the content knowledge students need to make social studies skills more meaningful and truly create the informed citizenry to which the discipline aspires.

* * *

Lessons and resources aiming to change and improve school climate—materials that emphasize, prioritize, and encourage students to speak about their own experiences and opinions—far outnumber those providing comprehensive portrayals and analyses of LGBTQ+ history. The two are not, however, and should not be treated as, mutually exclusive. Good history lessons, even those that don't explicitly ask students to apply what they learn to the present, inevitably awaken deeper consideration of students' lives and surroundings. This idea extends beyond LGBTQ+ history; lessons on slavery and civil rights, for example, if done well, should inspire students to ponder race relations in the twenty-first century. Similarly, the underlying goal of anti-bullying and climate-focused lessons parallels calls for ending harassment that students might learn about in their history and social studies classes, though this concept is more obtuse due to the relative lack of LGBTQ+ history in most students' school experience. Recognizing this overlap, then, and developing curricula that address multiple purposes and acknowledge the intrinsic link between a profound understanding of the past and positive change in the present, can fulfill and align with anti-bullying and social studies missions.

5

Two Steps Forward: LGBTQ+ History Resources and the Obstacles They Face

The LGBTQ+ community in the late 1960s and early 1970s and advocates for LGBTQ students in the late 1990s and 2000s sought to improve life for individuals targeted for the ways in which they were different and the fear those differences inspired in others. Both prioritized creating circumstances in which the probability of mental and/or physical harm decreased before focusing on other goals. For the LGBTQ+ rights movement as a whole, that meant first seeking an end to erasure from general society, harassment in public places, and access to health care, and then turning to issues like marriage equality. Ameliorating the bullying, ostracism, and assault that LGBTQ+ students face, which in some cases deprives them of their fundamental right to education, was similarly the first step taken by organizations and advocates focused on schooling. Incorporating LGBTQ+ history, therefore, could not have been on organizations' initial agenda because this larger goal was, and is, integral to LGBTQ+ student's overall educational experience. The delayed focus on history, then, was a reflection of the immense and ongoing energy necessary to make schools safe for LGBTQ+ students.

LGBTQ+-inclusive resources that seek to improve school climate and challenge students to rethink preconceived ideas and biases serve important social studies goals and reinforce civic-oriented skills that students need as part of the school community. Where these lessons and materials reference historical events or ask students to think about the mistreatment and discrimination that LGBTQ+ individuals endured, it is imperative that they also gain a deep understanding of the myriad ways in which that population advocated for rights and recognition as well as the LGBTQ+ community's role and contributions throughout US history. Social studies aims to instill discourse and debate skills, both of which demand concrete evidence to support one's position. Inclusive history lessons, already necessary to provide students with complete, honest, culturally sustaining portrayals of US history, are essential here, as well. These resources exist, but they need increased support from the institutions that create them and those where they might be implemented.

The University of Minnesota's Human Rights Resource Center was one of the first organizations to develop and publish LGBTQ+ history lessons for high school classes in 2000. The Resource Center's curriculum initiative, created to teach students about the rights they might "innately" know they have but with little understanding of the intricacies and implications, includes a nine-lesson unit on LGBT rights. Kristi Rudelius-Palmer, the Center's director, explained the decision to focus on LGBT rights at a time when few schools addressed this topic. She stated,

> We believed that one of the most prevalent human rights violations going on in schools was against individuals identifying as LGBTQ. LGBTQ terms were also being used to degrade, bully, and discriminate against students. We probably also had the partners at the table that said, "We really should take this on," and we knew that it was one of the most challenging issues in schools, and still, unfortunately, we think is today.[1]

The foundational lessons, which were written by scholar-practitioner Dave Donahue with additional organizational support of Amnesty International's Outfront Program and GLSEN, examine the process of change, laws criminalizing homosexual behaviors, and the battle for same-sex marriage;[2] Rudelius-Palmer claimed that she searched for similarly themed lessons created prior and discovered none.[3] There was a six-year gap, then, between the commencement of LGBT History Month in 1994 and the Human Rights Resource Center's promotion of this history in schools through the creation of comprehensive, activity-based lessons with a similar goal in 2000.

Though the Human Rights Resource Center received support from local groups in St. Paul and human rights and LGBT advocacy organizations like Amnesty International, Human Rights Educators' Network, and GLSEN,[4] its development of social studies lessons did not immediately lead to a widespread increase in historically focused LGBTQ resources. In the spring 2002 special issue of *Theory and Research in Social Education*, three authors examined efforts at implementing inclusive curriculum and engaging students in discussions of heteronormativity and homophobia, yet these were scholarly case studies rather than classroom-ready resources; Stephen Thornton's 2003 *Social Education* article "Silence on Gays and Lesbians in Social Studies Curriculum" lamented this absence. LGBTQ+ students' plights received more attention, but resources available to history and social studies teachers remained rare.

Beginning in 2003, the *New York Times* Learning Network began creating and posting LGBTQ+ history lessons to its website. That year, the Learning Network, in cooperation with the Bank Street School of Education, developed lessons entitled "Family Life," "Legally Wed," and "Aesthetics of Activism: Exploring the Ways the Arts Have Responded to AIDS"; the lessons explored complex family issues, the controversy surrounding same-sex marriage, and the role of art in AIDS activism, respectively.[5] The *Times* continued publishing lessons throughout the decade, including one that traced the evolution of gay and lesbian issues in the 1980s, 1990s, and 2000s in December 2007, a lesson entitled "The Culture Wars" in which students stated their opinion in a letter on a specific gay rights issue of their choice in 2009, and a lesson evaluating the arguments for and against repealing Don't Ask, Don't Tell in 2010.[6] These lessons, which impart LGBTQ+ history and build literacy and discussion skills, were a significant advancement in the pursuit of inclusive history curriculum at a time when the absence of such material was more a topic for scholarly articles than educator action.

As the national conversation regarding LGBTQ rights became increasingly prominent, including debates about Don't Ask, Don't Tell, same-sex marriage, and California's Proposition 8, advocacy organizations began to devise lessons that highlighted that community's history. Anti-bullying and school climate resources remained the priority, but history and civics lessons became more available, too. GLSEN published "When Did it Happen?" in 2009; the lesson introduced students to significant moments in LGBTQ+ history in the United States dating back to colonial times. In 2010 the ADL published "The Invisibility of LGBT People in History: 'Peculiar Disposition of the Eyes'" as part of its Curriculum Connections program; the lesson asked students to consider "historically marginalized groups in society" and use that context to "increase their awareness of the ways in which LGBT people have been made invisible in history" and "learn about historically significant LGBT people, topics and events."[7] "A Peculiar Disposition of the Eyes" names and addresses a distinct problem with the study of history in the United States and seeks to correct it; rendering a group invisible is, after all, a form of discrimination. Moreover, the idea of enhancing the visibility of important LGBTQ+ figures led activist educators to home in on historical actors whose sexuality and/or contributions to the LGBTQ+ rights movement were previously ignored, like Bayard Rustin, Frank Kameny, and Martha P. Johnson, about whom PBS Learning Media asks,

"In what ways was Johnson ahead of her time? If Johnson was still alive today, how might she be viewed by society?"[8] These lessons were housed on organizations' websites among materials on school climate and bullying—GLSEN, for example, has a page for educator resources but not one devoted specifically to history lessons—but their publication nevertheless offered teachers, many of whom were and are unfamiliar with this history, a mechanism through which to introduce LGBTQ+ history in their classrooms.

History UnErased, founded in 2014, is one of the few organizations singularly focused on offering comprehensive LGBTQ+ history lessons that teachers can use in class; though the organization's founders ardently support the idea of opening people's minds and increasing tolerance, they also believe that that goal can and should be served by the knowledge and context students glean from historical education rather than solely from lessons that seek to change the way young people interact.[9] The Berkeley History-Social Science Project also makes lessons on LGBTQ+ history available through their website, including eleventh grade materials on the Lavender Scare and McCarthyism through which students ponder, "How did the conditions of the Cold War lead to the criminalization of lesbian, gay, bisexual, transgender and queer Americans?"[10] Furthermore, Learning for Justice includes "The Role of Gay Men and Lesbians in the Civil Rights Movement," a unit that helps students draw connections between concurrent movements, in its roster of LGBTQ+-inclusive resources.[11]

Historical resources, then, do exist for teachers who seek them, though in less quantity than school climate resources. This echoes the institutional support both endeavors receive—fifty states have anti-bullying laws while only five have LGBTQ+ curriculum laws—and contributes to the gulf between the implementation of inclusive curriculum and historically inclusive curriculum. While the climate materials are often easily accessible to teachers regardless of their familiarity with the subject matter, historical lessons are frequently either mixed in among climate resources or require more independent research and learning.

Prioritizing History

LGBTQ+-inclusive curriculum, particularly that devoted to history, provides students—and, often, their teachers—with previously unknown information. Like lessons on words and bias, this, too, increases awareness and, if effective, positively impacts school climate. Learning about the past and understanding struggles that occurred years ago can be as valuable as discussions of students' immediate environment, especially where those struggles continue to exist;[12] doing so equips students to think critically about and draw important connections between the past, the present, and the future. Thus, advocates aiming to reduce or eradicate discrimination and bias, positively change local—including school-level—and national culture, and build relationships between people and groups that struggle to coexist promote the need for a greater understanding of history.

GLSEN's "When Did It Happen: An LGBT History Lesson"[13] was a comprehensive introductory lesson in which students discussed what they knew about LGBT history and, as a class, organized important moments in LGBT history from colonial times to the present into a timeline through interactive work and class discussion. Though the lesson provided snapshots more than in-depth analysis of LGBT history, it revealed details with which students were likely unfamiliar. Among the facts students learned were that Thomas Jefferson revised the punishment for sodomy under Virginia law and that the American Psychiatric Association voted unanimously to remove homosexuality from its list of disorders;[14] it illustrated the countless ways in which discrimination and bias affected the LGBTQ+ community over time, and the ways in which that community worked to triumph over the harassment it endured. It was replaced with "LGBTQ History Timeline," a lesson that similarly asks students to organize events and figures chronologically. The learning activity, according to the overview, "allows for the sharing of these often untold stories and also facilitates a much needed discussion about the erasure of LGBTQ history in what is considered American history, and the value of critical thinking in history classes."[15] The updated lesson includes Sylvia Rivera and Martha P. Johnson, transgender women who were prominent LGBTQ+ activists whose roles, like so much of this history, are too often omitted in high school classrooms.

Other lessons focus more specifically on a particular issue or event in LGBTQ+ history. Thirteen Ed Online, for example, addressed Don't Ask, Don't Tell and the role of gays in the military, contextualizing this restriction among those imposed on other groups throughout US history in a lesson entitled "Is Everyone Protected by the Bill of Rights?" This unit, published before the repeal of Don't Ask, Don't Tell, presented students with arguments on both sides of the issue in preparation for a debate. The scope of the unit begins broadly, as students consider multiple historic events, but becomes much more narrowly focused as students delve into the topic at the heart of the unit.[16] The ONE Archives lesson on the AIDS crisis asks students, "Why and how did activists respond to the AIDS crisis of the 1980s?" The lesson uses media, artwork, and primary sources to "engage [students] in the historical context of the AIDS crisis of the 1980s" and "analyze activist responses looking specifically at different goals and methods used by the activist organization ACT UP/LA."[17] These resources augment existing US history curricula and offer students the opportunity to learn about events and eras that they might not have accessed previously.

The ONE Archives, the nation's largest repository of LGBTQ+ history documents and artifacts, began producing lessons to support the FAIR Education Act's curriculum mandate for California schools. The lessons include selections from their primary source holdings, some of which are not available through other sites. Several of the resources focus on the LGBTQ+ rights movement, asking students to explore and evaluate the personal and political aspects of activism and the time period in which it occurred. In a lesson that asks, "How did the movement for LGBT equality go from assimilation to 'coming out' in the 1950s–1970s?" students review sources and mission statements from mid-twentieth-century gay rights organizations to acquire "greater understanding of the arguments, experiences and material conditions that shaped the movement."[18] "LGBTQ Civil Rights," meanwhile, asks students to consider "how various movements for equality [built] upon one another." This lesson, which contextualizes the struggle for LGBTQ rights within the larger atmosphere of reform and equality in the mid-late twentieth century, states in its overview, "While activists fighting for LGBT rights utilized similar tactics and had some shared goals of those fighting for Civil Rights broadly, LGBT people in racial minority communities faced additional discrimination. Moreover, many fighting for broader Civil Rights did not consider sexual preference or gender identity as a part of their fight"; students navigate these complexities to "determine to what extent the movement for LGBT rights was or was not part of the broader movement for Civil Rights of the 1970s and 1980s."[19]

One event, more than any other, remains the focal point for classroom discussions of LGBTQ+ rights if the topic comes up at all—Stonewall. Teachers include a brief mention of it as they discuss the multiple concurrent movements of the 1960s and 1970s, and textbooks, if they mention LGBTQ+ history, include a few lines on the riots. In 2019, this turning point in the movement received worldwide attention in honor of its fiftieth anniversary and increased calls for its integration into US history classes. Stanford History Education Group (SHEG), PBS Learning Media, and ADL attempt to meet that need with their lessons on the Stonewall riots and their impact. SHEG's lesson, which relies on primary source analysis, asks students to decipher "What caused the Stonewall Riots?"[20] PBS's "The LGBTQ Movement and the Stonewall Riots" builds on that, as students use a cause-and-effect lens to answer the question, "How did this event help spark a more visible LGBTQ movement?"[21] Furthermore, ADL's lesson, which positions Stonewall as "the beginning of the organized gay rights movement," challenges students to "reflect on LGBTQ rights and activism prior to and after Stonewall," query the differences between an uprising and a riot, and determine which term they would apply to Stonewall.[22] These lessons, and the analysis they require, push students to move beyond basic familiarity and into deeper comprehension of the multiple perspectives on this seminal event.

Many history-based LGBTQ+ resources emphasize same-sex marriage, an issue with which most students, regardless of their politics and location, are familiar. Although some scholars warn against relying too heavily on prior knowledge and solely focusing on this issue, it is, nevertheless, a significant moment in the fight for LGBTQ+ rights and present in many twenty-first-century students' lives. The Human Rights Resource Center and Learning for Justice, for example, created lessons focused specifically on same-sex marriage. The Human Rights Resource Center's lesson, "I Now Pronounce You ..." created after Vermont became the first state to legalize civil unions in 2000, invokes the Universal Declaration of Human Rights to contextualize marriage equality within "international humanitarian standards"; it also draws parallels to the idea of separate but equal that permeated American culture and discourse for a century and asks students to apply this concept to the same-sex marriage debate.[23] Learning for Justice and ADL, in their quest to eliminate discrimination and bias, invoke other examples of past bias and injustice in their lessons on the struggle for same-sex marriage. Learning for Justice's "Marriage Equality: Different Strategies for Attaining Equal Rights" situates the battle to legalize same-sex marriage in the "historical context of other struggles for equality,"[24] instructing students on constitutional rights and comparing executive, legislative, and judicial efforts on behalf of African American civil rights in the 1950s and 1960s with similar actions for marriage equality in the twenty-first century. ADL's "Winning the Right to Marry: Historic Parallels"[25] uses a similar strategy; students review evolving marriage laws including Jim Crow era restrictions and the Defense of Marriage Act and "analyze existing federal and state laws concerning same-sex marriage and consider whether or not [those] laws are in need of change."[26] ADL further built on this study of marriage with "Wedding Cake, Same Sex Marriage, and Discrimination," a lesson in which students learn about *Masterpiece Cakeshop v. Colorado Civil Rights Commission* (2018), develop their own opinions of the case and the Court's decision, and engage with classmates who hold different perspectives.[27]

These lessons, which are narrower in scope than surveys of LGBTQ+ history in the twentieth century, provide students with the opportunity to explore events and issues on their own and in context, reducing the sense of "otherness" that often accompanies LGBTQ+ history.[28] Lessons introducing students to the big picture of LGBTQ+ history are not without merit; students' knowledge of key events and individuals in LGBTQ+ history preceding the struggle for marriage equality undoubtedly aids their comprehension and grasp of this material. It is also important, though, for students to encounter lessons that interweave LGBT history and other topics, making it part of the curriculum rather than a separate entity. Lessons on marriage organically allow for that to happen.

The Zinn Education Project, which works to "introduce students to a more accurate, complex, and engaging understanding of United States history than is found in traditional textbooks and curricula,"[29] includes a document on Stonewall by Martin Duberman and accompanying questions in its unit "Women, Gays, and Other Voices of Resistance," a study of the sixties that goes beyond civil rights to examine the "general revolt in the culture against oppressive, artificial, previously unquestioned ways of living."[30] In a similar vein, Facing History and Ourselves, an organization that "uses lessons of history to challenge teachers and their students to stand up to bigotry and hate,"[31] published "LGBTQ History and Why It Matters," a lesson that uses GLSEN's timeline materials to "[give] students the opportunity to consider whose experiences are included in the history taught in schools, whose are often left out, and how that may reflect and perpetuate the 'in' groups and 'out' groups in our society."[32] It is imperative for students to learn LGBTQ+ history. It is also important that they understand the ramifications of omitting this, or any group, from the curriculum and learning experiences that comprise it. The Zinn Education Project and Facing History's resources aim to begin that conversation and have students evaluate this history and the impact of its absence.

"Unheard Voices," a collaboration between GLSEN, ADL, and StoryCorps, is one of the largest LGBTQ+ curriculum projects to date. It was published in 2011, "in response to the lack of representation of lesbian, gay, bisexual and transgender (LGBT) people in school curricula and disproportionate incidents of bullying and violence against LGBT youth ... [to] help educators to integrate LGBT history, people and issues into their instructional programs"[33] and based on oral histories conducted with "individuals who bore witness to or helped shape LGBT history in some way."[34] The information from these interviews comprise the foundation of lessons exploring the AIDS epidemic, Don't Ask, Don't Tell, LGBTQ+ family rights, and the twentieth-century homophile movement, among other topics.

The lessons also include supplementary materials to support the oral histories. Unlike history curricula that study significant moments through the perspective or actions of one, usually famous, individual, "Unheard Voices" uses individuals' experiences to make history relevant and help it resonate with students. The voices belong to "average" Americans with whom students might identify, thus decreasing the distance between students and the past they study and LGBTQ+ lifestyles in general. As historian John D'Emilio posited, a biographical approach is the optimal way to reach high school students, who learn well when they can relate to the information.[35] Though the lessons in "Unheard Voices" focus on specific events and issues, the curriculum as a whole is comprehensive, covering more than fifty years of history; it can thus be inserted into teachers' taught curriculum over the course of the year and integrated among other historical topics.

Studies of individuals, a strategy also used where history is a touchstone from which thematic lessons on bias and climate emerge as well as a proven device for effectively teaching high school history, extend beyond "Unheard Voices." Several organizations, in fact, develop curriculum focused on LGBTQ+ individuals whose historical and cultural contributions and experiences represent the struggles of this and other groups in US history. Learning for Justice's unit "The Role of Gay Men and Lesbians in the Civil Rights Movement" includes lessons on well-known African Americans who identified as LGBTQ+ and advocated for equality on multiple fronts; PBS Learning Media's "Understanding LGBTQ+ Identity: A Toolkit for Educators" focuses on many of the same figures. Learning for Justice's lesson on Lorraine Hansberry, the Pulitzer Prize-winning playwright of "A Raisin in the Sun," asserts that she "masked radical black politics through the construction of seemingly unthreatening African American characters"[36] as well as advocating for women's and LGBT rights. The lesson asks students, "What do Hansberry's writings and life illuminate about the intersections among civil rights, women's liberation, and the historic struggle for LGBT equality?"[37] as students learn about the politics and positions of a figure whose work they may have previously encountered. Similarly, through PBS Learning Media's resources "students learn about Hansberry's lasting impact and the intersectionality that defined her life."[38] Pauli Murray, a woman with whom high school students are likely less familiar, likewise fought to end discrimination on multiple fronts. PBS shows students "how her life intertwined with the Civil Rights and Women's Movement in the United States,"[39] and Learning for Justice's lesson asks students to evaluate the obstacles she faced in the mid-twentieth century fighting "Jane and Jim Crow."[40] "James Baldwin: Art, Sexuality, and Civil Rights" explores "how

[his] identity shaped his art and political activism. ... [and] the connections among self-identification, artistic expression, and political activism." Learning for Justice's lesson poses the essential question, "Why is it important that history recognize Baldwin not only as a black intellectual but also as a gay man whose ideas and artistry had an impact on politics, society, and culture?";[41] PBS Learning Media, too, asks students to examine "the intersectionality that defined and influenced Baldwin's career."[42] These lessons, in addition to delving into individuals' lives and work, accentuate the connective tissues winding through history and the importance of understanding the entirety of who someone was and what they believed.

Bayard Rustin, a civil rights activist who was one of the architects of the March on Washington, was also openly gay at time when that was distinctly uncommon. Rustin is often omitted from civil rights curricula that are more focused on Martin Luther King, Jr.'s and Malcolm X's contributions, yet his role in the movement offers students a rare, organic opportunity to see how the gay and civil rights movements overlapped and intersected. Learning for Justice offers an entire lesson dedicated to Rustin's advocacy which seeks, among other objectives, to illustrate that "Rustin was an instrumental figure in the modern civil rights movement" and "individuals have the ability to simultaneously advocate for multiple causes, even if they conflict or overlap."[43] In the essential questions, the lesson characterizes Rustin as "one of the twentieth century's most important political organizers" as well as "a gay man involved in the civil rights movement."[44] Rustin not only receives the recognition he deserves; teachers also have access to lessons that interweave concurrent movements, reduce the "otherness" and heteronormativity present in the majority of high school history lessons, and build important historical thinking skills.[45]

LGBTQ+-inclusive historical curriculum must extend beyond the overlap between civil rights and gay rights if history curricula are to be truly inclusive. In "Alan Turing: True to Himself" GLSEN asks, "Why might it be important to learn about the various identities of historical figures?" and encourages teachers to draw comparisons between Turing's treatment and the way in which LGBT individuals were targeted under McCarthyism.[46] PBS Learning Media's Understanding LGBTQ+ Identities site includes lessons on We'Wha, a Zuni lhamana who "traveled to Washington, D.C. to help document Indigenous Zuni culture" amid the Native American wars of the late nineteenth century,[47] Audre Lorde, "a Black feminist lesbian poet who believed that naming our full identities was an essential part of radical social change,"[48] and Alain Locke, the Black gay writer who was "the architect of the Harlem Renaissance."[49] Learning about these, and other, individuals' lives, battles, and advocacy opens a door to broader historical lessons, providing students with foundational knowledge of past struggles and the means to overcome them.

History UnErased (HUE) follows this idea as well, "bringing LGBTQ history into the mainstream curriculum" and "promoting genuine understanding and equality for all LGBTQ people."[50] HUE's lessons situate LGBTQ+ history within topics studied in classrooms throughout the nation; their "Intersections and Connections" curriculum "broadens history and the social sciences from Jamestown through the 21st century" and "ensures LGBTQ and all minorities are represented within a more complete, complex, and empowering story of America."[51] Their resources, which examine individuals' lives and significant events and eras in LGBTQ history, challenge students to rethink their ideas about US history and embrace figures like Jane Addams, Gladys Bentley, and Tom Cassidy in new ways. Miriam Morgenstern, one of HUE's founders, posited, "Children need to see themselves and their families reflected in the academic content in a classroom, but LGBTQ+ history, topics and people have been excluded from the curricula. We can't expect teachers to 'just do it.' They need resources and training to bring this erased content into their classrooms."[52] The curriculum and content produced by HUE, then, strives to undo this trend in a way that allows for the seamless inclusion of LGBTQ+ history in classrooms.

As encapsulated by Morgenstern, organizations developing LGBTQ+-inclusive curricula have similar goals, even when their tactics or semantics differ. LGBTQ+ students must feel safe and have positive associations with school if they are to learn, and, furthermore, they cannot be invisible in the resources and materials their teachers disseminate. US history classes may not be the place where students will consider and process the impact of their language and behavior on a regular basis, but it is where similar examples from the past, albeit often on a larger scale, will illustrate the same principles. Learning this history, then, is crucial to students' understanding and analysis of the past; the content and analysis it provokes serve a similar purpose to students' relationship with the present fulfilling a wide range of missions and objectives.

The lessons and units available online reflect advancing ideas on how to integrate omitted aspects of history into the classroom. They provide educators with packaged, well-researched lessons and resources on a topic with which many teachers are unfamiliar and/or uncomfortable. The lessons offered by PBS Learning Media, Learning for Justice, the ADL, and others are a remarkable entry point from which to begin introducing this history to a new generation of students. Furthermore, incorporating new material into the curriculum is a long and fraught process.[53] These lessons, even where they are too narrowly focused or excessively broad, exist as a starting point from which future curricula can grow. Though the disparate nature of these resources is potentially problematic in that it requires teachers to hunt for what they need, the materials and lessons indicate the increasing inclination to teach LGBTQ+ history and the work that goes into doing so.

The resources available to teachers offer high-quality options for making those wishing to make their classes more representative. Truly inclusive history curricula, though, require greater diversity of resources than what is currently available to the majority of teachers. Although some topics, like same-sex marriage and the Stonewall riots, are more accessible to students and therefore more viable as lessons, multiple organizations developing lessons on the same topics prevent the creation of resources on equally important topics like the Harlem Renaissance and the Second World War, time periods covered in US history classes that allow for organic integration of LGBTQ+ content. Furthermore, though there are clear connections between social reform movements, the cluster of lessons aligning the civil rights and gay rights movements do not meet educators' calls for materials that interweave LGBTQ+ history throughout US history. The similarities among resources available, though illustrative of the need for lessons on those topics, preclude broader historical learning. ONE Archives and PBS Learning Media intend to address these needs, but this lack of diversity prevents LGBTQ+ history from being implemented in US history classes as thoroughly as educators and scholars suggest it should be and as well as the number of available resources indicate that it could be.

In 2015, Carolyn Laub insisted that historically based curricula aiming to make LGBTQ+ individuals and events more visible must be distinct from anti-bullying and diversity lessons. She posited, "We're going to change what we are teaching and the way that we're teaching it so that LGBT Americans and their struggles and their stories are told in history. That is just so different than teaching about diversity, bias, or bullying [but] there hasn't really been a hunger for anyone to develop LGBT history lesson plans comprehensively."[54] Changes in the last five years met Laub's call, but this reform must persist. Marginalized groups are present throughout US history, and it benefits students for inclusive curriculum to encompass them all. Since GLSEN's founding in 1990 and as more organizations began creating LGBTQ+-inclusive resources, the majority targeted bullying and school climate. These topics seemed more societally acceptable and more imminently necessary, especially as national attention to bullying skyrocketed. In the twenty-first century, though, as LGBTQ+ issues have become and remain national news, organizations are rising to the challenge Laub addressed and developing resources that, to varying extents, invoke and convey this history. This recognition, and the work it spurs, are necessary and valuable steps for real change to happen.

One Step Back?

Kisha Webster, a former director of education and community engagement at Welcoming Schools, asserted that the most significant obstacles to taking these resources from the screen to the classroom are lack of administrative support and teachers' unfamiliarity with the material. She stated, schools "need to make sure that they have policies in place and resources associated with truly preparing educators to do this well"; she emphasized that LGBTQ+ history must be integrated properly, or it risks becoming insufficient and redundant.[55] Regardless of the number of available resources, without systemic support the materials will be used by a small cadre of individual educators rather than becoming an integral aspect of a US history survey course. Where ignorance and resistance abound, then, it is imperative to have accessible resources and information to thwart it. All of the organizations developing curriculum share this goal.

In order to incorporate new curricula in a major academic subject area in the current educational climate, it must align with state and national standards; any materials that do not explicitly comply have little chance of being used. In states where LGBTQ+ history is absent from standards, a significant obstacle considering the amount of material to be covered in ten months, resources must at least align with Common Core standards to be viable. Several organizations, therefore, prioritize compliance in an attempt to make their resources more acceptable and marketable; these organizations explicitly state their alignment with standards throughout their materials. Project Look Sharp's Sox Sperry underscored the importance of alignment, stating, "One of the most frequently visited parts of our website is the index for lessons around Common Core ... because a lot of teachers these days are being required to teach to tests that are tied to [those] standards."[56] Furthermore, ONE Archives includes Common Core and state standards as well as relevant sections of California's History and Social Science Framework in all of its materials. Learning for Justice's lessons reference the numbers of the Common Core standards addressed in each lesson at the end, and ADL is explicit about which standards each of its lessons meets. Jinnie

Spiegler, ADL's curriculum director, claimed, "Our lessons are always Common-Core aligned, have a social justice and anti-bias lens and include activities that are interactive."[57] Each of these organizations aims to create materials that appeal nationally and thus focus on aligning with Common Core over navigating fifty different, potentially contradictory, sets of standards.

The lack of requirements across the country to teach LGBTQ+ history is an oft-cited reason for its absence from classrooms and, therefore, stymies the use of available resources regardless of their purpose or content. Six states mandate teaching LGBTQ+ history. Where there is no mention, the chances that teachers will seek to incorporate this material significantly decrease. Aligning with Common Core and other national standards is essential, but it does not carry the gravitas of being entrenched in the state standards on which students are tested. This lack of institutional support detracts from the work that outside organizations do to develop materials by restricting teachers' opportunities to explore its impact in their classes. Despite education advocates' and developers' best efforts, bureaucratic restrictions pose significant hurdles to implementing LGBTQ+-inclusive curriculum in standards-based classes. LGBTQ+ history lessons, despite their value, depend on support beyond the academy and organizations that create and promote them.

As of 2021, five states (Alabama, Louisiana, Mississippi, Oklahoma, and Texas) have laws banning positive representations of LGBTQ+ individuals and issues in school settings. "No Promotion of Homosexuality"[58] legislation, referred to by LGBTQ+ rights advocates as "No Promo Homo" laws, "expressly forbid teachers from discussing gay and transgender issues (including sexual health and HIV/AIDS awareness) in a positive light—if at all."[59] These laws date back to the 1970s and John Briggs's efforts to ban LGBTQ content and teachers from public schools; they remain good law in the twenty-first century.

Unlike states that omit LGBTQ+ history from their standards, "No Promo Homo" laws codify restrictions on inclusive curriculum. The Alabama State Code, for example, declares,

> Any program or curriculum in the public schools in Alabama that includes sex education ... shall, as a minimum, include and emphasize the following ... An emphasis, in a factual manner and from a public health perspective, that homosexuality is not a lifestyle acceptable to the general public and that homosexual conduct is a criminal offense under the laws of the state.[60]

Similarly, Texas law states that educational materials must "state that homosexual conduct is not an acceptable lifestyle and is a criminal offense."[61] These laws, as well as those on the books in other states, circumvent any discussion of how to introduce LGBTQ+-inclusive curriculum by legally restricting the topic as a whole. Although specifically targeted to health and sex education classes, they are indicative of school culture and can be more widely applied. As recently as 2012, Tennessee and Missouri attempted to pass laws prohibiting any discussion or mention of homosexuality within school buildings, a bill thrice introduced in the Tennessee state legislature; both bills failed despite widespread conservative support due to the perceived homophobia attached to them.[62] In forty-five states, amending standards to include LGBTQ+ history is a necessary step to guarantee its place in taught curriculum. In the five states with "No Promotion of Homosexuality" legislation, the stumbling blocks are exponentially more significant.

* * *

LGBTQ+ history resources exist to a greater extent than ever before and educational and advocacy organizations develop new materials all the time. This helps overcome teachers' knowledge gaps and inexperience with this topic and offers students opportunities that they didn't have before. Educators and educational institutions now need to move past existing hurdles so these resources can be implemented. In Emily Hobson's opinion,

> everything that has kept LGBT history at somewhat of a fringe can be a way to introduce good historical method that then can be a pathway for students, who just think more critically about the past in general, think more critically about their learning in general, get excited about new areas, see the value ... political engagement, maybe get interested in teaching history because they don't have to just talk about World War II and the Cold War.[63]

Technical barriers like standards and testing, and societal and moral impediments, like the association of LGBTQ+ issues and sex,[64] have long posed obstacles to discussions of LGBTQ+ history in classrooms. Change is afoot, though. There is more attention now on the lack of LGBTQ+ history in public schools, the need for resources to teach it, and for those resources to be inquiry and/or project-based. History lessons, and the intention to teach them, remain grassroots. They require the same systemic backing that anti-bullying efforts receive in order to become similarly widespread, but the increasing number and quality of resources available indicate that Hobson's vision can become a reality.

6

The FAIR Act: A Legislative Victory for LGBTQ+ History Education

California, more than any other state, leads the nation in passing legislation protecting its LGBTQ+ population. These laws cover a broad spectrum of issues, from preventing housing and workplace discrimination to addressing gender identity to establishing legal parental rights for same-sex couples.[1] Since 2000, largely at the urging of then-assemblywoman Sheila Kuehl—the first openly gay member of the California state legislature and one of the founders of the state's LGBT Caucus—California also passed several laws intended to improve school climate, alleviate bullying, and create a more open environment for LGBTQ+ students. The Fair, Accurate, Inclusive, and Respectful (FAIR) Education Act, passed in 2011, was years in the making and the product of previous acts pertaining to education that built to it. Yet, it is also different from those acts. The FAIR Act, unlike anything successfully passed before it, requires social studies classes at all grade levels to include LGBTQ+ history and issues in their curricula. This key difference is groundbreaking, as it mandated revisions to general social studies and US history curricula from elementary through high school throughout the state. Supporters of the FAIR Act did not push it through the legislature to achieve guarantees of token mentions of LGBTQ+ history in social studies classes; rather, the act's mandate for inclusive curricula requires weaving LGBTQ+ events, figures, and issues throughout the history lessons to which students are currently exposed. The inclusiveness required by the FAIR Act should, in significant ways, make social studies education in California more relevant in the twenty-first century.

As the first law of its kind, the FAIR Act could only have passed in California, with its history of laws protecting the LGBTQ+ community. But, given that one of its primary goals was introducing potentially controversial issues in public school classes, its passage was not smooth. Though California is progressive, there is a vocal lobby and population devoted to preventing emphasis on and the expansion of LGBTQ+ rights, especially, in this case, where minors are involved. The legislative triumph of the FAIR Act, then, was representative of evolving thought and public opinion in California and nationwide in 2011, as well as an example of successful lobbying efforts on the part of LGBTQ+ advocacy organizations and the power of the state's Democratic majority.

The FAIR-est State of All

In 2010 and 2011, when the FAIR Act was introduced and passed by the state legislature, several things set California apart from other states in the rights and opportunities it granted to its LGBTQ+ population. According to Jo Michael, the former legislative director at Equality California (EQCA), beginning in the 1990s there was a significant push to take California from a state with limited legal protections to one with "the most comprehensive protection for LGBT people in the country."[2] Within ten years of its founding, EQCA claims, California became a leader in the rights and opportunities guaranteed to LGBT citizens, including, "protect[ion] from discrimination in securing employment and housing, accessing government services and participating in state-funded activities."[3]

Liberal cities in California began legislating change as early as the 1970s in the wake of the Stonewall riots and the protests they spurred. In 1972, San Francisco, a city with a prominent gay population, "banned the city, and those with city contracts, from discriminating based on race, gender, religion, or sexual orientation."[4] Six years later, in 1978, Harvey Milk was elected to the San Francisco board of supervisors and San Francisco passed an ordinance banning "discrimination in employment, housing, and public accommodations based on sexual preference," which, according to Milk, would "be the most stringent gay rights law in the country."[5] In 1984, newly incorporated West Hollywood became the first city in which the majority of lawmakers were gay. These cities, long known for liberal politics and politicians, took the first small steps toward greater acceptance—legally, at least—of LGBTQ+ Californians at a time when the population began to gain greater notice nationally. Not all Californians, inside or outside the state government, supported these policies—as previously mentioned, California State Senator John Briggs advocated for banning gay teachers from classrooms, pushing a ballot initiative that eventually failed in 1978—but the seeds of change were planted as cities and states around the country grappled with questions concerning a population no longer hidden.

California was also ahead of national politics and thinking on LGBTQ+ issues on a statewide level, decriminalizing all consensual sexual acts in 1975,[6] eleven years before the Supreme Court upheld Georgia's anti-sodomy laws in *Bowers v. Hardwick* (1986) and almost thirty years before the Court ruled such laws unconstitutional in *Lawrence v. Texas* (2003). By the 1990s, the state began its path toward the numerous protections it would begin to legislate for its LGBTQ+ population by the end of the decade. In 1992, Governor Pete Wilson signed into law a bill banning "job-related discrimination based on sexual orientation for virtually all state and private workers."[7] The law was not perfect—there was confusion over which professions were protected and it was a civil, rather than a criminal statute—but the law came at a time when several other states and the national government passed laws harmful to the LGBTQ+ community.[8] With this law, California became the seventh state to protect workers from discrimination based on sexual orientation, and it was by far the largest and most prominent at that time.[9]

Since the founding of the state legislature's LGBT Caucus in 1999, hundreds of bills were proposed, with many enacted into law; within a decade, California offered unprecedented protections to its LGBT population in multiple arenas. In its first year of existence, California created a statewide domestic partnership registry and passed laws prohibiting job discrimination and mandating life imprisonment for convicted murderers who committed their crime because of their victim's sexual orientation.[10] In the first decade of the twenty-first century, California enacted legislation intended to end discrimination in housing, jury selection, employment, insurance coverage, and public facilities, among others. At the same time, the state passed legislation to end school-based discrimination and harassment, strengthened its hate crimes laws and the penalties for committing such crimes, and augmented provisions for the prevention of and care for people with HIV and AIDS.[11] Moreover, bills that would restrict LGBT rights often died in committee. These advances, spurred by the efforts of the LGBT caucus and organizations like EQCA, were largely enacted during a Republican governor's administration, further emphasizing the importance of this legislation and the state's commitment to it. Several other states passed laws in the same time period expanding protections for their LGBT populations, but no other state did so to the same extent as California.

Despite California's outstanding legislative record on this subject, the general population remained much more divided with many Californians opposed to extending certain rights—marriage, in particular—to the LGBTQ+ community. Though it has a reputation as a progressive state, California's divisions—political and otherwise—run deep. The state is ethnically diverse; in 2000, the population was 47 percent white, 33 percent Latino, 12 percent Asian, and 6 percent African American.[12] Presidential election data from 2008 indicate that the state's coastal regions voted Democratic, while the interior, especially in the north, leaned Republican. This, according to the *New York Times*, resulted from a confluence of factors: in the post-Cold War era, conservative, affluent whites followed defense industry jobs out of the state; the Latino and Asian populations increased; and the filmmaking and technology industries flourished, bringing educated professionals to California's cities.[13] As these changes shifted party affiliation and electoral politics to the left, religion and culture continued to influence Californians' stance on social and civil rights issues like LGBTQ rights.

The fight for gay rights in California in 2008 centered on marriage as the state became embroiled in the controversy over Proposition 8 and the ensuing Supreme Court case. The battle not only revealed a lack of consensus on same-sex marriage, but it also brought nuanced divisions among Californians to light. A 2003 study, for example, revealed that "Blacks disapprove of homosexuality more strongly than whites" and "nearly three-quarters of Blacks say homosexual relations are always wrong."[14] A 2007 Pew Research survey indicated that Catholic and evangelical Christian Latinos tend to hold socially conservative beliefs, though they are also likely to vote Democratic.[15] Furthermore, responding to a 2008 *Los Angeles Times*/KTLA poll, approximately one-third of Asians, Blacks, Latinos, and whites strongly agreed with the statement, "If gays are allowed to marry, the institution of marriage will be degraded"; nearly the same proportion of Asians, Blacks, and Latinos strongly disagreed.[16]

On May 15, 2008, the California Supreme Court ruled in favor of same-sex marriage. Two weeks later, on June 2, Proposition 8, a ballot measure that "would amend the state Constitution to define marriage as a union 'between a man and a woman,'"[17] thereby overturning the Court's ruling, garnered over a million signatures and earned its place on the November ballot. In the next six months, campaigns urging people to vote "Yes" or "No" on 8 pervaded the state. With polling on the initiative close as November approached, the Mormon church, which viewed marriage as "a kind of firewall to be held at all costs," played an "extraordinary role" "in helping to pass [Proposition 8] with money, institutional support and dedicated volunteers."[18] California, then, became the focus of the growing nationwide debate over same-sex marriage. Proposition 8, and the strategies and resources employed by each side, revealed a deep divide on LGBTQ+ rights within a traditional institution as well as the efficacy and failure of tactics implemented to persuade voters[19]—many of the arguments and voices in this campaign would also be prominent in the public and media debates over the FAIR Act. Proposition 8 passed with 52 percent of the vote in the same election that saw Barack Obama decidedly win California. Seventy percent of Black voters, following their churches' lead, and 53 percent of Latino voters supported the measure, contributing significantly to its victory.[20] Though Proposition 8 was ultimately overturned and same-sex marriage legalized with the Supreme Court's decision in *Hollingsworth v. Perry* in 2013, the ramifications and impact of the battle were profound and instructive.

Thus, California was no stranger to first of its kind laws supporting and protecting LGBT citizens or protracted fights to defend them. Moreover, by 2010 the Democratic supermajority in the California state legislature was even more determined to take action to extend existing protections, both school-centered and societally,[21] especially after the uproar surrounding Proposition 8. Though other states include sexual orientation as a protected category and some, like Massachusetts, mandate anti-bias and bullying curriculum in schools—which California did, as well, beginning in 2000—the FAIR Act made California the first to require wholesale change to social studies curricula. Past efforts, and the political climate in 2011—including the inauguration of a Democratic governor—made it the most appropriate place for what supporters hoped would be groundbreaking legislation.

The Path to FAIR Legislation

California's efforts to improve the school environment and experience for LGBTQ+ students date back to the beginning of the twenty-first century, with the legislative push for greater protection of and equality for the LGBTQ+ population statewide and the legislative tenure of Sheila Kuehl, a Democrat from Santa Monica who served in the state assembly and, later, the state senate. Kuehl authored several bills aimed at extending existing antibias laws covering other underrepresented groups to further include gender and sexuality and promoted bias-free curricula across California, setting the precedent that would eventually lead to the FAIR Act and encountering similar struggles with opposition and implementation, albeit in a different, and potentially more adverse, climate.

Aiming to make schools safer and create an environment conducive to learning for all students, the California state legislature began debating bills meant to ameliorate the bullying and discrimination LGBTQ+ students regularly faced in the late 1990s. On October 2, 1999, Democratic Governor Gray Davis signed the California Student Safety and Violence Prevention Act of 2000 (AB 537), which added gender and sexual orientation to existing law that guaranteed equal rights and opportunities to all public school students "regardless of their sex, ethnic group identification, race, national origin, religion, or mental or physical disability";[22] this aligned legal code regarding education with hate crimes legislation that already offered wider coverage and protection. This law, then, treated schools as a microcosm of society aiming to create safe spaces in which students could learn without the fear or threat that their gender identity or sexuality would place them in harm's way.

Despite prohibiting violence and discrimination, the law provided no structure for implementation or enforcement. Thus, two years after the California Student Safety and Violence Prevention Act was passed and set to go into effect, few districts had implemented it. Kuehl, by this time a state senator, appealed to school superintendents. In a letter dated December 18, 2002, she wrote,

> We know that there is still substantial and documented harassment and discrimination against students who actually are or are perceived to be gay, lesbian, bisexual, or transgender, even though the law was first enacted more than two and one-half years ago. I believe this is, in part, due to the fact that the law has not, yet, been implemented or directly applied in many local school districts in California.[23]

The letter was accompanied by a resource intended to inform superintendents and districts how to implement the law and answer common questions. Despite these efforts, though, implementation was lax and discrimination persisted.

Four years later, and four years before Mark Leno would introduce the FAIR Act, Kuehl introduced a similarly minded bill to the California state senate. This bill, a response to the harassment and bullying LGBTQ+ students continued to face in schools, called for a bias-free curriculum that would increase awareness among heterosexual students and create a safer school environment for the LGBTQ+ population. In its original form, the Bias-Free Curriculum Act (SB 1437) focused more on classroom learning than its predecessor, mandating that "no textbook or other instructional materials shall be adopted by the state board or by any governing board for use in public schools that contains any matter reflecting adversely upon persons because of their race or ethnicity, gender, disability, nationality, sexual orientation, or religion," and "when adopting instructional materials for use in schools, government boards shall include only instructional materials which, in their determination, accurately portray, in an age-appropriate manner the cultural, racial, gender, and sexual orientation diversity of our society."[24] Following veto threats by Governor Schwarzenegger, who claimed that he would "veto any bill that, in his words, 'micromanaged' state education by requiring inclusion of LGBT individuals in textbooks,"[25] the Assembly passed an amended version of the bill that removed these curricular mandates.[26] Schwarzenegger, however, still vetoed it, claiming, "This bill offers vague protection when current law already provides clear protection against discrimination in our schools based on sexual orientation."[27] Schwarzenegger signed seven other bills that supported the LGBT community that year; he was unwilling, however, to pass the two education-related bills that crossed his desk. California maintained its burgeoning reputation for legally protecting its LGBTQ+ population, but it failed to further extend protection and improve circumstances in its schools.

Schwarzenegger's veto did not derail those in and outside the legislature who viewed the situation in schools as untenable. In 2007, Kuehl authored, and the Senate passed, SB 777, the Student Civil Rights Act. Unlike the Bias-Free Curriculum Act, this bill aimed at strengthening and clarifying existing state law rather than issuing new requirements. In its analysis of the bill, the Senate Judiciary Committee wrote, "This bill would create a consistency among statutes prohibiting various forms of discrimination based on specified personal characteristics by revising the list of prohibited bases of discrimination in Education Code ... consistent with the list in ... the Penal Code."[28] According to Kuehl,

> research has shown that inclusive school policies and curriculum make a difference: when students report that their schools have non-discrimination and anti-harassment policies that include sexual and gender identity, and when they say that they have learned about LGBT [Lesbian, Gay, Bisexual, and Transgender] issues at school, they report less harassment and they feel safer.[29]

EQCA also emphasized the need for clarity in its support of the law, claiming, "Lack of clarity in state law has resulted in lawsuits that cost taxpayers millions of dollars in unnecessary litigation and settlement costs. ... Individual school districts have paid anywhere between $45,000 and more than $1.1 million in settlements or judgments, not including attorney fees."[30] Despite the governor's veto message the previous year, stating that there was no need for law that simply recapitulated existing legislation, the problems those laws were meant to address persisted. The Student Civil Rights Act passed and was hailed as a success by the legislators and lobbyists who advocated for it.

Each of these acts, whether passed or vetoed by the governor, met with virulent backlash by conservative and family groups all centering on similar themes: interference with religious beliefs and family traditions, government overreach in education, and influencing students' sexual ideas and attitudes. In 2000, the Committee on Moral Concerns officially recorded its opposition to the bill with the state assembly, and the Senate's analysis of the bill reiterated a statement issued by the Traditional Values Coalition on AB 222, a similar bill vetoed the previous year, asserting, "Administrators already have the legal authority to prevent harassment of any student for any reason, including perceived homosexuality ... By specifically teaching the acceptance of homosexuality ... this bill will directly challenge ... strongly held religious beliefs."[31] In 2006, California State Senator Bill Morrow criticized the Bias-Free Curriculum Act for treating race and sexual orientation as similar categories, claiming that the former was biological fact and the latter a choice and thus cannot be treated as the same.[32] Karen England of the Capitol Resource Center, which would later be a major player in the battle against the FAIR Act, called the 2007 law "reverse discrimination" and "an outright attack on the religious and moral beliefs of California citizens."[33] Furthermore, the Campaign for Children and Families warned that the law would lead to "curriculum changes that include transvestite speakers and transsexual videos, classroom handouts on sex-change operations, and curriculum teaching children homosexual 'marriage' is completely normal"[34]—all in a bill with no mandate for curricular change. In 2007, in fact, legislation remained focus on eliminating bias and discrimination and guaranteeing equal protection to all students in California public schools.[35] This heightened awareness of the adverse circumstances LGBTQ+ students faced and the altruistic intent among LGBTQ+ rights advocates represented a victory for their cause, but opposition and vague provisions for enforcement presented significant obstacles.

Several things changed in California between 2007 and 2010. In 2008, Governor Schwarzenegger vetoed three laws acknowledging LGBTQ+ students and their plight. Additionally, the staunch division created by the battle over Proposition 8 and its resulting amendment to California's state constitution reverberated in decision-making related to other LGBTQ+ issues and changed the landscape and import of these decisions for many on both sides. In 2009, Mark Leno proposed a holiday in honor of Harvey Milk which the governor signed in the wake of the critical success of the film about his life, Sean Penn's Academy Award for the title role, and a strong lobbying effort by EQCA and students from Gay-Straight Alliances throughout California.[36] In 2010, Tyler

Clementi's suicide made national headlines and Jerry Brown, a Democrat with a record of supporting the LGBTQ+ community and its goals, was elected governor of a state with a Democratic majority in the state legislature. The idea of a curriculum bill once again gained support.

Thus, when Mark Leno introduced the FAIR Act in 2010 it was the most recent in a succession of attempts to enhance both education and the educational environment for all students, but especially for those who faced discrimination, bullying, and violence as a result of their real or perceived identity. Where the FAIR Act significantly differs from legislation enacted earlier, though, is its emphasis on curriculum and classroom instruction as the arenas through and in which to create change.

Legislating FAIR-ness

The 2000 and 2007 acts spearheaded and passed by Sheila Kuehl and her colleagues in the California state legislature represented meaningful accomplishments for LGBTQ+ students and the community as a whole, as well as for California, in general. As Mark Leno wrote in 2013, though,

> despite successful efforts in California during the past decade to pass laws intended to make schools safer for LGBT students, we continue to hear about young people who are bullied, at times violently, or are so mistreated by their own peers that they take their own lives. Clearly, our work to help promote understanding within our schools has only scratched the surface.[37]

The antidiscrimination policies prescribed by previous laws did not create the intended safe environment and connection to school community. Moreover, research indicates, "LGBT students in schools with an LGBT-inclusive curriculum ... felt more connected to their school community" and are less likely to encounter homophobia, miss school, or feel unsafe.[38] Further legislation was necessary, and attention again turned to curriculum.

Leno introduced the bill in December 2010,[39] arguing, "The historically inaccurate exclusion of LGBT Americans in social sciences instruction as well as the spreading of negative stereotypes in school activities sustains an environment of discrimination and bias in school throughout California."[40] Leno introduced SB 48, a bill pertaining to "prohibition of discriminatory content" in pupil instruction, on December 13, 2010.[41] Speaking on the bill at that time, Leno meshed the bullying epidemic that previous laws attempted to resolve with the curricular focus of the FAIR Act. He declared, "Our collective silence on this issue perpetuates negative stereotypes of LGBT people and leads to increased bullying of young people. We can't simultaneously tell youth it's OK to be yourself and live an honest, open life when we aren't even teaching students about historical LGBT figures or the LGBT equal rights movement."[42]

Specifically, the bill mandates that social science instruction include the contributions of several groups, among them lesbian, gay, bisexual, and transgender Americans, to the "economic, political, and social development of California and the United States"; neither instruction nor school sponsored activities may promote "a discriminatory bias on the basis of race or ethnicity, gender, religion, disability, nationality, sexual orientation"; and textbooks and instructional materials must "accurately portray the cultural and racial diversity of our society" including, among other contributions, those of LGBT Americans.[43] Many of the groups included in the FAIR Act's mandate—for example African Americans, Native Americans, and Mexican Americans—were previously included in educational legislation of a similar nature. Where the FAIR Act differs is in its inclusion of people with disabilities and, of course, lesbian, gay, bisexual, and transgender Americans.

The FAIR Act's journey through the California state legislature was illustrative of the political divide surrounding LGBTQ+ issues in California and throughout the nation. In both committee and floor votes in the Senate and Assembly, support for and opposition to the bill was largely determined by the side of the aisle on which a legislator sat. The legislative debate over the FAIR Act, then, was as much about politics as it was about education. In its analysis of the bill, the Education Committee referenced the vagueness of and potential problems with implementation, including the fact that the "bill does not specifically require the inclusion of lesbian, gay, bisexual, or transgender people in the History-Social Science Framework"—the document that details the social and historical information teachers and textbooks are meant to convey in each grade—and the state's moratorium on new instructional materials prior to the 2013–14 academic year.[44] Moreover, Republican Senator Robert Huff claimed that the bill, if passed, would "actively promot[e] a lifestyle."[45] The Judiciary Committee, too, noted the requisite delay in the changes the bill mandated resulting from California's budget crisis and the lack of available funds for new educational resources.

Support for the bill, however, trumped these concerns. Testifying in front of the Senate Education Committee, Carolyn Laub of the GSA asserted, "Bullying of lesbian, gay, bisexual, and transgender (LGBT) youth is a pervasive problem in our schools with serious consequences for students' mental health and academic achievement."[46] In addition, both committees cited the necessity of such a bill, reiterating Mark Leno's goal of making history properly inclusive, further clarifying and reducing confusion on what existing law entailed and, in the Judiciary Committee's assessment, referencing California's "history of requiring instruction that includes the various roles of different ethnic, gender, and minority groups ... to promote understanding, and to recognize the accomplishments of all groups of people."[47] The Senate Education and Judiciary Committees passed SB 48 along party lines in a Democratic triumph, 6–3 (one vote not recorded) and 3–2, respectively. Sent to the Senate floor, the FAIR Act passed 23–14, with three votes unrecorded;[48] no senator crossed the aisle.

The Assembly Committee on Education, which counted among its members Tommy Ammiano, the bill's sponsor in that chamber, likewise passed the FAIR Act along party lines with seven Democrats voting for and four Republicans against. The committee's analysis similarly acknowledged the expected delay in creating new instructional materials and amending state standards while also arguing,

> Instruction and instructional materials that portray the various roles and contributions of different ethnic and minority groups promote understanding of the diversity of the state and recognizes the accomplishments of all groups of people. Projecting such diversity gives pupils pride in his or her roots and a sense of equal opportunity. Hence it can be argued that by requiring instruction and textbooks to include the roles and contributions of persons with disabilities and LGBT Americans, this bill ensures equal representation of all people within the curriculum.[49]

The committee noted that, as advocates claimed, this revised curriculum could lead to the safe school environment sought for more than ten years. On July 5, 2011, the Democrat-dominated Assembly approved the bill by a vote of 50–26; the FAIR Act's legislative journey was significantly determined by—and benefitted from—the Democratic dominance in both houses. Liberal, urban Californians, and the political party that represented them, succeeded in passing the LGBTQ+ curriculum law Kuehl suggested was necessary in 2000, but the overwhelmingly positive Assembly vote indicated division even more than it did consensus.

Reactions to the bill as the state legislature considered it focused predominantly on the clauses pertaining to sexual orientation. Both the Senate and Assembly Committees' analyses of the bill include sizable lists of organizations that registered support for and opposition to the FAIR Act; many of these organizations maintained the stance taken regarding past legislation focused on LGBT rights. Human rights groups, teachers' organizations, and school districts in Los Angeles and San Francisco endorsed the bill. The California Teachers Association, for example, wrote, "CTA is pleased to support this measure to ensure the areas of social science instruction be expanded to include the contributions of LGBT individuals and other ethnic and cultural groups as such supporting the human and civil rights of all students."[50] California Church Impact, one of the few religious organizations to support the bill, stated, "We do not desire, from either political or moral positions, to consign the contribution of gay and lesbian members of our society to the hidden history we so easily ignore. Our faith principles uphold the equal humanity and therefore equal contributions of all members of our society."[51]

Meanwhile, many religious, family advocacy, and conservative organizations vehemently opposed the bill. The Calvary Christian Church, for example, claimed that the bill would "play with the minds of all California's students; even as young as Kindergarten!! Whatever the personal beliefs of adults on homosexuality, bisexuality, and transgender, the state has NO RIGHT trying to influence the beliefs, thinking and mindset of young students!"[52] Upon the bill's passage in the Assembly, Randi Thomasson of SaveCalifornia.com, one of the leading voices opposed to the FAIR Act, asserted, "Because of the raft of sexual indoctrination laws already in force, which promote homosexuality, bisexuality, and transsexuality under the guise of discrimination and harassment, the social engineers are already having their way with more than six million boys and girls, with or without SB 48"; he implored parents to remove their children from public schools.[53] The *Los Angeles Times* published an editorial criticizing legislative interference in education. It opined,

> These battles no doubt have a legitimate place in the social studies curriculum. But that's a decision for educators and textbook writers to make. If more is added to the social studies curriculum, something else will have to be deleted or treated more shallowly. Teachers already struggle to get through all the required material before the state's standardized tests are administered in the spring.[54]

Despite this opposition, the FAIR Act benefitted from a core of vocal and industrious supporters[55] and the Democratic supermajority; it was approved by the legislature and went to the governor.

On July 7, 2011, EQCA wrote to Governor Jerry Brown urging him to sign the FAIR Act into law. Roland Palencia, then EQCA's executive director, wrote,

While LGBT people represent a sizable and important part of the state, mention of the LGBT community's role in California history and contemporary society is virtually non-existent in textbooks and other school instructional materials. The FAIR Education Act would require that lesbian, gay, bisexual, and transgender (LGBT) Americans are included and recognized for their important historical contributions to the economic, political, and social development of California and the United States.[56]

EQCA and the GSA placed a great deal of hope in Governor Brown, with his long and documented history of supporting LGBT rights and causes. This hope was not misplaced: Brown signed the FAIR Act into law on July 14, 2011; it was set to go into effect on January 1, 2012. As in the legislature, the FAIR Act became law largely because the politics were in place to make it happen. Brown, a Democrat, and the Democratic legislative supermajority pushed through a bill that previously failed, and would likely have again under a Republican administration.

California, a leader in LGBTQ+ rights, was a clear place for potentially groundbreaking legislation; the FAIR Act extended California's protections in unprecedented ways. Upon signing the law, Governor Brown issued the following statement:

> History should be honest. This bill revises existing laws that prohibit discrimination in education and ensures that the important contributions of Americans from all backgrounds and walks of life are included in our history books. It represents an important step forward for our state, and I thank Senator Leno for his hard work on this historic legislation.[57]

The bill's advocates celebrated their victory as California passed legislation in the making since 2006, becoming the first state to mandate history and social science classes and curricula offer instruction in LGBTQ+ history and include information on LGBTQ+ individuals and lives and, through this, address bullying, discrimination, and violence in schools and in society at large. The opposition, however, did not accept defeat. The day Governor Brown signed the law, Randy Thomasson responded,

> It's ridiculous that Jerry Brown says he's making history "honest." ... The bill he signed prohibits teachers and textbooks from telling children the facts that homosexuality has the highest rate of HIV/AIDS and other STDs, higher cancer rates, and earlier deaths. ... This revisionist history will actually make more children believe a lie—that homosexuality is biological, which it's not, and healthy, which it isn't.[58]

The bill became law, but the battle was not over.

For the organizations that long supported including LGBTQ+ figures and history in the curriculum, the FAIR Act's passage was monumental. It was years in the making, the product of a confluence of factors, and, at the time it was passed, the only law in the nation specifically targeting social studies education as an arena in which LGBTQ+ history was a curricular necessity. The FAIR Act reflected emerging shifts in public opinion and attitudes, and the political success of an increasingly vocal and well-organized lobby that prioritized school-based protections and invested the time and resources to make them realities.

This political success, however, was complicated. The relative speed and ease with which the bill passed was more indicative of the Democratic power of California's legislative and executive branches than a true consensus around the law; thus, its enactment did nothing to take away, and in fact exacerbated, its controversial nature. Opponents seized on the clauses pertaining to gender and sexual orientation, ignoring the long list of other groups listed in the act, in a phenomenon reminiscent of the Rainbow Curriculum controversy nearly twenty-five years prior. Its subsequent path was fraught with continued attacks and opposition. The initial battle was over, but another would launch imminently as the political battle over educational change continued.

A FAIR Fight

Backlash to the FAIR Act, which emerged early in the legislative process, persisted and increased when it was voted into law. Stop SB 48, a coalition of religious and family-focused groups dedicated to placing a referendum on the June 2012 ballot to overturn the law, launched a petition to gather the signatures necessary to do so within two weeks of the law's enactment. Individuals and groups in favor of the law, many of whom recalled the sting of losing the battle over Proposition 8 three years prior and criticism of the "sub-par" campaign they ran at that time, including the obstinacy and inexperience of those in charge,[59] vowed to devote the resources and energy necessary to curtail this effort. Though the law had passed, the political maneuvering continued.

After Governor Brown signed the FAIR Act into law, opponents maintained their position that it would restrict parents' voices in their children's education; Randy Thomasson asserted, "Jerry Brown has trampled on the parental rights of the broad majority of California mothers and fathers who don't want their children to be sexually brainwashed."[60] Catholics for the Common Good, which also lobbied against the bill, released a statement reiterating protests recorded in 2006, declaring, "Politicians should not be co-opting school curricula and writing textbooks to push an ideological agenda, whether it be conservative or liberal."[61] DefendChristians.org portrayed the fight against the FAIR Act as a national struggle, claiming, "Because California is the largest consumer of textbooks, the content of California textbooks will likely end up in the textbooks of other states. Even if you don't live in California your help is urgently needed to stop this wicked curriculum."[62] According to SaveCalifornia.com, SB 48 would have a dangerous and life-changing impact on student learning, including, "teachers will be made to positively portray homosexuality, same-sex 'marriages,' bisexuality, and transsexuality, because to be silent can bring the charge of 'reflecting adversely' or 'promoting a discriminatory bias.'"[63] For these conservative groups, such alarming changes were unacceptable; there was no question that the FAIR Act had to be repealed.

The Stop SB 48 campaign launched shortly after Mark Leno introduced the bill in December 2010 in association with the Capitol Resource Institute, a socially conservative organization that "encourages churches to influence public policy."[64] It first focused on contacting and lobbying state representatives to vote against the bill. Though this initial effort proved unsuccessful, the Stop SB 48 campaign persisted, turning its attention to overturning the law through referendum. On its website, Stop SB 48 asserted, "The bill casts a wide-reaching net that includes all social sciences like economics, government, and cultural and social anthropology. ... Essentially teachers and administrators are being asked not to tolerate but to advocate";[65] the website also directed viewers to sign and distribute the referendum petition, donate to the effort, and follow Stop SB 48 on Facebook. In a press release announcing the launch of the petition, Brad Dacus, the president of the Pacific Justice Institute, an organization at the forefront of the campaign, posited, "Every Californian who believes in parental rights and passing down an unbiased history to our children is going to have to get involved. ... We need people to give like our future depends on it—because it does."[66] As the opposition coalesced around Stop SB 48's referendum, they found broader ways to spread their message, employing tactics designed to reach and persuade a large swath of voters to join their cause; this included YouTube videos and text messages delivered to all California cell phone numbers. For these organizations and their supporters, these statements and actions were commensurate with the grave danger that the FAIR Act posed to education.

Organizations like Calvary Chapel, the Family Research Council, and the Capitol Resource Institute opposed SB 48—like they did LGBT-related bills and laws in the past—from the moment it was introduced. With its passage, they used every resource at their disposal to lobby the people, whom they hoped would see the danger posed by this law and aid their cause. Similar to the battle over Proposition 8, in which conservative and religious organizations argued that same-sex marriage was harmful to children, they argued that teaching children about LGBTQ+ history and lives would adversely affect students. Unlike Proposition 8, though, the effort failed to gain the support of Mormon and Catholic churches and national Christian and conservative organizations; thus, it lacked access to the infrastructure and financial backing that such institutions and organizations provide.[67] The campaign was thus stymied by a severe lack of funds and an inexperienced, all-volunteer effort led by conservative Christian groups.

EQCA and like-minded organizations were determined to prevent the FAIR Act from being overturned. Previous experience, especially in the battle against Proposition 8, made them apprehensive about their chances of defeating the referendum; moreover, they faced the powerful tactics employed by the Stop SB 48 campaign which emphasized "kids learning about gays" as a scare tactic intended to rally support.[68] Guaranteeing the survival of the FAIR Act, though, emerged as a priority as Stop SB 48 gained momentum. Rick Jacobs, founder of the Courage Campaign, accused his opponents of using "fear tactics to prevent California high school students from learning history."[69] In a letter responding to Stop SB 48 and countering their claims about the law, he stated, "This new law has nothing to do with sex education. … The law merely requires that California schools integrate age-appropriate, factual information about social movements, current events and the social contributions of lesbian, gay, bisexual and disabled individuals into existing history and social studies lessons."[70] The Courage Campaign, along with EQCA, GSA Network, and the National Center for Lesbian Rights also collaborated on a "decline to sign campaign," countering Stop SB 48's efforts by dispatching "truth squads" to clarify the intentions and implications of the FAIR Act.[71] Learning from their mistakes in 2008, LGBTQ+ rights organizations used every resource and strategy at their disposal to ensure the defeat of the petition and referendum.

EQCA, one of the bill's original sponsors, launched its own fundraising campaign and recruitment effort to counter the referendum. In the 2008 battle over Proposition 8, gay rights groups found themselves on the losing side because, according to Garry South, a Democratic strategist, their effort "was essentially run by a committee of community activists who didn't trust any non-gay professionals and wouldn't take advice from more experienced campaign strategists on the outside who know what they're doing."[72] On August 25, 2011, they issued a press release announcing a coalition to protect the FAIR Act from repeal, encompassing "people of faith; labor organizations; lesbian, gay, bisexual, and transgender (LGBT) rights groups; disability rights advocates; racial justice organizations and many other groups who care about equality."[73] Moreover, on August 30, Executive Director Roland Palencia released the following statement in response to allegations made against the law by Tony Perkins of the Family Research Council: "It's critical that these groups are exposed for what they really are: fear-mongers who prey on good parents' deep, instinctive desire to protect their children in order to advance a hateful, anti-equality agenda."[74] EQCA's most politically minded move, though, was filing a complaint with California's Fair Practices Commission alleging that the primary organizations involved in the Stop SB 48 campaign—Stop SB 48, the Capitol Resource Center, and the Pacific Justice Institute—violated campaign finance laws.[75] Though these claims were refuted, they nevertheless marked the attempt at mounting a referendum as a political battle and effectively challenged the Stop SB 48 campaign in its final rush to accrue signatures.

Stop SB 48 faltered when the coalition failed to accumulate the 505,000 signatures needed to bring the referendum to ballot. On October 11, 2011, the ninety-day period allotted to gather signatures expired, and EQCA claimed victory. Mark Leno, who predicted the referendum would fail, said, "I'm glad to learn my early suspicions have been validated and from all indications it appears they failed by a wide margin."[76] The opposition, however, refused to acknowledge defeat. Stop SB 48 insisted, "To be sure, a referendum was the most direct route to stopping this misguided law in its tracks. ... But there are other tools available. An initiative involves a very similar process of gathering signatures, yet the citizens get more time to gather signatures."[77]

New groups, motivated by the referendum's defeat, emerged to continue the battle, including the Tea Party Patriots, the Christian Coalition of California, and the Committee for Parental Rights and Education. In its second attempt, Stop SB 48 submitted two ballot initiatives: the Children Learning Accurate Social Sciences (CLASS) Act—which removed the clauses pertaining to sexual orientation and religion, mandating instead, "Inclusion of the study of a person in social science instruction shall be accurate and based solely upon historical significance rather than membership in a protected class"[78]—and an initiative giving parents the right to opt out of LGBTQ+-related instruction if and when administered. Ultimately, this effort also failed—in fact, it collected fewer signatures than the first—and by July 2012, a year after the FAIR Act passed, the political campaign to repeal or reduce the law ceased.

As the political battle over the FAIR Act ensued, coupled with the uncertainty of whether it would remain good law, the focus remained on the politics and the struggle rather than on the significance of the law and the changes it mandated in curriculum and classroom settings. There is a standardized process for passing a law and denying a referendum thus facilitating political change—in as much as legislation equates with actual change in society. Educational change is a more nuanced, time-consuming process, requiring different, less conspicuous, actions and mobilization to yield success. The lack of funding in support of the law, coupled with the dearth of classroom resources available, made implementing the FAIR Act on the date it officially went into effect problematic under any circumstances; the political tumult surrounding the law exacerbated and added to these difficulties, maintaining the focus on political debate over schooling. Few districts outside of Los Angeles and San Francisco, which included LGBT history in its curriculum even before the law was passed,[79] took any action to implement the law when it officially went into effect, nor was there any instruction on how to do so. This would be the next, and a more complicated, battle.

Spreading FAIR-ness

Following in California's footsteps, four additional states developed and passed their own LGBTQ+ curriculum laws. Beginning on January 31, 2019, and over the course of eight months, New Jersey, Colorado, Oregon, and Illinois enacted legislation mandating the presence of LGBTQ+ topics in academic subjects, particularly history and social studies, in schools throughout the state. Each of these laws, like California's, aim to make coursework more inclusive and representative. Also, as in California, the legislatures voted on party lines and the laws were both celebrated and reviled by different groups for distinct reasons.

New Jersey, Colorado, Oregon, and Illinois's laws issue similar mandates, all akin to that established by the FAIR Act. New Jersey was the second state in the nation to pass an LGBTQ+ curriculum law. Like California, it had a history of laws supporting the LGBTQ+ population and a newly elected Democratic governor.[80] The law states, "A board of education shall include instruction on the political, economic, and social contributions of persons with disabilities and lesbian, gay, bisexual, and transgender people, in an appropriate place in the curriculum of middle school and high school students as part of the district's implementation of the New Jersey Student Learning Standards"; it directs boards of education to create policies and procedures to guide the selection of instructional materials to fulfill these goals.[81] Colorado echoed this call to teach "the history, culture, and social contributions of minorities," among them LGBTQ+ Americans, and "the intersectionality of significant social and cultural features within these communities."[82] Colorado, unlike California and New Jersey, added a funding provision to its bill to support its implementation allocating $37,495 for "content specialists."[83]

Oregon, meanwhile, included all of the subjects that encompass social studies in its law. HB 2023 specifies that "academic content standards for history, geography, economics and civics include sufficient instruction on the histories, contributions and perspectives of individuals who: (i) Are Native American; (ii) Are of African, Asian, Pacific Island, Chicano, Latino or Middle Eastern descent; (iii) Are women; (iv) Have disabilities; (v) Are immigrants or refugees; or (vi) Are lesbian, gay, bisexual or transgender."[84] Oregon's law, unlike others, explicitly calls for amending state standards, a key component in successful curriculum change. Illinois, the last of these five states to pass its LGBTQ+ curriculum law, established, "In public schools only, the teaching of history shall include a study of the roles and contributions of lesbian, gay, bisexual, and transgender people of this country and this state"; Illinois, like the states that preceded it, called for other marginalized groups' curricular inclusion, as well.[85] Each of these laws, like the FAIR Act, offered the promise of reform and inclusion. Moreover, the eight-year time difference between the FAIR Act and New Jersey, Colorado, Oregon, and Illinois's laws meant that the four latter states had a model from which to learn.

The Democratic majority in each state legislature was instrumental to the process. In New Jersey and Colorado, the laws passed almost entirely along party lines. In New Jersey, where the curriculum bill was signed into law on January 31, 2019, of the fifty-two votes in favor in the Assembly, fifty-one were Democrats; in the Senate, Democrats represented twenty-four of the twenty-seven votes for the law. All of the votes against—ten in the Assembly and eight in the Senate— were Republican.[86] The results were similar in Colorado, where the bill passed the House 40–24 and the Senate 24–11 almost entirely on party lines; one Republican senator crossed the aisle.[87] On May 28, 2019, the nation's first openly gay governor signed the bill. It was more bipartisan in Oregon, where, one week later, its bill "relating to inclusive education" received overwhelming legislative support. Nearly a quarter of the votes in favor in both the House and the Senate were Republican; opposition to the bill—twelve votes across both houses—was entirely Republican.[88] It was closer in Illinois, where the bill's journey was more protracted. In a 37–17 vote in the Senate, one Republican joined Democrats in support. All of the bill's support in the 60–42 vote in the House was Democratic; four Democrats, though, joined Republicans voting against it.[89] Despite small variations the pattern, as established in California, is clear: strong Democratic majorities, in states with liberal-leaning regions populated by people with social justice values, have the power and directive to pass these laws. Though this does not detract from the accomplishment, it renders the victories one-sided, a status that does not bode well when they call for profound and potentially controversial change.

In these states, as in California, advocacy groups celebrated while religious groups and concerned parents sought ways to opt out. LGBTQ+ activists in all four states triumphantly described laws that "get closer as a state to telling the whole story of our shared history"[90] and "cultivate respect towards minority groups, allow students to appreciate differences, and acquire the skills and knowledge needed to function effectively with people of various backgrounds,"[91] and through which "invisibility is being transformed into visibility."[92] In September 2020, the *Washington Blade*, an LGBTQ+ publication, published an article eagerly anticipating New Jersey and Illinois's laws going into effect.[93] Parents in New Jersey, meanwhile, sought avenues to opt out of LGBTQ+ curriculum; a Hackensack school board member claimed she was "disgusted and appalled" by the law.[94] Religious organizations and publications lamented the existence of additional laws intended to "indoctrinate children."[95] Regarding Oregon's law, Family Policy Alliance claimed, "If enacted, this bill would require history textbooks to include people based on their sexuality or internal feelings about gender. This means teachers will be forced to teach radical identity politics in the classroom, whether or not it has anything to do with the subject being taught."[96] Though none of the laws faced the same mass mobilization to repeal as the FAIR Act, each encountered similar resistance, ignorance, and backlash. Implementation, like the challenge facing advocates and curriculum designers in California, is the next frontier.[97]

7

Victory Deferred? Implementing LGBTQ+ Curriculum Laws

Passing laws and implementing them, especially in education, are distinctly different processes, especially when the law mandates changes that many people vehemently oppose. States whose laws were due to go into effect for the 2020–1 school year are just starting the process of navigating this reform. California, the pioneer, engaged in a years-long process to bring the FAIR Act's promise to fruition.

According to the legislation signed by Governor Brown, the FAIR Education Act should have gone into effect on January 1, 2012. At that time, though, it remained embroiled in uncertainty as the battle to repeal raged; it was good law, but it existed only on paper. By that summer, however, the FAIR Act was a reality with which California schools and the state education department had to contend. The political struggle was difficult and costly, but straightforward and short compared to the copious steps and considerations involved in bringing LGBTQ+ history into social science classes throughout the state. Where the political battle centered primarily on whether or not to pass—and then whether or not to repeal—the FAIR Act, implementing it led to far more questions and concerns. Despite limited progress and restrained optimism, meaningful change at the classroom level is slow in the making. The FAIR Act was, then, in microcosm, a tale of political mobilization and, for more than five years after it was enacted, educational stagnation.

In 2013, GSA's Carolyn Laub wrote an article, posted on the organization's website, advocating for implementation. She asserted, "Bullying starts with what young people are taught, so if they're taught to value some groups of people more than others, that shows up in their behavior towards their peers. With the enactment of California's FAIR Education Act, students can learn that these marginalized groups have actually made incredible contributions to this country's history."[1] Laub, and others who fought for and continued to support the FAIR Act and its implementation, looked at the landscape and saw that more than a year after it was meant to go into effect little had changed; in fact, many Californians remained unaware of the law and its mandate. Laub elucidated several obstacles to implementation, including lack of teacher training and district-level support;[2] both would impede any attempt at curricular change, never mind one with as much potential controversy. She also cited evidence and research proving that curriculum reform changes students' attitudes and leads to better school environments; these findings were echoed in several similar studies conducted by GLSEN, Human Rights Campaign, and other organizations.[3]

Significant obstacles to implementation existed within the bill itself and in the many stumbling blocks to curriculum change, in general, and amending California's standards, specifically. Introducing new information requires resources for both students and teachers and, in some cases, professional development. On a more intangible level, instructors, administrators, districts, and school boards need to buy into and support these changes. As San Francisco educator Lyndsey Schlax asserted, most administrators and teachers are unaware of, and therefore cannot teach or understand the necessity of teaching, this history.[4]

History illustrates that adding new, underrepresented groups to the curriculum is an even more arduous task.[5] In fact, there are clear parallels between the struggle to include LGBTQ+ history and efforts to better represent women and the civil rights movement in classes and resources. As second wave feminism gained traction in the 1970s, Janice Law Trecker's 1971 report "Women in U.S. History High-school Textbooks" spotlighted the inherent exclusivity in curriculum design; she stated, "Women are omitted both from topics discussed and by the topics chosen for discussion."[6] Subsequent attempts to integrate women in learning materials were undermined by the emphasis on standards that began in the 1980s and perpetuated throughout the No Child Left Behind and Common Core eras. Additionally, scholars assert, the historical narrative conveyed in most classrooms centers institutions and systems in which men are more prominent.[7] Civil rights, meanwhile, faced significant resistance to inclusion in the mid-twentieth century that continues, in many places, in the present. Mississippi did not mandate that students learn about the civil rights movement until 2011.[8] Moreover, according to the Southern Poverty Law Center, "as of 2011–2012, only 19 states specifically require[d] teaching *Brown v. Board of Education*, while 18 states require[d] coverage of MLK; 12, Rosa Parks; 11, the March on Washington; and six, Jim Crow segregation policies."[9] *Teaching the Movement*, the organization's report on this topic, reveals that twelve states' standards fail to include "recommended content," including identifying the movement's leaders, events, causes, and tactics.[10] These challenges are akin to those facing efforts to include LGBTQ+ history. It was all but inevitable, therefore, that the drive to incorporate LGBTQ+ figures and themes into the curriculum would encounter several stumbling blocks.

The Long Road to a FAIR Curriculum

First, and of major significance, the FAIR Act is an unfunded mandate.[11] The law did not provide for appropriations to create the materials students and teachers would need, nor did it provide for professional development or training.[12] Hence, though the state required reforms under the act, the cost of those changes, and the materials necessary to introduce them in classrooms, fell to the districts. Moreover, California's precarious fiscal situation at the time the bill was debated and passed delayed the adoption of new state-funded resources, namely, textbooks. According to the Assembly Committee on Education's analysis of the bill, "due to the suspension of instructional materials adoptions, the state will not consider the adoption of any new instructional materials until the 2015–2016 school year, and this bill does not require the adoption of new instructional materials prior to this date."[13] One reason EQCA and GSA mobilized to pass the FAIR Act in 2010 was to meet the 2012 textbook revision deadline;[14] the organizations spearheading this legislation understood the role that resources would play in this edict becoming a reality. The absence of funding provisions in the statute, coupled with the state's fiscal struggles, hindered the bill's progression from legal mandate to classroom reality.[15] In fact, a June 2013 editorial published by the Legal Aid Society of Orange County, California, asserted that the budget crisis enabled some districts to delay implementing the FAIR Act because they were not yet "technically obligated to make changes until the new textbook adoption takes place in 2015."[16] For districts reticent to implement the act, the lack of funding, and its various implications, offered a justifiable excuse. The act represented a hard-fought political victory without any real means of making it an educational reality.

The Assembly and Senate focused on textbooks in their discussion of instructional materials; it was widely acknowledged when the bill became law that classrooms would not have access to this valuable resource at the time it was set to go into effect. Textbooks, however, are not the only resource available to teachers and students.[17] Though revised textbooks were the ultimate goal, scholars, educators, and politicians who supported the law and the implementation process recognized that, until textbooks could be procured, alternate sources remained a viable option. Organizations that supported the FAIR Act concurred and began work to hasten implementation despite the lack of funding. In particular, ONE Archives mobilized to create a comprehensive curriculum that could be disseminated to schools throughout the state. According to Jamie Scot, the project and development manager at the ONE Archives Foundation until 2015, the authors meshed US history and LGBT history to create a curriculum that entwined the two and brought LGBT history into classrooms organically, rather than as a subject separate from the rest of the nation's history.[18] There were, then, options for teachers and schools that wished to comply with the FAIR Act sooner, rather than later. California, though, is diverse, and while this diversity distinguishes the state, it also means that localities and school districts differ in demographic makeup.[19] Materials were created and distributed, but many districts, due to opposition or apathy, continued to ignore the FAIR Act while the lack of required resources allowed them to do so.

While funding and stagnation at the highest levels posed huge hurdles, smaller issues, too, adversely affected implementation; scholars' opinions varied on these factors' impact. Rachel Reinhard, the director of UC Berkeley's History-Social Science Project, posited that bad timing was partly to blame, as the FAIR Act and the Common Core Standards were enacted and meant to go into effect at approximately the same time—prioritizing the Common Core put the FAIR Act on the backburner.[20] Sonoma State professor Don Romesburg, who played a key role in the implementation process, pointed to the "educational hodge podge"—the failure to agree on what topics should be taught and how to bring it into classrooms as a major flaw.[21]

Jamie Scot of the ONE Archives cited the lack of resources and teacher training as the most important misstep. She contended that, although there was little to no demand for teacher training in LGBT history prior to the FAIR Act, as teachers became aware of and excited about the act and the potential changes to the curriculum, the clamor grew; while the FAIR Act opened doors, teachers worried that they didn't have the knowledge or background to comfortably bring those issues into class or facilitate the conversation that might emerge.[22] A major component of the ONE Archives curriculum, therefore, was teacher training and professional development.[23] Reinhard concurred, asserting that many teachers were unaware of the law's existence, others knew of it but didn't know what to do about it, and many teachers didn't have the necessary content knowledge. Moreover, she claimed, allowing local districts to make decisions, a supposed benefit of the law, only exacerbated the statewide disparity.[24] All agreed that the decentralized nature of implementation in its early stages—as Jamie Scot declared, "It's like the Wild Wild West out here"[25]—greatly impeded progress. Years ago, textbook publishers and teachers only began including and teaching the civil rights movement when forced to do so by outside parties.[26] Scholars observing the situation in California believed the situation there was largely the same.

Beyond the availability of resources and professional development, educators and administrators are motivated to change their practices to remain aligned with state and national standards. After all, in the era of testing, the Common Core, and an expanded governmental role in education, classroom learning is propelled from on high. California educational standards derive from a state-sanctioned Framework that, according to the Department of Education, "provide[s] guidance for implementing the standards adopted by the State Board of Education."[27] Amending the Framework is a complicated process that involves multiple committees, comments, revisions, and the contributions of an ever growing and changing number of scholars.

Several attempts at revision, before and since the passage of the FAIR Act, stalled or failed for a variety of reasons. The Framework in place prior to the one approved in July 2016 was last updated in 2005, years before the FAIR Act, and failed to mention LGBTQ+ individuals or history.[28] According to Don Romesburg, more recent attempts at revision did not get off the ground, as in 2009, or failed to meet updated mandates and legislation, as in 2013.[29] The 2013 revision, which should have aligned the Framework with the FAIR Act, prescribed the bare minimum: lessons on Harvey Milk in fourth grade and incorporating Milk, the Lavender Scare, and same-sex marriage into the eleventh grade curriculum. In this case, Romesburg asserted, the Department of Education "didn't pay attention to their own law";[30] the revisions were tabled due to budgetary constraints. Most districts are not San Francisco, Los Angeles, or even Sacramento, where a task force assembled materials and encouraged lessons on Harvey Milk in 2011.[31] When government departments fail to support or enforce laws, there is little incentive—especially with something that provokes such strong reactions—for others to follow them.

Acknowledging the key role of standards in education and the importance of the Framework in amending California state standards, the Committee on LGBT History of the American Historical Association—some of the most renowned LGBT historians in the country—collaborated on a white paper entitled "Making the Framework FAIR" in 2014, suggesting age-appropriate revisions for grades two, four, five, eight, and eleven that mesh with the social studies curriculum at each level and promote greater, more organic inclusion of LGBTQ+ individuals, families, and historical events. The report contended,

> Students can only truly understand families, communities, social practices, and politics, for example, by understanding how they shaped and were shaped by same-sex relations and gender diversity—and how this changed over time. To make the history and social studies Framework truly transformative and representative of the published scholarship on LGBT history and the history of gender and sexuality over the past forty years, the California State Board of Education's Instructional Quality Commission (IQC) can afford to do no less.[32]

The vagueness of the FAIR Act, which allows schools and districts to decide how best to implement the law in their climate and environment, also leaves educators and administrators with little experience with LGBTQ+ history and, possibly, controversial or potentially sensitive matters, with no instruction or guidance on how to implement the law and revise curricula. Amending the Framework, therefore, was vital to implementation; it both obligated teachers to incorporate this material and provided benchmarks for student learning. The scholars who wrote "Making the Framework FAIR" thus created a document that makes LGBTQ+ history a part of family life, California history, and US history, similar to the ONE Archives curriculum. The goal of the FAIR Act was to make curriculum—and thereby school and society—more inclusive. Teaching LGBTQ+ history as "other" defeats that essential purpose.

Amending educational standards is a protracted bureaucratic process no matter the situation, but absolutely essential to real change at the classroom level. It is also the only certain way to make LGBTQ+-inclusive curriculum a reality. In the case of the FAIR Act, especially in light of California's fiscal restrictions, this was especially true. As Don Romesburg stated, "this moves, as bureaucracies do, at a glacial space. What we thought was going to be a long run has become an ultramarathon."[33] While the Framework languished the FAIR Act did, as well. In the summer of 2015, with funding reinstated, the Committee on LGBT History and the authors of "Making the Framework FAIR" prepared to once again work with the Board of Education's Instructional Quality Commission to amend the Framework to reflect the curricular changes mandated by the FAIR Act. Romesburg was hopeful that many of the committee's recommendations would be incorporated in the new Framework, stating, "It feels like they are headed not to a full inclusion of everything in 'Making the Framework FAIR,' and we never expected that. But maybe a third of it is going to make it in and that's huge."[34]

Romesburg was careful to point out that the Framework is not synonymous with the standards; major change to the former, though, can and should eventually lead to revision of the latter.[35] In a draft published in November 2015, the amended Framework included LGBTQ+ individuals' contributions to the Harlem Renaissance, the evolution of anti-gay state policies, the rise of lesbian and gay political movements, recognition of trans people in liberation struggles, marriage equality, and the AIDS epidemic in eleventh grade US history classes, exceeding the authors' expectations. The Framework at that time was open to a final round of public comment; it was approved in July 2016 to go into effect for the 2017–18 school year, more than five years after the original implementation date.[36] The approved Framework, which eradicated schools' and districts' claims that they are not technically obligated to incorporate LGBT history, was the enforcement tool advocates needed and the leverage they sought since the struggle to implement began. According to San Diego's ACLU chapter, "the new Framework will facilitate schools' LGBT-inclusive curricula and help create learning environments where students can thrive."[37] The approved Framework, a more belabored political victory in the struggle to include LGBTQ+ history in K–12 education than passing the law that necessitated it, made the FAIR Act's mandate real for schools across the state. Now not only did the legislation exist, teachers would be held accountable for implementing it.

Official approval of the Framework was a significant step in bringing the FAIR Act to fruition, but it did not indicate imminent change. Many California teachers did not have the knowledge, resources, or personal historical or educational background necessary to teach this curriculum; remedying this was a necessary next step for LGBTQ+-inclusive historical education to happen in a meaningful way. According to Don Romesburg, the Framework's approval led to "two major strands of activity": first, a textbook review and approval process and second, Framework rollout events, which would also provide professional development for California's teachers.[38]

Textbooks have been and continue to be inconsistent in their coverage of LGBTQ+ history. A variety of factors influence textbook authors' and publishers' decisions about the information they include and omit, among these the book's publication date and intended audience.[39] Textbook companies also publish regional editions to better appeal to different markets. California, one of the biggest markets, therefore holds sway over content. Implementation of the FAIR Act thus led to textbook revisions, review, and a months-long approval process that determined which books were and were not authorized for use in California classrooms in kindergarten through eighth grade.[40] As Don Romesburg described it, "there was a dramatic series of meetings" at which committees reviewed all of the textbooks submitted for approval where the "FAIR Education coalition went through line by line of every single textbook that was being proposed."[41] After several rounds of public comment and revision, additional suggestions to achieve compliance with the new Framework, and review by the Instructional Quality Commission and the State Board of Education, the California Department of Education approved ten textbooks—four elementary, six middle school level— on November 9, 2017.[42] "Of those that were approved," Romesburg stated, "all of them—by the time they were finally approved by the state in November of '17, all of them had somewhere around 75 to 80% of the LGBTQ+ content that is in the new Framework," an accomplishment he considered "hugely successful."[43] Textbooks, long considered an essential resource in social studies classes and a barometer of the topics teachers include, were also a significant consideration in implementing the FAIR Act. Hence, as exemplified in California, where the laws and educational frameworks change, the resources from which students learn do, as well.

The roll-out events, coordinated by the University of California's History-Social Science Project and the California Department of Education, happened in two phases; each featured ten events over the course of eighteen months in different parts of the state.[44] The first round, in 2017 and 2018, intended to educate teachers on the new Framework and the learning goals therein, as well as express the state's support for the FAIR Act and push teachers to put it into practice. Though Romesburg reported that he mostly encountered enthusiastic receptions, he also said, "There are still some very conservative parts of the state." Overall, as of 2018, he claimed, "Most teachers know what the law is, but almost no one has an implementation plan."[45] Romesburg, who facilitated the FAIR Act portion of the majority of roll-out events, stated that he told participants, "If you can do three or five things to integrate this into what you're already doing, you'll not only be light years ahead of where anyone else [is] … You will also be making a tremendous and memorable impact that students will remember for the rest of their lives whether they're straight or LGBTQ."[46] Greater awareness of the FAIR Act was a positive step, but the lag in classroom-level execution reflected long experienced curricular struggles. The difference, in this case, and a cause for limited optimism, was the weight of the state's Department of Education behind the mandate to teach LGBTQ+ history and the changes to which that support contributed.

Romesburg estimated that between twenty and forty teachers attended each roll-out event. At the conclusion of the first round, the History-Social Science

Project knew it was imperative to reach more teachers and received feedback that teachers who attended wanted more specific information on integrating LGBTQ+ history in their classes. The second round of events was born from these two needs. The sessions, offered in 2019 and 2020, went into greater depth on topics like Two-Spirit people, settler colonialism, the Harlem Renaissance, and the Lavender Scare, with Romesburg challenging teachers to think about how they might incorporate the material and resources into lessons they already taught. Many, he reported, responded that they saw the connections and intended to integrate their curricula. Romesburg is hopeful that this enthusiasm, and LGBTQ history, found its way into classrooms. There is anecdotal evidence that suggests it has, he stated, but no quantifiable data. He is concerned, moreover, that the lack of funding and attention paid to history education will ultimately impede this progress.[47]

For now, according to Romesburg, the UC Berkeley and UC Davis History-Social Science Projects and Our Family Coalition, the latter of which ultimately devoted more resources to this endeavor than its leaders ever imagined, create and disseminate most of the FAIR-aligned curriculum.[48] The History-Social Science Project at UC Berkeley offers lessons at multiple grade levels including elementary school resources on Charley Parkhurst and the California Gold Rush and same-sex marriage in early America, materials on Ancient Greece and Baron von Steuben for middle schools, and an award-winning lesson on the Lavender Scare for eleventh grade.[49] Our Family Coalition established the Teaching LGBTQ History website, a hub for K–12 resources that convey California LGBTQ+ history and information on the FAIR Act.[50] Romesburg asserted, "The inclusion of LGBT content can have a transformative effect, but that's belittled by the fact that history is considered so unimportant. [We will have to see] what the true impact can be, given the position of history education."[51]

Curricular change happens, but it is often a slow and grueling process. The larger world, in fact, moves at a much faster pace. In 2015, Don Romesburg stated,

> If you imagine the school life of a child, a child could have begun kindergarten and moved into middle school before what is mandated into law actually became the effective policy or road map of the state ... Think about an eighth grade gender non-normative kid ... They hear that the FAIR Act passed. "Oh, Hooray!" Now they will be—if indeed they make it through—they'll be graduating from high school before they ever see it.[52]

In the case of California, scholars say, real change did and continues to require grassroots activism and lobbying on the part of organizations like EQCA, Our Family Coalition, and GSAN as well as teachers, students, and parents advocating for reforms in what and how they learn.[53]

Students who learned of the law when it was passed, especially LGBTQ+ students, were "agitated" not to know more about it and eager for it to be implemented,[54] yet they had little control over what they learned. The examples of teachers throughout the state seeking additional professional development and/or introducing this material to their classes, even on a limited basis, and groups of educators uniting to plan lessons and units that incorporate LGBTQ+ issues and individuals continue to grow, but change in individual classrooms is not consensus around a law or statewide reform that one can specifically link to particular legislation.[55] The existence of the FAIR Act and the new Framework are significant steps, but grassroots work that compels people to act, a hallmark of the push to incorporate LGBTQ+ history in California and elsewhere—like that which led to the passage of the law and defeat of the referendum—will make these goals a reality.

The Road Extends

For eight years, advocates and educators in California grappled with myriad obstacles in their efforts to establish the infrastructure and resources necessary to see the FAIR Act implemented. For states and regions with newer mandates, their process is just beginning. Colorado's law includes provisions establishing a commission to review and make recommendations to revise state standards; that commission must include a member who identifies as LGBTQ+. The law also allocated funds to develop inclusive resources.[56] These are early steps on the path to inclusivity. In other states and counties, efforts are more advanced.

In Illinois, organizations that support the law and its implementation published "Inclusive Curriculum Implementation Guidance," meant to serve as a "quick start guide to support educators as they begin implementing the Inclusive Curriculum Law" in 2020. The guide lists resources for teaching LGBTQ+ history and charts indicating the ways in which doing so aligns with existing Illinois state standards.[57] The Legacy Project, one of the organizations that promoted and supports the law, followed with an inclusive curriculum law lesson plan search portal to facilitate teacher access to LGBTQ+ history and social studies lessons that meet their needs.[58] Additionally, Illinois Safe Schools

Alliance offered professional development sessions entitled "Deepening Our History: Implementing the Illinois Inclusive Curriculum Law" beginning in March 2021.[59] Like Colorado, then, actions taken by the law's advocates in Illinois indicate an awareness of the connection between standards and implementation and the need for quality resources.

In New Jersey, which passed its law at the beginning of 2019, organizations and individuals that supported the bill began planning for its implementation as it moved through the state legislature. Garden State Equality (GSE), which spearheaded this effort, conditionally secured $185,000 in grants from the Braitmayer Foundation and PSEG Foundation and brought together a coalition including teachers, administrators, parents, advocates, and the Department of Education to consider how best to implement the law and develop the curriculum necessary to do so.[60] Prior to the 2020–1 school year when the law was set to go into effect, GSE launched a pilot in which a diverse group of twelve schools around the state received access to the curriculum it produced for fifth, sixth, eighth, tenth, and twelfth grades; a curriculum coach; and additional professional development through an LGBTQ inclusive curriculum conference.[61] Ashley Chiappiano, GSE's former Safe Schools and Community Education Manager, said, "It's a full robust curriculum plus the research [to ascertain] what are some of the lessons learned for their particular school work and what they can focus on, and if there are challenges or triumphs in a particular area."[62] Schools that applied but were not accepted to the pilot received the curriculum minus the additional supports, and, ultimately, the intention is for all New Jersey schools to have free access to the lessons, thereby removing one obstacle to integration. Though the pilot was interrupted by school closures due to Covid-19, Garden State Equality continued to develop curriculum and work to build awareness of the law and the tools to implement it.[63]

Despite the availability of these resources, individual boards of education are free to choose how they implement the law. Chiappiano voiced concerns about the choices they might make, asserting, "What we're a little bit fearful of is that schools will choose resources that may be great with LGBT identity but not so great with trans identity ... If you're choosing a curriculum that is not talking about the full [LGBTQ+ experience], then it's not truly an inclusive curriculum." She also discussed the need to change state standards to align with the law and the reticence among parents who inquired about opting out;[64] in January 2020 Family Policy Alliance of New Jersey claimed to have over seven thousand signatures opposing LGBTQ+-inclusive instruction.[65] Overall, though, Chiappiano optimistically declared, "We're hoping we're in a positive spot, and the ball is rolling. We feel like we just need to keep it going. We're going to keep it moving."[66]

Massachusetts does not have an LGBTQ+ curriculum law, but it did revise its Framework in 2018. The updated Massachusetts State Framework offers teachers the option to discuss the Lavender Scare in units on the Cold War and Bayard Rustin in discussions on civil rights. It also lists LGBTQ+ history as a possibility for classroom study of social and political movements of the twentieth and twenty-first centuries, directing teachers to use primary and secondary sources to teach topics like "the impact of world wars on the demand for gay rights, the Stonewall Rebellion of 1969, the Gay Pride Movement, and ... the role of the Massachusetts Supreme Judicial Court in *Goodridge v. Department of Public Health* (2004),"[67] among others. To further this goal, the Massachusetts Department of Elementary and Secondary Education posted a lesson entitled "Defending Democracy at Home: Advancing Constitutional Rights, *Obergefell v. Hodges* (2015) Same-Sex Marriage" on its website and provides educators with a form to access additional materials.[68]

New York State standards currently list "gay rights and the LGBT movement" as one of nine options for teachers to introduce in a unit on twentieth-century civil rights movements.[69] The New York City Department of Education, however, began taking steps to make city classrooms more LGBTQ+-inclusive. Building on its "Hidden Voices" curriculum, which highlighted individuals who contributed to New York City history, the Office of Curriculum, Instruction, and Professional Learning developed a second edition focused on LGBTQ+ figures from the colonial era to the present about whom students can now learn. The guide, which offers information and primary sources on Thomasine Hall, Ma Rainey, Barbara Gittings, and Miguel Braschi, among others, aims to provide educators with the necessary information to bring previously untaught history into their classes.[70] Furthermore, the American Social History Project at City University of New York worked with scholars and educators to convert "Hidden Voices" into a series of lessons that all teachers can use with students at all grade levels.[71] This work, like the states that set precedents for it, identifies a gap in the curriculum and attempts to fill it. All of these efforts, like California's, take official mandates and build upon them. Doing so, these advocates and educators hope, makes them as meaningful in the classroom as they are in the legislature.

* * *

LGBTQ+ curriculum laws and the efforts to put them into practice lay the groundwork for reform that has the potential to make history classes more inclusive, as well as educate students on a topic prevalent in political and social spheres. California can, with the FAIR Act, establish model schools, resources, and curricula. Despite the protracted process to see the act's mandate come to fruition, teachers and schools throughout the state have started to understand what it entails and consider the curricular changes it necessitates; the state, meanwhile, is working to ensure that resources and materials match the FAIR Act's requirements. Other states have taken note, and through their laws and policies they are working to turn legislative edicts and framework revisions into realities at a faster pace; counties and cities are starting to advocate and create resources for LGBTQ+-inclusive history where state mandates do not yet exist. Obstacles and questions persist. Curricular reform requires funds that are in perpetually short supply and entrenched ideas do not change overnight. These laws, and the weight behind them, however, suggest that institutional support for LGBTQ+ history exists in ways that it did not a decade ago.

8

Compelled to Act: Teachers Who Include LGBTQ+ History

LGBTQ+-inclusive history, which enjoys growing but limited support from state governments and departments of education, is, for the most part, a grassroots, self-motivated endeavor. It is not yet a fixture in high school US history classes throughout the country, despite educators' and activists' work to make it so. It is not included in most states' standards or exams. Resources are available online for teachers who seek to incorporate this material,[1] but teachers must be inclined to search for it and know that it exists at all. It is, according to teachers and scholars, a subject with which many teachers have little to no experience; therefore, in many cases, this material is unconsciously omitted.[2] Among teachers who know this history, there are various reasons—including, in five states, laws prohibiting its mention[3]—that they do not include it.[4] There is, however, an embryonic movement to change this. A small number of high school social studies teachers do incorporate LGBTQ+ history and have a strong rationale for doing so. These teachers, though a minority now, believe they have the power to influence others and affect change among their students, schools, and communities.

It is impossible to explore what is happening in classrooms without talking to teachers. The twelve[5] teachers included represent different regions and their careers span decades (see Figure 8.1).[6] Eleven are from more liberal regions where one might expect LGBTQ+-inclusive curriculum to be considered acceptable: seven teach or taught in and around Los Angeles and San Francisco, California, from 1990 to the present; one taught in New York City from 2012 to 2015; one is a current teacher in northern New Jersey with more than a decade of experience; one taught in Portland, Oregon, for twelve years; a Chicago educator, currently working with students and with other teachers, has been working in education for nearly twenty years; and a rural Colorado teacher began her career in 2012. Five of the teachers are no longer in the classroom, though they are still professionally involved in education in some capacity; the seven who currently

NAME	CITY/REGION	YEARS TEACHING	LGBTQ+
Courtney Anderson	New York, NY Bay Area, CA	2009–14 2014–present	No
Danny M. Cohen	Chicago, IL	2014–present	Yes
Olivia Cole	Los Angeles, CA	2013–present	Yes
Fred Fox	Portland, OR	2006–present	Yes
Mitchell James	Northern New Jersey	2006–present	No
Hasmig Minassian	Bay Area, CA	2001–present	Yes
Felicia Perez	Los Angeles, CA	2000–10 2010–12	Yes
Dana Rosenberg	Bay Area, CA	1995–2008	Yes
Lyndsey Schlax	San Francisco, CA	2008–18	No
Will Scott	Los Angeles, CA San Francisco, CA	1990–98	Yes
Casey Sinclair	Brooklyn, NY	2012–15	Yes
Melanie Wells	Rural Colorado	2012–present	No

Figure 8.1 Participating teachers. List of teachers participating in this study, including location, years taught, and LGBTQ+ identity.

teach have been doing so for anywhere between seven and nineteen years. Eight of the teachers identify as LGBTQ+—five are lesbians and three are gay males; the others are heterosexual but sympathetic to LGBTQ+ issues and causes.

Unlike topics specifically addressed in state and national standards—those that students may be tested on at the end of the school year—teachers make a specific and conscious choice to include LGBTQ+ history in their US history classes. For some teachers there seems to be no choice at all; they identify as LGBTQ+ and believe that this often omitted history deserves to be included in the classes they teach.[7] For others, historical instruction is incomplete if it is not fully inclusive.[8] All of the teachers here, when asked, have direct and specific reasons for bringing LGBTQ+ history into their classes and, for each, the rationale derives from their own education and upbringing. LGBTQ+-inclusive history curriculum is not a niche field specific to teachers who identify as such and therefore seek to convey their own history; it is an endeavor undertaken by teachers who, through personal experiences and realizations, believe there are holes in traditional historical education that need to be filled. Though the work these teachers do is first and foremost to enrich their students' lives, they also recognize that, in teaching this history, they are doing something important and uncommon. In fact, all twelve stated that they never learned LGBTQ+ history in their K–12 education, regardless of their age or location. These teachers were excited that their stories would be told, and hope that their dedication to integration might influence others' practices, as well.

The Seeds: Teachers Who Incorporate LGBTQ+ History

While standards and curricula differ, students throughout the United States learn their country's history in a class devoted solely to that subject at least once, and often multiple times, during their academic careers. The material conveyed in those classes varies widely among states, districts, schools, and teachers; these decisions derive from internal and external sources and have the power to influence students' perception of history. US history teachers throughout the country, then, are faced with the decision of what to include—and omit—from the narrative they impart.

Many teachers, having never learned this material in their high school and college history classes, are not cognizant of leaving it out in their own classes;[9] their omission results from apathy or ignorance rather than hostility. For the few that prioritize this history and its importance to their students' education, though, it can become an essential part of their curriculum with the power to have a significant impact on their students.

The Early Adopters

In the 1990s and early 2000s, it was extremely rare to enter a classroom in which LGBT history was mentioned. Nine teachers in this study attended and graduated from high schools all over the country during this time period; none of them learned this history, and several reported that references to LGBTQ+ issues were conspicuously absent from their school environments.[10] Although Matthew Shepard's murder in 1998 raised awareness of the danger facing young people who identified as LGBT, the LGBTQ+ population and issues important to them were neither as frequently discussed nor as societally recognized as they would be ten years later.

Teachers who deemed this history important, then, were among a handful who integrated it into their classrooms.[11] Three teachers in this study, all of whom personally identify as LGBTQ+, implemented an inclusive curriculum at a time when few others did.

Dana Rosenberg taught from 1998 to 2008 at two different schools in Northern California. Rosenberg came into teaching with specific ideas about her role; as she stated, "I wanted school to be different than the way it was. ... My mission as a teacher was to disrupt."[12] Rosenberg turned to teaching because she "felt passionately about changing the systems of schools and how kids learned."[13] As a queer person, those changes included bringing LGBTQ+ issues into her classroom. At her first school, Rosenberg's students were middle and working class; of the two public high schools in town, according to Rosenberg, hers was "whiter with a bit more resources."[14] From 2005 to 2008 she taught at a Bay Area public alternative school focused on students pursuing their passions and working in the community. For Rosenberg, who considers herself "pretty political" and has been "out" her entire career, connecting with LGBTQ+ students and providing them with a safe space—including starting the school's GSA— was an inevitable, and beneficial, aspect of her teaching experience. Rosenberg left the social studies classroom in 2009, transitioning into sex education and administration.

Felicia Perez began teaching after working as an activist for LGBTQ+ youth advocating for students' right to establish a GSA at their school. Perez worked as a youth organizer for local and national organizations, including the ACLU, prior to entering the classroom. In that capacity, she worked with young people "teaching them information with regards to constitutional rights and amendment rights."[15] Guiding students through the process of understanding their rights and claiming their identity became part of her personal teaching philosophy. Similar to Rosenberg, Perez mentored students who identified as LGBTQ+, assisting those who struggled with their sexuality and identity. Unlike Rosenberg, from 1999 to 2012 Perez taught a largely Latinx and African American student population at two different schools in the Los Angeles Unified School District (LAUSD) that had few resources. Perez was open about her sexuality from the start. Including queer people in her history lessons was organic to Perez, who believes that if the curriculum highlights individuals from some cultures and societies it should include individuals from all.

Will Scott, meanwhile, taught from 1992 to 1999. After working as a prison educator following college, he decided to bring his skill set into the classroom. Scott stated that he was "at the intersection of social justice orientation and the desire to do … social justice work"; his experience and that philosophy brought him into the classroom.[16] As a gay, white, Canadian man teaching in an under-resourced Southern California school with a largely Latino and African American population in the early 1990s, it took time for Scott to find his voice and the confidence to insert the LGBT material he deemed necessary in the curriculum. Eventually, though, he recalled, "I began to feel that by checking parts of myself at the door, I was doing not only the queer kids in my classroom a disservice," because, he said, "I failed to provide [non-queer students] opportunities to discuss issues."[17] After moving to San Francisco in his fourth year of teaching, Scott found himself in a more diverse environment in which he felt safer and more comfortable with all the facets of his own identity. At that point, Scott began teaching from a social justice perspective and incorporating LGBTQ+ history where it fit thematically, though he knew that doing so could lead to his firing. Scott posited, "I was the teacher with all of the power in deciding the curriculum, but in another sense, I was a stranger in the communities in which I was teaching, not by the end but certainly in the beginning."[18] Scott left the classroom in 1999 to work for a teacher training organization.

Rosenberg, Perez, and Scott all entered teaching intending to inspire and awaken their students' consciences and guide them to use the history they learned as a springboard from which to think differently about the world. Their inclusion of LGBTQ+ history was especially radical at a time when, for many schools, establishing and attaining district support for a GSA was a significant struggle,[19] and larger society often remained silent on LGBTQ+ issues.

A More Inclusive US History Survey

The US history curriculum, regardless of teacher, school, or geographic location, is constantly evolving and, frequently, a challenge for even those teachers with outstanding time management skills. Choosing to include one historical event or era can often lead to omitting another. Additionally, teachers have for years insisted that getting much farther than the Second World War or the 1960s is nearly impossible in the course of an academic year. Teachers who include LGBTQ+ history, then, make a conscious decision to do so.

Mitchell James, who does not identify as LGBTQ+, lives and teaches in Northern New Jersey where he said "LGBTQ+ rights and families and, increasingly, students who are transitioning seem to be more apparent."[20] His school's student body is ethnically diverse and evenly split between male and female students. James began teaching in 2006, immediately after completing his master's; the open-minded philosophy and atmosphere of his school are, except for a brief stint student teaching, the only working conditions he's ever known. James has never been instructed to teach LGBTQ+ history, nor has he met opposition for doing so. He stated, "I felt fairly comfortable from the get go to teach topics that might be a little hands-off in other places."[21] James started incorporating LGBTQ+ history in his US history classes in his second or third year. While he could and would like to include more, his incorporation of LGBTQ+ history in his class "stems from the fact that [he] thinks it's something that needs to be taught."[22]

Melanie Wells began teaching in 2012 in rural Colorado; after encountering ineffective history teachers in her own schooling, she was determined to do and be better for her students. Considering this motivation, she asserted, "I wonder if there are some kind of connections between not having great origin stories and being willing to experiment a little bit more in service of the kids on the margins that need to be drawn in a little more."[23] Wells does not identify as LGBTQ+ and teaches in a conservative, predominantly white Colorado town that she compared to "a 1950s, 'Pleasantville,' 'Leave it to Beaver' style town."[24] According to Wells, her school is "a little slow to adopt other things," including progressive resources and curricula.[25] Teaching LGBTQ+ history is important to Wells because, she believes, it is an issue that resonates with students who need a place in which this history can be discussed and the language around it normalized. Despite the conservative atmosphere in the town where she teaches, Wells believes that her LGBTQ+ students need to see themselves in the history they learn.[26]

Wells and James include LGBTQ+ history in their Advanced Placement US History classes; both did so even before the College Board included a clause about gay rights in its Framework in 2014. They see this history as too important to exclude on an intellectual level, and relevant to their students' lives. Olivia Cole, who also infuses her US history classes with LGBTQ+ history, does so in a self-contained special education classroom. Moreover, Cole stated, "As a gay woman I already [felt] tied to the subject."[27] Cole claimed that LAUSD, where she's taught since 2012, supports teachers of all genders and sexualities.[28] She began focusing on curriculum, including LGBTQ+ history, in her second year after conquering significant classroom management challenges in her first year. The environment at her school and the freedom it allows, coupled with the relationship Cole is now able to cultivate with her students, create a space open to teaching LGBTQ+ history and helping students question the information they receive from other sources.

Courtney Anderson and Hasmig Minassian, who teach at the same Bay Area school, come from distinctly different backgrounds. Both women, though, believe it is essential to include LGBTQ+ history in their classes. Anderson, who does not identify as LGBTQ+, grew up "white, upper middle class, and privileged in Southern California." She began her teaching career at the age of twenty-two at a small New York City high school, where she taught from 2009 to 2014; she characterized it as an "openly LGBT friendly school" which, she stated, "was a big part of why we decided to be more inclusive with our curriculum."[29] Though the Bay Area school is, in her estimation, more traditional, she also said that "teachers have a lot of agency in their classrooms" and are "given the benefit of the doubt" when they want to try something new.[30] Anderson stated that, as a white person who was born in the United States, she always learned her history and, as a teacher, it is imperative that her students feel connected to the history they learn. As she said, "I firmly believe that history should reflect the community that you're a part of."[31]

Minassian, the daughter of Armenian immigrants who does identify as LGBTQ+, prioritizes normalizing LGBTQ+ figures and lives throughout history; she contended that the "bubble" in which she teaches is essential to her doing so. Though she did not immediately begin teaching LGBTQ+ history in her US history classes—she reported that she was "hesitant to teach it in her early years," felt vulnerable, and was worried she would be "accused of including this information because she was gay"—as she gained confidence as a teacher, she began to incorporate LGBTQ+ history in increasing amounts in the lessons that she teaches.[32]

Focus on LGBTQ+ History

Some teachers, like those aforementioned, include this history when and where they can in their existing US history classes. For others with the resources, freedom, and support, classes devoted to LGBTQ+ history are the answer. Although such courses are rare, they offer students an opportunity for in-depth learning on a topic that they often do not encounter in other classes. Scholars and the teachers in this study argue that LGBTQ+ history should be incorporated into US history surveys; while LGBTQ+ history is omitted from or remains peripheral in survey classes, specialized electives, and their ability to convey information excluded from other courses at the same school, serve as an entry point for inclusivity.

Lyndsey Schlax began teaching her elective on LGBTQ+ history in the fall of 2015 at an arts-focused high school in San Francisco; she began teaching seven years prior after three years as a paraeducator in various settings. Schlax, who does not identify as LGBTQ+, was asked by the district to create and teach a new course aligned with the FAIR Act. Though she focused on "undertold" histories prior to teaching her LGBTQ+ history elective, she did not specifically integrate LGBTQ+ history. Schlax's students at this specialized high school came from middle- to upper-middle-class homes with educated parents. The student body is diverse; it reflects the city, but it is whiter than other schools in the district.[33] Students in grades nine through twelve can take the LGBTQ+ history elective as a supplement to required history courses. With little previous exposure to this material, Schlax had to research and learn it in order to teach it.

Fred Fox likewise taught an elective on queer history at his public high school in Portland, Oregon, a city that he described as a "relatively liberal, progressive community."[34] Fox began teaching in 2005 after twelve years in the army. Fox, who is gay, recalled, "In hindsight I went into the army to not be gay and I thought it would fix me … it wasn't an environment where you could be gay."[35] His army career spanned the post-Cold War and War on Terror eras; it also coincided with Don't Ask, Don't Tell. Fox, then, is an intrinsic part of the history that he teaches. His school's student body was predominantly white, middle to upper class, and evenly split between males and females. According to Fox there was a small, open LGBTQ+ population among the students. Fox proposed his course in order to introduce these, and all, students to an underrepresented aspect of US history—one that, as a gay man, he never had the opportunity to learn—and was surprised in his research phase by how few history-centered resources he found. Fox therefore designed a class that translated college-level queer studies into a course accessible to high school students.

At an elective-based school in Brooklyn, students choose their own social studies courses. Survey courses, like those offered at more traditional high schools, are not part of the curriculum; students complete rigorous portfolio assessments rather than taking state tests. According to Casey Sinclair, who taught there from 2012 to 2015, the school's philosophy echoed her own: courses are often designed with students' requests in mind and respond to the direction in which students take them. Sinclair's classes on LGBTQ+ history and contemporary LGBTQ+ issues came from and followed this model. She recalled, "The LGBTQ+ curriculum had already been developed by a colleague and friend of mine" and, Sinclair said, "was a huge piece of where I fit in. I was really excited about teaching this material."[36] For Sinclair, this represented a relevant lens through which to teach US and New York history. Additionally, she was compelled by the idea that students would "see and learn and hear stories they don't get to hear and learn about … a whole part of their history and their life that they don't get to explore with other people in our collegial and academic environment."[37]

US History beyond the Classroom

A growing number of organizations outside the classroom now exist to fill the void and bring this information to students at different schools all over the country and educate teachers so that they can do the same.[38] Unsilence, a Chicago-based organization founded in 2014 by Danny M. Cohen, runs programs with young people in which they discuss the "hidden stories of human rights and … different modes of silencing."[39] Unsilence emerged from Cohen's long standing goal to "create educational experiences, learning experiences" and the curriculum he built and introduced to teachers in order to make that happen. The programs pay particular attention to the atrocities endured by homosexuals during the Holocaust. Though many students are familiar with Holocaust history, Unsilence focuses on a group of victims denied recognition for decades after the war. Representatives from Unsilence, including Cohen, run workshops in schools in which they reveal, teach, and engage students in discussions of this information. They conduct similar workshops with educators and public programs in states across the country to share their resources and provide comprehensive Holocaust education.

This diverse group of teachers, despite their differences, shares a dedication to teaching LGBTQ+ history. Doing so was/is easier for some than others, and their differences are a large part of the stories they tell. Ultimately, in their approach to teaching LGBTQ+ history, their similarities transcend their differences in meaningful ways.

Helping It Grow: The Motivation behind Teaching LGBTQ+-Inclusive History

The aforementioned teachers are among a minority nationwide incorporating LGBTQ+ history into their classes. The seven California teachers live and teach in the one of six states in the country that mandate LGBTQ+-inclusive history education; the most recent History and Social Science Framework dictates that colleagues in their schools and throughout the state join them in this endeavor, though many California teachers are still learning about how to implement this act. The others are part of the same grassroots movement; Mitchell James, Melanie Wells, and Danny M. Cohen also teach in states that now mandate LGBTQ+-inclusive curriculum. For all of these teachers, then, developing and teaching LGBTQ+-inclusive curricula is an intentional and willful act motivated by pedagogical, historical, political, and personal reasons that compel them to impart this information to their students (see Figure 8.2).

History as a Mirror

Some students, over the course of a school year, encounter a wealth of opportunities to see themselves or people "like" them in history, others less so. This dichotomy compelled Courtney Anderson to incorporate LGBTQ+ history in her teaching; because, she said, "I can't imagine being in a history class and feeling zero connection to what we're learning."[40] Similarly, Melanie Wells is motivated to expose her students to new perspectives on historical eras "so that the kids in my room who are LGBT have something where they recognize themselves in history."[41] Though Anderson and Wells teach in very different schools and communities, both are cognizant of the diversity within their classes and the need to consider it in curriculum planning. Their devotion to teaching LGBTQ+ history stems from a belief that students of every ethnicity, class, and gender need to see themselves in history. For them, including this material is one component of a larger desire for representation.

Anderson's desire for her students to see themselves in history derives from a personal academic history in which she was able to do just that. The opposite was true for Dana Rosenberg, whose impetus to teach LGBTQ+ history partly resulted from "holes in her own education." She asserted, "I was motivated in particular by students who were gay and lesbian ... who were terrified just to be in the world. They never felt like their experience was validated through a textbook or through the curriculum. ... I wanted them to see that history can be about them, too."[42] Having experienced history education that didn't reflect her identity and experiences, Rosenberg worked to ensure that her students experienced history differently. For her, righting the wrongs of the past determined her practice.

Fred Fox believes that while improving school climate is important work, it is not all that students need in order to feel safe. Fox was surprised when he began searching for resources for his course and found few focused on historical events,

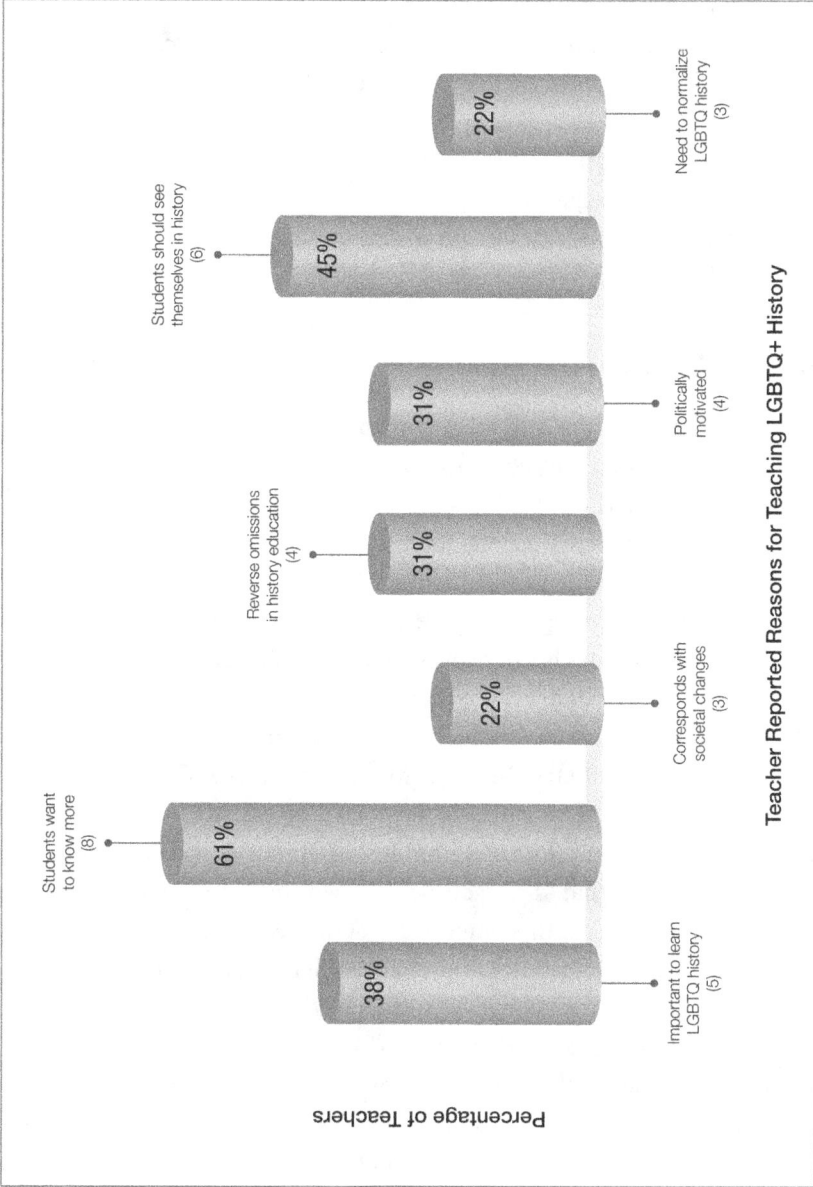

Figure 8.2 Motivation. Teacher reported motivation for including LGBTQ+ history. Note that each of the teachers reported more than one reason for including this history in their class. Each is discussed in greater detail in the following sections.

trends, and figures. As he said, "I found tons and tons of stuff about creating a safe space, and to support a classroom ... but not a lot about how to actually have students see themselves in a curriculum ... which is equally as important as just feeling safe."[43] Casey Sinclair similarly claimed that the connections that students make when they learn this history, a rare opportunity in an educational setting, are an important aspect of the school experience.[44] Many students' identities are complex, and it is essential that they see the important parts of themselves— especially those that might be frequently ignored or unacknowledged—in the history they learn. Thus, educators express, teaching LGBTQ+ history is integral to students connecting with classroom material, understanding who they are, and contextualizing others' experiences.

Reverse the Pattern of Omission

Beyond the desire for students to identify with the historical figures and events about which they learn, it is essential to several of these teachers that the history they teach is as complete as possible and free of the holes and omissions many of them noticed as students and in the resources at their disposal. None of the teachers interviewed for this study learned or heard mention of LGBTQ+ history in their own schooling (see Figure 8.3), an omission that left an indelible impression. A United States history course, for these teachers, is not complete if it fails to include the stories of every group.

LGBTQ+ history and individuals' contributions are less frequently acknowledged than military history, foreign policy, and other groups' struggles for equal rights at the K–12 level in a broad study of US history. Students may speculate on historical figures' identities, but discussion often goes no farther than that. Lyndsey Schlax, whose semester-long elective covered this material in depth, contended that not teaching LGBTQ+ history simply perpetuates this invisibility. She cites teachers' lack of knowledge as the cause of this omission; she believes it speaks to the need to remedy the lack of information conveyed to students.[45] Fred Fox, who, despite his own lived history, also had to learn the material before teaching his elective, contends that it is important to teach this history now so that future generations do not encounter the same ignorance as students in the past.[46] In states outside those with "No Promo Homo" laws the omission of LGBTQ+ history—as Schlax and Fox would testify—is much more a factor of apathy or ignorance than outright resistance. Reversing this trend, then, might change the way history is taught in the future.

Learned LGBTQ+ History in High School

No

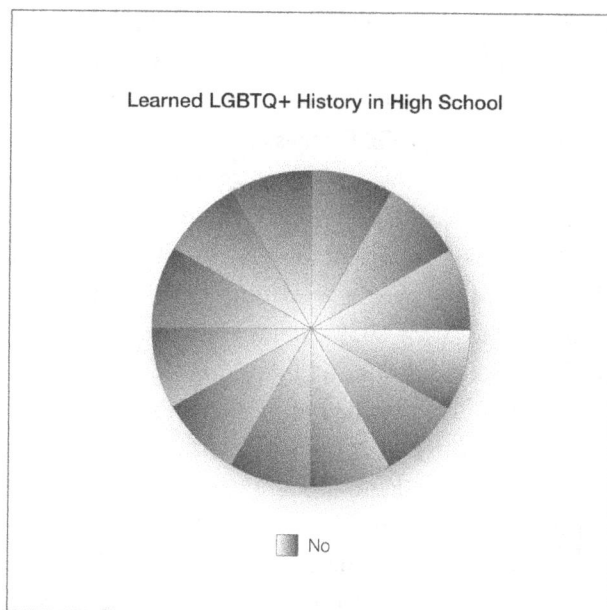

Figure 8.3 Teachers' background with LGBTQ+ history

Casey Sinclair, whose LGBT history course came about based on student requests, stated,

> It's not only that it was important to them because they get to see and learn and hear stories that they don't otherwise get to hear and learn about but also because it's really interesting, and it's like a whole part of their history and their life that they don't get to explore with other people in our collegial and academic environment.[47]

Danny M. Cohen, the founder of Unsilence, similarly believes that giving voice to these untold stories can be transformative for students and deepen their understanding of history. Moreover, according to Cohen, introducing topics through a historical lens provides students with a safe space in which to discuss potentially controversial topics due to the intellectual distance students place between themselves and the subject matter.[48] Learning history, then, is an important first step to conceptualizing and engaging with more current events.

A Thirst for Knowledge

High school students in the twenty-first century encounter discussions of LGBTQ+ issues in their daily lives. Perception and coverage of these matters varies, but news outlets across the political spectrum pontificate and social media debates rage on topics like transgender rights and depictions of gender identity and sexuality in movies and on television. As Melanie Wells stated, "My kids care about contemporary LGBT issues and … that is one of the things that they have very strong opinions on … that's one of these things that kids are very interested in and wish to know more about."[49] As students form their own ideas about the present, then, it is important for and to them to learn about the past.

Additionally, many young people are naturally curious and, when given the opportunity, will seek to learn about topics with which they are unfamiliar. Courtney Anderson recounted that 20 percent to 30 percent of her students chose to focus on LGBT history when given the option to do so for an end of year research project. As she said, "some [chose it] because they identified with it, some because they thought that they identified with it and wanted to explore that more, and others just because they're like, 'Well, I've never learned this and I want to learn more.' "[50] Sinclair similarly reported that students became immersed in the LGBTQ+ history that she taught.[51] For teachers with experience teaching LGBTQ+ history, their students' thirst for knowledge on this topic is remarkable. History can be repetitious for students required to take US history courses in several grades. The opportunity to break the monotony is, therefore, intriguing. The infrequency with which most students are introduced to these topics in a meaningful way makes the moments when they are even more eye opening.

The Demands of a Changing Society

Teachers claimed that the increasing presence of LGBTQ+ figures and attention to LGBTQ+-related issues in the media and across society demands the inclusion of LGBTQ+ history in their classes. It is social studies teachers' job to encourage civic mindedness; integrating the information necessary to do so is, for these teachers, imperative.

Mitchell James's motivation derived from the changes he saw in his environment. Though neither parents nor administrators specifically requested that he include LGBTQ+ history, he found changing attitudes and norms compelling. James recounted, "We are living in a more open society where students are, I can honestly say a lot more comfortable coming out now at least from my own interpretation even when I was in high school."[52] Courtney Anderson, too, cited acceptance and diversity among students as one reason that LGBTQ+-inclusive curriculum is important to her. Of her school in the Bay

Area, Anderson stated, the population "is incredibly open in terms of sexuality and gender" though there are many students who do not yet understand that gender is a spectrum and not a binary. This openness, however, "makes it a lot easier for [teachers] to continue to insert things and just try things out."[53] As James said, school and societal changes spurred him to act; he declared, "So my inclusion actually, I think, largely stems from the fact that I think it's something that needs to be taught. Not necessarily something that needs to be mandated from somebody else."[54]

Dana Rosenberg asserted that the way in which students learn history must reflect the society in which they live if progress is to be sustained.[55] As Felicia Perez contended,

> every day is something new that eventually you're going to have to teach if you stay in the profession long enough, but what that also means is there are definitely opportunities in looking back to see like, "What did we miss? What wasn't talked about in history like in terms of queer history? Who wasn't there and mentioned or who was there and wasn't mentioned?"[56]

In the same vein, Mitchell James, Will Scott, and Danny M. Cohen all discussed the need to educate students on LGBTQ+ issues in the Trump era when the rights secured by and for that population were under governmental attack;[57] national and international events, including shifts in power, necessarily impact the course of history and the way in which it is conveyed.

Political Motivation

Introducing students to subject matter that some might consider controversial, too mature, or simply unnecessary is, in and of itself, a political act. Most of the teachers interviewed teach in schools and communities where the decision to teach this history is accepted, if not wholeheartedly supported. For some the decision to introduce this material can be especially fraught. Under any circumstances, it is difficult to discuss teaching LGBTQ+ history without discussing the political motivation and/or implications in doing so.

To Fred Fox, teaching LGBTQ+ history was another step toward "chipping away at the lack of diversity in [the] curriculum," something he believed was important but others in his department resisted. Fox stated that, in his opinion, he received approval for his queer history course because of where he lives and previously offered courses focused on other marginalized groups. As he asserted, "if this was the first non-normative history class being offered, I don't think it would slide."[58] Lyndsey Schlax's personal interest in politics and grassroots revolution made the prospect of teaching LGBTQ+ history enticing; she took the opportunity to combine her own interests with what she believed was important and largely unknown subject matter and created a class that would open students to history they otherwise might never have discovered.[59]

Teachers who view their profession as inherently political, especially when they identify as LGBTQ+, have multiple motives for teaching this history. When Dana Rosenberg pursued her degree at a small women's liberal arts college, she subscribed to the institution's edict of teaching as a political act. Teaching this history in the late 1990s was overtly political. She came into teaching determined to teach LGBTQ+ history and change LGBTQ+ students' lives and found ways to implement her ideas. Felicia Perez believes that people in positions of power—specifically, in this case, teachers—have a responsibility to act as role models for their students. She stated,

> Being out in the classroom is just as important, has just as much of an effect and a massive impact as seeing a gay character on TV, as seeing a gay character in cartoons, in books. There's the exact same impact and that you're seeing a teacher, somebody who is a person of knowledge … teaching you something and exposing you to something and as an authority figure, and someone that you might admire and even look up to or even somebody that you might seek out for help and guidance is somebody who is queer.[60]

Becoming a role model, empowering students, giving them a safe space, and providing them with knowledge were essential aspects of teaching to Perez, who carried her activist background into her classroom. When learning translates into students having a voice, education becomes political.

Steps toward Normalcy

Nationwide, teachers who incorporate LGBTQ+ history into their courses are in the minority. Among the teachers interviewed, many reported that their decision to teach this material was their own and not something that was a priority (or, in some cases, acceptable) for their colleagues or the district. Those who do teach this history, though, echo scholars' findings calling for an end to "othering."[61] Part of their motivation in teaching inclusive curriculum is to normalize the history and experience of being LGBTQ+ in the United States.

Hasmig Minassian believes that LGBTQ+ figures and events should be "folded in" to the curriculum in the same way as other groups and individuals and that they should be discussed in a "normal, non-sexual way just like anyone else." Minassian espoused that something as simple as "changing the language, which seems like it's something that is so basic ... would be so meaningful to day-to-day life."[62] Full integration can accomplish that goal. Melanie Wells, who teaches in a more conservative environment in rural Colorado, focuses on reducing stigma and increasing acceptance through LGBTQ+ history. As she contended, "the thing I can do is at least normalize it and make it seem like it's not as big a deal as it might be." Wells attempts to capture her students' passion and teach about things that are important in their world. By making those subjects more accessible, she posited, they become more relevant, more memorable, and more openly discussed.[63] In Los Angeles, meanwhile, Olivia Cole teaches in a school that supports "tak[ing] the mystery out" of LGBTQ+ history and lifestyles.[64] Omitting this history reinforces the idea that the LGBTQ+ population is different or less important than groups that are more prominent in the US history curriculum: when students grow accustomed to not hearing about something it becomes "other" or abnormal. Teaching this history, and making it as much a part of the curriculum as the Civil War and the Progressive Era, can reverse that trend and accomplish the goal of removing the mystery.

* * *

Querying and assessing why teachers believe it is important to teach LGBTQ+ history is significant to this practice becoming more widespread. Inclusive curriculum cannot be—or be perceived as being—a niche filled only by LGBTQ+ teachers and tailored to or only meaningful for LGBTQ+ students; it must appeal to many different groups and enhance learning experiences regardless of how a student identifies. Evaluating teachers' different reasons and goals, then, makes it clear that teaching LGBTQ+ history is not narrow in scope and intention and that a diverse group of teachers believe it is necessary for all students' historical learning and participation in twenty-first-century society. These voices, and the diversity among them, lay the foundation for more widespread support of this endeavor; only by building this support among teachers and within the institutions that govern and determine educational policy and standards in the states and the national government will this grassroots movement grow.

9

Innovations at the Grassroots Level: LGBTQ+ History in High School Classroom Instruction

The paucity of teachers integrating LGBTQ+ history into their lessons illustrates how important the motivation to do so is among those who teach this material. Personal motivation, though, is not the only factor in determining whether students learn LGBTQ+ history. School and classroom environments conducive to introducing this material are also essential factors. In fact, strong support systems in environments that foster creativity and discussion were deemed integral to including LGBTQ+ history.[1] The classroom experiences described by the teachers featured in this chapter, then, are the product of their investment in this topic and its necessity as well as the knowledge that there is some level of support and/or an audience for this endeavor.

Teachers' experiences, strategies, and ideas about teaching LGBTQ+ history strongly indicate that for this material, like other topics in US history, there is no one way, or a correct way, to convey this information to students. While all believe in its significance as part of students' historical learning, they have different ideas about how to introduce the material, on which topics and events to focus, the tactics they use in class to disseminate and discuss this history, and the best ways for students to access it (see Figure 9.1).

These differences are determined not only by teachers' personal ideas and philosophies but also by the student population in their classes, the school environment, the political atmosphere in the community, and their own life experience. In many ways, then, teaching LGBTQ+ history is quite similar to any other topic or era in a US history class.

LGBTQ HISTORY TOPICS TAUGHT

- Relationships among Native Americans
- Women in the Civil War
- Gay identity among cowboys
- LGBTQ influences in the Settlement House movement
- Portland vice scandal
- Harlem Renaissance
- LGBTQ communities in the Second World War
- Lavender Scare
- Immigration and banning "sexual deviants"
- Culture of the Beat Generation
- Stonewall

- Gay Rights Movement of the 1960s and 1970s
- Queer reaction to Vietnam
- Harvey Milk
- AIDS epidemic/ACT UP
- Don't Ask, Don't Tell
- Battle for same-sex marriage
- Relevant Supreme Court cases
- US history through lens of marginalized groups (including a week of LGBTQ history)
- LGBTQ individuals (i.e., Bayard Rustin, Jane Addams)
- Lesbian feminism
- LGBTQ artists in US history

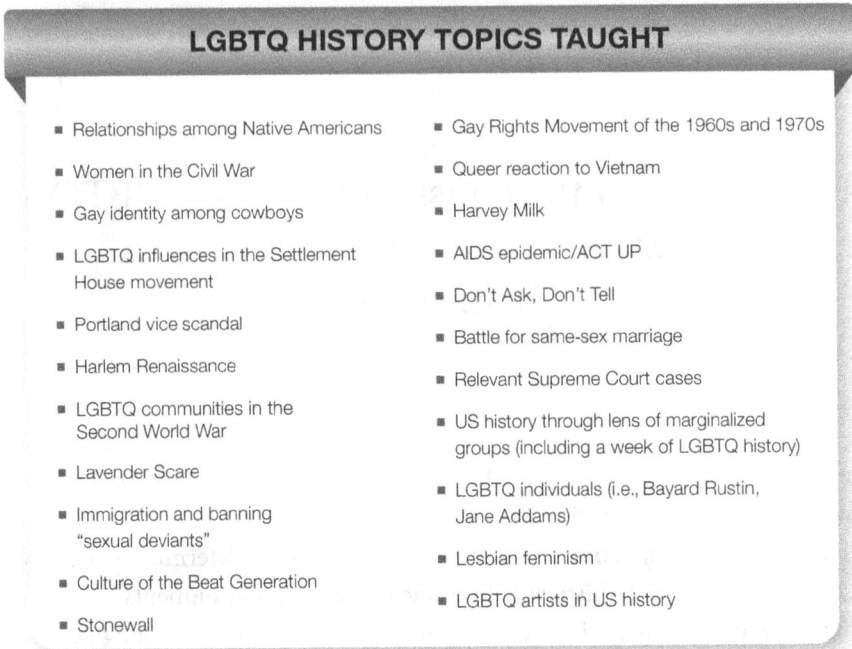

Figure 9.1 Topics taught. The teachers interviewed for this study reported integrating LGBTQ+ history in an array of topics, including both national and local events.

Integrating LGBTQ+ History into the US History Curriculum

Most of the teachers interviewed believe that LGBTQ+ history is a part of the larger history of the United States and teach it as such, integrating it into the curriculum where they believe it belongs. As Melanie Wells asserted, "I try to just weave it in as I go. A lot of what I do is just drop in references about … 'This is how this connects to that issue.'"[2] For many, lessons on the Harlem Renaissance and the civil rights movements of the 1960s were/are natural places to discuss LGBTQ+ history and the roles of LGBTQ+ individuals; all of the teachers, though, incorporated LGBTQ+ history in different ways and eras over the course of the year. As Felicia Perez stated, "I don't think that you can have a queer history if that's the only history you're going to have … if we can show the relationship between individuals and topics and historical moment, that it is the relationship that is going to allow us to see these things are all intersectional."[3] Moving away from heteronormativity and "othering" in social studies classes and making LGBTQ+ history a part of the larger historical narrative are prevailing themes among these teachers' practices.

There are multiple entry points for studying LGBTQ+ history throughout US history. The civil rights era of the 1960s is one of the most popular among the teachers interviewed. This is not the first time that many of the teachers incorporate LGBTQ+ history—Sinclair, for example, discusses gay identity among cowboys in the 1800s[4]—but it is the most common among those in the study. Olivia Cole, who also includes LGBTQ+ history in lessons on the Harlem Renaissance and teaches her students about the Lavender Scare, called civil rights the "entry point" and said that she "frames it in this context."[5] Wells, for example, incorporates the Stonewall riots in her unit on civil rights, segueing from one group's fight for equality and recognition to another and asking students to discuss the impact of those struggles.[6] Similarly, Fred Fox included queer rights and Stonewall in lessons on civil rights, asking students to think about how events in the 1960s and 1970s contributed to prominent LGBTQ+ issues today.[7]

Hasmig Minassian, meanwhile, presents topics related to the gay rights movement in the 1950s, 1960s, and 1970s concurrently with topics related to other civil rights movements of the time. Minassian reported that she disseminates a list of terms and topics to research this era, and that Daughters of Bilitis, Mattachine Society, Stonewall, and Harvey Milk are all on it. Bayard Rustin, too, is on her list; Minassian believes that Rustin is especially important for his contributions to both Black civil rights and gay rights.[8] Teaching civil rights is a complicated matter regardless of the material on which a teacher focuses or the strategies implemented. For these teachers, presenting the civil rights era as encompassing several different groups' struggles provides students the opportunity to mine the complexities and significance of that time in a way that they might not be able to by studying the movements in a vacuum. Including key aspects of the LGBTQ+ rights movement of that time is, to them, a necessary aspect to making it more complete.

Studying civil rights, though, is not only learning about the people, organizations, and events of the era. Several teachers present this topic thematically, establishing social change movements or the experiences of marginalized groups as an overall framework and asking students to evaluate the era and all of its parts as a whole, rather than differentiating between overlapping movements at the start. Dana Rosenberg discussed a unit she taught in her US history class in the early 2000s on social change movements, saying, "We basically used this theoretical framework for 'What is a social change movement?' and then try to follow that framework for all of those social change movements that [the students] researched."[9] Rosenberg explicitly stated that she included gay rights and the Free Speech Movement in this unit, among others. Using this framework, students could compare and contrast "bigger change moments" and backlash across movements and get a larger sense of the era as a whole.[10]

Will Scott similarly created a social justice-oriented curriculum, investigating US history through the theme of violence.[11] Scott's students considered questions including, "When is violence acceptable? When is it not? What does it mean?"[12] In the late 1990s, this unit weaved together gay rights, the civil rights movement, and second wave feminism; while Scott believed that imparting LGBTQ+ history was important in general, he also believed it essential at a time when many were dying of AIDS. Courtney Anderson, meanwhile, taught twentieth century US history using the plight of marginalized groups as a lens. Anderson contended, "Twentieth century history was our focal point and we used the term the rights movements because I don't think civil rights is just black and white. There are several rights movements that existed and they co-existed."[13] When she taught in New York, her unit included a week on LGBT rights and activism, with particular attention on Stonewall because, given the geographic context, that provided students with a landmark with which they connected; this week was part of a larger unit that incorporated and asked students to examine several other group's struggles, as well.[14] In asking students to consider multiple movements as part of one larger quest for social change, Rosenberg, Scott, and Anderson all required their students to conduct research and complete projects that synthesized this information. For them, this method opened students' eyes to the similarities between groups and the way that their struggles endure in the present. Integrating gay rights and LGBTQ+ history in this way, then, was a natural fit. Social movements borrow from and foster each other; including gay rights in a study of the civil rights era represents this overlap, achieving the intersectionality for which teachers in this study strive.

The teachers interviewed asserted that civil rights and twentieth century social movements are natural entry points for educators inclined to build an inclusive curriculum, especially when they first set out to do so.[15] The prominence of Stonewall over other LGBTQ+ topics in US history textbooks and other LGBTQ+-inclusive resources attests to that notion, as well. Many of these teachers and scholars in the field note, however, that LGBTQ+ history neither began nor ended with Stonewall. There are other important topics and eras in US history where these educators believe it is important to integrate LGBTQ+ individuals and issues.

The Harlem Renaissance is often taught as a period of creativity and self-expression during which Black people in Harlem and other northern cities pondered and asserted their identity and role in America through diverse art forms. For Olivia Cole and Courtney Anderson, this is also an important era in LGBTQ+ history. Cole asserted that devoting class time to the LGBT artist community facilitates discussion of LGBTQ+ history across several eras. She therefore includes the role and contributions of LGBTQ+ individuals in the Harlem Renaissance; she opted to focus on "some of the singers during that time period who were openly gay" using materials provided by History UnErased.[16] The Harlem Renaissance is part of a larger unit on race in Anderson's ninth-grade ethnic studies class. Guided by the notion that no group exists alone in history, she includes a lesson on the LGBT community during the Harlem Renaissance; for Anderson a unit on race is not limited to that construct alone.[17] Lyndsey Schlax, meanwhile, tied the Harlem Renaissance to the larger narrative of the 1920s with lessons on rent parties and evolving ideas of marriage expressed in the literature of the time.[18] The freedoms experienced by people who existed in the enclaves where the Harlem Renaissance thrived extended to marginalized groups and individuals outside of the African American community who also lived their lives on the periphery. The Harlem Renaissance, then, offers ample entry points for teachers who wish to present a more inclusive picture of US history.

Wars are a prominent part of any US history curriculum. War, however, is not simply battles, victory, or defeat. Learning about war also entails understanding its human, national, and international impact. Felicia Perez and Fred Fox both navigate wars' effects on the LGBTQ+ population in their classes. Perez, for example, introduced the idea of women dressing as men to join the Civil War and asked students to evaluate the way in which some groups, including LGBTQ+ soldiers and civilians, were targeted during the First and Second World Wars, both by the United States' enemies and within the US military.[19] Moreover, Perez expanded her students' comprehension of the anti-war movement of the 1960s and 1970s by discussing not only why people generally opposed the Vietnam War but also "why queer folks would be against the war."[20] Fox, an army veteran, also challenged his students to consider the impact of war on people's ideas about gender. As he said, "I'm really excited about looking at wars and how the changing gender norms impacted openness and created enclaves, and allowed women to wear pants ... So that lesbian women could wear what they felt comfortable in and they could identify themselves better."[21] While many works of literature focus on the full spectrum of human experience in wartime, US history classes often present a narrower version of the human cost of war. Thinking about the way that war changes people's lives and environments can help make these lessons relevant to students; learning that LGBTQ+ individuals experienced repression and oppression against the backdrop of some of history's greatest struggles provides context and makes evident often unacknowledged complexities, as well.

Although the 1950s is often portrayed as an era of suburban conformity, *Rebel without a Cause* illustrates the opposite perspective. According to Melanie Wells, the movie shows "both how things should be and how 1950s society doesn't quite live up to that idea."[22] Wells uses this film, and the character of Plato, to expose students to gay life and gay individuals' plight in 1950s America. Wells helps her students understand Plato's experiences and the larger implications of being different in a time when it was so important to appear the same. Ultimately Wells's students understand that in the context of the time "there's just no space for him to be there."[23] Mitchell James also challenges his students to juxtapose 1950s conformity against people existing outside of what was considered acceptable, discussing LGBTQ+ history in the context of the Beat Generation. James stated, "We do talk about the existence for being a marginalized person that was designated as gay at that point in time. It was considered a psychological disorder. We talked about it in the frame of reference of the 1950s where you see these conservative values."[24] It is generally acknowledged that the social movements of the late 1950s and 1960s would not have happened if everyone in the country had been included in the postwar prosperity. Often, though, this era's impact on closeted gays is omitted from classroom discussions. Including it, as Wells and James would attest, provides meaningful context for subsequent lessons.

Supreme Court cases are an excellent barometer of the atmosphere in the United States. Moreover, learning about these cases instills in students an understanding of the Constitution and how it works. Looking at Supreme Court cases, then, can be instructive for students as they think about gay rights, especially when LGBTQ+ history and relevant cases are integrated with precedents established in other areas. Hasmig Minassian asserted, "I always taught *Loving v. Virginia* and I always compare the anti-miscegenation cases to gay and lesbian marriage because [even before the Court's decision upholding same-sex marriage] when I was teaching it at the time, I knew. I knew we were headed that way."[25] Minassian uses this landmark case to contextualize current events that, she believes, remain unsettled.[26] Marriage equality, like myriad other aspects of the LGBTQ+ rights movement, has deep connections to other historical struggles.[27] Olivia Cole, meanwhile, uses cases pertaining to gay rights—she specifically mentioned *Lawrence v. Texas* (2003)—to teach her students about the court system. In discussing her LGBTQ+-related lesson plans, she said, "Gay rights within the Supreme Court, the different rulings of the Supreme Court and the different levels. It's one way that I teach the different levels of the court systems so that they can understand the appeal process and how things get to the Supreme Court."[28] It is vital for Cole's special education students that her lessons are focused, structured, and specific. Following one case and taking the time to analyze and evaluate it therefore serves the dual purpose of helping students understand an essential function of the US government as well as one group's fight for equal rights.

These teachers are united in the idea that LGBTQ+-inclusive curriculum is necessary and essential. Beyond that, though, the ways in which they incorporate this history are diverse. In general, teachers prioritize different topics and create curriculum based on different sets of circumstances; the same is true of integrating LGBTQ+ history. Mitchell James, for example, devotes significant class time to the AIDS epidemic of the 1980s and the impact of the Christian conservative movement on the spread of and reaction to HIV and AIDS. James believes that the conservatism of the 1980s continues to impact US politics and society today, thus making this particular area of study important. He reported, "We really focus on it within the context of this time when Reagan and his administration refused to even acknowledge its existence ... how does a population that is a minority in a sense—how does one respond to get their voice heard in a country that is seemingly unwilling to discuss the issue?"[29] For many teachers, reaching the 1980s before the end of the school year is difficult; for James, it's a concrete part of his curriculum.

Danny M. Cohen's organization, Unsilence, aims to reveal the "hidden stories of human rights and ... talk about different modes of silencing." Much of Unsilence's work pertains to the Holocaust and the silence that continues to exist around many aspects of it; he pays particular attention to LGBTQ+ individuals' experiences—stories that, in part or in their entirety, are largely ignored. Cohen contended that discussing LGBTQ+ history in a historical context enhances students' comfort level with a potentially sensitive topic. He stated, "We were also able to give permission to the young people to talk about LGBT history and sexual violence at the same time, opening that up in a kind of safe way" because of students' chronological distance from the Holocaust.[30] Moreover, because homosexuality was illegal in several nations in the 1940s, many survivors faced additional discrimination and, potentially, imprisonment after the war. Cohen referred to this as the "false liberation of homosexual prisoners";[31] his organization works to educate students now about their suffering and struggles in the larger context of a catastrophic event.

LGBTQ+ history is also often omitted from units on the Red Scare, or McCarthyism, in the 1950s despite the fact that this population endured discrimination and consequences similar to those accused of communism during this era. During the Lavender Scare, labeling homosexuals as subversive—the same label given to communists—led to the mass firing of anyone suspected of homosexuality within the federal government and publicly revealed their identity. Olivia Cole infuses her lessons on the 1950s with both the Red and Lavender Scares, both of which, she believes, had an important impact on the country and influence the history she teaches subsequently.[32] For Cohen, Cole, and the other teachers in this study, persecution is not something experienced by one group at a time and therefore should not be taught as such.

Fred Fox and Courtney Anderson incorporate LGBTQ+ history in their lessons on immigration, another topic with current implications. As Fox considered his unit on immigration he thought, "Let's talk about sexuality because they were banned. 'Sexual deviants' were banned from immigrating to the country. It doesn't have to be the focus of the lesson; it just needs to be acknowledged that queer folk weren't allowed to immigrate."[33] This practice presents a powerful and important idea—the more teachers mention LGBTQ+ individuals and events throughout the curriculum the more integrated and normalized this history becomes. By making LGBTQ+ history present in small and large ways over the course of the year, the omission of the past can slowly be reversed.

Community

Many communities offer resources that facilitate or deepen students' comprehension of LGBTQ+ history. Five of the teachers explicitly discussed the way in which events, landmarks, museums, exhibits, and archives in their community play a role in determining their topic selection or making the material more authentic to students' lives.

San Francisco has a thriving LGBTQ+ community and a wealth of history. Among the teachers in that area, Lyndsey Schlax, Hasmig Minassian, and Dana Rosenberg used the city and its history and resources to enliven their lessons and units. Schlax, for example, used the Castro to enhance students' understanding of "gayborhoods." Students looked at images of a place that they've likely visited throughout their lives, discussed the artwork, graffiti, and representations of gay life that they see there, evaluated how and why such enclaves arose in certain cities, and analyzed what these neighborhoods, and the sense of belonging they offered to members of the gay community, might mean.[34] This task situates history in a place with which students are familiar and an idea—community— with which they can identify.

Minassian and Rosenberg believe that living and teaching in the San Francisco area, where AIDS ravaged the community, demands teaching that epidemic. As Minassian said, "definitely teach about the HIV/AIDS movement in San Francisco in particular. This is a very local history movement for us, in terms of the struggles that happened here ... I came into teaching through a lens of the HIV/AIDS movement."[35] Minassian recalled how immersed she was in this chapter of San Francisco history as a teenager there, leading to her conclusion that bringing it into her own classes was necessary.[36] Rosenberg's students visited the AIDS Memorial at the LGBT Center in San Francisco and interviewed people who were involved in ACT UP. Rosenberg's teaching career spanned the late 1990s and early 2000s; the activists her students interviewed, then, were deeply involved with advocating for AIDS patients at the height of the epidemic. Her students immersed themselves in that time period and used the resources available to them in the city in which they lived.[37] San Francisco offers a wealth of opportunities for students to explore this history and its impact in and outside of the classroom, something these teachers incorporated in their instruction.

In Portland, Fred Fox focused on the Portland vice scandal. He very excitedly related, "So there was this huge scandal here in Portland at the end of the Victorian era [focused on] an underground homosexual group and what's so fascinating [is] that it's local history so I think it's going to blow kids' minds just to make that sort of connection."[38] This scandal, Fox stated, in which upper-class white men were arrested for sodomy for the first time, crosses and blurs race, class, and sexuality lines, challenging students to think about how all of these factors intersect.[39] The Portland vice scandal does not appear in history textbooks available nationally, and few students likely learn about it in their classes. For Fox's students, though, it made their learning of LGBTQ+ history different, relatable, and relevant.

Courtney Anderson has experience teaching in two regions with significant LGBTQ+ populations: New York and the Bay Area. As a new teacher on the Lower East Side of New York teaching twentieth century social movements, she realized that she had access to an important and compelling resource that could make history seem more real, and less distant, to her students—Stonewall. Anderson remembered, "We really focused a lot on the Stonewall riots because they're in New York City and a lot of our kids live in that general region so they could walk by the bar and be like, 'Oh my God. This is such a momentous thing for New York City history and I can also identify with it.'"[40] Students often complain that there is little reason to learn history and that they have no interest in things that happened decades or centuries ago. When the places where history was made are a part of their immediate environment, its significance becomes more apparent. Community events, whether well known (Stonewall) or on a smaller scale (Portland vice scandal), can be powerful learning tools.

Focus on Individuals

A preponderance of history education entails learning about major events and their ramifications; focusing on individuals—beyond the major historical figures covered in most schools' curricula—is rarer. Students better identify with classroom material, though, when presented with a personal lens or perspective on the events and phenomena about which they learn. Four of the teachers, therefore, pay specific attention to LGBTQ+ individuals who contributed to the larger historical moments students study.

According to Felicia Perez, students can access history by learning about individuals and the events and circumstances of their lifetimes. Discussing Harvey Milk and Sylvia Rivera, two figures whose lives and contributions Perez introduced to her students, she asserted, "They would find out about these individuals and these people and then that would inherently lead them down this road of finding out these events that we might not cover, that might not come out in a particular event or we might not be able to spend a lot of time there but you should know who these people are."[41] Perez named several people and groups of people whom she specifically referenced in her class including the Taino and Sarah Edmonds, a woman who dressed as a man to fight in the Civil War, because their lives and experiences are historically important and rich and because learning about LGBTQ+ lives in the past can help immerse students in history in the present.[42]

Olivia Cole also uses figures from the past to engage her students and help them understand the larger concepts she teaches. For Cole's students, many of whom have little experience with the LGBTQ+ population in their personal lives and for whom there is a negative connotation attached to LGBTQ+ individuals, starting the year looking at people, as opposed to mass movements, increases their comfort with this topic. She related that she will often show her students a picture of Calamity Jane and ask them to describe the individual they see. As she said, "everyone back in the day is wearing these floppy hats and they look really sullen and they all looked kind of dirty. You can't tell but just leaving it up there, I could see their little wheels turning and I called on one of the kids … He was like, 'Well miss, that's a woman.' "[43] Although Cole willingly answers students' questions about her own life, asking them to study LGBTQ+ history was an additional leap for a group that, she stated, "still [wasn't] comfortable using the term gay and girlfriend and things like that. They were still bad words to them."[44] Starting their study with individuals, then, laid a foundation for the material Cole would teach later.

For Hasmig Minassian and Casey Sinclair, it is necessary to focus on individuals to reverse their absence from people's historical memory. Minassian prioritizes including LGBTQ+ people over activism in her classes because, in her opinion, it is the people who so often go unnoticed and unacknowledged. Minassian contended that, unlike other minority groups, there are no immediately defining physical characteristics of the majority of LGBTQ+ historical figures and, therefore, their sexuality, and the fact that a gay man or woman played a vital role in a movement or era, goes largely and erroneously ignored.[45] Minassian, therefore, tries to incorporate LGBTQ+ figures with whom students are not familiar and LGBTQ+ lifestyles of figures that they know in an attempt to make these people and their lives more visible. Similarly, Sinclair declared, "Because so much of the history is erased, because these people's stories didn't get told there are so many questions about who they were and what they really did."[46] She pays specific attention to Jane Addams and the women in the settlement house movement, challenging students to evaluate not only what they accomplished for others but also how their own identities existed in and outside of that environment.[47] Through this study, Sinclair's students learn about important historical figures and a movement that changed thousands of people's lives as well as how this movement influenced and was influenced by the lives of those who sustained it. Moreover, as students learn about the ways that people in the past submerged their true selves these individuals become less hidden.

Putting the Spotlight on LGBTQ+ History

Integrating LGBTQ+ history throughout the US history curriculum in an authentic, organic way is an ideal goal, one that a majority of the teachers interviewed implemented. The nature of history education, though, is that throughout the course of an academic year, particular groups' history or contributions to history become the focus of a lesson or unit. Although total integration is the goal for many, the demands of the discipline and the time— especially as teachers continue to figure out how best to bring this information into their classes—may also lead to lessons, units, and classes specifically focused on LGBTQ+ history.

California in the twenty-first century has been the focus of significant national attention as a battleground for LGBTQ+ rights. It is not surprising, then, given the prominence of these issues, that more than half of the teachers (seven in total) participating in this study teach/taught in California. Among them, Courtney Anderson, Hasmig Minassian, and Felicia Perez devote specific time in their required classes to events and individuals involved with and affecting the LGBTQ+ population. Anderson's unit on sex, gender, and sexuality, the intention for which is to "blow open the spectrum a little bit about traditional gender roles among other things," aims to promote "different understandings about what we call the LGBT community and what [that has meant] throughout history."[48] Felicia Perez, meanwhile, decorated her room with posters she gathered from the ACLU "of queer people who were making history and had made history, and it talked about how they were queer, how they were gay, how they were these prolific and important people." Teaching in a third-floor classroom with no windows, Perez was left on her own to find a way to open her room to the outside world. She chose to do so by exposing students to individuals and accomplishments they might not have known about previously and, through these posters and discussion of them, indicated the history students would learn.[49] In addition to units that integrate LGBTQ+ history thematically, Hasmig Minassian devotes time to exploring important events in LGBTQ+ history, like Stonewall and the AIDS epidemic, on their own merit. Making connections between moments and events in history is a priority, but focusing on aspects of history of which students, as Minassian said, have "zero knowledge"[50] is important, as well. Without specific content knowledge, after all, key components are omitted when those larger, thematic connections are made.

For a few teachers the best way to convey LGBTQ+ history was to design and teach classes solely devoted to this topic. In these classes, time becomes easier to manage, students are aware of the subject matter they will learn, and the nuances of LGBTQ+ history can be explored in depth in ways that might not happen in a survey course. Though electives are wonderful in conveying in-depth information and offering students the opportunity to mine a topic in more profound ways, relying on electives as a primary means to teach LGBTQ+

history can be problematic. First, as previously stated, electives are a privilege most often available in well-funded schools or schools with alternative curricula. Second, not all students take them, and those that do self-select. Third, teaching LGBTQ+ history as its own elective, separate from a comprehensive telling of US history, maintains this distinction. In fact, Fred Fox pushed for his elective because he believed in the value of this material and, though survey courses at his school began to integrate information on Stonewall, he believed that more had to be done and was not.[51]

Teaching an elective was not a choice for Casey Sinclair. Given the instructional design of her school, it was not a matter of whether to teach an elective but what the subject matter would be. The curriculum development group with which she worked was motivated to bring LGBTQ+ history into US history classrooms, thus a course was born. Sinclair recalled, "We really took an intersectional lens. We really looked at people's identities and who they were and what people they were representing and all those kinds of things; what about that was important for that historical moment."[52] For Sinclair, her students' ability to examine and profoundly understand this community and its history was of the utmost importance. As she stated, "I think part of it is identifying texts that show the fluidity of sexuality and then look for many different characters in history and try to imagine and understand the various pressures that were on people and how they are different from what we see now ... and how have things evolved and how have they not."[53] In a traditional US history survey class, Sinclair would not have the same freedom or flexibility in her approach. Here, she could prioritize engagement and deep, internalized comprehension over breadth of coverage.

When Lyndsey Schlax was approached about teaching an LGBTQ+ history elective, she first had to learn the information that she would be expected to know at its helm. Having never learned this history herself, it was as new to her as it would be to her students. She had, however, learned about other movements for social justice and already valued this lens as an overall theme in her teaching. An LGBTQ+ history class, then, corresponded with her established philosophy.[54] Schlax designed her class around students' discoveries; it was important to her that her students realize all the history they missed in their previous studies. She asserted, "I wanted them to have that, 'Oh my gosh! I see it. I see this experience. I see these people. I see that they've always been around and I see that they haven't been represented' [moment]."[55] To accomplish that, Schlax used a diverse set of resources that tended heavily toward podcasts and began with the history of gender and sexuality, the differences between them, and the idea that "there have always been gender nonconforming people, they just don't end up in your history books."[56] Schlax applied these ideas throughout her semester-long class, in which students examine LGBTQ+ history throughout the twentieth and twenty-first centuries. Her unit on marriage equality, for example, focuses not only on whether same-sex couples are entitled to this right, but dissent on the topic within the LGBTQ+ community. She explained, "We talked a lot about— there are a lot of people who are fighting for the right to get married. There's a whole pile of people who are fighting just to destroy marriage because nobody should have to get married because that's a pile of BS. So, like this push and pull of subversive and confrontation and desire for legitimacy."[57] Only in this kind of elective do most teachers have time to immerse students in a study of this issue's complexities.

Fred Fox's class likewise explored queer history in a nonbinary way, evaluating the multiple experiences of people and groups that identify as LGBTQ+ or are gender nonconforming. These labels, and their impact, are important to Fox, who intended to begin his class by looking at "profiles of pre-gay, nineteenth, eighteenth century Americans who are gender nonconforming, who today we might call transgender or we might call a lesbian" and consider whether these modern labels can be appropriately applied to people and lifestyles in the past.[58] For Fox, who taught at a school where a two-day unit on Stonewall in US history classes was an accomplishment for LGBTQ+ history education—as it is and would be in schools across the country—looking at the history students know from a completely different perspective was an exciting prospect. Like Schlax, Fox's class included the impact of world wars, immigration, and current issues; he later included colonialism and its impact on queer communities and cultures.[59] Students often complain that they learn the same history multiple times over the course of their education. In Fox's class, as well as in Schlax and Sinclair's classes, the events might be the same but the perspective is not.

Building Historical Skills

Effectively teaching LGBTQ+ history, like other topics, involves more than disseminating information. Students must evaluate and digest this subject matter like they would any other, especially considering that for many students this information, studied in an historical context, is brand new. The teachers in this study, therefore, understand that it is not enough to simply introduce LGBTQ+ history; they must also guide their students in building the skills to understand

RESOURCES & STRATEGIES

Resources include:

- Visual sources – photographs, artwork, posters, images, etc.

- Text sources – primary and secondary sources, excerpted readings, biographies, scholarly articles, essays, etc.

- Timelines

- Supreme Court decisions

- Multimedia sources – movies, podcasts, music, etc.

- Language analysis

- Local newspapers and archives

- Student-written and -produced plays

- Oral histories and interviews

- *Queer History of the United States*

- Current events materials

- Field Trips (including museums)

Assignments and Strategies:

- Weave LGBTQ history throughout the curriculum

- Focus on language and vocabulary

- Make connections to students' lives

- Research papers/presentations

- Socratic seminars/class discussion

- Written, artistic, and creative assignments

- Social justice oriented curriculum

- Student-conducted interviews with parents and community members

- Text analysis/differentiated reading assignments/evaluating multiple perspectives

- Exploration of "erased" history

- Use of current events to connect past and present

- Project-based curriculum

Figure 9.2 Teacher resources and strategies. The teachers reported using a variety of tactics to convey LGBTQ+ history to their students.

and apply it. The requirements for doing so differ as student populations and school resources do. Nevertheless, each of these educators discussed specific ways in which their students learned LGBTQ+ history and expressed their historical discoveries (see Figure 9.2).

Often when students learn a new topic, they must also learn the language and vocabulary necessary to discuss that material. This is especially true of potentially sensitive or controversial topics like LGBTQ+ history, where it is imperative that students understand specific terminology and use it appropriately, as well as grasp the ways in which language might be used offensively. Building language and vocabulary skills are the foundation of this unit for Olivia Cole. She said, "The first thing I normally have to deal with is the language. What are they using? What kind of words do they use to describe and how do they explain and speak in a sensitive and not a derogatory way? That's the first step."[60] While

Lyndsey Schlax's students didn't face the same learning obstacles as Cole's, she, too, focused on language development to start her course. Schlax's students spent a semester navigating this material, and it was therefore important that they understood not only the language and terminology that they used but also the nuances in language as it applied to gender and sexuality in English and other languages.[61] Fred Fox, meanwhile, considered language from a different perspective. History students have a tendency to apply present day standards and ideas to the past; therefore, in planning his course, Fox questioned the use of twenty-first-century labels in a class that spans decades. He questioned, "How fair is it to impose a modern understanding on the past?"[62] Schlax and Fox have more time and opportunity to discuss evolving terminology and ideas relating to gender and sexual identity, providing their students with context that they likely wouldn't receive in a survey course. Considering the plethora of ways that language is invoked around this topic, to Schlax and Fox this study is significant.

The teachers in this study incorporate a vast array of sources in their classes, from text to visual images to film and other forms of media to field trips that explore students' communities. Reading and evaluating primary and secondary sources and using them to compare, contrast, and make connections remain key aspects in comprehending history at the secondary level. Sinclair, for example, selected and presented her students with truncated readings and questions to guide them, often asking what might be controversial and what evidence the reading presented for students to defend their positions.[63] Through this practice, students build reading comprehension and argumentation skills. Students in Danny M. Cohen's Unsilence workshops participate in interactive text analysis, navigating personal histories by choosing the part of the story with which they want to engage next. "The Son," for example, presents students with testimony written by a gay son of Holocaust survivors in which he discusses the tragedy they endured and his experience watching his peers die of AIDS. Students consider how this story resonates with them and make authentic connections as they read.[64] Melanie Wells also asks students to analyze documents around her lessons on LGBTQ+ history, particularly in connection with her unit on *Rebel without a Cause* if time allows. The document analysis enriches the students' experience and understanding of the film and provides them with greater context of the era portrayed. Wells also provides students with scholarly articles on this topic as a summer assignment, making them available for extra credit owing to the timing and difficulty of the sources.[65]

The flexibility of the elective format allowed Lyndsey Schlax to incorporate several different types of sources, including text and visual primary sources.

Schlax described a class period as a time in which students listened to music from a particular era while they analyze primary sources from that time period; she provided the example of listening to Bessie Smith while students read documents about the Harlem Renaissance. Schlax also devoted class time to honing this skill with her students. She stated, "I walk them through how to analyze a primary document: How do you question this document? Who is the audience? Who created it? Who's likely to see it? … What bias may have existed in this document?"[66] These skills were important for students' success in Schlax's class, especially as they examined and evaluated loaded topics and questions. Additionally, developing a command of these skills allows students to be successful beyond Schlax's class and in other academic endeavors.

Among the indications of what students have learned are the ways in which they can reflect upon and apply that knowledge. For many of these teachers, assessment is not a test; it is a more in-depth measure of students' facility with all they learned about LGBTQ+ history. Dana Rosenberg, Hasmig Minassian, and Courtney Anderson require students to research and write about a specific topic pertaining to social movements, with many focusing on some aspect of LGBTQ+ history. Mitchell James's students interview their parents about the AIDS epidemic and write papers on their findings. James posited, "I want my students to speak with people who lived through it to get a sense of how they viewed the epidemic … what they were aware of with regard to the gay population, what they knew of with regard to the gay population that was in fact fighting for research funding and drug testing and access to better drugs."[67] James thus put a twist on the traditional term paper, asking students to work as historians to gather original information. Will Scott's students wrote and performed a play about the information they learned, presenting their history of violence dramatically as well as writing investigative papers on a related topic.[68] Fred Fox's students designed and presented personal interest research projects, producing, for example, documentary films and wall murals.[69] Lyndsey Schlax, meanwhile, engaged students in an art analysis project, in which, after studying LGBTQ+ artists and their contribution to the community, students "chose a piece of art," created a placard for it, and "put on a gallery opening."[70] For Schlax, who taught at a specialized arts school, this project both reflected what students learned in her class and engaged their talents and sensibilities. Material effectively conveyed can contribute to a variety of outcomes and expressions. Students' buy-in to their lessons on LGBTQ+ history is evident in the work they are able to produce when these units or classes conclude.

Research indicates that innovative approaches and immersive experiences can be meaningful to students' ability to retain and internalize the information that they learn.[71] Projects like James's, Scott's, Schlax's, and Fox's are the types of educational experiences that make an impact. It is essential to evaluate not only how much students learn or how much time they spend learning it but also whether or not the ways they learn it are effective. Based on teacher observations and assessments, learning this history expands students' ideas and knowledge base about LGBTQ+ history and the practice of "doing history" in general. This, then, indicates that the strategies are effective, an important first step as the presence of the content increases in these, and other, classrooms.

Bringing the Past into the Present

Several of the teachers in this study, regardless of their sexual orientation, claimed that including LGBTQ+ history in their classrooms was a part of their effort to reverse years of omission and silence.[72] The lessons, units, projects, and resources they described have the power to do just that. Danny M. Cohen, whose organization is named for this purpose, believes in the importance of and supports all efforts at Holocaust education; his work is different than other organizations oriented around that goal because, in addition, it promotes students and teachers discovering and discussing the "silenced" narrative of that time. Revealing and asking students to ponder and discuss the Holocaust through the lens of gay victims and survivors is new terrain for most of the student groups and educators with whom he works.[73] Casey Sinclair, whose students engaged in in-depth explorations of LGBTQ+ history and individuals, maintained this focus and intensity "because so much of the history is erased, because these people's stories didn't get told, there are so many questions about who they were and what they really did."[74]

Fred Fox and Courtney Anderson thought more specifically about the role of the storyteller, and that person's power to influence what generations of students know about US history. Fox began his class by "talking about the process of history because we're going to be looking at how much of this history has been erased."[75] Anderson, too, stated, "Actually what we're focusing on right now is looking at omission and sugarcoating in history, who writes history, who gets to decide that, and why does it matter";[76] she applies this query to the broad scope of history, LGBTQ+ history included.

These educators, then, through the work they do in their classrooms and with their students, harness their power as the storyteller to share important and relevant information to which so few are exposed. Their classroom practices begin the work of unsilencing and acknowledging history that is as much a part of the American experience as the majority of what students regularly learn in their US history classes.

10

Impact at the Grassroots: Challenges and Rewards in Teaching LGBTQ+ History

Surviving the Darkness: Challenges to Teaching LGBTQ+ History

Teaching sensitive, potentially controversial material, regardless of teacher motivation or community open-mindedness, is not without its challenges. Resistance to change in education is historically well documented[1] and, in many cases, expected. The lack of support for teachers incorporating LGBTQ+ history in their classes is itself testament to the slow pace of and obstacles to significant curricular and classroom change. Moreover, there are widespread and often competing opinions on what should happen in schools and classrooms; even in the most progressive environments, teachers encounter backlash when their approach to a topic or situation meets with student, parent, or administrative disapproval. Ten of the twelve teachers encountered resistance at some level, whether from other teachers, administrators, or members of the community (Figure 10.1). They encountered challenges from people in and outside their schools who claimed that this was not "real history" and didn't need to be taught,[2] had to respond to parents and colleagues who deemed their sources inappropriate,[3] and battled long-standing ignorance or misperceptions of LGBTQ+ history and issues.[4] Some teachers reported persisting in their goal of teaching LGBTQ+-inclusive history despite the constraints of the school year and requirements imposed by standards-based education, both of which posed significant stumbling blocks in this case as they do in many other attempts at curricular change. Given the array of challenges present, these teachers' efforts to incorporate LGBTQ+ history into the curriculum reflect their beliefs about its necessity and significance in students' education.

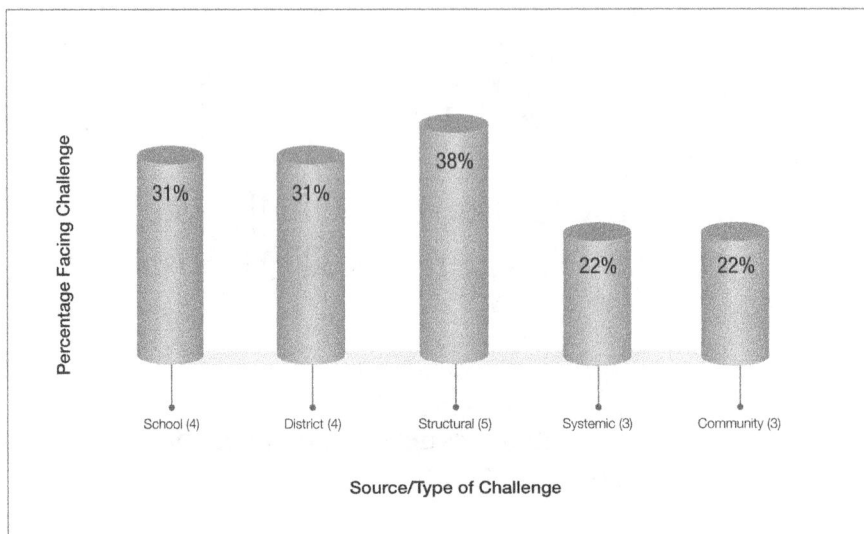

Figure 10.1 Teacher challenges. Teachers reported facing challenges from a variety of sources. Systemic challenges included standards and testing, and structural challenges refer to the way in which a school day or year is organized.

School-Based Challenges

Classes that integrate or focus on LGBTQ+ history, and plans to establish them, were sources of discontent for students and/or teachers at four teachers' schools in this study.[5] Fred Fox, for example, faced multiple obstacles in his attempt to win approval for his queer history elective. Although many of his colleagues supported his endeavor, some of the more conservative members of his department expressed concerns. Fox recalled, "One [colleague] actually did say that he is not opposed to the class in general; he is just concerned that if we start getting too specialized we won't be teaching the real history."[6] Though Fox's class and the written proposal he prepared for it demonstrated how it adhered to state standards, colleagues who believed in more traditional US history courses were reticent to support a class in which history would be viewed through a new lens. In fact, Fox stated, the same colleague was so opposed to his elective that he "told all of the counselors that the class wasn't going to run and they shouldn't let students sign up for it."[7] Though the situation was remedied, it indicated the lengths to which someone would go to defeat that which they opposed and the tenacity necessary to see it through.

For eight of the teachers in this study, student interest in the topic was a primary reason for pursuing LGBTQ+-inclusive curriculum. Not all students, though, are interested in or willing to learn about LGBTQ+ history. Teachers in this study who taught before LGBTQ+ issues were more openly discussed, as well as current teachers in more conservative regions, encountered students who explicitly and implicitly resisted or refused to learn this material. Additionally, teachers in this study opine that student and parent opposition to including LGBTQ+ history is among the most significant reasons why it is not present in more classrooms; in the regions where these teachers work, this reticence is often based more on a lack of awareness or resistance to change than hostility or homophobia.[8] Dana Rosenberg, who taught in the 1990s and early 2000s, related that, while many of her students appreciated that she incorporated this material, each year there were some for whom she had to offer alternative assignments after they refused to participate in her LGBTQ+ history research project. While she surmised that several used their belief systems as an excuse to avoid work altogether, it was nevertheless significant that, each year, homophobia seemed an appropriate and compelling argument against completing a class assignment.[9] Furthermore, Lyndsey Schlax, whose LGBTQ+ history elective was first offered in 2015, reported that, although she encountered no negative parental reaction and students intentionally signed up for her class, some changed their minds when they understood its scope and purpose. She said, "I lost a couple of kids at the beginning of the year when I sent home the syllabus and it said in big bold letters, 'We're going to be talking about sexuality … because of the nature of this class and our connection to arts there may be some exposure to nudity and mature topics.'"[10] She never heard from the students or parents; they simply dropped the class.

Hasmig Minassian commented on the heteronormativity in classroom settings, and the way in which it has the potential to hinder LGBTQ+-inclusive curriculum and create a feeling of "otherness" among students who identify as LGBTQ+. As she asserted, the additional steps necessary to prepare a class to learn this material and the way in which teachers need to rethink their language and perspective in order to do so might be too difficult for some teachers to undertake. Comparing this to other marginalized groups, she contended, "At first, we had to make people feel good about being a woman and then including them in history became a lot easier, but this is a dual step that we don't have with white men who are straight. I didn't ever have to make my white students feel good about being white and then teach them history."[11] For Minassian, preparing her students to learn this history, and, in particular, encouraging LGBTQ+ students for whom learning this history might have the greatest benefit to embrace their identity and open themselves to that experience, was a challenge specific to teaching LGBTQ+ history. The perspectives and biases with which students enter class, then, can pose a significant obstacle to this particular curricular change.

Administrative Resistance

Opposition from one's superiors can have a chilling effect on intentions and practices, especially in education where school administrators and district and Board of Education officials can dictate what and how information is conveyed. Even in districts where administrative officials rarely participate at the classroom level, where significant change is afoot or controversy might arise, those in power, the teachers reported, often become involved.

Some administrators prioritize the possible problems with integrating potentially controversial information, which might be conceived as inappropriate by people whose needs schools attempt to meet. Administrative reaction to LGBTQ+-inclusive curriculum differed widely. Teachers like Olivia Cole and Courtney Anderson feel wholeheartedly supported by their administrations in this endeavor.[12] Mitchell James, meanwhile, noted the relative silence he faces regarding LGBTQ+-inclusive curriculum; for James, this gives him the freedom to do as he sees fit.[13] Others, though, encountered explicit resistance. Will Scott, for example, hoped to bring the conversation about LGBTQ+ history and experiences into his classroom when he taught in the 1990s. Because his school viewed this material as appropriate mainly as it applied to violence prevention, administrators prioritized bringing in outside speakers over using teachers and class time as resources.[14]

Furthermore, administrators' personal interpretations of teachers' practices and results can pose obstacles. Lyndsey Schlax, who collected data from her students to assess their opinions on her class and what they learned, related that the head of her social studies department misrepresented this data to the Board of Education to suggest that the only compelling aspect of Schlax's class was her guest speakers, thus severely undermining her efforts and presenting an inaccurate portrayal of the impact of her course.[15] These diverse reactions can hamper teachers' efforts to make their curriculum more inclusive. When the administrators whose support teachers seek withhold it, it is that much more difficult to attempt something new.

Backlash against teaching LGBTQ+ history comes from officials beyond the school level, as well. Dana Rosenberg, Fred Fox, and Lyndsey Schlax were all forced to overcome pushback regarding teaching practices and materials at the district level in order to proceed. Dana Rosenberg encountered backlash "from the district in trying to use materials they didn't feel were appropriate and mostly because they were too political or they want textbooks." She said, however, that though she "had to confront a lot of bigotry in that district," once she entered her classroom she felt free from those constraints; she was, she said, "in her own world" and "had a lot of autonomy."[16] The district's response, then, did not prevent Rosenberg from fulfilling her teaching philosophy.

Fox and Schlax shared similar experiences of defending the necessity of their electives to district representatives. Fox described navigating policies, prejudices, and officials' ideas of appropriateness in his effort to win approval for his elective. He related, "One of the weird obstacles ... was the fact that the district has a problem with us offering this class because ... they said queer history should be in a regular history classroom, why isn't it?" Though Fox would personally like to see greater integration in US history classrooms, resistance in his district prevented that from occurring; this comment to him, therefore, was both odd and hypocritical.[17] Schlax faced a similar situation, defending her class against the argument, "We have a US history class. Let's just infuse it there"; she, too, added, "Knowing that that's not going to work because you've been telling people to just infuse it there for ages and you've got like five people doing it."[18] In Schlax's estimation, "it can be really hard working within a complex bureaucratic system and trying to do something radical."[19] Arguments for broader inclusion in survey courses, which to that point had not happened in Fox's or Schlax's district, seem like positive steps at face value; to Fox and Schlax, though, they were backhanded attempts to curtail the more immersive experiences that the two teachers proposed.[20] Moreover, Fox's district's legal committee stalled on approving his class because though they searched for other examples of such courses to serve as precedent, they had trouble locating that information; for Fox this, too, represented the need for, rather than a reason to deny, his class.[21] The dearth of LGBTQ+ history education in schools, based on Schlax's and Fox's cases, can therefore be self-perpetuating.

Structural and Systemic Issues

Time is one of teachers' greatest enemies. There is never enough of it, either in a class period or in an academic year. This is an oft-cited reason among teachers who do not include LGBTQ+ history in their classes and a stumbling block for those intent on doing so. Two of the teachers, Mitchell James and Melanie Wells, explicitly stated that they wished they had the time to include more.[22]

Wells modifies her unit on *Rebel without a Cause* and gay life in the 1950s each year, deciding which materials she will and will not be able to include based on the time remaining in the school year.[23] Similarly, Mitchell James stated, "I can say that in my AP history class sometimes time does not afford us to cover as much as we would like"; he often chooses, therefore, to do one in-depth unit on LGBTQ+ history rather than "throw it in willy-nilly as just a mere mention."[24]

Time precludes people from incorporating LGBTQ+ history because, with very few exceptions, there is little to nothing about it in state or local standards. The emphasis on standards-based education and assessment, according to Hasmig Minassian, means that students do not hear about LGBTQ+ history until high school, if at all, as teachers race to cover mandated topics and often omit others.[25] Felicia Perez concurs. She argued, "I don't believe that our best foot forward is spending so much money on testing and on test prep and on getting our students to—will they be able to accurately assess if letter C is better than letter E"; this, she pointed out, gets in the way of real curriculum development.[26] Struggles that all teachers face on a daily basis, then, even more adversely impact upon attempts to bring LGBTQ+ history, or anything slightly divergent, into the curriculum. Moreover, LGBTQ+ history's absence from state standards and the impact of this omission are a thread through each aspect of this effort from the creation of resources to attempts to make history classes move inclusive. It therefore makes sense that the teachers interviewed would cite standards and testing as a challenge to incorporating LGBTQ+ history in their classrooms.

Debates about the state of education, meanwhile, frequently focus on class size, resource availability, and teacher training. Each of these factors, the teachers interviewed claimed, impact one's ability to incorporate LGBTQ+ history. Parents and educators throughout the country advocate for smaller classes, which studies show improve students' learning.[27] Olivia Cole, whose self-contained special education classes are, by law and necessity, small, contended that class size is significant to her ability to interact with and meet her students' needs. She asserted that she would not be able to include LGBTQ+ history in a larger setting.[28] Felicia Perez also referred to smaller classes, positing that funds allocated for testing would be better spent on decreasing class size and supporting resource development. Effective teaching, Perez contended, is based on providing high quality, appropriate resources for students. The lack of this, in addition to the lack of uniformity in resources and textbooks, make it more difficult to teach in general and certainly more difficult to teach complicated and new subject matter.[29]

Teachers cannot teach what they do not know. While this is certainly a matter of being comfortable in the classroom, it is even more because when teachers are unaware of historical events and contributions they also have no idea that they are omitting them from the curriculum. Lyndsey Schlax knew little about LGBTQ+ history before she was approached to teach her elective; she now believes that this ignorance and the absence of this information in teacher-training programs must be remedied for LGBTQ+ history to be meaningfully included in the curriculum. She asserted, "I think it's important to look at the education that our future teachers are getting. If you don't know what you don't know, then you're not going to include it when you become a teacher and we're just going to perpetuate stuff. We're going to perpetuate invisibility."[30]

Will Scott and Felicia Perez, too, claimed that teachers' knowledge gap is a significant obstacle to incorporating LGBTQ+ history. Scott transitioned into teacher education when he left the classroom. In this role, Scott coaches "with LGBT sensitivity in mind" and works with teachers to "figure out how to teach LGBT history in classrooms."[31] Changing teacher education, as Wendy Rouse is trying to do at San Jose State University, and preparing teachers intellectually and emotionally to facilitate lessons on LGBTQ+ history, is an integral first step in making inclusive curriculum more widespread.

Community Reaction

Americans tend to have opinions about the state of education and what students learn. Many want schools, especially those that their children attend, to propagate beliefs and ideas similar to their own. Teaching controversial issues and integrating "new" information into history classes—whether it is LGBTQ+ history in the twenty-first century or civil rights in the mid to late twentieth century—has the power to upset these desires and expectations. Resistance, then, comes not only from the people connected to the school but also from the community at large.

Melanie Wells discussed the ways in which she is mindful of the conservative community in which she teaches when she incorporates LGBTQ+ history in her US history classes. She stated, "I try to weave it in a little bit and touch on it and make references without beating kids over the head with it."[32] This strategy helps Wells fulfill her goal of normalizing this history while also ensuring that, for the most part, students are comfortable with the information presented. Because she is careful, tactical, and respectful of the community in which she teaches,

Wells is able to implement her own philosophy without meeting resistance in a community that she described as heavily populated by people who supported Donald Trump and his policies leading up to the 2016 election.[33] Working within the confines of her environment enables Wells to balance everyone's needs.

Resistance to inclusive curriculum is not specific to conservative communities. Even in more left-leaning environments, there are people who oppose the inclusion of information with which they disagree or that they believe is inappropriate for a school setting. In San Francisco, home to one of the nation's largest LGBTQ+ populations, Lyndsey Schlax encountered significant backlash. Schlax recalled, "I got several threatening letters delivered to the school and emails, people trying to save me ... that's a pretty standard experience for people who are doing LGBT activism work ... but it is new for a lot of social studies teachers."[34] Though the threats abated, they represented a high level of resistance for which Schlax, an educator, was not prepared. Extreme backlash, then, can exist in the most unexpected places and can have the power to scare a teacher away from exploring something that could engender such a negative reaction.

The existence of LGBTQ+ inclusive curriculum as well as queer history electives does not always equate with school or community acceptance of these endeavors. Although there is some safety in the comfort of one's classroom, teacher testimony suggests it is likely that one will face a reaction, either positive or negative, on the other side of the door where LGBTQ+-inclusive curriculum is concerned. The most significant challenge, then, is how teachers—especially those in regions where there will be as many or more people supporting the effort to integrate LGBTQ+ history as those who oppose it[35]—move past the obstacles in their way to incorporate information that is, in fact, a part of the historical narrative they teach.

Impact at the Grassroots

Educators who incorporate LGBTQ+ history in their curricula believe that doing so creates positive change among their students, in their classes, and, hopefully, in the larger school community. Though most of their efforts remain local, they believe it is possible for these efforts to become more widespread.[36] It is impossible and inaccurate to apply twelve teachers' experiences to the wider field of historical education; the work they do in their classrooms and the changes that they believe it creates happen, for now, in their own classrooms and communities. They are a beachhead in this movement in the same vein as the educators developing curriculum and the activists who fought for the FAIR Education Act. Their personal reflections speak to the positive impact of their inclusive curricula and the possibilities that exist when students find themselves in situations where the information they receive opens their minds. For these teachers and their students, then, LGBTQ+-inclusive historical curricula enhance students' historical knowledge, allow them to make connections between the past and the present, and provide students with the more complete historical narrative to which their teachers believe they are entitled. According to the teachers, their students—regardless of their sexuality or gender identity—and, to varying extents, other members of the school or local community benefit from learning LGBTQ+ history.

Knowledge Acquired

Education seeks to do many things. First and foremost, though, educators impart knowledge, the acquisition and retention of which among students represents success. The majority of teachers in this study reported that, in their assessment, students left their classes feeling more knowledgeable about LGBTQ+ history and better able to think critically about LGBTQ+-relevant issues. Lyndsey Schlax and Danny M. Cohen reached this conclusion based on survey data and written responses, while others, like Olivia Cole and Fred Fox, noticed students' increased comfort level and ability to converse about LGBTQ+-related topics. These and other signs of success, as well as students' overall ability to retain and apply this information, were personally and professionally meaningful.

Lyndsey Schlax, Olivia Cole, and Hasmig Minassian each stated that most or all of their students had "zero exposure" to LGBTQ+ history before entering their classes. All three also reported, though, that most or all of their students felt better versed in this history than at the start of the year when their classes concluded. In order to demonstrate the merits of her elective, Schlax conducted an end-of-term survey to assess student takeaways and reactions. According to her data, "75% of students reported that they knew little or nothing about LGBTQ+ history before taking the class. And after taking the class, 100% of them report that they believe they know a lot, which was described as 'more than most people my age.'"[37] Cole, who estimated that 90 percent of her students have no prior exposure to this history, stated that they leave her class aware of and comfortable discussing this history. She said, "The best part is my little advocates and these kids who went from not being able to say the word gay and thinking girlfriend was a bad word to now they can communicate with me and communicate with others about it."[38] For Cole and her students, this is a significant victory. Minassian reported that students leave her class equipped with knowledge of Stonewall and the AIDS epidemic and, more importantly, a sense that the LGBTQ+ population is not different or separate from every other group that students learn about and encounter in their daily lives.[39] The work of these three teachers, then, results in over one hundred students each year knowing about and understanding the nuances of LGBTQ+ history.

Learning something new, something of which one was previously unaware, can, in certain circumstances, be equivalent to removing blinders that they have worn up to that point. Mitchell James, Melanie Wells, and Fred Fox referred to this eye-opening effect in evaluating the impact of LGBTQ+-inclusive history education on their students. James's AIDS unit, he stated, exposes students to information in a way that they've never received it before, facilitating their understanding of the subject matter and the world at large.[40] Wells, meanwhile, talked about watching her students' facial reactions as they understood that Plato in *Rebel without a Cause* was gay and all the implications surrounding that; she also commented that students are savvier in identifying that aspect of Plato's character than in the past.[41] According to Fox, "kids were just blown away. They were like, 'I cannot believe it,' because they're like, 'How did I never know this happened? How did I never know that they used to think gays were diseased and they would put them in jail?'"[42] For Fox, this moment of enlightenment is one of the reasons he feels compelled to teach LGBTQ+ history. Assessing his students' learning, he stated, "It wasn't a room full of queer students and yet they still found these amazing personal connections to the topics, so that is also very rewarding."[43]

Courtney Anderson similarly described students' engagement and excitement when they begin to use what they learned about LGBTQ+ history to make connections between this population and other groups. She recalled, "That's when our discussion becomes really, really helpful for some of the students who weren't making those larger connections to other more historical events and that's where they get to be like, 'Oh, yes, you're right. I never thought about that.' That's a really cool aha moment to see on a kid's face."[44] Teacher observations suggest that this level of understanding, in which students wordlessly react to the information they learn, indicates the extent to which incorporating LGBTQ+ history can build knowledge and understanding as well as change a student's relationship to his or her learning experience as a whole.

Shifting Perspectives

The information students receive in class can have the power to better inform or change their ideas as well as dispel biases. Four of the teachers, in fact, remarked that they observed a sea change among their students based on the information disseminated and discussions in which they participated in class.

Hasmig Minassian, whose overall goal is to normalize her students' views and ideas about the LGBTQ+ community, spoke specifically about working to break down students' prejudices. She stated, "You spend a lot of time in your classroom working through people's individual homophobias and I think that's just real."[45] Minassian strives to help her students understand that identifying as LGBTQ+ is not synonymous with a negative lifestyle and that this population has, historically and presently, made meaningful contributions to society.[46] Minassian strongly believes and sees it as a sign of success when students let go of the idea that there is an "other."[47] Melanie Wells's goals are similar, though her tactics are subtler. By inserting small mentions about LGBTQ+ history throughout the year, Wells removes the stigma for many of her students and builds their comfort level, as well. Wells's students, she asserted, are curious about this information; by the end of the year, it's simply part of the conversation.[48]

Courtney Anderson, meanwhile, instills the idea of intersectionality in her students through their study of LGBTQ+ history. Anderson sees history as intersectional and laments that is it too often taught as compartmentalized events. Teaching social movements together allows her to share this intersectional lens with her students in an accessible, organic way. She asserted, "The best way of going about this is to do it in a way you're integrating organically … so the civil rights … women's rights … gay rights … every other rights movement is happening at the same time." Intersectionality, an important and complicated concept, is thus easier to comprehend because, as Anderson deduced, "we understand that we can fit into multiple groups but when those groups are interacting on a broader level and intersecting on a broader level, it's hard to compartmentalize history."[49] Changes in perspective do not require radical shifts in a person's thought process. A new perspective can derive from refocusing how one sees and conceptualizes their surroundings or a better understanding of a new idea or philosophy. For these teachers, integrating LGBTQ+ history enables these changes, big and small, to occur.

Teachers have many different reasons for including LGBTQ+ history in their classes. Among Olivia Cole's goals is "to take away some of these things that they've been taught over and over and over again." She stated, "I always want to expand their minds. I want them to go further."[50] Cole's goals are admirable, yet potentially challenging when students' backgrounds and home lives have already instilled particular perspectives. By the end of the year, though, Cole has witnessed real change. She said, "I no longer hear any [derogatory] words in my classroom. They've learned and if they hear someone else they correct each other, which is pretty cool. I was like, 'I'm never going to see the changes. Gay is always going to be an insult,' but I saw it happen in my little classroom universe."[51] As Cole witnessed, providing students access to facts and historical information and guiding them in the process of making connections can positively impact the way in which students think about people they once perceived as different or inferior.

Improving School Climate

Evaluating the accomplishments of her LGBTQ+ history classes, Casey Sinclair stated,

> I mean it was liberating to just be able to talk about this, to have a safe, supportive, inquisitive, curious environment where sometimes students would be like, what you just said was offensive, and that was okay ... maybe that's because we don't all know everything yet, right? So fostering that kind of environment where you're both protecting students from, not protecting them but facilitating both growth and also safety, right? But not sacrificing growth for safety is really important.[52]

A preponderance of the literature on and efforts to build LGBTQ+-inclusive curriculum focus on school climate and creating safe, accepting environments. Anti-bullying initiatives and changing the language and terminology students use—the latter a focal point for history teachers, as well—therefore frequently takes precedence over teaching history. As Sinclair attested, though, history classes and the discussions that they foster can significantly change the way students relate to each other and their teachers.

According to Dana Rosenberg, instruction is more authentic, and students are more engaged, when the subject matter is important to the teacher and not a random topic plucked from a school's history curriculum.[53] Doing this, she believes, facilitates the student–teacher relationship; teachers become real people as opposed to standards-spouting cogs and students, by virtue of their teachers' authenticity, feel acknowledged, as well. This connection was important to Rosenberg as a teacher, as she declared, "it was almost always a coming out process to teach the unit because it's so personal, and I guess that it's made a lot more engaging because that is always one of my qualities as a teacher, to have a really close relationship with my students."[54] Olivia Cole acknowledged a similar phenomenon, in which sharing her life and inserting herself in what she teaches fosters an environment of trust and compassion. Because of this, she related, learning occurs in more meaningful ways for all of her students, most or all of whom do not identify as LGBTQ+, than if she, as the teacher, was an aloof authority figure.[55]

For students who identify as LGBTQ+, the inclusion of this history and the presence of an accepting teacher can make a real difference in their lives. Felicia Perez, who mentored several students in her time as a teacher, forming lasting bonds with them and their families, credited the freedom to make her own pedagogical choices with making her classroom a safe and engaging place in which students thrived. Having the space to introduce, discuss, and navigate LGBTQ+ history with her students, and provide them with the opportunity to feel less alone was, for Perez, a defining aspect of her career.[56] A great deal of the history students learn in every unit of study is in some way about people forging identities, engaging in conflict, resolving disputes, and struggling to be seen. These are valuable lessons that are extraordinarily relevant to the LGBTQ+ experience and necessary for all regardless of their sexual orientation and gender identity. In fact, Lyndsey Schlax asserted that, in the years since her school began offering her LGBTQ+ history elective, "the school, as a whole, is better at being responsive."[57] It makes sense, then, that these teachers assert that exploring these ideas, in and outside the context of LGBTQ+ history, will build on and build from the relationships established in a collaborative classroom.

Leave Them Wanting More

When students are immersed in what they learn and engaged by new discoveries, the end of a class or a semester comes too soon; there is so much more to know than what may feasibly be squeezed into a class period. Five of the teachers in this study experienced this with their students. Having learned and analyzed information that stunned them and, in some cases, angry at an educational system that previously hid this history from them, students exposed to LGBTQ+ history continued to seek answers and became advocates for its inclusion.

LGBTQ+ history, to an extent, is a study of human rights violations. Several of the topics that teachers cover in their classes, from immigration to the Lavender Scare to the Supreme Court, illustrate the ways in which the LGBTQ+ population has been excluded, restricted, and discriminated against in US history. Rights violations, regardless of the group in question, are subjects that tend to engage and enrage high school students; in an LGBTQ+-inclusive class, this reaction is exacerbated by the fact that unlike other groups, many students are learning of this mistreatment and the laws and actions that supported and bolstered it for the first time. Courtney Anderson, who devotes class time to studying legal restrictions that LGBTQ+ Americans faced, explained her students' interest in this history with a simple statement: "Once you get kids pissed, their buy-in is so much better."[58] Students, Anderson and others posited, are angered not only by what they learn but also by the fact that this information wasn't previously revealed. Felicia Perez stated that queer history, the importance of which was abundantly clear to her students by the way she decorated her room, "was not something they had learned before." Rather than fear the new material, though, she said, "It was making them angry. They were like, 'Why didn't we learn about this in the elementary school? Why didn't we learn about this in junior high? I'm so glad we're learning about this now.'"[59] Teacher evidence suggests that this anger, regardless of whether it derives from what students learn or the fact that they have never learned it before, sustains their investment in the subject matter after the discussion or class concludes.

It is impossible to know what one does not know. It is a conundrum that historians and scholars have pondered and reflected upon ad nauseum. It is also a question that Lyndsey Schlax, Felicia Perez, and their students encounter repeatedly in their study of LGBTQ+ history, the elusive answer to which motivates students to search for knowledge even after class ends and grades are entered. Schlax's end of semester survey asks students "What else do you want to know? What else do you want to learn?" and the most common response is, "I don't know, because I don't know what I don't know." In Schlax's estimation, "That realization is huge. They came to the end of this class and they're like, 'Oh gosh! There's so much stuff that I don't know, and I have no idea what it is.'"[60] Though this is frustrating for some of Schlax's students, it is an impetus to discovery for others. Similarly, after their introduction to queer history and its nuances, Perez's students questioned what they do and do not learn in their history classes and the reasons behind inclusion and exclusion. Perez contended that it is imperative to consider these questions, saying, "As they leave the classroom they need to be able to have these frames that they're constantly looking at and considering, in terms of who is and isn't being talked about and why ... Is that done deliberately? Are people being left out on purpose? Who's not involved in this story? Who's telling the story?"[61] In other words, then, Perez hoped her students would continue to search for and find the information and the stories that they did not know and consider whether those stories were complete.

Schlax stated that, through her class, she hopes her students will see the world differently; go from being color blind to seeing the entire spectrum of colors. Recognizing and understanding that there is a world of knowledge to explore fulfills that goal.[62] Awakening students' curiosity and having them realize how much there is to discover, teachers assert, is a powerful impact of LGBTQ+-inclusive history. Students encounter the same historical events and trends so often throughout their education that the idea that there is more to learn on these topics can seem preposterous. Schlax's and Perez's students' reactions illustrate that when presented with new, controversial information, students are flooded by innumerable questions and the realization that there is, in fact, so much of which they are unaware. Learning LGBTQ+ history in school can compel students to ask questions outside of it.

Effective history and civics education has the power to inspire students to act. Casey Sinclair witnessed this effect in her LGBTQ+ history class. She recalled, "I saw a lot of people really grow into activists during that time. Some people who were already activists and who just grew more and became more interested and involved and vocal and confident in themselves."[63] Furthermore, Cole shared that one of her students, a male who knew little about the LGBTQ+ community before her class, later advocated for a transgender teammate on the school's baseball team when others opposed his participation.[64] Moreover, Fox's students advocated for and conducted research to support the need for a "lavender graduation" for LGBTQ+ students; though they did not have enough time to turn that goal into a reality when they came up with the idea, subsequent groups of students continue to work for this cause.[65] Meaningful, engaging education that challenges students to think about the world and their place in it can be extremely powerful. The LGBTQ+ community and rights movement have accomplished a lot in a relatively short period of time, but their struggles continue and are increasingly prominent in the national conversation. Teacher testimony and the stories they share indicate that learning this history contextualizes current events and provides students with a foundation they can use to support their own evolving opinions. Not all students are activists, but, as these anecdotes show, given the tools, all students can be active.

History Revealed

According to Dana Rosenberg, "our society does not have a historical memory and it's really devastating to our future."[66] Rosenberg delivered this lament while discussing her desire for history to feel like a living thing for her students, though she worried that this was difficult, if not impossible. This historical amnesia, willful and involuntary acts of forgetting and silencing, is the focus of teachers and organizations dedicated to integrating LGBTQ+ history into classrooms and people's general consciousness. These educators' efforts contribute to making that goal a reality; all of their students are more aware of and able to speak to the complex and complicated narrative that is LGBTQ+ history. LGBTQ+ history has long been suppressed and erased, not only in classrooms but also in more general retellings of history; this creates a vicious cycle in which people unaware of this history unintentionally perpetuate the silence around it. Felicia Perez asserted that teaching LGBTQ+ history pushes students to talk about things that largely remain unsaid.[67] These teachers' efforts, and their students' knowledge, retention, inquisitiveness, and application of these concepts, therefore, illustrate that LGBTQ+-inclusive history education is indeed impactful.

* * *

Each of these educators offers his or her students a historical learning experience that includes LGBTQ+ history in meaningful ways. They all do so differently, operating within the structures, circumstances, and environments specific to their schools and the classes that they teach. For all, including LGBTQ+ history enriches their teaching and their students' education in myriad ways. Their students, they contend, are more aware and knowledgeable of LGBTQ+ history and issues than their peers.

In addition, the teachers hope that others will accept their actions and, possibly, follow the precedent they set. In fact, those who have left the classroom mentor teachers who wish to incorporate LGBTQ+ history. They are aware of, and have faced, the challenges to inclusive curriculum, some to a greater extent than others. Yet, they not only continue and refine their practice but also took the time to contribute their experiences to this study in the hope of reaching other, similarly inclined educators. They are, therefore, the roots of a movement to the same extent as the founders of GLSEN and GSA. A grassroots movement, after all, requires multiple seeds.

The teacher reported impact of these classes and this information on students offers initial proof that LGBTQ+ history is essential to students' study of US history. Students learn to critically evaluate the past and the present, applying historical lessons to current events like transgender rights.[68] They learn to think differently and question sources and information, delving deeper into what they think they know to find out the answers that they have not yet discovered.[69] Students are inspired to learn and their minds are opened to possibilities that they didn't previously know existed, largely because their teachers showed them that there was so much left for them to discover.[70] Lastly, history builds understanding and compassion, especially as students discover it together. As Lyndsey Schlax posited, "[the LGBTQ+ history class] showed me quite a lot about the power that visibility and responsive curriculum can have not only on an individual student or a classroom, but a school, and the teacher, and the wider community that the school is located in."[71] Regardless of the LGBTQ+ content teachers choose to convey, the observed outcomes of their efforts reflect the power of this subject matter.

The vast majority of these teachers (eleven) work in liberal-minded areas. Many of them, especially among those currently in the classroom, reported that their students are aware of LGBTQ+ issues in the news today.[72] Melanie Wells, who asserted that many of her students and their parents support Donald Trump, also stated that her students are aware of and curious to learn more about the issues facing the LGBTQ+ community.[73] Some of the teachers reflected upon their students' lack of personal experience with LGBTQ+ individuals and current events pertaining to that community. Olivia Cole, for example, posited that she was the first LGBTQ+ person that many of her students encountered,[74] and, in the 1990s, Will Scott felt uncomfortable revealing his own sexuality or bringing up history or issues important to the LGBTQ+ community in his class in Los Angeles.[75] Moreover, though many of the students were aware of and had opinions about issues facing the LGBTQ+ population today, few knew anything of the history preceding those current events.[76] Liberal enclaves, then, provide a forum in which exploring this material is acceptable and, in many cases, welcomed; this acceptance, though, does not replace the need for context and information. As the teachers reported, augmenting students' knowledge of present-day issues with the history that led to this point helps students to contextualize and better understand the discussions happening around them today. As with many other topics covered in a history class, the baseline knowledge with which students enter requires the supporting evidence that historical education can provide.

Environment is a key factor for many of these teachers. Hasmig Minassian, for example, claimed, "My gay teacher friends in [more conservative] Orange County say they could never do what I do."[77] Students' readiness to learn and their predisposition to support the LGBTQ+ community offer entry points for curriculum not traditionally taught; the liberal bubble, in this way, provides a safety net for a practice that might be riskier, and possibly not attempted, elsewhere. It is the rare teacher who is willing to put his or her job on the line to teach material that he or she is specifically instructed not to discuss. Though there are instances of this happening to teachers who strongly believe in the need for LGBTQ+-inclusive education[78]—these teachers are necessary, after all, if a grassroots movement is to be successful—a negative environment in the educational arena more often has a chilling effect than a rebellious one.

None of the teachers in this study encountered LGBTQ+ history in their K–12 education. Five were exposed to it as college undergraduates in their women's studies and history classes,[79] but the others were not. Growing up and attending high school in the 1980s and 1990s, though, these teachers were exposed to lessons on other marginalized groups struggling for recognition and existence, many of which also fought for their place in the curriculum. These lessons, and the trend toward inclusion and representation in history classes, prepared them to act as pioneers on this new frontier. As such, they constantly refine their practice, seeking new information and ways to convey it. In 2020, for example, Courtney Anderson related, "We've spent the last few years amping up our social living curriculum's gender and sexuality unit."[80] Furthermore, Melanie Wells shared that she established a "genius hour" in her US history classes during which students engage in year-long research projects; "some of the most promising projects," she said, "were focused on LGBTQ history."[81] For Anderson, Wells, and others, LGBTQ+-inclusive history teaching is a constantly evolving endeavor.

Teacher education programs and classes can also play a stronger role in augmenting educators' knowledge of or facility with this material. As Lyndsey Schlax posited, until LGBTQ+ history is a component of teacher education programs its presence in classrooms, where many teachers don't realize the scope of what they're omitting, will remain stagnant.[82] Two of the educators in this study, Will Scott, who works with new and emerging teachers, and Danny M. Cohen, whose organization seeks to equip teachers to introduce LGBTQ+ history into their classes, seek to expand the number of LGBTQ+-inclusive history classes through their work with educators; both understand the need to increase teacher awareness and buy-in for progress to occur.[83] While it remains reasonable to assume that the majority of teachers do not learn this information in their own schooling, teacher education programs can prepare their students to integrate LGBTQ+ history into their classes where, hopefully, it self perpetuates.

Teachers' assessments and anecdotal evidence related to students' historical knowledge bolster the rationale and support scholars' arguments in favor of LGBTQ+-inclusive curriculum. Teacher testimony pertaining to how learning LGBTQ+ history changes school culture and community provides further evidence of why it is a necessary part of a well-rounded and complete historical education and why it is as necessary as school climate and anti-bullying curricula. Though the conclusions drawn from this study are based on teachers' own work and observations and the sample size, and thus evidence gathered, is small in scope, understanding the impact of inclusive history curricula on a small scale gives credence to arguments for these curricular changes on a larger scale. Moreover, the success that these teachers report working on their own indicates the larger potential of inclusive curriculum if the obstacles that prevent other teachers from incorporating this history into their classes were to be removed. The positive experiences and outcomes shared by the teachers in this study are a powerful rejoinder to the arguments against inclusive curriculum.

LGBTQ+ history education, by and large, happens in an echo chamber; many students who are most unaware of this history and for whom it might be most transformative have no chance, for now, of learning it in their US history classes. Including this information, though, is powerful regardless of the overall political atmosphere in the region where that instruction occurs. Given the political divisions regarding support for and opposition to LGBTQ+ rights in the United States, and considering the mission of social studies education, including LGBTQ+ history in the curriculum is essential to this subject fulfilling its goals. As Mitchell James posited in 2017, "it became a lot more common of a topic throughout the year ... particularly because of what was going on also politically in the election of Trump, and the people that he stigmatized and continues to do so along the way. I think it became sort of a more common topic just as a necessity to talk about what was going on in our country."[84] The 2020 presidential election ushered in a new administration committed to restoring, respecting, and upholding LGBTQ+ rights, but societal rifts remain. These teachers' work is a small and necessary step in addressing a larger problem and, though it is as or more important in states where it is banned, those big moves require the foundation provided by these smaller acts.

Fred Fox credited the courses developed before his queer history class for opening a space in which his class can exist. Fox declared, "There are all kinds of little seeds that have been planted along the way." He is grateful for the efforts of those who forged paths and started conversations and classes focusing on marginalized groups before him because, he said, "A queer history class would not have been the first minority lens acceptable."[85] Because others came first, Fox's class was approved. Now Fox's class and the classes and practices of all of the teachers in this study are the seeds for what comes next.

Conclusion: The Future of LGBTQ+ History Instruction

When I began this research eight years ago, the landscape for LGBTQ+-inclusive history education was much different. Fewer resources were available online; there was far less attention paid to the presence of this material in classrooms. The FAIR Education Act had passed, but its implementation prospects seemed distant. Teachers in liberal regions were far more defensive about including this material in their classrooms; a teacher whom I asked about a resource she used in class was reticent to discuss it until I explained my work. Keeping up with the changes that occurred as I researched was daunting at times but also indicative of what happens as a movement seeking to create change takes hold. The future of this enterprise, then, is brighter now than it was less than a decade ago.

The African American Civil Rights Movement and the women's rights movement did not appear in US history curricula as they occurred or in their immediate aftermath; they remain underrepresented in many states' standards and classroom instruction today despite the fact that the civil rights movement itself focused on schooling and advocated for the inclusion of Black history. The push to include these major historical moments encountered significant resistance, especially in the South where "mint julep" versions of textbooks omitted the civil rights movement even as northern schools began learning about it.[1] Advocates for incorporating LGBTQ+ history similarly navigate the controversy engendered by curricular reforms as well as confronting the decades-long debates over sex education which, unlike civil rights and women's rights, involves and potentially offends individuals' religious beliefs. Advocates for LGBTQ+ inclusive history classes and resources insist that this topic is purely historical; the opposition is highly motivated to prevent its appearance in history classes, conflating it with the studies of sexuality and sex education that they stand vehemently against. Fully grasping the struggle to integrate LGBTQ+ history, then, requires understanding arguments in favor of inclusion as well as the opposition this movement faces relative to other historical topics and the additional sources of resistance with which it must contend.

The movement to include LGBTQ+ history is both top-down and bottom-up; change has, and must, come from both directions. Legislation and framework revisions must be implemented by teachers if they are to have a real impact; administrative and governmental support is necessary bolster teachers' inclination to incorporate LGBTQ+ history. The areas in which progress has been made illustrate the potential effects of both this partnership and the different entities encompassed within it; the way in which obstacles persist show their limitations.

Classroom change does not happen without teachers who are willing to implement it. As we enter the third decade of the twenty-first century, more teachers are interested in and/or willing to introduce LGBTQ+ history to their students than in the past. Though it was difficult to find teachers who engaged in this practice five years ago, in the intervening years more teachers began including LGBTQ+ history; some who already incorporated it became more open to speaking about their practices than they were in the past.[2] In 2014, less than twenty people attended the NCSS session on the *How to Survive a Plague* unit; in 2017, more than thirty attendees at the same conference signed in and engaged in extended conversations at a poster presentation on teachers' efforts to include LGBTQ+ history in their classrooms.[3] A roundtable discussion at the American Historical Association (AHA) in 2018 entitled "Words that Shape the World: Historians, Teachers, and Partnerships for LGBT History" was similarly well attended, with teachers sharing their experiences teaching this material and inquiring about extending their practice. In 2019, the Committee on LGBT History awarded the first biyearly Don Romesburg Prize, named for the Sonoma State scholar who spearheaded efforts to change California's Framework, to Rachel Reinhard and Bay Area educator Emily Richards of UC Berkeley's History-Social Science Project for its lesson on the Lavender Scare. The prize recognizes K–12 teachers who present and investigate "intersectional and research-driven LGBT history content" with their students;[4] such an award would be neither possible nor necessary without a pool of teachers committed to and immersed in this work. State governments and Departments of Education, then, are not alone in reconsidering the role of LGBTQ+ history in social studies classrooms; change is happening concurrently among teachers with the motivation and ability to create more inclusive learning experiences.

Beyond government and classroom-centered movements for change, discussions of LGBTQ+ history's place in social studies classes have become more prominent in the media. In an era of sound bites and "listicles," increased coverage of this topic in the popular press clearly indicates that it is an issue about which people outside educational circles are thinking; the speed with which information is shared also means that these articles reach a broad audience relatively quickly. In October 2017, for example, *U.S. News and World Report* published "Don't Overlook LGBTQ+ History in High School" in which author Alexandra Pannoni claimed, "There is a burgeoning movement to cover the contributions of gay, lesbian, bisexual, transgender and queer individuals in public schools."[5] Pannoni went on to offer suggestions to teachers interested in incorporating LGBTQ+ history based on the advice of one California teacher already doing so. Tris Mamone published "I Wish I Had Learned LGBTQ+ History in High School" on HuffPost, a website that previously posted similarly themed articles, in 2018. Writing in response to Illinois's then-proposed LGBTQ+ history bill, Mamone asserted, "LGBTQ+ people have existed throughout history and made tremendous contributions to American culture, yet no one talked about them in school … If I had known about them, I might not have suffered through years of alienation, confusion and self-hatred."[6] More recently, *Time* magazine's 2019 article "As More States Require Schools to Teach LGBTQ History, Resources for Teachers Expand" discussed increased attention to inclusive classroom resources.[7] Teachers' efforts and advocacy for change in schools and the halls of government, then, garner greater and more positive attention than in the past. Reform is afoot and the media has taken notice; change, and conversations referencing it, have long been and continue to be indicators of progress.

The possibilities that exist in some parts of the country, however, are not present in other states and regions. Though in a positive step three states— Utah (2017), Arizona (2019), and South Carolina (2020)—recently repealed or overturned their "No Promo Homo" laws, five states maintain them; if anything, the movement toward inclusive curriculum in other parts of the country strengthened these states' resolve to prohibit discussions of LGBTQ+ history, issues, and lifestyles in their schools.[8] Similar atmospheres and thought processes are evident in conservative regions outside these five states, as well. Evangelical opposition to LGBTQ+-inclusive curriculum continues to thrive in these areas, as well as in states that passed and are moving to implement curriculum laws; it often increases in proportion to the success advocates experience. A spokesperson for Focus on the Family, one of the organizations most vehemently opposed to the presence of LGBTQ+ issues in schools, told NBC News, "Policies should offer both across-the-board protection for every student, as well as respect for the fact that parents have the most intimate knowledge of their children, and therefore, should have the power to decide when, if and how their kids are introduced to controversial sexual topics."[9] Furthermore, this opposition is far better funded than the state mandates calling for integrating LGBTQ+ history and the individual teachers doing so, a factor Don Romesburg emphasized in discussing his concerns about the FAIR Act's future, especially when the funding attached to the Framework revisions expires.[10] Thus, though the movement to introduce LGBTQ+ history in US history classes has gained traction in more liberal parts of the country it is entirely possible that there are limits to the extent of this progress. This does not detract from the movement's success, but it suggests that nationwide change might currently be an unrealistic goal.

The most prevalent impediment to change on this front is the aforementioned absence of LGBTQ+ history from state standards and the tests generated to assess students' facility with the information therein. Despite educators' and scholars' arguments against the need for and the dependence on standards and testing, their place in education and their influence over schooling have not wavered. While this poses an obstacle, then, it is also a source of promise. California's FAIR Education Act, despite the struggle to implement it on a widespread basis, remains a significant victory in the fight to incorporate LGBTQ+ history in US history classes, as do similar laws in New Jersey, Colorado, Oregon, Illinois, and Nevada and the framework revision in Massachusetts. They proved that such legislation was possible, especially in states with Democratic legislative majorities. Additionally, the diligence and tenacity of the scholars and educators who worked to change California's Framework and create resources in other states and counties serve as an example to additional states that might be similarly inclined. Where standards are among the most significant obstacles to incorporating LGBTQ+ history, amending them is a meaningful step toward more inclusive curriculum. Though top-down actions do not lead to immediate change, they lay important groundwork for continued progress. The most meaningful obstacle, then, is also the one with the most realistic chance to become an opportunity. As the FAIR Education Act was the domino leading to change in New Jersey, Colorado, Oregon, Illinois, and Nevada, so too might changes in six states lead others to amend their guidelines for student learning.

The movement to incorporate LGBTQ+ history in high school US history classes is therefore on the precipice of real success. Teachers and advocates have established a foundation from which these reforms can grow and a trajectory marked by slow and steady progress from top-down and bottom-up perspectives. Increased attention to these reform efforts, greater awareness of advocates' accomplishments and the continuing need for change, and sustained discussion of inclusive curriculum in the public forum have the potential to build upon the success generated by existing efforts. Nationwide change might not be feasible, but the increasing curricular prominence of a subject rarely spoken of in society thirty years ago represents progress nonetheless.

LGBTQ+-inclusive curriculum has expanded beyond the handful of US history classrooms in which it was present five or ten years ago. Additional reforms and greater support are necessary if it is to become an entrenched aspect of US history classrooms. In 2019, NCSS issued "Contextualizing LGBT+ History within the Social Studies Curriculum," a position statement that "asserts that contextualizing LGBT+ history within the story of America through an inquiry-based, non-judgmental critical analysis of primary sources is a reflection of what unifies caretakers of the social studies, irrespective of their political affiliations or ideologies"; the statement urged educators to ponder how they might create "more accurate and empowering curriculum."[11] This stance, from an organization that counts thousands of social studies teachers among its members, is the type of institutional support necessary to propel this movement forward. Political and educational LGBTQ+ activist organizations must make curricular change a priority to counter a focused, well-funded opposition. There will always be individual teachers who, believing a topic is important, work to ensure its inclusion and/or prominence in their classroom. These teachers are the grassroots of this movement and they are essential, but they cannot grow it on their own. Standards and institutional support—within and outside the educational arena—are vital to continued and increasing progress, especially considering the obstacles that will remain steadfast.

As battles for equality, recognition, and access persist in the United States, it remains essential for students to understand the history of those struggles in order to comprehend the problems and divisions facing the nation today. Education, in fact, encompasses the transmission of culture among generations and occurs in an array of forums including the home, religious institutions, voluntary organizations, social circles, the media, and society at large. High school students do not solely rely on class discussions for the knowledge and ideas they acquire, but these conversations and the way in which information is conveyed in school, as versus other settings, broadens and contextualizes how students comprehend LGBTQ+ history and the issues facing the population today.

Renewed emphasis on the plight of marginalized groups in this country began prior to the 2016 election; it has intensified since and reached new levels in the spring and summer of 2020. In March 2021, President Biden issued an executive order directing the Secretary of Education to review and enforce regulations "guarantee[ing] an educational environment free from ... discrimination on the basis of sexual orientation or gender identity."[12] Incorporating LGBTQ+ history as that population continues to navigate questions about rights and representation serves the mission of social studies and connects the classroom and the world outside of it in a way that prepares students to engage in difficult conversations in meaningful ways. Moreover, this history's omission from US history classes becomes less viable as LGBTQ+ rights and debates pertaining to them remain part of the national conversation; teachers, school districts, and departments of education cannot legitimately claim to educate students in this discipline and foster participatory citizenship while leaving out a central aspect of the nation's narrative. Though history and social studies receive less attention among educational policy makers in the twenty-first century than literacy and math, within the classroom it remains imperative for the subject to fulfill its mission.

When Kevin Jennings established the organization that became GLSEN in 1990, he hoped that he might be able to support LGBT teachers struggling with their identity and their sense of belonging in school communities where they felt compelled to hide their true selves. Nearly thirty years later, GLSEN is the single largest organization supporting LGBTQ+ students and teachers and providing curriculum and professional development to schools around the country. Its research is published and cited in the academic and popular press, and its advocacy efforts have made schools more welcoming and curriculum more inclusive for thousands of students. GLSEN today exists far beyond the scope of anything its founders could have imagined. The movement to integrate LGBTQ+ history into US history classrooms has similarly, but so far on a smaller scale, come farther than advocates ever thought possible. It has farther to go still and realities and obstacles with which to contend, but it also has a strong foundation of its own and powerful role models to follow. In the places where progress is possible, then, continued efforts and the passage of time indicate it can be accomplished. The fight, as Lyndsey Schlax declared, however prolonged, is worth it.

Appendix A

List of Teacher Interviews

Courtney Anderson, telephone interview, November 1, 2016
Courtney Anderson, telephone interview, August 10, 2017
Courtney Anderson, email conversation, October 27, 2020
Danny M. Cohen, video chat interview, November 16, 2016
Danny M. Cohen, video chat interview, August 8, 2017
Danny M. Cohen, video chat interview, October 21, 2020
Olivia Cole, telephone interview, December 8, 2016
Olivia Cole, telephone interview, September 6, 2017
Fred Fox, telephone interview, May 24, 2016
Fred Fox, telephone interview, August 7, 2017
Mitchell James, telephone interview, October 30, 2016
Mitchell James, telephone interview, August 8, 2017
Hasmig Minassian, telephone interview, November 23, 2016
Hasmig Minassian, telephone interview, January 26, 2017
Hasmig Minassian, telephone interview, September 25, 2017
Felicia Perez, telephone interview, September 25, 2016
Felicia Perez, telephone interview, December 6, 2016
Felicia Perez, telephone interview, August 14, 2017
Dana Rosenberg, telephone interview, December 6, 2016
Dana Rosenberg, email interview, September 25, 2017
Lyndsey Schlax, telephone interview, March 16, 2016
Lyndsey Schlax, telephone interview, January 12, 2017
Lyndsey Schlax, telephone interview, September 7, 2017
Will Scott, telephone interview, November 15, 2016
Will Scott, telephone interview, August 16, 2017

Casey Sinclair, in person interview, November 22, 2016
Casey Sinclair, telephone interview, September 27, 2017
Melanie Wells, telephone interview, September 20, 2016
Melanie Wells, telephone interview, August 17, 2017
Melanie Wells, email conversation, July 20, 2020

Appendix B

List of Activist and Scholar Interviews

University-Based Scholars

Robert Cohen, New York University, May 2013
John D'Emilio, University of Illinois at Chicago (emeritus), July 7, 2016
John D'Emilio, University of Illinois at Chicago (emeritus), July 13, 2016
John D'Emilio, University of Illinois at Chicago (emeritus), July 16, 2016
Emily Hobson, University of Nevada-Reno, June 8, 2016
Don Romesburg, Sonoma State University, February 6, 2015
Don Romesburg, Sonoma State University, June 16, 2015
Don Romesburg, Sonoma State University, March 11, 2016
Don Romesburg, Sonoma State University, May 2, 2017
Don Romesburg, Sonoma State University, May 30, 2018
Don Romesburg, Sonoma State University, August 6, 2020
Wendy Rouse, San Jose State University, October 26, 2018
Wendy Rouse, San Jose State University, August 8, 2020
Stephen Thornton, University of South Florida, June 24, 2014

Organization-Based Educators and Advocates

Debra Fowler, History UnErased, June 24, 2016
Debra Fowler, History UnErased, November 20, 2018
Debra Fowler and Miriam Morgenstern, History UnErased, July 6, 2016
Debra Fowler and Miriam Morgenstern, History UnErased, April 23, 2018
Kevin Jennings, founder of GLSEN, June 28, 2013
Kevin Jennings, founder of GLSEN, January 3, 2018
Kevin Jennings, founder of GLSEN, January 17, 2018
Kevin Jennings, founder of GLSEN, July 25, 2018

Geoffrey Kors, former director of Equality California, March 26, 2015
Carolyn Laub, GSA, July 9, 2015
Jo Michael, Equality California, July 30, 2014
Miriam Morgenstern, History UnErased, June 24, 2016
Miriam Morgenstern, History UnErased, August 10, 2016
Rachel Reinhard, Berkeley Social Science Project, January 29, 2015
Kristi Rudelius-Palmer, Human Rights Resource Center, September 14, 2016
Jamie Scot, ONE Archives (formerly), February 26, 2015
Sox Sperry, Project Look Sharp, June 13, 2016
Jinnie Spiegler, Anti-Defamation League, July 16, 2015
Jinnie Spiegler, Anti-Defamation League, August 8, 2016
Kisha Webster, Welcoming Schools, July 8, 2015
Kisha Webster, Welcoming Schools, July 15, 2015

Additional Interviews

David France, filmmaker, September 16, 2013

Appendix C

Online Resources for Teaching LGBTQ History

The following list includes LGBTQ history resources available online. The resources were developed and published by the education departments of LGBTQ and human rights advocacy groups and address different topics and issues pertinent to the LGBTQ community. All of these resources are available at the URL listed as of March 2021, but organizations do periodically replace their online resources. Please note: this list is not exhaustive.

History Surveys

"The Invisibility of LGBT People in History: 'Peculiar Disposition of the Eyes,'" Anti-Defamation League, 2010, accessed October 20, 2020.

This lesson, part of the ADL's Curriculum Connections program, mines the concept of invisibility and the way in which minority groups have been marginalized throughout history, culminating in an activity in which students learn about historical figures who identify as LGBTQ and the way in which this identity is often omitted from discussions of their lives and contributions. The goal of this lesson is for students to understand "the ways in which LGBTQ people have been made invisible in history."

https://www.adl.org/media/6779/download

"LGBTQ History Timeline Lesson," GLSEN, 2019, accessed October 20, 2020.

"LGBTQ History Timeline Lesson" is a comprehensive introductory lesson in which students discuss what they know about LGBTQ history and, as a class, organize important moments in LGBTQ history from colonial times to the present into a timeline through interactive work and class discussion. Among the facts students learn are that Thomas Jefferson revised the punishment for sodomy under Virginia law and that the American Psychiatric Association voted unanimously to remove homosexuality from its list of disorders.

https://www.glsen.org/activity/lgbtq-history-timeline-lesson

"LGBTQ History and Why It Matters," Facing History and Ourselves, accessed October 8, 2020.

Facing History's lesson uses the materials from GLSEN's "LGBTQ History Timeline" to challenge students to consider how the way in which they learn about and conceive of historical eras can further entrench divisions in society. Students learn about important events in LGBTQ+ history and reflect upon the ways that other history resources—textbooks, for example—cover this material. Ultimately, students think about how inclusive curriculum would change the way they learn and how omissions in history education perpetuate invisibility.

https://www.facinghistory.org/educator-resources/current-events/lgbtq-history-and-why-it-matters

"Out and Affirmed," Project Look Sharp, accessed October 20, 2020.

This lesson asks students to consider not only the information they receive but also the sources disseminating it as they examine topics from the Mattachine Society to Don't Ask, Don't Tell and individuals including Anita Bryant and Matthew Shepard. "Out and Affirmed" uses sources with which students are familiar—including newspapers, websites, and advertisements—to teach this history and build the twenty-first-century skills at the center of the organization's guiding principles.

https://www.projectlooksharp.org/front_end.php?kit_id=7#

The Learning Network, "Teaching and Learning About Gay History and Issues," *New York Times*, last modified June 2016, accessed October 20, 2020.

In 2003 the *New York Times* Learning Network began creating and posting LGBTQ history lessons to its website. That year, the Learning Network, in cooperation with the Bank Street School of Education, developed lessons entitled "Family Life," "Legally Wed," and "Aesthetics of Activism: Exploring the Ways the Arts Have Responded to AIDS"; the lessons explored complex family issues, the controversy surrounding same-sex marriage, and the role of art in AIDS activism, respectively. The *Times* continued publishing lessons throughout the decade, including one that traces the evolution of gay and lesbian issues in the 1980s, 1990s, and 2000s in December 2007, a lesson entitled "The Culture Wars" in which students state their opinion in a letter on a specific gay rights issue of their choice in 2009, and a lesson evaluating the arguments for and against repealing Don't Ask, Don't Tell in 2010. Furthermore, the Learning Network's website provides additional resources and materials from the *New York Times'* archive and other sources.

https://learning.blogs.nytimes.com/2011/11/22/teaching-and-learning-about-gay-history-and-issues/

Biographical Resources (alphabetical by individual)

"James Baldwin," PBS Learning Media, accessed October 26, 2020.

This lesson challenges students to explore the "intersectionality that defined and influenced Baldwin's career." Students read Baldwin's literature and speeches and consider the ways in which his work and his life influenced American history and culture.

https://www.pbslearningmedia.org/resource/fp18-lgbtq-baldwin/james-baldwin/

"James Baldwin: Art, Sexuality, and Civil Rights," Learning for Justice, accessed March 2, 2021.

This lesson, the first in Learning for Justice's unit "The Role of Gay Men and Lesbians in the Civil Rights Movement," explores "how [his] identity shaped his art and political activism ... [and] the connections among self-identification, artistic expression, and political activism." The lesson poses the essential question, "Why is it important that history recognize Baldwin not only as a black intellectual but also as a gay man whose ideas and artistry had an impact on politics, society, and culture?"

    https://www.learningforjustice.org/classroom-resources/lessons/james-baldwin-art-sexuality-and-civil-rights

"Lorraine Hansberry: LGBT Politics and Civil Rights," Learning for Justice, accessed March 2, 2021.

This is the second lesson in Learning for Justice's unit, "The Role of Gay Men and Lesbians in the Civil Rights Movement." Lorraine Hansberry, the Pulitzer Prize-winning playwright of "A Raisin in the Sun," "masked radical black politics through the construction of seemingly unthreatening African American characters" as well as advocating for women's and LGBT rights. The lesson asks students, "What do Hansberry's writings and life illuminate about the intersections among civil rights, women's liberation, and the historic struggle for LGBT equality?"

    https://www.learningforjustice.org/classroom-resources/lessons/lorraine-hansberry-lgbt-politics-and-civil-rights

"Lorraine Hansberry," PBS Learning Media, accessed October 26, 2020.

A Raisin in the Sun, Hansberry's famous play about an African American family in Chicago in the 1950s, has been an English class staple for decades. This social studies lesson explores her life and the way that her public and private identities influenced her work and her activism.

    https://www.pbslearningmedia.org/resource/fp19.lgbtq.hansberry/lorraine-hansberry/

"Activism: Marsha P. Johnson," PBS Learning Media, accessed October 26, 2020.

PBS Learning Media uses a short documentary about Marsha P. Johnson and her role in the LGBTQ rights movement to impart the information that students need to consider the causes they support and how they might advocate for change. PBS also supplies discussion questions and organizational handouts to help students evaluate and apply what they learn.

　　https://www.pbslearningmedia.org/resource/fp18.lgbtq.marsha.p.johnson/activism-marsha-p-johnson/support-materials/

"Alain Locke," PBS Learning Media, accessed October 26, 2020.

This lesson uses a *First Person: Classroom* video, as well as primary sources and discussion questions, to introduce students to Alain Locke, his work, and his ideas. Students examine Locke's significance within the Harlem Renaissance and his relationship with other African American leaders of the time to get a sense of the person behind the work he produced.

　　https://www.pbslearningmedia.org/resource/fp20-alain-locke/alain-locke-first-person-classroom-understanding-lgbtq-identity-educators-toolkit/

"Audre Lorde," PBS Learning Media, accessed October 26, 2020.

Audre Lorde was a Black feminist lesbian and civil rights activist who, through her writing and her advocacy, addresses issues relating to race, gender, and sexuality. In this lesson, students analyze Lorde's work, delve into ideas pertaining to intersectionality, and ponder Lorde's significance to the people she fought for and represented.

　　https://www.pbslearningmedia.org/resource/fp19.lgbtq.lorde/audre-lorde/

"Pauli Murray: Fighting Jane and Jim Crow," Learning for Justice, accessed March 2, 2021.

This lesson, the third part of Learning for Justice's unit, "The Role of Gay Men and Lesbians in the Civil Rights Movement," focuses on Pauli Murray, a woman who fought to end discrimination on multiple fronts. Murray, a black woman, confronted prejudice and obstacles because of her race and her gender; she also attended Yale Law School and was an ordained Episcopal priest. Learning for

Justice's lesson asks students to evaluate the challenges she faced in the mid-twentieth century fighting "Jane and Jim Crow."

   https://www.learningforjustice.org/classroom-resources/lessons/pauli-murray-fighting-jane-and-jim-crow

"Pauli Murray," PBS Learning Media, accessed October 26, 2020.

Pauli Murray was a lawyer and activist who worked on behalf of the civil rights and women's rights movements, including as a founder of the National Organization for Women. She experienced discrimination because of her race and her sex, which compelled her to try to dismantle the systems that enabled such prejudice. Murray also questioned her gender and sexual identity. PBS Learning Media's lesson asks students, "Why is it important to acknowledge that Murray questioned her gender identity? Why does it matter?" as they consider her influence over civil rights movements and politics.

   https://ny.pbslearningmedia.org/resource/fp20-vid-pauli-murray/pauli-murray/

"Bayard Rustin: The Fight for Civil and Gay Rights," Learning for Justice, March 2, 2021.

The last lesson in Learning for Justice's unit on the gay men and lesbians in the civil rights movement is dedicated to Rustin's advocacy. It seeks, among other objectives, to illustrate that "Rustin was an instrumental figure in the modern civil rights movement," and "individuals have the ability to simultaneously advocate for multiple causes, even if they conflict or overlap." In the essential questions, the lesson characterizes Rustin as "one of the twentieth century's most important political organizers" as well as "a gay man involved in the civil rights movement."

   https://www.learningforjustice.org/classroom-resources/lessons/bayard-rustin-the-fight-for-civil-and-gay-rights

Youth in Motion, "Brother Outsider: The Life of Bayard Rustin Curriculum Guide," Frameline, 2012, accessed October 20, 2020.

Youth in Motion's curriculum guide, which accompanies the documentary *Brother Outsider: The Life of Bayard Rustin*, offers an in-depth exploration of the civil rights movement of which Rustin was a significant part, includes guidelines on facilitating conversations on LGBTQ issues, encountering and responding to homophobia in schools and communities, and the use of art and media to create social change.

http://rustin.org/wp-content/uploads/Discussion%20Guide%20-%20 Brother%20Outsider.pdf

Leslea Newman, GLSEN, The Matthew Shepard Foundation, and Candlewick Press, "He Continues to Make a Difference: Commemorating the Life of Matthew Shepard," GLSEN, 2014, accessed October 20, 2020.

In this lesson, the authors' goal is to increase awareness and sensitivity and reduce incidents of bullying. "He Continues to Make a Difference," the foundation of which is a recent historical event, offers a variety of options for teachers in different disciplines to use in their classrooms; the curriculum guide includes deconstructing and analyzing the poem "October Mourning: A Song for Matthew Shepard" as well as social studies questions contextualizing the events surrounding and implications of Matthew Shepard's murder.

https://www.glsen.org/activity/ela-and-history-resource-matthew-shepard-grades-9-12

"Matthew Shepard and James Byrd, Jr. Hate Crimes Prevention Act," Anti-Defamation League, accessed October 20, 2020.

This lesson examines hate crimes, in general, and the circumstances surrounding Shepard's and Byrd's deaths, specifically. According to the ADL, "this lesson provides an opportunity for … students to understand the Matthew Shepard and James Byrd, Jr. Hate Crimes Prevention Act, learn about how hate escalates, connect the understanding of the escalation of hate with [their] murders and consider what young people can do … to prevent hate crimes."

https://www.adl.org/education/educator-resources/lesson-plans/ matthew-shepard-and-james-byrd-jr-hate-crimes-prevention

"Alan Turing: True to Himself," GLSEN, 2015, accessed October 20, 2020.

This lesson asks students to consider choices they've made and stances they've taken in light of what they learn about Turing's life, as well as examining Turing's work during the Second World War and the impact of his sexuality on his life subsequently. The lesson asks students to think about historical figures' identities and encourages teachers to draw comparisons between Turing's treatment and the way in which LGBT individuals were targeted under McCarthyism.

https://www.glsen.org/activity/alan-turing-true-himself

"We'Wha," PBS Learning Media, accessed October 26, 2020.

We'Wha was a Zuni lhamana (nonbinary person) who traveled to Washington, DC, in the late 1800s where she demonstrated Zuni practices and met President McKinley and other government officials. In this material culture lesson students learn about and evaluate the impact of her life and interaction, set against the backdrop of concurrent military action against indigenous people in the West. Students examine a bowl We'Wha created which is now on display at the Smithsonian Institute and consider what they might learn about We'Wha and her life through an item she produced.

https://www.pbslearningmedia.org/resource/fp20-we-wha/wewha-first-person-classroom/

"Unheard Voices: Stories and Lessons for Grades 6–12," GLSEN, 2011, accessed October 20, 2020.

"Unheard Voices," a collaboration between GLSEN, the ADL, and StoryCorps, is one of the largest LGBTQ curriculum projects to date. It was published in 2011 and is based on oral histories conducted with "individuals who bore witness to or helped shape LGBT history in some way." The information from these interviews comprises the foundation of lessons exploring the AIDS epidemic, Don't Ask, Don't Tell, LGBT family rights, and the twentieth-century homophile movement, among other topics. The lessons also include supplementary materials to support the oral histories. "Unheard Voices" uses individuals' experiences to make history relevant and help it resonate with students. Though the lessons in

"Unheard Voices" focus on specific events and issues, the curriculum as a whole is comprehensive, covering more than fifty years of history.

https://www.glsen.org/unheardvoices.html
https://www.adl.org/media/4699/download

ADL, GLSEN, and StoryCorps, "In-Group, Out-Group: The Exclusion of LGBT People from Societal Institutions," GLSEN, 2011, accessed October 20, 2020.

This collaboratively developed resource, part of the Unheard Voices curriculum, investigates the inclusion and exclusion of certain groups in public life and the role of fear and prejudice in this ostracism. The goal of the lesson, ultimately, is for students to "increase their awareness about the ways in which LGBT people are currently included/excluded from societal institutions."

https://www.glsen.org/sites/default/files/UV%20Lessons.pdf

Topics in LGBTQ+ History

The Lavender Scare

"The Lavender Scare," Berkeley History-Social Science Project, 2013, accessed October 20, 2020.

This lesson, created for eleventh-grade US history classes to facilitate compliance with California's FAIR Education Act, asks students to consider the plight of and discrimination against the LGBTQ population during the McCarthy era. Students study the Cold War and the rise of McCarthy, the presence of gay and lesbian individuals in the government, and the way in which the atmosphere of the time led to shifting perspectives on and the criminalization of LGBTQ individuals.

http://ucbhssp.berkeley.edu/content/lavender-scare

The Stonewall Riots

Bay Breeze Educational Resources, "Stonewall and Beyond: Gay and Lesbian Issues," Thirteen ed online, 2011, accessed October 20, 2020.

This unit is dedicated to evaluating anti-gay bias and media representations of the LGBTQ community; students are prompted to evaluate the biases they witness, as well as those that they personally hold. Students study the Stonewall riots on the second day of the unit as a means of contextualizing the progress, or lack thereof, made by the gay rights movement since that time. Among the unit's objectives, authors state that students will "develop an understanding of how bias and negative stereotypes affect the civil rights of gays and lesbians."
    https://www.thirteen.org/edonline/lessons/stonewall/

"Stonewall Riots," Stanford History Education Group, accessed October 20, 2020.

In this lesson, students analyze the causes of the Stonewall riots on June 28, 1969. In doing so, they evaluate events and activism that preceded the riots including the Lavender Scare and marches in Philadelphia and Washington, DC. Students also evaluate Stonewall's impact and context in the twenty-first century.
    https://sheg.stanford.edu/history-lessons/stonewall-riots

"The LGBTQ Movement and the Stonewall Riots," PBS Learning Media, accessed October 26, 2020.

In this lesson, students learn about the LGBTQ movement in the mid-twentieth century and the causes and effects of the Stonewall riots in 1969. The lesson starts with videos that provide information on these topics, after which students look more deeply at important figures in the LGBTQ movement and the factors that made the Stonewall riots effective.
    https://www.pbslearningmedia.org/resource/fp18-socst-lgbtq-stonewall/the-lgbtq-movement-and-stonewall-riot/

"The Stonewall Uprising," Anti-Defamation League, accessed October 26, 2020.

This lesson positions Stonewall as "the beginning of the organized gay rights movement" and challenges students to "reflect on LGBTQ rights and activism prior to and after Stonewall." Students learn to query the differences between an uprising and a riot and determine which term they would apply to Stonewall.

Students also contextualize Stonewall within the activism that led to and followed it.

https://www.adl.org/education/educator-resources/lesson-plans/the-stonewall-uprising

LGBTQ Rights Movement

"LGBTQ Civil Rights," ONE Archives, accessed October 9, 2020.

In this intersectional lesson, students consider the ways in which LGBTQ individuals in "racial minority communities" endured greater discrimination than others as well as the ways in which the civil rights movement failed to include LGBTQ rights as one of its goals. Using primary sources from ONE Archives' collection, students investigate the ways in which social justice movements in the 1970s and 1980s overlapped and existed separately from each other.

https://www.onearchives.org/wp-content/uploads/2019/02/one-archives-foundation-civil-rights.pdf

"LGBTQ Equality, 1950–1970," ONE Archives, accessed October 9, 2020.

In this lesson, students learn about the LGBTQ movement in the mid-twentieth century, including organizations like the Mattachine Society, Daughters of Bilitis, and the Gay Liberation Front. Students also analyze primary sources from these organizations and other LGBTQ publications from the 1950s, 1960s, and 1970s. Ultimately, students engage in a role play activity in which they represent these organizations and their goals. At the end of the lesson students should be able to answer the inquiry question, "How did the movement for LGBT equality go from assimilation to 'coming out' in the 1950s-1970s?"

https://www.onearchives.org/wp-content/uploads/2019/02/one-archives-foundation-coming-out.pdf

Same-Sex Marriage

"I Now Pronounce You ... Same Sex Marriage Legislation," Human Rights Resource Center, 2000, accessed October 20, 2020.

Created after Vermont became the first state to legalize civil unions in 2000, this lesson invokes the Universal Declaration of Human Rights to contextualize marriage equality within "international humanitarian standards"; it also draws parallels to the idea of separate but equal that permeated American culture and discourse for a century and asks students to apply this concept to the same sex marriage debate.

http://www1.umn.edu/humanrts/edumat/hreduseries/TB3/act6/act6f.html

"Winning the Right to Marry: Historic Parallels," Anti-Defamation League, 2010, accessed October 20, 2020.

This lesson reviews evolving marriage laws including Jim Crow era restrictions and the Defense of Marriage Act (1996) as well as "past injustices within the institution of marriage" to "analyze existing federal and state laws concerning same-sex marriage and consider whether or not [those] laws are in need of change." Students also consider the plight of an individual affected by restrictive marriage laws.

https://www.adl.org/media/6790/download

"Wedding Cake, Same Sex Marriage, and Discrimination," Anti-Defamation League, accessed October 20, 2020.

This lesson provides students with the opportunity to consider constitutional and LGBTQ rights issues through a study of the *Masterpiece Cake Shop* case on which the Supreme Court ruled in 2018; the lesson "provides an opportunity for students to learn more about this important case and its related constitutional principles, to reflect on their own opinions and the views of others, and to explore different points of view about the case in order to write an opinion essay of their own."

https://www.adl.org/media/10779/download

AIDS

"AIDS and HIV Activism," ONE Archives, accessed October 8, 2020.

In this lesson students evaluate events related and the government's response to the AIDS epidemic in the 1980s. They discuss the LGBT community's reaction to the government's, and other major institutions', apathy and the activism that their anger inspired. Students specifically consider ACT-UP/LA in their study of AIDS-focused advocacy.

https://www.onearchives.org/wp-content/uploads/2019/02/one-archives-foundation-los-angeles-aids-crisis.pdf

Civil Rights and Human Rights Lessons

"Debating Tolerance in a New Democracy: A Role Play," Human Rights Resource Center, 2000, accessed October 20, 2020.

"Debating Tolerance in a New Democracy" requires students to "stage a parliamentary committee hearing in the newly independent Eastern European country of Boldovistan." This lesson, developed in 2000 at a time when many Eastern European nations were defining their identities, integrates important world events and attitudes into a discussion of legal consensual relations.

http://hrlibrary.umn.edu/edumat/hreduseries/TB3/act4/act4f.html

"Rights Abuses around the World," Human Rights Resource Center, 2000, accessed October 20, 2020.

In this lesson, the Human Rights Resource Center provides students with information on the difficulties gay and lesbian citizens of Romania faced as of 2000, using these facts to compel students to "develop and implement appropriate strategies for addressing human rights abuses in the world." Moreover, an examination of the Universal Declaration of Human Rights asks students to compare the promises in that document with LGBT rights as of 2000.

http://hrlibrary.umn.edu/edumat/hreduseries/TB3/act8/act8f.html

Jack Bareilles, "Women, Gays, and Other Voices of Resistance," in
***Voices of a People's History of the United States: Teacher's Guide*, ed.**
Gayle Olson-Raymer (New York: Seven Stores Press, 2005), 235–46.

This unit from the Zinn Education Project, which works to "introduce students to a more accurate, complex, and engaging understanding of United States history than is found in traditional textbooks and curricula" includes a document on Stonewall by Martin Duberman and accompanying questions in this unit, a study of the sixties that goes beyond civil rights to examine the "general revolt in the culture against oppressive, artificial, previously unquestioned ways of living."

   https://www.zinnedproject.org/materials/women-gays-and-other-voices-of-resistance/

Notes

Foreword

1 See Blanche Wiesen Cook, "The Historical Denial of Lesbianism," *Radical History Review* (Spring/ Summer, 1979), 62–3; Blanche Wiesen Cook, *Eleanor Roosevelt, Volume 1, The Early Years, 1884–1933* (New York: Viking, 1992), 479; Robert Cohen, "Out of the Closet and Into History? The Eleanor Roosevelt-Lorena Hickok Affair," *Reviews in American History* (June 2017), 314–22.

2 One sign of this shift from bigotry to dignity appeared in the *New York Times* on the day we wrote this foreword. The *Times* story told of the homophobic denial of a varsity letter to a New Jersey high school distance runner in 1958 and its aftermath. That athlete, Tom Ammiano, would go on to become a California State Assemblyman and gay rights leader in San Francisco, who would sponsor California's FAIR Education Act (see Chapter 6), which mandated including LGBTQ+ history in K–12 social studies classes. Sixty-three years after Ammiano's graduation, his New Jersey high school finally acted to reverse its discriminatory act, notifying Ammiano that he would be awarded the varsity letter he had earned in his youth (Carol Pogash, "He Won a Varsity Letter at 16. He Finally Got It When He Was 79," *New York Times*, February 28, 2021).

Introduction

1 In 1981, the CDC reported on an illness affecting homosexual men. The disease, spread through intercourse, breastfeeding, and intravenous drug use, came to be known as Acquired Immune Deficiency Syndrome (AIDS); homosexual men were among the groups hit hardest by it. In 1987, after years of government apathy and pharmaceutical price gauging, ACT UP formed to advocate for AIDS patients with the entities whose recognition and assistance they needed to fight and learn more about this disease.

2 The terminology used to identify the population now referred to as LGBTQ+ (or some variation thereof) has evolved since the middle of the twentieth century. Previously referred to clinically as "homosexuals," those who identified as such adopted the term "gay" in the late 1950s and early 1960s. Women, who felt excluded

from an identification that they believed largely applied to men, adopted the term "lesbian" in the 1960s and 1970s. The acronym LGBT first appeared in the late 1980s and was intended to include bisexuals and transgender individuals, groups theretofore marginalized in the gay community. The acronym has evolved and expanded over time. This book uses LGBT (lesbian, gay, bisexual, transgender), LGBTQ (lesbian, gay, bisexual, transgender, queer), and LGBTQ+. More recent iterations expand to LGBTQQIIAA+ (lesbian, gay, bisexual, transgender, queer, questioning, intersex, intergender, asexual, ally, and beyond). Though sections of this narrative refer to eras before the adoption of these acronyms, it is an impartial and current method of identifying this community and is therefore used throughout.

3 David France, interview with the author, September 16, 2013, Brooklyn, NY, tape/notes/transcript in the author's possession.

4 Ibid.

5 Robert Cohen, conversation with the author, May 2013, New York, notes in the author's possession.

6 See, for example, Robert Cohen, " 'Two, Four, Six, Eight, We Don't Want to Integrate': White Student Attitudes Toward the University of Georgia's Desegregation," *Georgia Historical Quarterly* 80, no. 3 (Fall 1996): 616–45; Robert Cohen, *Freedom's Orator: Mario Savio and the Radical Legacy of the 1960s* (New York: Oxford University Press, 2009); Robert Cohen and David J. Snyder, eds., *Rebellion in Black and White: Southern Student Activism in the 1960s* (Baltimore: Johns Hopkins University Press, 2013).

7 I taught this unit at a large Brooklyn high school to four different Participation in Government classes over the course of a week. Each class met four times.

8 George Chauncey, *Why Marriage?: The History Shaping Today's Debate over Gay Equality* (New York: Basic Books, 2005), 95.

9 California's Proposition 8, a ballot referendum that passed in November 2008, amended the state constitution to ban same-sex marriage. Its passage heightened a simmering debate about the legality and morality of same-sex marriage nationwide. See Chapter 6 for more detail.

10 "Attitudes on Same-Sex Marriage," Pew Research Center, May 14, 2019, https://www.pewforum.org/fact-sheet/changing-attitudes-on-gay-marriage/; Justin McCarthy, "Record High 60% of Americans Support Same-Sex Marriage," Gallup, May 19, 2015, https://news.gallup.com/poll/183272/record-high-americans-support-sex-marriage.aspx.

11 Supreme Court of the United States, "*Lawrence v. Texas* (02-102)," Legal Information Institute, June 26, 2003, https://www.law.cornell.edu/supct/html/02-102.ZO.html.

12 "Inaugural Address by President Barack Obama," The White House, January 21, 2013, https://obamawhitehouse.archives.gov/the-press-office/2013/01/21/ inaugural-address-president-barack-obama.

13 The act was repealed one year later.

14 Tal Kopan and Eugene Scott, "North Carolina Governor Signs Controversial Transgender Bill," CNN, March 24, 2016, https://www.cnn.com/2016/03/23/politics/ north-carolina-gender-bathrooms-bill/index.html.

15 Adam Liptak, "In Narrow Decision, Supreme Court Sides With Baker Who Turned Away Gay Couple," *New York Times*, June 4, 2018, https://www.nytimes. com/2018/06/04/us/politics/supreme-court-sides-with-baker-who-turned-away-gay-couple.html.

16 Dave Philipps, "New Rule for Transgender Troops: Stick to Your Birth Sex, Or Leave," *New York Times*, March 13, 2019, https://www.nytimes.com/2019/03/13/us/ transgender-troops-ban.html.

17 President Joe Biden overturned that ban with a January 2021 Executive Order that "immediately prohibit[ed] any service member from being forced out of the military on the basis of gender identity." (Lolita C. Baldor and Zeke Miller, "Biden Reverses Trump Ban on Transgender People in Military," AP News, January 25, 2021, https://apnews.com/article/biden-reverse-ban-transgender-military-f0ace4f98 66e0ca0df021eba75b3af20).

18 Talya Minsberg, "'Boys Are Boys and Girls Are Girls': Idaho Is First State to Bar Some Transgender Athletes," *New York Times*, April 1, 2020, https://www.nytimes. com/2020/04/01/sports/transgender-idaho-ban-sports.html. The state also banned transgender individuals from amending their birth certificates to reflect their gender identity.

19 Gloria T. Alter, "LGBTQ+ Issues in Social Education: Understanding, Inclusion, and Advocacy," *Social Education* 81, no. 5 (2017): 277–8.

20 Keith C. Barton and Linda S. Levstik, *Teaching History for the Common Good* (New York: Routledge, 2004); Marilynne Boyle-Baise and Carl A. Grant, "Citizen/ Community Participation in Education," in *Critical Issues in Social Studies TeacherEeducation*, ed. Susan Adler (Greenwich, CT: Information Age, 2004), 145–64; David Kobrin, *Beyond the Textbook: Teaching History Using Documents and Primary Sources* (Portsmouth, NH: Heinemann, 1996); Gloria Ladson-Billings, "Crafting a Culturally Relevant Social Studies Approach," in *The Social Studies Curriculum: Purposes, Problems, and Possibilities*, ed. E. Ross (Albany, NY: SUNY Press, 2001), Chapter 10.

21 Stephen Thornton, *Teaching Social Studies That Matters: Curriculum for Active Learning* (New York: Teachers College, 2005).

22 Though the terms social studies and history are often used interchangeably, they have different pedagogical meanings. History education, as defined by the

American Historical Association in 1899, focuses on strict historical learning. Social studies, meanwhile, encompasses a wider lens of study including, but not limited to, history, geography, civics, and economics. Though history is a part of social studies, its importance is weighted equally with the discipline's other components. The following chapters focus on historical learning and US history classes, but because US history classes are part of a larger course of social studies learning in high schools around the country, they consider social studies literature, resources, and pedagogy and the philosophy behind the discipline, as well.

23 Unless otherwise noted, the information and analysis in this book refers to high school classes.

24 Geneva Gay, "Social Studies Teacher Education for Urban Classrooms," in *Critical Issues in Social Studies Teacher Education*, ed. Susan Adler (Greenwich, CT: Information Age, 2004), 75–96.

25 John D'Emilio and Estelle B. Freedman, *Intimate Matters: A History of Sexuality in America* (Chicago: University of Chicago Press, 2012). D'Emilio is the former chair of the Committee on LGBT History.

26 Stuart Biegel, *The Right to Be Out* (Minneapolis: University of Minnesota Press, 2010).

27 David Campos, "Battling the Bullying of LGBTQ+ Students," *Social Education* 81, no. 3 (October 2017): 288–95.

28 Kevin Jennings, interview with the author, January 3, 2018, Brooklyn, NY, tape/notes/transcript in the author's possession.

29 Don Romesburg, interview with the author, May 30, 2018, Brooklyn, NY, tape/notes/transcript in the author's possession.

30 Stephen Thornton, interview with the author, June 24, 2014, New York, tape/notes/transcript in the author's possession.

31 Lyndsey Schlax, interview with the author, January 12, 2017, Brooklyn, NY, tape/notes/transcript in the author's possession.

1 Making History: The LGBTQ+ Movement's Evolving Struggle for Acknowledgment and Inclusivity

1 Patricia A. Cain, "Litigating for Lesbian and Gay Rights: A Legal History," *Virginia Law Review* 79, no. 7 (October 1993): 1551–641.

2 Craig Kaczorowski, "Mattachine Society," GLBTQ archive, accessed March 19, 2018, http://www.glbtqarchive.com/ssh/mattachine_society_S.pdf.

3 Elizabeth A. Armstrong and Suzanna M. Crage, "Movements and Memory: The Making of the Stonewall Myth," *American Sociological Review* 71, no. 5 (October

2006): 724–51; Timothy Stewart-Winter, "Queer Law and Order: Sex, Criminality, and Policing in the Late Twentieth-Century United States," *Journal of American History* 102, no. 1 (June 2015): 61–72.

4 "Our Story," PFLAG, accessed March 16, 2018, https://www.pflag.org/our-story.

5 Ibid.

6 Lambda Legal began in 1973 as "a band of volunteer lawyers struggling to break new ground for LGBT people in the American justice system"; it uses the court system to win rights and recognition for the LGBTQ+ community. The National LGBTQ+ Task Force was founded in 1973 to fight legal barriers to opportunity and equality. The National Center for Lesbian Rights began in 1977 as "a national legal organization committed to advancing the civil and human rights of lesbian, gay, bisexual, and transgender people and their families through litigation, legislation, policy, and public education." Lastly, the Human Rights Campaign is a political action committee founded in 1980 to promote LGBTQ+ equality. "Lambda Legal History," Lambda Legal, accessed March 16, 2018, https://www.lambdalegal.org/about-us/history; "About: Mission and History," National LGBTQ+ Task Force, accessed March 16, 2018, http://www.thetaskforce.org/about/mission-history.html; "Mission and History," National Center for Lesbian Rights, accessed March 16, 2018, http://www.nclrights.org/about-us/mission-history/; "HRC Story: Mission Statement," Human Rights Campaign, accessed March 16, 2018, http://www.hrc.org/hrc-story/mission-statement.

7 Mark Z. Barabak, "Gays May Have the Fastest of All Civil Rights Movements," *Los Angeles Times*, last modified May 20, 2012, http://articles.latimes.com/2012/may/20/nation/la-na-gay-rights-movement-20120521.

8 "Lambda Legal History," Lambda Legal.

9 Ibid.

10 "About: Mission and History," National LGBTQ+ Task Force.

11 "ACT UP Accomplishments and Partial Chronology," ACT UP, accessed March 16, 2018, https://endaids.actupny.com/the-community.

12 Curriculum change is a slow process regardless of the subject matter. Other reform movements' achievements, which most states include in their standards in the twenty-first century, met with resistance when textbook publishers first began including this information in their resources. There was, though, more of a push among advocates to include this information in the curriculum. Jonathan Zimmerman, "Where the Customer Is King: The Textbook in American Culture," in *A History of the Book in America, Volume 5: The Enduring Book: Print Culture in Postwar America*, eds. David Paul Nord, Joan Shelley Rubin, and Michael Schudson (Chapel Hill: University of North Carolina Press, 2009), 304–24.

13 "Gay Liberation Front: Manifesto," Fordham University, accessed January 18, 2019, https://sourcebooks.fordham.edu/pwh/glf-london.asp.

14 "About Mission and History," National LGBTQ+ Task Force.

15 "HRC Story: HRC Foundation," Human Rights Campaign, accessed March 16, 2018, https://www.hrc.org/hrc-story/hrc-foundation.

16 Clifford Rosky, "Anti Gay Curriculum Laws," *Columbia Law Review* 117, no. 6 (October 2017): 1478.

17 Jay Clarke, "Gay Rights Fight Shaping Up in Miami," *Washington Post*, March 27, 1977, https://www.washingtonpost.com/archive/politics/1977/03/27/gay-rights-fight-shaping-up-in-miami/e4f596c1-f8e0-4785-b528-599077a478ba/?utm_term=.04a11f177c6e.

18 Ibid.

19 Stuart Hinds, "Anita Bryant: Hate Monger Descends on Kansas City," *Phoenix Newsletter*, October/November 2015, https://library.umkc.edu/content/images/glama/timeline/1977-bryant.pdf.

20 Rosky, "Anti Gay Curriculum Laws."

21 Ibid., 1479.

22 Ibid., 1480.

23 Ibid., 1477.

24 Kevin Jennings, interview with the author, January 3, 2018, Brooklyn, NY, tape/notes/transcript in the author's possession. This is a significant difference between the gay rights movement and the African American Civil Rights Movement in the mid-twentieth century. In the latter, children and young adults participated in protests and marches, most famously in Birmingham in 1963. The African American Civil Rights Movement also made school desegregation a central issue. Early gay rights organizations like the Mattachine Society and the Gay Liberation Front prioritized legislation and discriminatory practices that targeted adults.

25 NCLR Annual Report 2016–17, National Center for Lesbian Rights, accessed March 16, 2018, http://www.nclrights.org/wp-content/uploads/2017/12/NCL17CA-AR-Web-Version-No-Donors.pdf. The Utah law, which was successfully repealed in 2017, was one of those passed in the wake of "Save Our Children."

26 "Cultivating Respect: Safe Schools for All," PFLAG, accessed March 16, 2018, https://www.pflag.org/cultivating-respect-safe-schools-all. PFLAG received a grant from Suburu in 2017 to update this program's materials.

27 "Creating Safe and Welcoming Schools For All Children & Families," Welcoming Schools, accessed March 16, 2018, http://www.welcomingschools.org.

28 Kevin Jennings, interview with the author, January 3, 2018, Brooklyn, NY, tape/notes/transcript in the author's possession.

29 Ibid.

30 Ibid.

31 Ibid.

32 Jennings asserted that there is a connection between GLSEN's emerging success and the increase in GSAs. In response to a question about proof of GLSEN's early success, he replied, "The rapid spread of Gay Straight Alliances and things like that." Kevin Jennings, interview with the author, January 3, 2018, Brooklyn, NY, tape/notes/transcript in the author's possession.

33 "History and Accomplishments," GSA Network, accessed March 28, 2018, https://gsanetwork.org/about-us/history.

34 Ibid. The type of support system does not exist in the same cohesive way for curriculum development, but the success of GSA offers proof of its necessity and effectiveness.

35 "Read, Watch, Collaborate: GLSEN PD for Educators," GLSEN, accessed April 13, 2018, https://www.glsen.org/educate/professional-development.

36 "Our Approach," GSA Network, accessed March 28, 2018, https://gsanetwork.org/about-us.

37 Kevin Jennings, interview with the author, January 3, 2018, Brooklyn, NY, tape/notes/transcript in the author's possession.

38 Ibid. Jennings stated, "Virtually every major LGBT organization I can think of has some kind of program dealing with schools now."

39 "Staff," Our Family Coalition, accessed April 20, 2018, http://www.ourfamily.org/about/our-staff; "Welcoming and Inclusive Schools Program," Our Family Coalition, accessed April 18, 2018, www.ourfamily.org/schools/wisp.

40 "Time to Thrive," Human Rights Campaign, 2018, accessed April 20, 2018, timetothrive.org.

41 Learning for Justice was founded as Teaching Tolerance. The organization changed its name in 2021, stating, "The fact is, tolerance is not justice. It isn't a sufficient description of the work we do or of the world we want." (Jalaya Liles Dunn, "Our New Name: Learning for Justice," Learning for Justice, February 3, 2021, https://www.learningforjustice.org/magazine/our-new-name-learning-for-justice.)

42 "Program History," Welcoming Schools, accessed April 18, 2018, http://www.welcomingschools.org/our-program/history/.

43 This number changes as Learning for Justice creates new resources and changes the content on its website. The number sixty-seven is accurate as of March 2021. Twenty-nine of those lessons are for high school social studies, history, and civics classes.

44 "Lessons," Learning for Justice, accessed March 3, 2021, https://www.learningforjustice.org/classroom-resources/lessons?keyword=&field_topic%5B6%5D=6.

45 Kisha Webster, interview with the author, July 8, 2015, Brooklyn, NY, tape/notes/transcript in the author's possession.

46 Steven Lee Myers, "Ideas & Trends; How a 'Rainbow Curriculum' Turned into Fighting Words," *New York Times*, December 13, 1992, accessed April 24, 2018, https://www.nytimes.com/1992/12/13/weekinreview/ideas-trends-how-a-rainbow-curriculum-turned-into-fighting-words.html.

47 Ibid.

48 Josh Barbanel, "Under 'Rainbow,' a War: When Politics, Morals and Learning Mix," *New York Times*, December 27, 1992, accessed April 24, 2018, https://www.nytimes.com/1992/12/27/nyregion/under-rainbow-a-war-when-politics-morals-and-learning-mix.html.

49 Lally Weymouth, "Mrs. Cummins's Triumph," *Washington Post*, January 8, 1993, accessed April 25, 2018, https://www.washingtonpost.com/archive/opinions/1993/01/08/mrs-cumminss-triumph/4b23129f-a0e3-49ed-a11c-64e473b45d09/?utm_term=.1f338993de2e.

50 Ibid.

51 Myers, "Ideas & Trends," *New York Times*.

52 Joseph A. Fernandez with John Underwood, *Tales Out of School: Joseph Fernandez's Crusade to Rescue American Education* (Boston: Little, Brown, 1993), 239.

53 "The Rainbow, Revised," *New York Times*, January 30, 1993, accessed April 24, 2018, https://www.nytimes.com/1993/01/30/opinion/the-rainbow-revised.html.

54 George Will, "Just Another Kind of Love," *Washington Post*, December 6, 1992, accessed April 25, 2018, https://www.washingtonpost.com/archive/opinions/1992/12/06/just-another-kind-of-love/42ef9eca-5f3b-4bf2-9a6c-780b8bb14ecc/?utm_term=.80b0e305c59b.

55 Peter Schmidt, "N.Y.C. Debate over 'Rainbow' Curriculum Still Raging in Many Board Races," *Education Week*, March 24, 1993, accessed April 24, 2018, https://www.edweek.org/ew/articles/1993/03/24/26board.h12.html.

56 Myers, "Ideas & Trends," *New York Times*.

57 Kevin Jennings, interview with the author, January 3, 2018, Brooklyn, NY, tape/notes/transcript in the author's possession.

58 William Celis III, "Schools Across U.S. Cautiously Adding Lessons on Gay Life," *New York Times*, January 6, 1993, https://www.nytimes.com/1993/01/06/us/schools-across-us-cautiously-adding-lessons-on-gay-life.html.

59 "LGBT History Month: Rodney Wilson," Pride Center of Vermont, October 31, 2017, http://www.pridecentervt.org/news/item/lgbt-history-month-rodney-wilson.

60 Rodney Wilson, "Knowing LGBT History Is Knowing Yourself," *The Advocate*, October 1, 2015, https://www.advocate.com/commentary/2015/10/01/knowing-lgbt-history-knowing-yourself.

61 Ibid. Although June was already established as LGBT Pride Month, the founders of LGBT History Month intended to differentiate their educational movement from

the celebration of LGBT identity. They chose October because October 11 was already designated as Coming Out Day.

62 Kevin Jennings, interview with the author, July 25, 2018, Brooklyn, NY, tape/notes/ transcript in the author's possession.

63 Original LGBT History Month Committee Members, "Op-ed: The Story Behind the First LGBT History Month," *The Advocate*, September 2, 2015, https://www. advocate.com/commentary/2015/09/02/op-ed-story-behind-first-lgbt-history- month.

64 Kevin Jennings, interview with the author, July 25, 2018, Brooklyn, NY, tape/notes/ transcript in the author's possession.

65 "Lesbian, Gay, Bisexual, Transgender Pride Month: About," Library of Congress, accessed July 30, 2018, https://www.loc.gov/lgbt-pride-month/about/.

66 Kevin Jennings stated that he believes that LGBT History Month was important for promoting the idea that LGBT history had a place in students' education. Although he asserted that this history should be taught throughout the year and not just within the confines of this month, the establishment of a commemorative month and the positive reception it received was meaningful. (Kevin Jennings, interview with the author, July 25, 2018, Brooklyn, NY, tape/notes/transcript in the author's possession.)

67 Original LGBT History Month Committee Members, "Op-ed: The Story Behind the First LGBT History Month."

68 Ibid.

69 Wilson, "Knowing LGBT History Is Knowing Yourself."

70 Kari Hudnell, "GLSEN Statement on the Start of LGBT History Month," GLSEN, October 1, 2015, https://www.glsen.org/article/glsen-statement-start-lgbt-history- month.

71 Maria Newman, "Board Adopts a Curriculum About AIDS," *New York Times*, January 19, 1995, accessed April 25, 2018, https://www.nytimes.com/1995/01/19/ nyregion/board-adopts-a-curriculum-about-aids.html.

72 "About," Illinois Family Institute, accessed July 30, 2018, https://illinoisfamily.org/ about/.

73 Laurie Higgins, "Back to School: Teachers Who Exploit Their Position," Illinois Family Institute, August 13, 2013, https://illinoisfamily.org/education/ back-to-school-teachers-who-exploit-their-position/.

74 Barbara Anderson, "Clips from a Minnesota Child Protection League Presentation," presentation, Southwest Metro Tea Party, November 18, 2013, https://www.youtube. com/watch?v=vFIxKtcaOJA.

75 "About," Focus on the Family, accessed July 30, 2018, https://www.focusonthefamily. com/about.

76 "Capturing Children's Minds," True Tolerance—a Project of Focus on the Family, accessed July 30, 2018, https://www.truetolerance.org/2011/capturing-childrens-minds/.

77 Peter Sprigg, "Homosexuality in Your Child's School," Family Research Council, 2006, https://downloads.frc.org/EF/EF06K26.pdf.

78 Kevin Jennings, interview with the author, January 3, 2018, Brooklyn, NY, tape/notes/transcript in the author's possession.

79 John D'Emilio, email interview with author, July 16, 2016, Brooklyn, NY, digital files/notes in the author's possession. D'Emilio is the author of *Sexual Politics, Sexual Communities: The Making of a Homosexual Minority in the United States* and a former professor at University of Illinois, Chicago.

80 Kisha Webster, interview with the author, July 8, 2015, Brooklyn, NY, tape/notes/transcript in the author's possession.

81 Emily Hobson, interview with the author, June 8, 2016, Brooklyn, NY, tape/notes/transcript in the author's possession; Kevin Jennings, interview with the author, January 3, 2018, Brooklyn, NY, tape/notes/transcript in the author's possession.

2 Building a Model: LGBTQ+ History and Higher Education

1 "The History of LGBTS at Yale," Yale University Lesbian, Gay, Bisexual, and Transgender Studies, accessed April 15, 2018, https://lgbts.yale.edu/history-lgbts-yale.

2 "LGBT Studies," Hobart and William Smith Colleges, accessed April 24, 2018, http://www.hws.edu/academics/lgbt/history.aspx.

3 Toni McNaron, *Poisoned Ivy: Lesbian and Gay Academics Confronting Homophobia* (Philadelphia: Temple University Press, 1996).

4 UCLA psychologist Evelyn Hooker's work on gay men's psychological health led to homosexuality's removal from the DSM IV as a psychiatric disorder and UCLA doctors performed some of the first gender reassignment surgeries.

5 "History," UCLA Lesbian, Gay, Bisexual, Transgender, and Queer Studies, accessed April 15, 2018, https://lgbtqstudies.ucla.edu/about/history/.

6 Ibid.

7 "The History of LGBTS at Yale," Yale University Lesbian, Gay, Bisexual, and Transgender Studies.

8 "About CLAGS," CLAGS Center for LGBTQ+ Studies, accessed April 23, 2018, clags.org/about-clags/.

9 John D'Emilio, interview with the author, July 7, 2016, Brooklyn, NY, tape/notes/transcript in the author's possession; Emily Hobson, interview with the author, June 8, 2016, Brooklyn, NY, tape/notes/transcript in the author's possession.

10 Among those not mentioned are Kent State University, Webster College, Indiana University of Pennsylvania, Cornell University, and several schools in the University of California system. In addition, UMass Amherst collaborates with Mount Holyoke College, Smith College, Amherst College, and Hampshire College on a Five-College Queer and Sexuality Studies course. This list is not exhaustive.

11 Lists on this topic are inconclusive, with different institutions included in different compilations. Moreover, the number of universities offering this minor changes each year; available lists might not be updated as often as necessary. There were more than thirty colleges and universities offering LGBT studies minors at the time of this writing.

12 "The History of LGBT Studies at Maryland," University of Maryland, accessed June 16, 2014, http://www.lgbts.umd/edu/lgbthistory.html.

13 Ibid.

14 The program lists fifty-two courses in its course descriptions. Sixteen courses counting toward the LGBT studies minor and certificate were offered in the fall 2020 semester. "Department of Women's Studies," University of Maryland, accessed October 1, 2020, http://wmst.umd.edu/academics/courses; "Fall 2020 WMST, LGBT, & Black WMST Undergraduate Courses, Department of Women's Studies," University of Maryland, accessed October 1, 2020, http://wmst.umd.edu/academics/courses.

15 "LGBT Studies: History," Hobart and William Smith Colleges, accessed April 24, 2018, http://www.hws.edu/academics/lgbt/history.aspx.

16 Ibid.

17 San Diego State University was the second institution to offer this major in 2012. "Lesbian, Gay, Bisexual and Transgender Studies | What Can I Do with This Major?," San Diego State University, accessed April 24, 2018, https://go.sdsu. edu/student_affairs/career/lesbiangaybisexualtransgender.aspx. City College of San Francisco became the first community college to offer this major in 2012, as well. "Lesbian, Gay, Bisexual and Transgender Studies AA Major—Active," City College of San Francisco, accessed April 24, 2108, http://www.ccsf.edu/dam/ccsf/documents/OfficeOfInstruction/Catalog/Programs/LesbianGayBisexualandTransgenderStudies/LesbianGayBisexualandTransgenderStudiesMajor.pdf.

18 "Lesbian, Gay, Bisexual and Transgender Studies AA Major—Active," City College of San Francisco, accessed October 1, 2020, https://ccsf.curricunet.com/Report/GetReport?entityId=1137&entityType=Program&reportId=29. Among these courses is a history course entitled "LGBT American History." The course description states, "Survey of the origins, development, and current status of the Lesbian, Gay, Bisexual, and Transgender reform and liberation movements in the United States, with particular emphasis since WWII. Includes the lives, communities, organizations, and resistance movements created by LGBT peoples

from diverse racial, ethnic, and class backgrounds." "History," City College of San Francisco, accessed October 1, 2020, https://www.ccsf.edu/academics/ccsf-catalog/courses-by-department/history.

19 LGBTQ+ Studies, "About," DePaul College of Liberal Arts and Social Sciences, accessed April 23, 2018, https://las.depaul.edu/academics/lgbtq-studies/about/Pages/default.aspx.

20 Jason Derose, "DePaul University to Offer Minor in 'Queer Studies,'" NPR, accessed April 22, 2018, https://www.npr.org/templates/story/story.php?storyId=5173232.

21 LGBTQ+ Studies, "Lesbian, Gay, Bisexual, Transgender, and Queer Studies," University of Colorado Boulder, accessed May 12, 2014, http://lgbt.colorado.edu.

22 Berkeley Academic Guide, "About the Program," Lesbian, Gay, Bisexual, and Transgender Studies, accessed April 21, 2018, http://guide.berkeley.edu/undergraduate/degree-programs/lesbian-gay-bisexual-transgender-studies/.

23 Steven Lee Myers, "Ideas & Trends; How a 'Rainbow Curriculum' Turned into Fighting Words," *New York Times*, December 13, 1992, accessed April 24, 2018, https://www.nytimes.com/1992/12/13/weekinreview/ideas-trends-how-a-rainbow-curriculum-turned-into-fighting-words.html.

24 Don Romesburg, Stacie Brensilver Berman, David Duffield, Daniel Hurewitz, Rachel Reinhard, and Wendy Rouse, "Words That Shape the World: Historians, Teachers, and Partnerships for LGBT History" (panel discussion, American Historical Association Annual Meeting, Washington, DC, January 5, 2018). Historians at this panel debunked the perception that LGBTQ+ history courses are prevalent at universities, claiming that though some institutions offer LGBTQ+ history courses, the majority do not and where they are offered there are few faculty members with the expertise to teach them. In a separate conversation, Emily Hobson, a history professor at University of Nevada, Reno, asserted the same. (Emily Hobson, interview with the author, June 8, 2016, Brooklyn, NY, tape/notes/transcript in the author's possession.)

25 "HIST 490:004 Special Topics in American History: U.S. Lesbian, Gay, Bisexual, and Transgender Histories," Committee on Lesbian, Gay, Bisexual, and Transgender History, accessed June 16, 2014, http://clgbthistory.org/wp-content/uploads/2013/03/HIST-490-U.S.-LGBT-Histories1.pdf.

26 "Syllabi," Committee on Lesbian, Gay, Bisexual & Transgender History, accessed April 23, 2018, http://clgbthistory.org/projects/syllabi.

27 Trudy Ring, "Morehouse to Offer Course in Black LGBT History, Culture," *The Advocate*, December 20, 2012, accessed April 24, 2018, https://www.advocate.com/society/education/2012/12/20/morehouse-offer-course-black-lgbt-history-and-culture.

28 Emily Hobson, interview with the author, June 8, 2016, Brooklyn, NY, tape/notes/transcript in the author's possession.

29 Ibid.

30 Wendy Rouse, interview with the author, October 26, 2018, Brooklyn, NY, tape/notes/transcripts in the author's possession. The FAIR Education Act (2011) is a California law mandating that K–12 teachers incorporate LGBTQ+ history in their social studies curriculum. See Chapters 6 and 7.

31 Wendy Rouse, interview with the author, August 8, 2020, Ridgefield, CT, tape/notes/transcripts in the author's possession.

32 Wendy Rouse, interview with the author, October 2, 2018, Brooklyn, NY, tape/notes/transcripts in the author's possession; Wendy Rouse, interview with the author, August 8, 2020, Ridgefield, CT, tape/notes/transcripts in author's possession.

33 Wendy Rouse, interview with the author, August 8, 2020, Ridgefield, CT, tape/notes/transcripts in the author's possession. Rouse's program is more than three years old, and its students are beginning to finish their credentialing programs and enter the classroom. The initial results are positive. She reported that alumni reach out to ask for LGBTQ+ history resources for their classrooms and attend professional development sessions, but that it will take a couple more years before the impact of San Jose State's social science major can truly be measured.

34 Wendy Rouse, interview with the author, August 8, 2020, Ridgefield, CT, tape/notes/transcripts in the author's possession.

35 Lyndsey Schlax, conversation with the author, March 16, 2016.

36 John D'Emilio, interview with the author, July 7, 2016, Brooklyn, NY, tape/notes/transcript in the author's possession.

37 Emily Hobson, interview with the author, June 8, 2016, Brooklyn, NY, tape/notes/transcript in the author's possession.

38 Ibid.

39 Emily K. Hobson and Felicia T. Perez, "Questions, Not Test Answers: Teaching LGBT History in Public Schools" in *Understanding and Teaching U.S. Lesbian, Gay, Bisexual, and Transgender History*, ed. Leila J. Rupp and Susan K. Freeman (Madison: University of Wisconsin Press, 2014), 77–91.

3 Expanding Awareness: LGBTQ+ Content in Students' Lives

1 Deborah Hastings, "L.A. Law Kiss Hailed by Gay Rights Group," Associated Press, February 9, 1991, accessed April 30, 2018, https://apnews.com/62a4f9c94e3839eddb95916ee43d54f6.

2 GLAAD Media Institute, *Where We Are on TV '19–'20* (New York: GLAAD Media Institute, 2019), https://www.glaad.org/sites/default/files/GLAAD%20WHERE%20WE%20ARE%20ON%20TV%202019%202020.pdf, 8. The 2019–20 report included the full slate of television, cable, and streaming platform programming and offers

a complete picture of representation on TV. The 2020–1 report found a decrease in representation on television, largely in scripted cable shows. The report attributed that decrease to production shutdowns and irregular filming patterns related to the Covid-19 pandemic, and therefore, hopefully, not indicative of an ongoing downward trend (Raina Deerwater, "Where We Are on TV 2020–2021," GLAAD, January 14, 2021, https://www.glaad.org/blog/glaads-where-we-are-tv-report-despite-tumultuous-year-television-lgbtq-representation-holds).

3 GLAAD Media Institute, *Where We Are on TV '19-'20*, 10, 12, and 16. GLAAD also reported that the number of bisexual characters decreased despite a growing number of LGBTQ+ people identifying as bisexual.

4 GLAAD Media Institute, *Where We Are on TV '19-'20*, 4.

5 Ibid.

6 Pew Research Center, *A Survey of LGBT Americans: Attitudes, Experiences and Values in Changing Times* (Washington, DC: Pew Research Center, 2013), http://www.pewsocialtrends.org/files/2013/06/SDT_LGBT-Americans_06-2013.pdf; Proctor & Gamble and GLAAD, *LGBTQ Inclusion in Advertising and Media: Executive Summary* (New York: GLAAD, 2020), https://www.glaad.org/sites/default/files/P%26G_AdvertisingResearch.pdf.

7 "Great LGBTQ+ Inclusive Picture and Middle Grade Books," Welcoming Schools, accessed April 15, 2018, http://www.welcomingschools.org/pages/books-inclusive-of-LGBTQ+-family-members-and-characters/.

8 Carolyn Kellogg, "Once Controversial, 'Heather Has Two Mommies' Is Now Collectible," *Los Angeles Times*, May 11, 2017, accessed April 15, 2018, http://www.latimes.com/books/jacketcopy/la-ca-jc-heather-has-two-mommies-20170511-story.html. According to this article, *Heather Has Two Mommies* was the ninth most challenged book of the 1990s. *Heather Has Two Mommies* was one of the books at the heart of the Children of the Rainbow controversy.

9 Leslea Newman, "Kids Books," Leslea Kids, accessed April 23, 2018, http://www.lesleakids.com/mommy.html.

10 Sherri Machlin, "Banned Books Week: And Tango Makes Three," New York Public Library, September 23, 2013, accessed April 23, 2018, https://www.nypl.org/blog/2013/09/23/banned-books-week-and-tango-makes-three.

11 J. J. Austrian, *Worm Loves Worm* (New York: HarperCollins, 2016).

12 "Great LGBTQ+ Inclusive Picture and Middle Grade Books," Welcoming Schools.

13 Malinda Lo, "LGBTQ+ YA by the Numbers: 2015–2016," Malinda Lo, accessed April 23, 2018, https://www.malindalo.com/blog/2017/10/12/lgbtq-ya-by-the-numbers-2015-16. Lo breaks this down further on her website, looking at gender representation and more specific LGBTQ+ content. In this earlier study Lo found seventy-nine books focusing on LGBTQ characters and issues in 2016.

14 Malinda Lo, "A Decade of LGBTQ YA since Ash," Malinda Lo, May 14, 2019, https://www.malindalo.com/blog/2019/3/18/a-decade-of-lgbtq-ya-since-ash. In this report, too, Lo evaluated gender representation and genre. She also makes clear that the books in her report forefront LGBTQ+ characters and themes; they are not peripheral to the story.

15 Danika Leigh Ellis, "The 38 Best Queer YA Novels," *Vulture*, June 21, 2018, https://www.vulture.com/2018/06/38-best-lgbtq-ya-novels.html.

16 GLSEN, *The 2019 National School Climate Survey: The Experiences of Lesbian, Gay, Bisexual and Transgender Youth in Our Nation's Schools* (New York: Gay, Lesbian, and Straight Education Network, 2020), 60.

17 Christine Gentry, conversation with the author, March 4, 2021, Brooklyn, NY, communication, transcript, and notes in the author's possession.

18 "Diverse Gender Expression and Gender Non-Conformity Curriculum in English Grades 7–12," National Council of Teachers of English, July 1, 2014, https://ncte.org/statement/gender-curriculum-7–12/.

19 Ibid.

20 "About," National Council of Teachers of English, accessed October 19, 2020, https://ncte.org/about/.

21 "Safe Schools Program for LGBTQ Students," Mass.gov, accessed October 19, 2020, https://www.mass.gov/info-details/safe-schools-program-for-lgbtq-students#inclusive-curriculum-materials-.

22 Leslea Newman, GLSEN, The Matthew Shepard Foundation, and Candlewick Press, "He Continues to Make a Difference: Commemorating the Life of Matthew Shepard," GLSEN, 2014, accessed October 19, 2020, http://www.glsen.org/matthewshepard, 19. The social studies aspects of this lesson are discussed in the next chapter.

23 "Love, Simon: Coming Out & Invisible Identities Lesson," GLSEN, accessed October 19, 2020, https://www.glsen.org/article/love-simon-coming-out-invisible-identities-lesson.

24 Christine Gentry, conversation with the author, March 4, 2021, Brooklyn, NY, communication, transcript, and notes in the author's possession. Gentry mentioned applying this lens to *Twelfth Night*, Circe in Homer's *Odyssey*, and nonfiction articles, among other works.

25 Christine Gentry, conversation with the author, March 4, 2021, Brooklyn, NY, communication, transcript, and notes in the author's possession.

26 Ibid.

27 Lauren Jensen, email conversation with the author, October 25, 2020, Brooklyn, NY, communication and notes in the author's possession.

28 Rebecca McBride, email conversation with the author, October 21, 2020, Brooklyn, NY, communication and notes in the author's possession.

29 Lauren Jensen, email conversation with the author, October 25, 2020, Brooklyn, NY, communication and notes in the author's possession.

30 Christine Gentry, conversation with the author, March 4, 2021, Brooklyn, NY, communication, transcript, and notes in the author's possession.

31 "Health Education," New York City Department of Education, accessed October 19, 2020, https://www.schools.nyc.gov/learning/learn-at-home/activities-and-supports/health-education.

32 "Sex and HIV Education," Guttmacher Institute, October 12, 2020, https://www.guttmacher.org/state-policy/explore/sex-and-hiv-education#. Those states include California, Colorado, Connecticut, Delaware, Iowa, Maryland, New Jersey, New Mexico, Oregon, Rhode Island, and Washington. According to GLSEN's survey, 5.1 percent of all students surveyed and 26.6 percent of students who claimed their school conveyed positive representations of the LGBTQ+ population learned about gender and sexuality in health classes. (GLSEN, *The 2019 National School Climate Survey: The Experiences of Lesbian, Gay, Bisexual and Transgender Youth in Our Nation's Schools*, 60.)

33 "Sexual Health Education," Washington State Department of Health, accessed October 19, 2020, https://www.doh.wa.gov/CommunityandEnvironment/Schools/SexualHealthEducation. States such as Iowa, Colorado, and California have similar laws.

34 "Home," FLASH, accessed October 19, 2020, https://www.etr.org/FLASH/.

35 "Lesson Selection Tool," FLASH, accessed October 19, 2020, https://www.etr.org/FLASH/.

36 Kathe Taylor, *Comprehensive Sexual Health Education Data Survey* (Olympia, WA: Office of Superintendent of Public Instruction, 2019), https://www.k12.wa.us/sites/default/files/public/communications/2019-12-Sexual-Health-Education-Data-Survey.pdf, 4.

37 "Toward Understanding … Some of Us Are Lesbian or Gay," ReCAPP, 2007, accessed August 1, 2018, http://recapp.etr.org/recapp/index.cfm?fuseaction=pages.LearningActivitiesDetail&PageID=170.

38 "Who We Are: About Advocates for Youth," Advocates for Youth, 2021, accessed May 4, 2021, https://www.advocatesforyouth.org/about/.

39 "I Am Who I Am," Advocates for Youth, 2005, last modified December 8, 2017, https://advocatesforyouth.org/wp-content/uploads/3rscurric/documents/7-Lesson-6-3Rs-IAmWhoIAm.pdf.

40 "About Us," Safe Schools Coalition, accessed August 1, 2018, http://www.safeschoolscoalition.org/about_us.html#OurMission; "Stories," sex, etc., accessed August 1, 2018, https://sexetc.org/sex-ed/info-center/stories/.

4 Creating Community: LGBTQ+ Content in Social Studies Classes

1 Department of the Interior Bureau of Education, *The Social Studies in Secondary Education* (Washington, DC: Government Printing Office, 1916), 9.

2 Jo Ann Webb, "U.S. Department of Education Continues Work after First-Ever Federal Summit on Bullying," US Department of Education, August 16, 2010, accessed April 26, 2018, https://www.ed.gov/news/press-releases/us-department-education-continues-work-after-first-ever-federal-summit-bullying.

3 "U.S Education Department Releases Analysis of State Bullying Laws and Policies," US Department of Education, December 6, 2011, accessed April 26, 2018, https://www.ed.gov/news/press-releases/us-education-department-releases-analysis-state-bullying-laws-and-policies.

4 "Laws & Policies," stopbullying.gov, September 2017, accessed April 25, 2018, https://www.stopbullying.gov/laws/index.html.

5 "After Rutgers Suicide Columnist Promises 'It Gets Better,'" National Public Radio, October 5, 2010, https://www.npr.org/templates/story/story.php?storyId=130349924.

6 "Our Misson/Vision/People," It Gets Better Project, accessed January 29, 2019, https://itgetsbetter.org/initiatives/mission-vision-people/.

7 GLSEN began conducting its National School Climate Survey in 1999. This survey, which consistently spotlights the harassment and bullying LGBTQ+ students face at school and the resources necessary to help them, is one of the most frequently cited statistical sources in studies of and articles about LGBTQ-related bullying.

8 Sue Hyde, "School Doors Open, with Deadly Consequences," National LGBTQ Task Force, accessed April 24, 2018, http://www.thetaskforce.org/school-doors-open-with-deadly-consequences/.

9 "LGBTQ Youth," stopbullying.gov, September 24, 2017, accessed April 24, 2018, https://www.stopbullying.gov/at-risk/groups/lgbt/index.html.

10 Anne O'Brien, "Inclusive Anti-Bullying Policies Create a Safer Environment for LGBT Students," George Lucas Educational Foundation, October 27, 2015, accessed April 24, 2018, https://www.edutopia.org/blog/inclusive-anti-bullying-policies-create-safer-environment-lgbt-students-anne-obrien.

11 Diana Hess, "Teaching About Same-Sex Marriage as a Policy and Constitutional Issue," *Social Education* 73, no. 7 (2009): 344–9; Kevin Jennings, "'Out' in the Classroom: Addressing Lesbian, Gay, Bisexual and Transgender Issues in Social Studies Curriculum," in *The Social Studies Curriculum*, ed. E. Wayne Ross (Albany: State University of New York Press, 2006), 255–64; Stephen Thornton, "Silence on Gays and Lesbians in Social Studies Curriculum," *Social Education* 67, no. 4 (2003): 226–30.

12 "Policy Maps," GLSEN, updated August 2020, accessed October 2, 2020, https://www.glsen.org/policy-maps. In comparison, by August 2020 five states had laws mandating LGBTQ+-inclusive history curricula.

13 GLSEN, *The 2013 National School Climate Survey: The Experiences of Lesbian, Gay, Bisexual and Transgender Youth in Our Nation's Schools* (New York: Gay, Lesbian, and Straight Education Network, 2014); "Growing Up LGBT in America: HRC Youth Survey Report Key Findings," Human Rights Campaign, 2012, https://assets2.hrc.org/files/assets/resources/Growing-Up-LGBT-in-America_Report.pdf?_ga=2.144728948.1389147936.1533265876-1406905136.1424747565.

14 GLSEN, *The 2019 National School Climate Survey: The Experiences of Lesbian, Gay, Bisexual and Transgender Youth in Our Nation's Schools* (New York: Gay, Lesbian, and Straight Education Network, 2020), xiii.

15 Ibid., 16.

16 Ibid., 66. Of those who had access to sex education, 22.9 percent said it included LGBTQ+ topics (61).

17 GLSEN, *The 2019 National School Climate Survey*, 57. Nearly half (48.9 percent), though, said they had access to LGBTQ+ topics in their school library.

18 GLSEN, *The 2019 National School Climate Survey*, 60. In 2017, 35.2 percent of respondents reported learning LGBTQ+ topics in their academic classes. (GLSEN, *The 2017 National School Climate Survey: The Experiences of Lesbian, Gay, Bisexual and Transgender Youth in Our Nation's Schools* (New York: Gay, Lesbian, and Straight Education Network, 2018), 58.)

19 GLSEN, *The 2019 National School Climate Survey*, 62. 42.3 percent of respondents said they could identify more than ten teachers or staff members who supported LGBTQ+ students and 42.4 percent said that the administration at their school was very or somewhat supportive.

20 In 2017, 11.4 percent of total respondents reported learning LGBTQ+ history and 58.5 percent of those who experienced positive representations did so in history classes (GLSEN, *The 2017 National School Climate Survey*, 59). In 2019, for comparison, those numbers were 11.6 percent and 60.3 percent.

21 "About Project Look Sharp," Project Look Sharp, last modified April 2018, https://www.projectlooksharp.org/?action=about_pls.

22 Sox Sperry, interview with the author, June 13, 2016, Brooklyn, NY, tape/notes/transcript in the author's possession.

23 "Who We Are," Anti-Defamation League, accessed July 31, 2018, https://www.adl.org/who-we-are.

24 Jinnie Spiegler, interview with the author, July 16, 2015, Brooklyn, NY, tape/notes/transcript in the author's possession.

25 "Introduction: Understanding Lesbian, Gay, Bisexual, and Transgender Rights as Human Rights," Human Rights Resource Center, 2000, http://hrlibrary.umn.edu/edumat/hreduseries/TB3/details.htm.

26 Daryl Presgraves, "Schools across the Country Celebrate 10th Anniversary of GLSEN's No Name-Calling Week," GLSEN, January 20, 2014, https://www.glsen.org/article/10th-anniversary-glsens-no-name-calling-week.

27 GLSEN, "ThinkB4YouSpeak Guide for Educators of Grades 6–12," GLSEN, 2008, accessed July 17, 2015, http://www.glsen.org/sites/default/files/Guide%20to%20ThinkB4YouSpeak.pdf.

28 "What's So Bad about That's So Gay?," Learning for Justice, accessed March 3, 2021, https://www.learningforjustice.org/classroom-resources/lessons/whats-so-bad-about-thats-so-gay.

29 "Challenging Gender Stereotyping and Homophobia in Sports," Learning for Justice, accessed March 3, 2021, https://www.learningforjustice.org/classroom-resources/lessons/challenging-gender-stereotyping-and-homophobia-in-sports.

30 "Creating an LGBT-Inclusive School Climate," Teaching Tolerance, 2013, accessed August 1, 2018, https://www.tolerance.org/sites/default/files/2017-11/Teaching-Tolerance-LGBT-Best-Practices-2017-WEB-Oct2017.pdf.

31 "The History and Impact of Anti-LGBT Slurs," Anti-Defamation League, 2010, accessed August 1, 2018, https://www.adl.org/media/6788/download.

32 "Understanding Homophobia/Heterosexism and How to Be an Ally," Anti-Defamation League, accessed July 16, 2015, http://www.adl.org/education-outreach/lesson-plans/c/understanding-homophobia-heterosexism-ally.html#.VbBf1Iu4n5Y.

33 "Transgender Identity and Issues," Anti-Defamation League, 2014, accessed October 6, 2020, https://www.adl.org/media/4767/download.

34 "Words Really Matter," Human Rights Resource Center, 2000, accessed August 1, 2018, http://hrlibrary.umn.edu/edumat/hreduseries/TB3/details.htm.

35 "Media Construction of Social Justice: Case Study: Gay Affirmative or Gay Negative?," Project Look Sharp, 2014, accessed July 17, 2015, http://www.projectlooksharp.org/?action=justice.

36 Department of the Interior Bureau of Education, *The Social Studies in Secondary Education*, 53.

37 Sox Sperry, interview with the author, June 13, 2016, Brooklyn, NY, tape/notes/transcript in the author's possession.

38 Leslea Newman, GLSEN, The Matthew Shepard Foundation, and Candlewick Press, "He Continues to Make a Difference: Commemorating the Life of Matthew Shepard," GLSEN, 2014, accessed October 19, 2020, http://www.glsen.org/matthewshepard, 1. Newman was also the author of *Heather Has Two Mommies*, the book at the center of the Rainbow Curriculum controversy.

39 "Matthew Shepard and James Byrd, Jr. Hate Crimes Prevention Act," Anti-Defamation League, accessed July 6, 2015, http://www.adl.org/education-outreach/lesson-plans/c/matthew-shepard-and-james-byrd-jr.html#.VbBUYu4n5Y.

40 "Critiquing Hate Crimes Legislation," Learning for Justice, accessed March 3, 2021, https://www.learningforjustice.org/classroom-resources/lessons/critiquing-hate-crimes-legislation.

41 Kisha Webster, interview with the author, July 15, 2015, Brooklyn, NY, tape/notes/transcript in the author's possession.

42 Youth in Motion, "Brother Outsider: The Life of Bayard Rustin Curriculum Guide," Frameline, 2012, accessed July 15, 2015, https://ticketing.frameline.org/_uploaded/curriculumguidebrotheroutsider_377065.pdf.

43 "Caitlyn Jenner and the Power of Coming Out," Anti-Defamation League, accessed July 16, 2015, http://www.adl.org/education-outreach/lesson-plans/c/caitlyn-jenner-and-the-power-of-coming-out.html#.VbBfg4u4n5Y.

44 "Introduction: Understanding Lesbian, Gay, Bisexual, and Transgender Rights as Human Rights," Human Rights Resource Center, last modified 2000, http://hrlibrary.umn.edu/edumat/hreduseries/TB3/details.htm.

45 ADL, GLSEN, and StoryCorps, "In-Group, Out-Group: The Exclusion of LGBT People from Societal Institutions," GLSEN, 2011, accessed August 1, 2018, https://www.glsen.org/sites/default/files/UV%20Lessons.pdf, 27.

5 Two Steps Forward: LGBTQ+ History Resources and the Obstacles They Face

1 Kristi Rudelius-Palmer, interview with the author, September 14, 2016, Brooklyn, NY, tape/notes/transcript in the author's possession.

2 Vermont legalized civil unions shortly before these lessons were published.

3 Kristi Rudelius-Palmer, interview with the author, September 14, 2016, Brooklyn, NY, tape/notes/transcript in the author's possession.

4 Ibid.

5 The Learning Network, "Teaching and Learning about Gay History and Issues," *New York Times*, last modified June 2016, https://learning.blogs.nytimes.com/2011/11/22/teaching-and-learning-about-gay-history-and-issues/.

6 Ibid.

7 "The Invisibility of LGBT People in History: 'Peculiar Disposition of the Eyes,'" Anti-Defamation League, accessed July 31, 2018, https://www.adl.org/media/6779/download.

8 "Activism: Marsha P. Johnson," PBS Learning Media, accessed October 9, 2020, https://www.pbslearningmedia.org/resource/fp18.lgbtq.marsha.p.johnson/activism-marsha-p-johnson/support-materials/.

9 Debra Fowler and Miriam Morgenstern, interview with the author, April 23, 2018, Brooklyn, NY, tape/notes/transcript in the author's possession.

10 "The Lavender Scare," Berkeley History-Social Science Project, 2013, accessed April 23, 2018, http://ucbhssp.berkeley.edu/content/lavender-scare.

11 "The Role of Gay Men and Lesbians in the Civil Rights Movement," Learning for Justice, accessed March 3, 2021, https://www.learningforjustice.org/classroom-resources/lessons/the-role-of-gay-men-and-lesbians-in-the-civil-rights-movement.

12 Debra Fowler, interview with the author, June 24, 2016, Brooklyn, NY, tape/notes/transcript in the author's possession.

13 "When Did It Happen" was accessible online on GLSEN's website in July 2015; however, as of May 2016 it was no longer accessible online and searches for this lesson yield an error message. Searches for other GLSEN materials, including resources on *Lawrence v. Texas* and diversity within the LGBT community, end in similar results, indicating that GLSEN updates, and takes down, its curricular offerings.

14 "When Did It Happen: An LGBT History Lesson," GLSEN, 2009, accessed July 1, 2015, http://www.glsen.org/sites/default/files/When%20Did%20it%20Happen%20Lesson%20Plan_0.pdf.

15 "LGBTQ History Timeline," GLSEN, accessed October 7, 2020, https://www.glsen.org/activity/lgbtq-history-timeline-lesson.

16 Peter Denegre, "Is Everyone Protected by the Bill of Rights?" Thirteen ed online, 2011, accessed August 1, 2018, https://www.thirteen.org/edonline/lessons/billofrights/.

17 "AIDS and HIV Activism," ONE Archives, accessed October 8, 2020, https://www.onearchives.org/wp-content/uploads/2019/02/one-archives-foundation-los-angeles-aids-crisis.pdf.

18 "LGBTQ Equality, 1950–1970," ONE Archives, accessed October 9, 2020, https://www.onearchives.org/wp-content/uploads/2019/02/one-archives-foundation-coming-out.pdf. This lesson focuses on the Mattachine Society, ONE, Inc., Daughters of Bilitis, Gay Liberation Front, and Radicalesbians. The site also has a separate lesson on Daughters of Bilitis and the ways they supported lesbians in the 1950s.

19 "LGBTQ Civil Rights," ONE Archives, accessed October 9, 2020, https://www.onearchives.org/wp-content/uploads/2019/02/one-archives-foundation-civil-rights.pdf.

20 "Stonewall Riots," Stanford History Education Group, accessed October 9, 2020, https://sheg.stanford.edu/history-lessons/stonewall-riots. One of the primary sources is a speech by Sylvia Rivera, a transgender woman whose role in the

Stonewall riots and the LGBTQ+ movement as a whole is essential, though often unacknowledged in classrooms.

21 "The LGBTQ Movement and the Stonewall Riots," PBS Learning Media, accessed October 9, 2020, https://www.pbslearningmedia.org/resource/ fp18-socst-lgbtq-stonewall/the-lgbtq-movement-and-stonewall-riot/.

22 "The Stonewall Uprising," Anti-Defamation League, accessed October 9, 2020, https://www.adl.org/media/12966/download.

23 "I Now Pronounce You … Same-Sex Marriage Legislation," Human Rights Resource Center, 2000, accessed July 1, 2015, http://www1.umn.edu/humanrts/edumat/ hreduseries/TB3/act6/act6f.html.

24 "Marriage Equality: Different Strategies for Attaining Equal Rights," Learning for Justice, accessed March 3, 2021, https://www.learningforjustice.org/classroom-resources/lessons/marriage-equality-different-strategies-for-attaining-equal-rights.

25 This lesson, like others in the ADL Curriculum Connections collection, uses an oral history interview and the accompanying resources from the Unheard Voices program as a key resource for students.

26 "Winning the Right to Marry: Historic Parallels," Anti-Defamation League, 2010, accessed August 1, 2018, https://www.adl.org/media/6790/download.

27 "Wedding Cake, Same Sex Marriage, and Discrimination," Anti-Defamation League, 2018, accessed October 8, 2020, https://www.adl.org/media/10779/download.

28 Carolyn Laub, interview with the author, July 9, 2015, Brooklyn, NY, tape/notes/ transcript in the author's possession; Kisha Webster, interview with the author, July 8, 2015, Brooklyn, NY, tape/notes/transcript in the author's possession.

29 "Zinn Education Project," Howard Zinn.org, accessed August 2, 2018, https://www. howardzinn.org/related-projects/zinn-education-project/.

30 Jack Bareilles, "Women, Gays, and Other Voices of Resistance," in *Voices of a People's History of the United States: Teacher's Guide*, ed. Gayle Olson-Raymer (New York: Seven Stores Press, 2005), 235–46.

31 "Our Mission," Facing History and Ourselves, accessed October 8, 2020, https:// www.facinghistory.org/about-us.

32 "LGBTQ History and Why It Matters," Facing History and Ourselves, accessed October 8, 2020, https://www.facinghistory.org/educator-resources/current-events/ lgbtq-history-and-why-it-matters.

33 "Unheard Voices: Stories of LGBT History," Anti-Defamation League, accessed July 21, 2018, https://www.adl.org/media/4699/download.

34 "Unheard Voices: Stories and Lessons for Grades 6–12," GLSEN, 2011, accessed July 31, 2018, https://www.glsen.org/unheardvoices.html.

35 John D'Emilio, interview with the author, July 7, 2016, Brooklyn, NY, tape/notes/ transcript in the author's possession.

36 "Lorraine Hansberry: LGBT Politics and Civil Rights," Learning for Justice, accessed March 3, 2021, https://www.learningforjustice.org/classroom-resources/lessons/lorraine-hansberry-lgbt-politics-and-civil-rights.

37 Ibid.

38 "Lorraine Hansberry," PBS Learning Media, accessed October 8, 2020, https://www.pbslearningmedia.org/resource/fp19.lgbtq.hansberry/lorraine-hansberry/.

39 "Pauli Murray," PBS Learning Media, accessed October 8, 2020, https://www.pbslearningmedia.org/resource/fp20-vid-pauli-murray/pauli-murray/.

40 "Pauli Murray: Fighting Jane and Jim Crow," Learning for Justice, accessed March 3, 2021, https://www.learningforjustice.org/classroom-resources/lessons/pauli-murray-fighting-jane-and-jim-crow.

41 "James Baldwin: Art, Sexuality, and Civil Rights," Learning for Justice, accessed March 3, 2021, https://www.learningforjustice.org/classroom-resources/lessons/james-baldwin-art-sexuality-and-civil-rights.

42 "James Baldwin," PBS Learning Media, accessed October 8, 2020, https://www.pbslearningmedia.org/resource/fp18-lgbtq-baldwin/james-baldwin/.

43 "Bayard Rustin: The Fight for Civil and Gay Rights," Learning for Justice, accessed March 3, 2021, https://www.learningforjustice.org/classroom-resources/lessons/bayard-rustin-the-fight-for-civil-and-gay-rights.

44 Ibid.

45 PBS Learning Media and ONE Archives also offer lessons on Bayard Rustin.

46 "Alan Turing: True to Himself," GLSEN, 2015, accessed August 2, 2018, https://www.glsen.org/sites/default/files/Alan%20Turing%20True%20to%20Himself-Final.pdf. Alan Turing was a British mathematician and cryptanalyst whose work broke the Nazi Enigma code during the Second World War. Turing was openly gay and was punished for his sexual orientation in the 1950s. He committed suicide in 1954.

47 "We'Wha," PBS Learning Media, accessed October 8, 2020, https://www.pbslearningmedia.org/resource/fp20-we-wha/wewha-first-person-classroom/. In Zuni culture, lhamana were nonbinary individuals who were elevated above other members of their tribe because they embodied multiple spirits. The term "Two Spirit," coined in the 1990s, refers to transgender and nonbinary indigenous people.

48 "Audre Lorde," PBS Learning Media, accessed October 8, 2020, https://www.pbslearningmedia.org/resource/fp19.lgbtq.lorde/audre-lorde/.

49 "Alain Locke," PBS Learning Media, accessed October 8, 2020, https://www.pbslearningmedia.org/resource/fp20-alain-locke/alain-locke-first-person-classroom-understanding-lgbtq-identity-educators-toolkit/.

50 "History Unerased," History UnErased, accessed May 5, 2021, https://unerased.org/.

51 "Curriculum," History UnErased, accessed May 5, 2021, https://unerased.org/resource/curriculum.

52 Miriam Morgenstern, interview with the author, June 24, 2016, Brooklyn, NY, tape/notes/transcript in the author's possession.

53 David Tyack and Larry Cuban, *Tinkering toward Utopia: A Century of Public School Reform* (Cambridge: Harvard University Press, 1995); Jonathan Zimmerman, *Whose America? Culture Wars in the Public Schools* (Cambridge: Harvard University Press, 2002).

54 Carolyn Laub, interview with the author, July 9, 2015, Brooklyn, NY, tape/notes/transcript in the author's possession.

55 Kisha Webster, interview with the author, July 15, 2015, Brooklyn, NY, tape/notes/transcript in the author's possession.

56 Sox Sperry, interview with the author, June 13, 2016, Brooklyn, NY, tape/notes/transcript in the author's possession.

57 Jinnie Spiegler, interview with the author, July 16, 2015, Brooklyn, NY, tape/notes/transcript in the author's possession.

58 According to Clifford Rosky's article in the *Columbia Law Review*, "the phrase 'no promo homo' was originally coined by Nan Hunter to describe the Briggs Initiative, a 1978 California ballot proposal allowing the termination of any public school teacher who engaged in 'advocating, soliciting, imposing, encouraging, or promoting of private or public homosexual activity.'" (Rosky, "Anti Gay Curriculum Laws," *Columbia Law Review* 117, no. 6 (October 2017): 1468.)

59 "'No Promo Homo' Laws," GLSEN, accessed April 11, 2017, https://www.glsen.org/learn/policy/issues/nopromohomo. Six states maintained "No Promo Homo" laws at the start of 2020. A US district court declared South Carolina's "No Promo Homo" law unconstitutional in March of that year, ruling it violated the Fourteenth Amendment.

60 "Alabama Code Title 16. Education § 16-40A-2," FindLaw, accessed July 31, 2018, https://codes.findlaw.com/al/title-16-education/al-code-sect-16-40a-2.html.

61 "Texas Health and Safety Code § 85.007. Educational Materials for Minors," FindLaw, accessed October 8, 2020, https://codes.findlaw.com/tx/health-and-safety-code/health-safety-sect-85-007.html.

62 Paige Hamby Barbeauld, "'Don't Say Gay' Bills and the Movement to Keep Discussion of LGBT Issues Out of Schools," *Journal of Law and Education* 43, no. 1 (Winter 2014): 137–46.

63 Emily Hobson, interview with the author, June 8, 2016, Brooklyn, NY, tape/notes/transcript in the author's possession.

64 John D'Emilio, interview with the author, July 7, 2016, Brooklyn, NY, tape/notes/transcript in the author's possession; Kevin Jennings, interview with the author, January 3, 2018, Brooklyn, NY, tape/notes/transcript in the author's possession.

6 The FAIR Act: A Legislative Victory for LGBTQ+ History Education

1 "Past Legislation," California Legislative Lesbian, Gay, Bisexual, and Transgender Caucus, accessed March 16, 2016, http://lgbtcaucus.legislature.ca.gov/legislation.

2 Jo Michael, interview with the author, July 30, 2014, Brooklyn, NY, tape/notes/transcript in author's possession.

3 "Issues: Non-Discrimination," Equality California, accessed June 27, 2015, http://www.eqca.org/site/pp.asp?c=kuLRJ9MRKrH&b=4026611.

4 Matthew Bajko, "40 Years Ago, San Francisco Adopted Historic Gay Rights Law," *Bay Area Reporter*, April 12, 2018, https://www.ebar.com/news/news//258422; Marc Stein, *Rethinking the Gay and Lesbian Movement (American Social and Political Movements of the 20th Century)* (New York: Routledge, 2012).

5 Les Ledbetter, "Bill on Homosexual Rights Advances in San Francisco," *New York Times*, March 22, 1978, https://www.nytimes.com/1978/03/22/archives/bill-on-homosexual-rights-advances-in-san-francisco.html.

6 "Gay Events Timeline 1970–1999," SOIN Sexual Orientation Issues in the News; "California's Senate Votes Bill Repealing Sexual Prohibitions," *New York Times*, May 2, 1975, https://www.nytimes.com/1975/05/02/archives/californias-senate-votes-bill-repealing-sexual-prohibitions.html. The California state assembly referred to the bill as the "Consenting Adult Sex Bill."

7 Jane Gross, "California Governor, in Reversal, Signs a Bill on Gay Rights in Jobs," *New York Times*, September 26, 1992, http://www.nytimes.com/1992/09/26/us/california-governor-in-reversal-signs-a-bill-on-gay-rights-in-jobs.html.

8 The Clinton administration created the Don't Ask, Don't Tell policy and the Defense of Marriage Act in the early to mid-1990s, in addition to state laws that supported discriminatory practices aimed at the LGBTQ+ community.

9 Gross, "California Governor, in Reversal, Signs a Bill on Gay Rights in Jobs." California's law was preceded by laws in Wisconsin, Massachusetts, Hawaii, Connecticut, Vermont, and New Jersey.

10 Eric Astacaan, "1999 Legislation," California Legislative Lesbian, Gay, Bisexual, and Transgender Caucus, accessed March 16, 2016, http://lgbtcaucus.legislature.ca.gov/1999-legislation.

11 "Past Legislation," California Legislative Lesbian, Gay, Bisexual, and Transgender Caucus.

12 "Just the Facts: California's Population," Public Policy Institute of California, April 2020, https://www.ppic.org/publication/californias-population/#:~:text=No%20race%20or%20ethnic%20group,the%202018%20American%20Community%20Survey. Those numbers shifted by 2020. Latinos (39 percent) and Asians

(15 percent) make up a larger proportion of the population, and 37 percent of Californians are white.

13 Micah Cohen, "In California, Growing Diversity First Made Its Mark," *New York Times*, October 8, 2012, https://fivethirtyeight.blogs.nytimes.com/2012/10/08/in-california-growing-diversity-first-made-its-mark/.

14 Gregory B. Lewis, "Black-White Differences in Attitudes towards Homosexuality and Gay Rights," *Public Opinion Quarterly* 67, no. 1 (Spring 2003): 75.

15 "Changing Faiths: Latinos and the Transformation of American Religion," Pew Research Center, April 25, 2007, https://www.pewresearch.org/hispanic/2007/04/25/changing-faiths-latinos-and-the-transformation-of-american-religion/.

16 Marisa Abrajano, "Are Blacks and Latinos Responsible for the Passage of Proposition 8? Analyzing Voter Attitudes on California's Proposal to Ban Same-Sex Marriage in 2008," *Political Research Quarterly* 63, no. 4 (December 2010): 927.

17 "Timeline: Proposition 8," *Los Angeles Times*, November 30, 2012, https://www.latimes.com/local/la-prop8-timeline-story.html.

18 Jesse McKinley and Kirk Johnson, "Mormons Tipped Scale in Ban on Gay Marriage," *New York Times*, November 14, 2008, https://www.nytimes.com/2008/11/15/us/politics/15marriage.html.

19 Chris Cillizza and Sean Sullivan, "How Proposition 8 Passed in California—and Why It Wouldn't Today," *Washington Post*, March 26, 2013, https://www.washingtonpost.com/news/the-fix/wp/2013/03/26/how-proposition-8-passed-in-california-and-why-it-wouldnt-today/.

20 Ibid.

21 Rachel Reinhard, interview with the author, January 29, 2015, Brooklyn, NY, tape/notes/transcript in author's possession.

22 California State Assembly, "AB 537 Assembly Bill—Chaptered," *Legislative Counsel's Digest*, February 18, 1999, http://www.leginfo.ca.gov/pub/99-00/bill/asm/ab_0501-0550/ab_537_bill_19991010_chaptered.html.

23 Sheila Kuehl, "Letter to School Superintendents," GSA Network, December 18, 2002, https://www.gsanetwork.org/files/resources/SKLetter.pdf.

24 California State Senate, "SB 1437 Amended," *Legislative Counsel's Digest*, May 1, 2006, http://leginfo.legislature.ca.gov/faces/billTextClient.xhtml?bill_id=200520060SB1437.

25 Lori Arnold, "Gov. Schwarzenegger Vows to Veto Gay-Friendly Curriculum Bill," *Christian Examiner*, June 9, 2006, http://www.christianexaminer.com/article/gov.schwarzenegger.vows.to.veto.gay.friendly.curriculum.bill/43205.htm; "Governor Says He Will Veto Bill Protecting Students and Fostering Tolerance in Schools," Equality California, May 25, 2006, http://www.eqca.org/site/apps/nlnet/content2.aspx?c=kuLRJ9MRKrH&b=4025925&ct=5195357.

26 Roger Brigham, "Kuehl Waters Down Textbook Bill," *Bay Area Reporter Online*, August 10, 2006, http://www.ebar.com/news/article.php?article=1069&sec=news.

27 Senate Judiciary Committee, "Instruction: Prohibition of Discriminatory Content," Sacramento, CA, April 5, 2011, http://www.leginfo.ca.gov/pub/11-12/bill/sen/ sb_0001-0050/sb_48_cfa_20110404_134404_sen_comm.html. The quote from then-governor Arnold Schwarzenegger is cited in this document.

28 Senate Judiciary Committee, "Discrimination: The California Student Civil Rights Act," *SB 777 Senate Bill—Bill Analysis*, April 9, 2007, ftp://leginfo.ca.gov/pub/07-08/ bill/sen/sb_0751-0800/sb_777_cfa_20070418_124057_sen_comm.html, 4.

29 Ibid., 3.

30 "Governor Signs Six LGBT Bills, Secures Protections for LGBT Youth," Equality California, October 12, 2007, http://www.eqca.org/site/apps/nlnet/content2.aspx?c= kuLRJ9MRKrH&b=4026083&ct=5198249.

31 Assembly Committee on Education, "Discrimination Based on Sexual Orientation in Instructional Services and Programs," Bill Analysis AB 222—As Amended March 24, 1999, April 7, 1999, http://www.leginfo.ca.gov/pub/99-00/bill/asm/ab_0201- 0250/ab_222_cfa_19990407_112400_asm_comm.html, 4.

32 Roger Brigham, "Kuehl Waters Down Textbook Bill," *Bay Area Reporter Online*, August 10, 2006, http://www.ebar.com/news/article.php?article=1069&sec=news. Morrow's contention was wrong; in 2003 CA made sexual orientation a protected class.

33 Karen England, "Outrageous Homosexual Bill Passes California Senate—SB 777 a Serious Assault on Religious Freedom and Morality in Schools," *Christian News Wire*, May 24, 2007, http://www.christiannewswire.com/news/933623242.html.

34 Campaign for Children and Families, "They're BAACCKK: California 'Gay' Brainwashing Bills (SB 777 and AB 394)," Americans for Truth, March 26, 2007, https://americansfortruth.com/2007/03/27/ theyre-baacckk-california-gay-brainwashing-bills-sb-777/.

35 California State Senate, "SB 777 Senate Bill—Chaptered," *Legislative Counsel's Digest*, February 23, 2007, http://www.leginfo.ca.gov/pub/07-08/bill/sen/sb_0751-0800/ sb_777_bill_20071012_chaptered.html; "Governor Signs Six LGBT Bills, Secures Protections for LGBT Youth," Equality California; Senate Judiciary Committee, "Discrimination: The California Student Civil Rights Act," *SB 777 Senate Bill—Bill Analysis*.

36 "Governor Signs 3 Gay Rights Bills, Vetoes 2," *GSA Network*, October 15, 2009, http://www.gsanetwork.org/news/governor-signs-3-gay-rights-bills- vetoes-2/101509; Mark Tran, "Arnold Schwarzenegger Signs Law Establishing Harvey Milk Day," *The Guardian*, October 13, 2009, http://www.theguardian.com/ world/2009/oct/13/schwarzennegger-law-harvey-milk-day.

37 Mark Leno, "California's FAIR Education Act: Addressing the Bullying Epidemic by Ending the Exclusion of LGBT People and Historical Events in Textbooks and Classrooms," *QED: A Journal in GLBTQ Worldmaking*, inaugural issue (Fall 2013), 106.

38 GLSEN, *The 2013 National School Climate Survey The Experiences of Lesbian, Gay, Bisexual and Transgender Youth in Our Nation's Schools* (New York: Gay, Lesbian, and Straight Education Network, 2014), xx; the sentiment is also expressed in Leno, "California's FAIR Education Act."

39 A former community activist who once held Harvey Milk's seat on the San Francisco Board of Supervisors, Leno was elected to the California state assembly in 2002 and the state senate in 2008. Leno had proven himself a staunch advocate for LGBTQ+-related issues and had an established relationship with the organizations promoting the bill.

40 Senate Rules Committee, "Instruction: Prohibition of Discriminatory Content," Sacramento, CA, March 29, 2011, http://www.leginfo.ca.gov/pub/11-12/bill/sen/ sb_0001-0050/sb_48_cfa_20110408_104724_sen_floor.html, 4.

41 California Legislative Information, "SB-48 Pupil Instruction: Prohibition of Discriminatory Content," California Legislative Information, July 14, 2011, http:// leginfo.legislature.ca.gov/faces/billNavClient.xhtml?bill_id=201120120SB48.

42 "Senator Mark Leno Introduces FAIR Education Act," Equality California, December 13, 2010, http://www.eqca.org/site/apps/nlnet/content2.aspx?c=kuLRJ9 MRKrH&b=4869041&ct=8971441. The It Gets Better Project, established the same year, similarly encouraged LGBTQ+ youth to make connections, build community, and believe in their value as individuals.

43 California State Senate, "FAIR Education Act: Senate Third Reading," 2011, https:// leginfo.legislature.ca.gov/faces/billNavClient.xhtml?bill_id=201120120SB48.

44 Senate Committee on Education, "Instruction and Instructional Materials: Sexual Orientation," Sacramento, CA, March 23, 2011, http://www.leginfo.ca.gov/pub/11-12/bill/sen/sb_0001-0050/sb_48_cfa_20110322_113330_sen_comm.html, 5–6.

45 Susan Brinkmann, "California's 'Pro-Gay Indoctrination' Bill Advances in Same Week that Priest Is Accused of 'Anti-Gay Indoctrination,'" *WOG Blog*, March 30, 2011, http://www.womenofgrace.com/blog/?p=7547.

46 Carolyn Laub, "FAIR Education Act's 1st Victory!," *GSA Network Blog*, March 23, 2011, https://www.gsanetwork.org/news/blog/fair-education-act's-1st-victory/03/23/11.

47 Senate Judiciary Committee, "Instruction: Prohibition of Discriminatory Content," 5.

48 California Legislative Information, "SB-48 Pupil Instruction: Prohibition of Discriminatory Content."

49 Assembly Committee on Education, "Instruction: Prohibition of Discriminatory Content," Sacramento, CA, June 22, 2011, http://www.leginfo.ca.gov/pub/11-12/bill/sen/sb_0001-0050/sb_48_cfa_20110621_104537_asm_comm.html, 3.

50 Senate Judiciary Committee, "Instruction: Prohibition of Discriminatory Content," 4; and Senate Rules Committee, "Instruction: Prohibition of Discriminatory Content," 9. The Judiciary and Rules Committees' analyses of the bill include quoted material from organizations outside of the state government that submitted documentation in support of or opposed to the FAIR Act.

51 Senate Rules Committee, "Instruction: Prohibition of Discriminatory Content," 10.

52 Senate Judiciary Committee, "Instruction: Prohibition of Discriminatory Content," 8.

53 "Pro-Family Response to Jerry Brown's Signing of SB 48," SaveCalifornia.org, July 14, 2011, http://savecalifornia.com/7-14-11-pro-family-response-to-jerry-brown-signing-lgbt-role-models-bill.html.

54 Los Angeles Times Editorial Board, "Gays in Textbooks: Best Told by Historians, Not by Politicians," *Los Angeles Times*, April 8, 2011, http://articles.latimes.com/2011/apr/08/opinion/la-ed-textbook-20110408.

55 Leno, "California's FAIR Education Act."

56 Roland Palencia, "Letter to Governor Jerry Brown: EQCA Urges Your Signature Re: SB 48- F.A.I.R. Education Act (Leno)," Equality California, July 7, 2011, http://www.eqca.org/atf/cf/%7B34F258B3-8482-4943-91CB-08C4B0246A88%7D/SB%2048%20EQCA%20Governor%20Letter.pdf.

57 "Governor Signs FAIR Education Act—LGBT History Bill," KQED News, accessed July 16, 2018, https://www.kqed.org/news/33986/governor-signs-fair-education-act-lgbt-history-bill.

58 Adam Bink, "Stop SB 48 Campaign: 'We're Working on an Initiative'," Equality on Trial, 2011, accessed June 2, 2015, http://www.equalityontrial.com/category/fair-education-act/page/2/.

59 Cillizza and Sullivan, "How Proposition 8 Passed in California—and Why It Wouldn't Today"; Seth Hemmelgarn, "EQCA: No Illusion on Stop SB 48," *Bay Area Reporter Online*, September 1, 2011, http://ebar.com/new/article.php?sec=news&article=6005; Cynthia Laird, "EQCA to Fight SB 48 Referendum," Edge Media Network, July 30, 2011, http://www.edgemedianetwork.com/news/local/news//122766/eqca_to_fight_sb_48_referendum; Patrick Range McDonald, "Stop SB 48 Campaign Seeks to Repeal California's Gay History Law," *LA Weekly*, July 25, 2011, http://www.laweekly.com/news/stop-sb-48-campaign-seeks-to-repeal-californias-gay-history-law-2390481.

60 Jim Christie, "California Orders Gay History in School Textbooks," Reuters, July 14, 2011, https://www.reuters.com/article/us-gays-california-history/california-orders-gay-history-in-school-textbooks-idUSTRE76D7QT20110715.

61 "Governor Ignores Thousands of Phone Calls; CCG Evaluating Next Step," Catholics for the Common Good, July 14, 2011, http://ccgaction.org/node/1084.

62 "Urgent: Help Stop Radical Bill from Manipulating Our Kids," DefendChristians.org, September 27, 2011, http://defendchristians.org/news/urgent-help-stop-radical-bill-from-manipulating-our-kids.

63 "Pro-Family Response to Jerry Brown's Signing of SB 48," SaveCalifornia.org, July 14, 2011, http://savecalifornia.com/7-14-11-pro-family-response-to-jerry-brown-signing-lgbt-role-models-bill.html.

64 "Group Fighting California's Gay-Inclusive Education Law Short on Signatures, Accused of Violations," The American Independent Institute, September 2011, http://www.americanindependent.com/197541/group-trying-to-repeal-cas-lgbt-inclusive-education-law-short-on-signatures-accused-of-violations.

65 "SB 48 and the Churches," Stop SB 48, 2011, accessed June 20, 2015, http://archive.constantcontact.com/fs078/1100422530046/archive/1107189511593.html.

66 "Stop SB 48 Petitions Now Available," Pacific Justice Institute, July 28, 2011, http://www.pacificjustice.org/press-releases/stop-sb-48-petitions-now-available.

67 Lisa Leff, "Calif. Gay History Referendum Faces Uphill Battle," Associated Press, September 3, 2011, http://news.yahoo.com/calif-gay-history-referendum-faces-uphill-battle-220939816.html.

68 Hemmelgarn, "EQCA: No Illusion on Stop SB 48."

69 Seth Hemmelgarn, "Decline to Sign Campaign Developing," *Bay Area Reporter Online*, August 4, 2011, http://www.ebar.com/news/article.php?sec=news&article=5912.

70 Rick Jacobs, "Letter to the Editor: Courage Campaign Asks for Truth in Dialogue about SB 48," *San Diego Gay & Lesbian News*, August 24, 2011, http://sdgln.com/tags/courage-campaign?page=1#sthash.aMzVtPzP.dpbs.

71 Hemmelgarn, "Decline to Sign Campaign Developing."

72 Cillizza and Sullivan, "How Proposition 8 Passed in California—and Why It Wouldn't Today."

73 "Equality Organizations Launch Coalition to Protect FAIR Education Act," Equality California, August 25, 2011, http://www.eqca.org/site/apps/nlnet/content2.aspx?c=kuLRJ9MRKrH&b=6493233&ct=1119989.

74 "Hate Groups Backing FAIR Education Act Referendum Must Be Exposed," Equality California, August 30, 2011, http://www.eqca.org/site/apps/nlnet/content2.aspx?c=kuLRJ9MRKrH&b=6493233&ct=1120262.

75 "Group Fighting California's Gay-Inclusive Education Law Short on Signatures, Accused of Violations," The American Independent Institute; Roland Palencia,

"Letter to Fair Political Practices Commission," EQCA, September 28, 2011, http://www.eqca.org/atf/cf/{34f258b3-8482-4943-91cb-08c4b0246a88}/SB%2048%20COMPLAINT%20TO%20FPPC%2009-28-2011.PDF.

76 Wyatt Buchanan, "Group Fighting LGBT Teachings Fails Petition Drive," *SF Gate*, October 13, 2011, http://www.sfgate.com/bayarea/article/Group-fighting-LGBT-teachings-fails-petition-drive-2327869.php.

77 Adam Bink, "Stop SB 48 Campaign: 'We're Working on an Initiative.'"

78 Kevin T. Snider, "Request to Prepare Circulating Title and Summary Using the Amended Language," State of California Department of Justice: Office of the Attorney General, December 21, 2011, http://oag.ca.gov/system/files/initiatives/pdfs/11–0093%20(i1038_11-0093_ais_(stop_sb_48)).pdf.

79 Leno, "California's FAIR Education Act."

80 Ashley Chiappiano, interview with the author, January 15, 2020, Brooklyn, NY, tape/notes/transcript in author's possession.

81 New Jersey State Legislature, "An Act Concerning Instruction and Instructional Materials in Public Schools and Supplementing Chapter 35 of Title 18A of the New Jersey Statutes," Trenton, NJ, January 31, 2019, https://www.njleg.state.nj.us/2018/Bills/PL19/6_.HTM.

82 General Assembly of the State of Colorado, "House Bill 19-1192," Denver, Colorado, May 28, 2019, https://leg.colorado.gov/sites/default/files/2019a_1192_signed.pdf, 2 and 7.

83 Ibid.

84 Oregon Legislative Assembly, "House Bill 2023," Salem, Oregon, May 23, 2019, https://olis.leg.state.or.us/liz/2019R1/Downloads/MeasureDocument/HB2023/Enrolled, 1.

85 101st General Assembly, State of Illinois, "HB0246," Springfield, IL, August 9, 2019, https://www.ilga.gov/legislation/fulltext.asp?DocName=10100HB0246&GA=101&SessionId=108&DocTypeId=HB&LegID=114183&DocNum=0246&GAID=15&Session=.

86 "Vote: Senate Floor: Third Reading—Final Passage," LegiScan, accessed October 14, 2020, https://legiscan.com/NJ/rollcall/S1569/id/768662; "Vote: Assembly Floor: Third Reading—Final Passage," LegiScan, accessed October 14, 2020, https://legiscan.com/NJ/rollcall/S1569/id/780779.

87 "HB 19-1192: Inclusion of American Minorities in Teaching Civil Government," Colorado Education Association, accessed October 14, 2020, http://scorecard.coloradoea.org/2019/bills/hb-19-1192/.

88 "2019 Session: House Bill 2023," *The Oregonian*, accessed October 14, 2020, https://gov.oregonlive.com/bill/2019/HB2023/. Oregon's bill passed 51–7 (twelve Republicans in favor) in the House and 21–5 (five Republicans in favor) in the Senate.

89 "Vote: Third Reading in the House," LegiScan, accessed October 14, 2020, https://legiscan.com/IL/rollcall/HB0246/id/820403; "Vote: Third Reading in the Senate," LegiScan, accessed October 14, 2020, https://legiscan.com/IL/rollcall/HB0246/id/870676.

90 "LGBTQ Inclusive Curriculum Bill Approved by Illinois Gov. JB Pritzker," Equality Illinois, accessed October 14, 2020, https://www.equalityillinois.us/%EF%BB%BFlgbtq-inclusive-curriculum-bill-approved-by-illinois-gov-jb-pritzker/.

91 "Governor Phil Murphy Signs LGBTQ-Inclusive Curriculum Legislation—Second in the Nation," Garden State Equality, accessed October 14, 2020, https://www.gardenstateequality.org/curriculum_legislation.

92 Scott Weiser, "Legislation Expands Mandatory Civics and History Education to Include Asians and LGBTQ Minority Groups," *Complete Colorado*, April 12, 2019, https://pagetwo.completecolorado.com/2019/04/12/legislation-expands-mandatory-civics-and-history-education-to-include-asians-and-lgbtq-minority-groups/.

93 Phillip Van Slooten, "LGBTQ-Inclusive Curriculum Laws Take Effect in N.J., Ill.," *Washington Blade*, September 9, 2020, https://www.washingtonblade.com/2020/09/09llo/lgbtq-inclusive-curriculum-laws-take-effect-in-n-j-ill/. The same article mentions that counties in Maryland and Virginia passed similar curricular mandates.

94 Hannan Adely, "Can Parents Opt Out of New Jersey's LGBTQ Curriculum Law?" *North Jersey*, June 26, 2019, https://www.northjersey.com/story/news/education/2019/06/26/teaching-lgbtq-in-schools-can-nj-parents-opt-out/1549151001/.

95 "Oregon Law Now Requires Schools Teach LGBTQ Curriculum to All Ages," *Pulpit and Pen*, July 23, 2019, https://pulpitandpen.org/2019/07/23/oregon-law-now-requires-schools-teach-lgbtq-curriculum-to-all-ages/.

96 "OREGON: Ask Governor Kate Brown to Veto Legislation Mandating LGBT Content in ALL School History, Geography, Economics and Civics Curriculums," Family Policy Alliance, June 5, 2019, https://familypolicyalliance.com/issues/2019/06/05/oregon-ask-governor-kate-brown-veto-legislation-mandating-lgbt-content-school-history-geography-economics-civics-curriculums/.

97 New Jersey, Colorado, Oregon, and Illinois's laws were meant to go into effect in the 2020–1 school year.

7 Victory Deferred? Implementing LGBTQ+ Curriculum Laws

1 Carolyn Laub, "It Doesn't Inevitably Get Better: Implement the FAIR Education Act," GSA Network, January 17, 2013, https://www.gsanetwork.org/news/it-doesn't-inevitably-get-better-implement-fair-education-act/011713.

2 Ibid.

3 GLSEN, *The 2013 National School Climate Survey The Experiences of Lesbian, Gay, Bisexual and Transgender Youth in Our Nation's Schools* (New York: Gay, Lesbian, and Straight Education Network, 2014); Laub, "It Doesn't Inevitably Get Better: Implement the FAIR Education Act"; Mark Leno, "California's FAIR Education Act: Addressing the Bullying Epidemic by Ending the Exclusion of LGBT People and Historical Events in Textbooks and Classrooms," *QED: A Journal in GLBTQ Worldmaking*, inaugural issue (Fall 2013).

4 Lyndsey Schlax, interview with the author, March 16, 2016, Brooklyn, NY, tape/notes/transcript in the author's possession.

5 David Tyack and Larry Cuban, *Tinkering Toward Utopia: A Century of Public School Reform* (Cambridge: Harvard University Press, 1995); Jonathan Zimmerman, "Where the Customer Is King: The Textbook in American Culture," in *A History of the Book in America, Volume 5: The Enduring Book: Print Culture in Postwar America*, eds. David Paul Nord, Joan Shelley Rubin, and Michael Schudson (Chapel Hill: University of North Carolina Press, 2009).

6 Janice Law Trecker, "Women in U.S. History High-school Textbooks," in *Sex Bias in the Schools: The Research Evidence*, eds. Janice Pottker and Andrew Fishel (Madison, NJ: Fairleigh Dickinson University Press, 1977), 148.

7 Elizabeth Weingarten, "Is This the End of the Crusade for Gender-Equal Curricula?," *The Atlantic*, June 15, 2017, https://www.theatlantic.com/education/archive/2017/06/is-this-the-end-of-the-crusade-for-gender-equal-curricula/530493/.

8 Sierra Mannie, "Why Students Are Ignorant about the Civil Rights Movement," The Hechinger Report, October 1, 2017, https://hechingerreport.org/students-ignorant-civil-rights-movement/.

9 Henry Louis Gates, Jr., "What Was the Civil Rights Movement?," PBS, accessed October 16, 2020, https://www.pbs.org/wnet/african-americans-many-rivers-to-cross/history/what-was-the-civil-rights-movement/.

10 Teaching Tolerance, *Teaching the Movement: The State of Civil Rights Education in the United States in 2011* (Montgomery, AL: Southern Poverty Law Center, 2011), 8 and 17.

11 California State Senate, "FAIR Education Act: Senate Third Reading," 2011, https://leginfo.legislature.ca.gov/faces/billNavClient.xhtml?bill_id=201120120SB48; Senate Committee on Education, "Instruction and instructional materials: sexual orientation," Bill Analysis, last modified December 13, 2010, http://www.leginfo.ca.gov/pub/11–12/bill/sen/sb_0001-0050/sb_48_cfa_20110322_113330_sen_comm.html.

12 Rachel Reinhard, interview with the author, January 29, 2015, Brooklyn, NY, tape/notes/transcript in the author's possession; Don Romesburg, interview with

the author, June 16, 2015, Brooklyn, NY, tape/notes/transcript in the author's possession; Jamie Scot, interview with the author, February 26, 2015, Brooklyn, NY, tape/notes/transcript in the author's possession; Senate Rules Committee, "Instruction: Prohibition of Discriminatory Content," Bill Analysis, last modified March 29, 2011, http://leginfo.ca.gov/pub/11–12/bill/sen/sb_0001-0050/sb_48_cfa_20110408_105410_sen_floor.html.

13 Assembly Committee on Education, "Instruction: Prohibition of discriminatory content," Bill Analysis, last modified June 22, 2011, http://www.leginfo.ca.gov/pub/11-12/bill/sen/sb_0001-0050/sb_48_cfa_20110621_104537_asm_comm.html.

14 Geoffrey Kors, interview with the author, March 26, 2015, Brooklyn, NY, tape/notes/transcript in the author's possession. Oregon and Illinois's laws specifically refer to adopting textbooks that include LGBTQ+ history and individuals.

15 Don Romesburg, interview with the author, June 16, 2015, Brooklyn, NY, tape/notes/transcript in the author's possession; Jamie Scot, interview with the author, February 26, 2015, Brooklyn, NY, tape/notes/transcript in the author's possession.

16 Hayley Penan, "Fair Education Act," *The Notice*, June 3, 2013, http://thenoticeca.com/2013/06/03/fair-education-act/.

17 See Chapter 5 and Appendix C for more information on resources available to teachers.

18 Jamie Scot, interview with the author, February 26, 2015, Brooklyn, NY, tape/notes/transcript in the author's possession. Scot left ONE Archives while this was still a work in progress. As she described the process, curriculum developers combed through US history textbooks to find entry points throughout the timeline to integrate LGBTQ+ history so that it would be woven throughout the year.

19 Jo Michael, interview with the author, July 30, 2014, Brooklyn, NY, tape/notes/transcript in the author's possession.

20 Rachel Reinhard interview with the author, January 29, 2015, Brooklyn, NY, tape/notes/transcript in the author's possession.

21 Don Romesburg, interview with the author, June 16, 2015, Brooklyn, NY, tape/notes/transcript in the author's possession.

22 Jamie Scot, interview with the author, February 26, 2015, Brooklyn, NY, tape/notes/transcript in the author's possession.

23 Ibid.

24 Rachel Reinhard, interview with the author, January 29, 2015, Brooklyn, NY, tape/notes/transcript in the author's possession.

25 Jamie Scot, interview with the author, February 26, 2015, Brooklyn, NY, tape/notes/transcript in the author's possession.

26 Zimmerman, "Where the Customer Is King: The Textbook in American Culture."

27 "Curriculum Frameworks & Instructional Materials," California Department of Education, last modified December 28, 2017, https://www.cde.ca.gov/ci/cr/cf/.

28 "History-Social Science Framework for California Public Schools: 2005 Edition with New Criteria for Instructional Materials," California Department of Education 2005, reposted June 5, 2009, https://www.cde.ca.gov/ci/cr/cf/documents/histsocsciframe.pdf; Don Romesburg, conversation with the author, June 16, 2015.

29 Don Romesburg, interview with the author, June 16, 2015, Brooklyn, NY, tape/notes/transcript in the author's possession.

30 Ibid.

31 Matthew S. Bajko, "CA Schools Already Teaching Gay History," Bay Area Reporter Online, April 21, 2011, http://www.ebar.com/news/article.php?article=5645&sec=news.

32 Don Romesburg, Leila J. Rupp, and D. M. Donahue, *Making the Framework FAIR: California History-Social Science Framework Proposed LGBT Revisions Related to the FAIR Education Act* (San Francisco, CA: Committee on Lesbian, Gay, Bisexual, and Transgender History, 2014), 6.

33 Don Romesburg, interview with the author, June 16, 2015, Brooklyn, NY, tape/notes/transcript in the author's possession.

34 Ibid.

35 Don Romesburg, interview with the author, March 11, 2016, Brooklyn, NY, tape/notes/transcript in the author's possession. As per Romesburg, once the Framework changes are approved the state legislature must move to open the standards for revision; thus, the committee's work will not be done when the Framework is approved. The Framework is instructive for textbook publishers, though, with these amendments leading to significant changes in the resources available to teachers.

36 Don Romesburg, interview with the author, March 11, 2016, Brooklyn, NY, tape/notes/transcript in the author's possession.

37 "New California History-Social Science Framework Approved by State Ed Board: LGBT Advocates and Scholars Applaud the New Standards," ACLU San Diego and Imperial Counties, July 14, 2016, https://www.aclusandiego.org/lgbt-framework/.

38 Don Romesburg, interview with the author, May 30, 2018, Brooklyn, NY, tape/notes/transcript in the author's possession.

39 Stacie Brensilver Berman, "Books Have Their Own Stories: LGBTQ History in United States History Textbooks, 1990–2015," in *Comparative Perspectives on School Textbooks: Analyzing Shifting Discourses on Nationhood, Citizenship, Gender, and Religion*, ed. Alexander Wiseman and Dobrochna Hildebrandt-Wypych (London: Palgrave Macmillan, 2021).

40 Don Romesburg, interview with the author, May 30, 2018, Brooklyn, NY, tape/notes/transcript in the author's possession. Romesburg also stated that the state oversees the textbook approval process for kindergarten through eighth grade, but districts determine which books high schools use. There is less awareness, then, of

the content in high school textbooks than elementary and middle school books. He also expressed the hope that California rejecting books that did not comply with the Framework would compel publishers to include more LGBTQ+ history in future editions.

41 Ibid.

42 "2017 History-Social Science Adoption," California Department of Education, last modified October 9, 2018, https://www.cde.ca.gov/ci/hs/im/hssadoptedprograms. asp. Two books were not adopted, both of which were published by Houghton Mifflin. According to Don Romesburg, that company was slower to accept and adopt changes than others and had not made substantive enough revisions by the deadline.

43 Don Romesburg, interview with the author, May 30, 2018, Brooklyn, NY, tape/ notes/transcript in the author's possession.

44 Don Romesburg, interview with the author, August 6, 2020, Ridgefield, CT, tape/ notes/transcript in the author's possession.

45 Ibid.

46 Ibid.

47 Don Romesburg, interview with the author, August 6, 2020, Ridgefield, CT, tape/ notes/transcript in the author's possession.

48 Ibid.

49 "LGBTQ History," Berkeley History-Social Science Project, accessed October 23, 2020, https://ucbhssp.berkeley.edu/teacher-resources/lgbtq.

50 "Home," Teaching LGBTQ History, accessed October 24, 2020, http://www. lgbtqhistory.org/.

51 Don Romesburg, interview with the author, August 6, 2020, Ridgefield, CT, tape/ notes/transcript in the author's possession.

52 Don Romesburg, interview with the author, June 16, 2015, Brooklyn, NY, tape/ notes/transcript in the author's possession.

53 Rachel Reinhard, interview with the author, January 29, 2015, Brooklyn, NY, tape/notes/transcript in the author's possession; Don Romesburg, interview with the author, February 6, 2015, Brooklyn, NY, tape/notes/transcript in the author's possession; Jamie Scot, interview with the author, February 26, 2015, Brooklyn, NY, tape/notes/transcript in the author's possession.

54 Jamie Scot, interview with the author, February 26, 2015, Brooklyn, NY, tape/notes/ transcript in the author's possession.

55 Rachel Reinhard, interview with the author, January 29, 2015, Brooklyn, NY, tape/ notes/transcript in the author's possession.

56 General Assembly of the State of Colorado, "House Bill 19–1192," Denver, Colorado, May 28, 2019, https://leg.colorado.gov/sites/default/files/2019a_1192_ signed.pdf.

57 Equality Illinois, Illinois Safe Schools Alliance, a program of Public Health Institute of Metropolitan Chicago, and The Legacy Project, "Inclusive Curriculum Implementation Guidance, Condensed Edition," Illinois Inclusive Curriculum Advisory Council, accessed October 17, 2020, https://www.isbe.net/Documents/Support-Students-Implementation-Guidance.pdf, 2.

58 "How to Use the Search Portal," Illinois Inclusive Curriculum Advisory Council, 2021, accessed May 6, 2021, https://icl.legacyprojectchicago.org/search.

59 "Virtual Professional Development Sessions," Illinois Safe Schools Alliance, 2020, accessed May 6, 2021, https://www.ilsafeschools.org/virtual-pd-sessions?emci=b1d2deb2-33f7-ea11-99c3-00155d039e74&emdi=4df6b9d4-cb12-eb11-96f5-00155d03affc&ceid=2304351.

60 Ashley Chiappiano, interview with the author, January 15, 2020, Brooklyn, NY, tape/notes/transcript in the author's possession.

61 The twelve schools represent urban, suburban, and rural districts. The student populations among the schools differ, as well, in terms of ethnicity, socioeconomic status, and grade levels. (Ashley Chiappiano, interview with the author, January 15, 2020, Brooklyn, NY, tape/notes/transcript in the author's possession.)

62 Ashley Chiappiano, interview with the author, January 15, 2020, Brooklyn, NY, tape/notes/transcript in the author's possession.

63 GSE hosted a conference for educators in October 2020 to share LGBTQ+-inclusive resources.

64 Ibid.

65 Melanie Burney, "LGBTQ Education Is Now Mandatory in N.J. Schools. Here's How Teachers Are Preparing," *Philadelphia Inquirer*, January 20, 2020, https://www.inquirer.com/education/nj-lgbtq-education-curriculum-lesson-plans-mandate-20200120.html.

66 Ibid.

67 Massachusetts Department of Elementary and Secondary Education, *2018 History and Social Science Framework, Grades Pre Kindergarten to 12* (Malden: Massachusetts Department of Elementary and Secondary Education, 2018), 135–6.

68 "Safe Schools Program for LGBTQ Students," Massachusetts Department of Elementary and Secondary Education, accessed October 17, 2020, https://www.doe.mass.edu/sfs/lgbtq/.

69 "New York State Grades 9–12 Social Studies Framework," New York State Education Department, January 2015, http://www.nysed.gov/common/nysed/files/programs/curriculum-instruction/ss-framework-9-12.pdf. State Senator Brad Hoylman introduced an LGBTQ+ curriculum bill in 2019. It languished in committee.

70 NYC Department of Education, "Hidden Voices: LGBTQ+ Stories in United States History," *WeTeachNYC*, accessed March 11, 2021, https://www.weteachnyc.org/

media2016/filer_public/e4/6e/e46e71d1-f2ca-4ce3-89d2-6ce2db1decda/hv_lgbtq_
v13_ada.pdf.

71 "LGBTQ+ Curriculum Project for NYC Department of Education Completed,"
American Social History Project: Center for Media and Learning, September 18,
2020, https://ashp.cuny.edu/news/lgbtq-curriculum-project-nyc-department-
education-completed.

8 Compelled to Act: Teachers Who Include LGBTQ+ History

1 See Chapter 5.

2 Lyndsey Schlax, interview with the author, March 16, 2016, Brooklyn, NY, tape/
notes/transcript in the author's possession; Kisha Webster, interview with the
author, July 8, 2015, Brooklyn, NY, tape/notes/transcript in the author's possession.

3 States with laws prohibiting the discussion of LGBTQ+ issues in schools include
Alabama, Louisiana, Mississippi, Oklahoma, and Texas.

4 Gloria T. Alter, "Discovery, Engagement, and Transformation," *Social Education* 81,
no. 5 (2017): 279; "No Promo Homo Laws," GLSEN, accessed December 12, 2017,
https://www.glsen.org/learn/policy/issues/nopromohomo; Emily K. Hobson and
Felicia T. Perez, "Questions, Not Test Answers: Teaching LGBT History in Public
Schools," in *U.S. Lesbian, Gay, Bisexual, and Transgender History*, eds. Leila J. Rupp
and Susan K. Freeman (Madison: University of Wisconsin Press, 2014), 77–91.

5 I interviewed thirteen teachers. One ultimately opted against having their stories
included in this book. Some of the teachers' names were changed at their request.

6 Finding teachers to interview was difficult, especially because though there are
thousands of teachers, relatively few focus on LGBTQ+ history consistently or
in depth, if at all. I knew only one of the teachers prior to conducting this study.
The others I located in a variety of ways: friends and colleagues introduced me to
educators whom they thought might teach this material, I initiated a social media
campaign to spread my interview request through a web of contacts in different
regions, and I reached out to teachers whose efforts on this topic were the subjects
of articles I read. I interviewed each educator multiple times; the conversations
lasted between sixty and ninety minutes.

7 Olivia Cole, interview with the author, September 6, 2017, Brooklyn, NY, tape/
notes/transcript in the author's possession; Hasmig Minassian, interview with the
author, September 25, 2017, Brooklyn, NY, tape/notes/transcript in the author's
possession; Dana Rosenberg, interview with the author, December 6, 2016,
Brooklyn, NY, tape/notes/transcript in the author's possession; Will Scott, interview
with the author, August 16, 2017, Brooklyn, NY, tape/notes/transcript in the
author's possession.

8 Courtney Anderson, interview with the author, August 10, 2017, Brooklyn, NY, tape/notes/transcript in the author's possession; Mitchell James, interview with the author, August 8, 2017, Brooklyn, NY, tape/notes/transcript in the author's possession; Melanie Wells, interview with the author, August 17, 2017, Brooklyn, NY, tape/notes/transcript in the author's possession.

9 Danny M. Cohen, interview with the author, November 16, 2016, Brooklyn, NY, tape/notes/transcript in the author's possession; Felicia Perez, conversation with the author, September 25, 2016; Lyndsey Schlax, interview with the author, March 16, 2016, Brooklyn, NY, tape/notes/transcript in the author's possession.

10 Courtney Anderson, interview with the author, August 10, 2017, Brooklyn, NY, tape/notes/transcript in the author's possession; Olivia Cole, interview with the author, September 6, 2017, Brooklyn, NY, tape/notes/transcript in the author's possession; Danny M. Cohen, interview with the author, August 8, 2017, Brooklyn, NY, tape/notes/transcript in the author's possession; Fred Fox, interview with the author, August 7, 2017, Brooklyn, NY, tape/notes/transcript in the author's possession; Hasmig Minassian, interview with the author, September 25, 2017, Brooklyn, NY, tape/notes/transcript in the author's possession; Mitchell James, interview with the author, August 8, 2017, Brooklyn, NY, tape/notes/transcript in the author's possession; Felicia Perez, interview with the author, August 14, 2017, Brooklyn, NY, tape/notes/transcript in the author's possession; Lyndsey Schlax, interview with the author, September 7, 2017, Brooklyn, NY, tape/notes/transcript in the author's possession.

11 Kevin Jennings, interview with the author, January 3, 2018, Brooklyn, NY, tape/notes/transcript in the author's possession. According to Kevin Jennings, one of the reasons he founded the organization that would become GLSEN in 1990 was to unite teachers across the country attempting to establish GSAs or discuss LGBT issues in a school-based setting something, he recalled, few teachers did and for which there was little support. Jennings asserted that any discussion around this issue throughout the 1990s was, in many places, taboo.

12 Dana Rosenberg, interview with the author, December 6, 2016, Brooklyn, NY, tape/notes/transcript in the author's possession.

13 Dana Rosenberg, email exchange with the author, September 25, 2017, Brooklyn, NY, electronic files in the author's possession.

14 Dana Rosenberg, interview with the author, December 6, 2016, Brooklyn, NY, tape/notes/transcript in the author's possession.

15 Felicia Perez, interview with the author, August 14, 2017, Brooklyn, NY, tape/notes/transcript in the author's possession.

16 Will Scott, interview with the author, August 16, 2017, Brooklyn, NY, tape/notes/transcript in the author's possession.

17 Ibid.

18 Will Scott, interview with the author, November 15, 2016, Brooklyn, NY, tape/notes/transcript in the author's possession.

19 Kevin Jennings, interview with the author, January 3, 2018, Brooklyn, NY, tape/notes/transcript in the author's possession.

20 Mitchell James, interview with the author, October 30, 2016, Brooklyn, NY, tape/notes/transcript in the author's possession.

21 Mitchell James, interview with the author, August 8, 2017, Brooklyn, NY, tape/notes/transcript in the author's possession.

22 Mitchell James, interview with the author, October 30, 2016, Brooklyn, NY, tape/notes/transcript in the author's possession. James lives in a state that, as of 2019, mandates LGBTQ+-inclusive curriculum.

23 Melanie Wells, interview with the author, August 17, 2017, Brooklyn, NY, tape/notes/transcript in the author's possession.

24 Melanie Wells, interview with the author, September 20, 2016, Brooklyn, NY, tape/notes/transcript in the author's possession.

25 Ibid.

26 Ibid.

27 Olivia Cole, interview with the author, December 8, 2016, Brooklyn, NY, tape/notes/transcript in the author's possession.

28 Ibid.

29 Courtney Anderson, interview with the author, August 10, 2017, Brooklyn, NY, tape/notes/transcript in the author's possession.

30 Ibid.

31 Courtney Anderson, interview with the author, November 1, 2016, Brooklyn, NY, tape/notes/transcript in the author's possession.

32 Hasmig Minassian, interview with the author, September 25, 2017, Brooklyn, NY, tape/notes/transcript in the author's possession.

33 Lyndsey Schlax, interview with the author, January 12, 2017, Brooklyn, NY, tape/notes/transcript in the author's possession.

34 Fred Fox, interview with the author, May 24, 2016, Brooklyn, NY, tape/notes/transcript in the author's possession.

35 Fred Fox, interview with the author, August 7, 2017, Brooklyn, NY, tape/notes/transcript in the author's possession. Fox relocated after the 2017–18 school year.

36 Casey Sinclair, interview with the author, September 27, 2017, Brooklyn, NY, tape/notes/transcript in the author's possession.

37 Casey Sinclair, interview with the author, November 22, 2016, Brooklyn, NY, tape/notes/transcript in the author's possession.

38 See Chapter 5.

39 Danny M. Cohen, interview with the author, November 16, 2016, Brooklyn, NY, tape/notes/transcript in the author's possession.

40 Courtney Anderson, interview with the author, November 1, 2016, Brooklyn, NY, tape/notes/transcript in the author's possession.

41 Melanie Wells, interview with the author, September 20, 2016, Brooklyn, NY, tape/notes/transcript in the author's possession.

42 Dana Rosenberg, interview with the author, December 6, 2016, Brooklyn, NY, tape/notes/transcript in the author's possession.

43 Fred Fox, interview with the author, May 24, 2016, Brooklyn, NY, tape/notes/transcript in the author's possession.

44 Casey Sinclair, interview with the author, November 22, 2016, Brooklyn, NY, tape/notes/transcript in the author's possession.

45 Lyndsey Schlax, interview with the author, March 16, 2016, Brooklyn, NY, tape/notes/transcript in the author's possession.

46 Fred Fox, interview with the author, August 7, 2017, Brooklyn, NY, tape/notes/transcript in the author's possession.

47 Casey Sinclair, interview with the author, November 22, 2016, Brooklyn, NY, tape/notes/transcript in the author's possession.

48 Danny M. Cohen, interview with the author, November 16, 2016, Brooklyn, NY, tape/notes/transcript in the author's possession.

49 Melanie Wells, interview with the author, September 20, 2016, Brooklyn, NY, tape/notes/transcript in the author's possession.

50 Courtney Anderson, interview with the author, November 1, 2016, Brooklyn, NY, tape/notes/transcript in the author's possession.

51 Casey Sinclair, interview with the author, November 22, 2016, Brooklyn, NY, tape/notes/transcript in the author's possession.

52 Mitchell James, interview with the author, October 30, 2016, Brooklyn, NY, tape/notes/transcript in the author's possession.

53 Courtney Anderson, interview with the author, November 1, 2016, Brooklyn, NY, tape/notes/transcript in the author's possession.

54 Mitchell James, interview with the author, October 30, 2016, Brooklyn, NY, tape/notes/transcript in the author's possession.

55 Dana Rosenberg, interview with the author, December 6, 2016, Brooklyn, NY, tape/notes/transcript in the author's possession.

56 Felicia Perez, interview with the author, December 6, 2016, Brooklyn, NY, tape/notes/transcript in the author's possession.

57 Danny M. Cohen, interview with the author, August 8, 2017, Brooklyn, NY, tape/notes/transcript in the author's possession; Mitchell James, interview with the author, August 8, 2017, Brooklyn, NY, tape/notes/transcript in the author's

possession; Will Scott, interview with the author, August 16, 2017, Brooklyn, NY, tape/notes/transcript in the author's possession.

58 Fred Fox, interview with the author, May 24, 2016, Brooklyn, NY, tape/notes/transcript in the author's possession.

59 Lyndsey Schlax, interview with the author, September 7, 2017, Brooklyn, NY, tape/notes/transcript in the author's possession.

60 Felicia Perez, interview with the author, September 25, 2016, Brooklyn, NY, tape/notes/transcript in the author's possession.

61 Sandra Schmidt, "Queering Social Studies: The Role of Social Studies in Normalizing Citizens and Sexuality in the Common Good," *Theory and Research in Social Education* 38, no. 3 (2010).

62 Hasmig Minassian, interview with the author, November 23, 2016, Brooklyn, NY, tape/notes/transcript in the author's possession.

63 Melanie Wells, interview with the author, September 20, 2016, Brooklyn, NY, tape/notes/transcript in the author's possession.

64 Olivia Cole, interview with the author, December 8, 2016, Brooklyn, NY, tape/notes/transcript in the author's possession.

9 Innovations at the Grassroots Level: LGBTQ+ History in High School Classroom Instruction

1 Courtney Anderson, interview with the author, November 1, 2016, Brooklyn, NY, tape/notes/transcript in the author's possession; Courtney Anderson, interview with the author, August 10, 2017, Brooklyn, NY, tape/notes/transcript in the author's possession; Olivia Cole, interview with the author, December 8, 2016, Brooklyn, NY, tape/notes/transcript in the author's possession; Olivia Cole, interview with the author, September 6, 2017, Brooklyn, NY, tape/notes/transcript in the author's possession; Mitchell James, interview with the author, October 30, 2016, Brooklyn, NY, tape/notes/transcript in the author's possession; Mitchell James, interview with the author, August 8, 2017, Brooklyn, NY, tape/notes/transcript in the author's possession; Felicia Perez, interview with the author, September 25, 2016, Brooklyn, NY, tape/notes/transcript in the author's possession.

2 Melanie Wells, interview with the author, September 20, 2016, Brooklyn, NY, tape/notes/transcript in the author's possession.

3 Felicia Perez, interview with the author, September 25, 2016, Brooklyn, NY, tape/notes/transcript in the author's possession.

4 Casey Sinclair, interview with the author, November 22, 2016, Brooklyn, NY, tape/notes/transcript in the author's possession.

5 Olivia Cole, interview with the author, December 8, 2016, Brooklyn, NY, tape/notes/transcript in the author's possession.

6 Melanie Wells, interview with the author, September 20, 2016, Brooklyn, NY, tape/notes/transcript in the author's possession.

7 Fred Fox, interview with the author, May 24, 2016, Brooklyn, NY, tape/notes/transcript in the author's possession.

8 Hasmig Minassian, interview with the author, November 23, 2016, Brooklyn, NY, tape/notes/transcript in the author's possession.

9 Dana Rosenberg, interview with the author, December 6, 2016, Brooklyn, NY, tape/notes/transcript in the author's possession.

10 Ibid.

11 Will Scott, interview with the author, November 15, 2016, Brooklyn, NY, tape/notes/transcript in the author's possession.

12 Ibid.

13 Courtney Anderson, interview with the author, November 1, 2016, Brooklyn, NY, tape/notes/transcript in the author's possession.

14 Ibid.

15 Courtney Anderson, interview with the author, November 1, 2016, Brooklyn, NY, tape/notes/transcript in the author's possession; Fred Fox, interview with the author, August 7, 2017, Brooklyn, NY, tape/notes/transcript in the author's possession; Hasmig Minassian, interview with the author, November 23, 2016, Brooklyn, NY, tape/notes/transcript in the author's possession; Lyndsey Schlax, interview with the author, March 16, 2016, Brooklyn, NY, tape/notes/transcript in the author's possession; Lyndsey Schlax, interview with the author, January 12, 2017, Brooklyn, NY, tape/notes/transcript in the author's possession; Melanie Wells, interview with the author, September 20, 2016, Brooklyn, NY, tape/notes/transcript in the author's possession.

16 Olivia Cole, interview with the author, December 8, 2016, Brooklyn, NY, tape/notes/transcript in the author's possession.

17 Courtney Anderson, interview with the author, November 1, 2016, Brooklyn, NY, tape/notes/transcript in the author's possession.

18 Lyndsey Schlax, interview with the author, January 12, 2017, Brooklyn, NY, tape/notes/transcript in the author's possession.

19 Felicia Perez, interview with the author, December 6, 2016, Brooklyn, NY, tape/notes/transcript in the author's possession.

20 Ibid.

21 Fred Fox, interview with the author, May 24, 2016, Brooklyn, NY, tape/notes/transcript in the author's possession.

22 Melanie Wells, interview with the author, September 20, 2016, Brooklyn, NY, tape/notes/transcript in the author's possession.

23 Ibid.
24 Mitchell James, interview with the author, October 30, 2016, Brooklyn, NY, tape/notes/transcript in the author's possession.
25 Hasmig Minassian, interview with the author, November 23, 2016, Brooklyn, NY, tape/notes/transcript in the author's possession.
26 Ibid.
27 Among the organizations creating classroom resources on LGBTQ+ history, the Human Rights Resource Center and Learning for Justice offer lessons connecting the battle for same-sex marriage with the struggle for interracial marriage.
28 Olivia Cole, interview with the author, December 8, 2016, Brooklyn, NY, tape/notes/transcript in the author's possession.
29 Mitchell James, interview with the author, October 30, 2016, Brooklyn, NY, tape/notes/transcript in the author's possession.
30 Danny M. Cohen, interview with the author, November 16, 2016, Brooklyn, NY, tape/notes/transcript in the author's possession.
31 Ibid.
32 Olivia Cole, interview with the author, December 8, 2016, Brooklyn, NY, tape/notes/transcript in the author's possession.
33 Fred Fox, interview with the author, May 24, 2016, Brooklyn, NY, tape/notes/transcript in the author's possession.
34 Lyndsey Schlax, interview with the author, January 12, 2017, Brooklyn, NY, tape/notes/transcript in the author's possession.
35 Hasmig Minassian, interview with the author, November 23, 2016, Brooklyn, NY, tape/notes/transcript in the author's possession.
36 Ibid.
37 Dana Rosenberg, interview with the author, December 6, 2016, Brooklyn, NY, tape/notes/transcript in the author's possession.
38 Fred Fox, interview with the author, May 24, 2016, Brooklyn, NY, tape/notes/transcript in the author's possession.
39 Ibid.
40 Courtney Anderson, interview with the author, November 1, 2016, Brooklyn, NY, tape/notes/transcript in the author's possession.
41 Felicia Perez, interview with the author, December 6, 2016, Brooklyn, NY, tape/notes/transcript in the author's possession.
42 Ibid.
43 Olivia Cole, interview with the author, December 8, 2016, Brooklyn, NY, tape/notes/transcript in the author's possession.
44 Ibid.
45 Hasmig Minassian, interview with the author, November 23, 2016, Brooklyn, NY, tape/notes/transcript in the author's possession.

46 Casey Sinclair, interview with the author, November 22, 2016, Brooklyn, NY, tape/notes/transcript in the author's possession.

47 Ibid.

48 Courtney Anderson, interview with the author, November 1, 2016, Brooklyn, NY, tape/notes/transcript in the author's possession.

49 Felicia Perez, interview with the author, September 25, 2016, Brooklyn, NY, tape/notes/transcript in the author's possession.

50 Hasmig Minassian, interview with the author, November 23, 2016, Brooklyn, NY, tape/notes/transcript in the author's possession.

51 Fred Fox, interview with the author, May 24, 2016, Brooklyn, NY, tape/notes/transcript in the author's possession.

52 Casey Sinclair, interview with the author, November 22, 2016, Brooklyn, NY, tape/notes/transcript in the author's possession.

53 Ibid.

54 Lyndsey Schlax, interview with the author, January 12, 2017, Brooklyn, NY, tape/notes/transcript in the author's possession.

55 Lyndsey Schlax, interview with the author, March 16, 2016, Brooklyn, NY, tape/notes/transcript in the author's possession. Schlax offers her curriculum to any teacher starting their own LGBTQ+ history elective.

56 Ibid.

57 Lyndsey Schlax, interview with the author, January 12, 2017, Brooklyn, NY, tape/notes/transcript in the author's possession.

58 Fred Fox, interview with the author, May 24, 2016, Brooklyn, NY, tape/notes/transcript in the author's possession.

59 Ibid.

60 Olivia Cole, interview with the author, December 8, 2016, Brooklyn, NY, tape/notes/transcript in the author's possession.

61 Lyndsey Schlax, interview with the author, March 16, 2016, Brooklyn, NY, tape/notes/transcript in the author's possession.

62 Fred Fox, interview with the author, May 24, 2016, Brooklyn, NY, tape/notes/transcript in the author's possession.

63 Casey Sinclair, interview with the author, November 22, 2016, Brooklyn, NY, tape/notes/transcript in the author's possession.

64 Danny M. Cohen, interview with the author, October 21, 2020, Brooklyn, NY, tape/notes/transcript in the author's possession.

65 Melanie Wells, interview with the author, September 20, 2016, Brooklyn, NY, tape/notes/transcript in the author's possession.

66 Lyndsey Schlax, interview with the author, March 16, 2016, Brooklyn, NY, tape/notes/transcript in the author's possession.

67 Mitchell James, interview with the author, October 30, 2016, Brooklyn, NY, tape/notes/transcript in the author's possession.

68 Will Scott, interview with the author, November 15, 2016, Brooklyn, NY, tape/notes/transcript in the author's possession.

69 Fred Fox, interview with the author, August 7, 2017, Brooklyn, NY, tape/notes/transcript in the author's possession.

70 Lyndsey Schlax, interview with the author, January 12, 2017, Brooklyn, NY, tape/notes/transcript in the author's possession

71 Keith C. Barton and Linda S. Levstik, *Teaching History for the Common Good* (New York: Routledge, 2004); Gloria Ladson Billings, "Crafting a Culturally Relevant Social Studies Approach," in *The Social Studies Curriculum: Purposes, Problems, and Possibilities*, ed. E. Ross, chapter 10 (Albany, NY: SUNY Press, 2001); Linda S. Levstik and Keith C. Barton, *Doing History: Investigating with Children in Elementary and Middle Schools* (Mahwah, NJ: Lawrence Erlbaum Associates, 1997).

72 Courtney Anderson, interview with the author, November 1, 2016, Brooklyn, NY, tape/notes/transcript in the author's possession; Danny M. Cohen, interview with the author, November 16, 2016, Brooklyn, NY, tape/notes/transcript in the author's possession; Dana Rosenberg, interview with the author, December 6, 2016, Brooklyn, NY, tape/notes/transcript in the author's possession; Lyndsey Schlax, interview with the author, March 16, 2016, Brooklyn, NY, tape/notes/transcript in the author's possession; Casey Sinclair, interview with the author, November 22, 2016, Brooklyn, NY, tape/notes/transcript in the author's possession.

73 Danny M. Cohen, interview with the author, November 16, 2016, Brooklyn, NY, tape/notes/transcript in the author's possession.

74 Casey Sinclair, interview with the author, November 22, 2016, Brooklyn, NY, tape/notes/transcript in the author's possession.

75 Fred Fox, interview with the author, May 24, 2016, Brooklyn, NY, tape/notes/transcript in the author's possession.

76 Courtney Anderson, interview with the author, November 1, 2016, Brooklyn, NY, tape/notes/transcript in the author's possession.

10 Impact at the Grassroots: Challenges and Rewards in Teaching LGBTQ+ History

1 David Tyack and Larry Cuban, *Tinkering Toward Utopia: A Century of Public School Reform* (Cambridge: Harvard University Press, 1995); Jonathan Zimmerman, "Where the Customer Is King: The Textbook in American Culture," in *A History of the Book in America, Volume 5: The Enduring Book: Print Culture in Postwar*

America, ed. David Paul Nord, Joan Shelley Rubin, and Michael Schudson (Chapel Hill: University of North Carolina Press, 2009).

2 Fred Fox, interview with the author, May 24, 2016, Brooklyn, NY, tape/notes/ transcript in the author's possession.

3 Dana Rosenberg, interview with the author, December 6, 2016, Brooklyn, NY, tape/ notes/transcript in the author's possession; Will Scott, interview with the author, November 15, 2016, Brooklyn, NY, tape/notes/transcript in the author's possession; Lyndsey Schlax, interview with the author, January 12, 2017, Brooklyn, NY, tape/ notes/transcript in the author's possession.

4 Olivia Cole, interview with the author, September 6, 2017, Brooklyn, NY, tape/ notes/transcript in the author's possession; Fred Fox, interview with the author, May 24, 2016, Brooklyn, NY, tape/notes/transcript in the author's possession; Dana Rosenberg, interview with the author, December 6, 2016, Brooklyn, NY, tape/notes/transcript in the author's possession; Will Scott, interview with the author, November 15, 2016, Brooklyn, NY, tape/notes/transcript in the author's possession; Lyndsey Schlax, interview with the author, January 12, 2017, Brooklyn, NY, tape/notes/transcript in the author's possession; Melanie Wells, interview with the author, August 17, 2017, Brooklyn, NY, tape/notes/transcript in the author's possession.

5 Among the other teachers interviewed, four teachers replied that several teachers at their school include LGBTQ+ history, albeit in different ways. Three others stated that they received support from colleagues who did not teach an integrated curriculum themselves. Two worked in schools where there was little interaction between department members.

6 Fred Fox, interview with the author, May 24, 2016, Brooklyn, NY, tape/notes/ transcript in the author's possession.

7 Ibid.

8 Dana Rosenberg, interview with the author, December 6, 2016, Brooklyn, NY, tape/ notes/transcript in the author's possession; Melanie Wells, interview with the author, September 20, 2016, Brooklyn, NY, tape/notes/transcript in the author's possession.

9 Dana Rosenberg, interview with the author, December 6, 2016, Brooklyn, NY, tape/ notes/transcript in the author's possession.

10 Lyndsey Schlax, interview with the author, March 16, 2016, Brooklyn, NY, tape/ notes/transcript in the author's possession.

11 Hasmig Minassian, interview with the author, November 23, 2016, Brooklyn, NY, tape/notes/transcript in the author's possession.

12 Olivia Cole, interview with the author, December 8, 2016, Brooklyn, NY, tape/ notes/transcript in the author's possession; Courtney Anderson, interview with the author, November 1, 2016, Brooklyn, NY, tape/notes/transcript in the author's possession.

13 Mitchell James, interview with the author, October 30, 2016, Brooklyn, NY, tape/notes/transcript in the author's possession.

14 Will Scott, interview with the author, November 15, 2016, Brooklyn, NY, tape/notes/transcript in the author's possession.

15 Lyndsey Schlax, interview with the author, January 12, 2017, Brooklyn, NY, tape/notes/transcript in the author's possession.

16 Dana Rosenberg, interview with the author, December 6, 2016, Brooklyn, NY, tape/notes/transcript in the author's possession.

17 Fred Fox, interview with the author, May 24, 2016, Brooklyn, NY, tape/notes/transcript in the author's possession.

18 Lyndsey Schlax, interview with the author, January 12, 2017, Brooklyn, NY, tape/notes/transcript in the author's possession.

19 Ibid.

20 Fred Fox, interview with the author, May 24, 2016, Brooklyn, NY, tape/notes/transcript in the author's possession; Lyndsey Schlax, interview with the author, January 12, 2017, Brooklyn, NY, tape/notes/transcript in the author's possession.

21 Fred Fox, interview with the author, May 24, 2016, Brooklyn, NY, tape/notes/transcript in the author's possession.

22 Mitchell James, interview with the author, October 30, 2016, Brooklyn, NY, tape/notes/transcript in the author's possession; Melanie Wells, interview with the author, September 20, 2016, Brooklyn, NY, tape/notes/transcript in the author's possession.

23 Melanie Wells, interview with the author, September 20, 2016, Brooklyn, NY, tape/notes/transcript in the author's possession.

24 Mitchell James, interview with the author, October 30, 2016, Brooklyn, NY, tape/notes/transcript in the author's possession.

25 Hasmig Minassian, interview with the author, January 26, 2017, Brooklyn, NY, tape/notes/transcript in the author's possession.

26 Felicia Perez, interview with the author, September 25, 2016, Brooklyn, NY, tape/notes/transcript in the author's possession.

27 "Why Class Size Matters Today," National Council for Teachers of English, April 1, 2014, accessed January 21, 2018, http://www2.ncte.org/statement/why-class-size-matters/.

28 Olivia Cole, interview with the author, December 8, 2016, Brooklyn, NY, tape/notes/transcript in the author's possession.

29 Felicia Perez, interview with the author, September 25, 2016, Brooklyn, NY, tape/notes/transcript in the author's possession.

30 Lyndsey Schlax, interview with the author, March 16, 2016, Brooklyn, NY, tape/notes/transcript in the author's possession. Schlax is not alone in this contention. Scholars and university professors concerned about the lack of LGBTQ+ history in

schools also focus on the dearth of college and university-based options available to teachers who wish to or might be able to include this material (Daniel Hurewitz, Don Romesburg, and Wendy Rouse, "Words That Shape the World: Historians, Teachers, and Partnerships for LGBT History," presentation, American Historical Association Annual Meeting, Washington, DC, January 5, 2018).

31 Will Scott, interview with the author, November 15, 2016, Brooklyn, NY, tape/ notes/transcript in the author's possession.

32 Melanie Wells, interview with the author, September 20, 2016, Brooklyn, NY, tape/ notes/transcript in the author's possession.

33 Ibid.

34 Lyndsey Schlax, interview with the author, January 12, 2017, Brooklyn, NY, tape/ notes/transcript in the author's possession.

35 States with "No Promo Homo" laws present their own distinct challenges and obstacles in this case.

36 Danny M. Cohen, interview with the author, November 16, 2016, Brooklyn, NY, tape/notes/transcript in the author's possession; Don Romesburg, interview with the author, March 11, 2016, Brooklyn, NY, tape/notes/transcript in the author's possession; Lyndsey Schlax, interview with the author, January 12, 2017, Brooklyn, NY, tape/notes/transcript in the author's possession.

37 Lyndsey Schlax, interview with the author, March 16, 2016, Brooklyn, NY, tape/ notes/transcript in the author's possession.

38 Olivia Cole, interview with the author, December 8, 2016, Brooklyn, NY, tape/ notes/transcript in the author's possession.

39 Hasmig Minassian, interview with the author, January 26, 2017, Brooklyn, NY, tape/ notes/transcript in the author's possession.

40 Mitchell James, interview with the author, October 30, 2016, Brooklyn, NY, tape/ notes/transcript in the author's possession.

41 Melanie Wells, interview with the author, September 20, 2016, Brooklyn, NY, tape/ notes/transcript in the author's possession.

42 Fred Fox, interview with the author, May 24, 2016, Brooklyn, NY, tape/notes/ transcript in the author's possession.

43 Fred Fox, interview with the author, August 7, 2017, Brooklyn, NY, tape/notes/ transcript in the author's possession.

44 Courtney Anderson, interview with the author, November 1, 2016, Brooklyn, NY, tape/notes/transcript in the author's possession.

45 Hasmig Minassian, interview with the author, November 23, 2016, Brooklyn, NY, tape/notes/transcript in the author's possession.

46 Ibid.

47 Hasmig Minassian, interview with the author, January 26, 2017, Brooklyn, NY, tape/ notes/transcript in the author's possession.

48 Melanie Wells, interview with the author, September 20, 2016, Brooklyn, NY, tape/notes/transcript in the author's possession.

49 Courtney Anderson, interview with the author, November 1, 2016, Brooklyn, NY, tape/notes/transcript in the author's possession.

50 Olivia Cole, interview with the author, December 8, 2016, Brooklyn, NY, tape/notes/transcript in the author's possession.

51 Ibid.

52 Casey Sinclair, interview with the author, November 22, 2016, Brooklyn, NY, tape/notes/transcript in the author's possession.

53 Dana Rosenberg, interview with the author, December 6, 2016, Brooklyn, NY, tape/notes/transcript in the author's possession.

54 Ibid.

55 Olivia Cole, interview with the author, December 8, 2016, Brooklyn, NY, tape/notes/transcript in the author's possession.

56 Felicia Perez, interview with the author, September 25, 2016, Brooklyn, NY, tape/notes/transcript in the author's possession.

57 Lyndsey Schlax, interview with the author, September 7, 2017, Brooklyn, NY, tape/notes/transcript in the author's possession.

58 Courtney Anderson, interview with the author, November 1, 2016, Brooklyn, NY, tape/notes/transcript in the author's possession.

59 Felicia Perez, interview with the author, September 25, 2016, Brooklyn, NY, tape/notes/transcript in the author's possession.

60 Lyndsey Schlax, interview with the author, March 16, 2016, Brooklyn, NY, tape/notes/transcript in the author's possession.

61 Felicia Perez, interview with the author, December 6, 2016, Brooklyn, NY, tape/notes/transcript in the author's possession.

62 Lyndsey Schlax, interview with the author, March 16, 2016, Brooklyn, NY, tape/notes/transcript in the author's possession.

63 Casey Sinclair, interview with the author, November 22, 2016, Brooklyn, NY, tape/notes/transcript in the author's possession.

64 Olivia Cole, interview with the author, September 6, 2017, Brooklyn, NY, tape/notes/transcript in the author's possession.

65 Fred Fox, interview with the author, August 7, 2017, Brooklyn, NY, tape/notes/transcript in the author's possession. According to Fox, the Black Student Union in his district hosts their own graduation ceremony each year in addition to the school-wide graduation. His students built on that idea in seeking an LGBTQ+ graduation ceremony.

66 Dana Rosenberg, interview with the author, December 6, 2016, Brooklyn, NY, tape/notes/transcript in the author's possession.

67 Felicia Perez, interview with the author, September 25, 2016, Brooklyn, NY, tape/notes/transcript in the author's possession.

68 Olivia Cole, interview with the author, December 8, 2016, Brooklyn, NY, tape/notes/transcript in the author's possession; Olivia Cole, interview with the author, September 6, 2017, Brooklyn, NY, tape/notes/transcript in the author's possession; Fred Fox, interview with the author, August 7, 2017, Brooklyn, NY, tape/notes/transcript in the author's possession; Hasmig Minassian, interview with the author, November 23, 2016, Brooklyn, NY, tape/notes/transcript in the author's possession.

69 Courtney Anderson, interview with the author, November 1, 2016, Brooklyn, NY, tape/notes/transcript in the author's possession; Felicia Perez, interview with the author, September 25, 2016, Brooklyn, NY, tape/notes/transcript in the author's possession; Felicia Perez, interview with the author, December 6, 2016, Brooklyn, NY, tape/notes/transcript in the author's possession; Lyndsey Schlax, interview with the author, March 16, 2016, Brooklyn, NY, tape/notes/transcript in the author's possession.

70 Danny M. Cohen, interview with the author, November 16, 2016, Brooklyn, NY, tape/notes/transcript in the author's possession; Dana Rosenberg, interview with the author, December 6, 2016, Brooklyn, NY, tape/notes/transcript in the author's possession; Lyndsey Schlax, interview with the author, January 12, 2017, Brooklyn, NY, tape/notes/transcript in the author's possession; Casey Sinclair, interview with the author, November 22, 2016, Brooklyn, NY, tape/notes/transcript in the author's possession.

71 Lyndsey Schlax, interview with the author, September 7, 2017, Brooklyn, NY, tape/notes/transcript in the author's possession.

72 Courtney Anderson, interview with the author, November 1, 2016, Brooklyn, NY, tape/notes/transcript in the author's possession; Fred Fox, interview with the author, August 7, 2017, Brooklyn, NY, tape/notes/transcript in the author's possession; Mitchell James, interview with the author, October 30, 2016, Brooklyn, NY, tape/notes/transcript in the author's possession; Lyndsey Schlax, interview with the author, January 12, 2017, Brooklyn, NY, tape/notes/transcript in the author's possession; Casey Sinclair, interview with the author, November 22, 2016, Brooklyn, NY, tape/notes/transcript in the author's possession.

73 Melanie Wells, interview with the author, September 20, 2016, Brooklyn, NY, tape/notes/transcript in the author's possession.

74 Olivia Cole, interview with the author, September 6, 2017, Brooklyn, NY, tape/notes/transcript in the author's possession.

75 Will Scott, interview with the author, November 15, 2016, Brooklyn, NY, tape/notes/transcript in the author's possession.

76 Courtney Anderson, interview with the author, November 1, 2016, Brooklyn, NY, tape/notes/transcript in the author's possession; Hasmig Minassian, interview with

the author, November 23, 2016, Brooklyn, NY, tape/notes/transcript in the author's possession; Felicia Perez, interview with the author, September 25, 2016, Brooklyn, NY, tape/notes/transcript in the author's possession; Lyndsey Schlax, interview with the author, March 16, 2016, Brooklyn, NY, tape/notes/transcript in the author's possession.

77 Hasmig Minassian, electronic correspondence with the author, February 4, 2018, Brooklyn, NY, electronic files in the author's possession.

78 Don Romesburg, "Words That Shape the World: Historians, Teachers, and Partnerships for LGBT History," presentation, American Historical Association Annual Meeting, Washington, DC, January 5, 2018.

79 Hasmig Minassian, interview with the author, September 25, 2017, Brooklyn, NY, tape/notes/transcript in the author's possession; Dana Rosenberg, interview with the author, December 6, 2016, Brooklyn, NY, tape/notes/transcript in the author's possession.

80 Courtney Anderson, email conversation with the author, October 27, 2020, Brooklyn, NY, communication/notes in the author's possession.

81 Melanie Wells, email conversation with the author, July 20, 2020, Ridgefield, CT, communication/notes in the author's possession.

82 Lyndsey Schlax, interview with the author, March 16, 2016, Brooklyn, NY, tape/notes/transcript in the author's possession.

83 Danny M. Cohen, interview with the author, November 16, 2016, Brooklyn, NY, tape/notes/transcript in the author's possession; Danny M. Cohen, interview with the author, August 8, 2017, Brooklyn, NY, tape/notes/transcript in the author's possession; Will Scott, interview with the author, August 16, 2017, Brooklyn, NY, tape/notes/transcript in the author's possession.

84 Mitchell James, interview with the author, August 8, 2017, Brooklyn, NY, tape/notes/transcript in the author's possession.

85 Fred Fox, interview with the author, May 24, 2016, Brooklyn, NY, tape/notes/transcript in the author's possession.

Conclusion: The Future of LGBTQ+ History Instruction

1 Jonathan Zimmerman, "Where the Customer Is King: The Textbook in American Culture," in *A History of the Book in America, Volume 5: The Enduring Book: Print Culture in Postwar America*, eds. David Paul Nord, Joan Shelley Rubin, and Michael Schudson (Chapel Hill: University of North Carolina Press, 2009).

2 As I discuss this work with an increasing network of people, I find more teachers who excitedly respond that they include this information and/or wish they could devote more time to it. In addition, people outside education circles have put me in contact with teachers they know who focus on this material. It is a sign of progress

that more teachers are invested in and open about including LGBTQ+ history in their classes.

3 Approximately forty teachers attended a session on LGBTQ+ history resources for K–12 students at the 2019 NCSS conference.

4 "Don Romesburg Prize," Committee on Lesbian, Gay, Bisexual, and Transgender History, accessed January 5, 2019, http://clgbthistory.org/prizes/don-romesburg-prize.

5 Alexandra Pannoni, "Don't Overlook LGBTQ+ History in High School," *U.S. News and World Report*, October 16, 2017, www.usnews.com/high-schools/blogs/high-school-notes/articles/2017-10-16/dont-overlook-LGBTQ+-history-in-high-school.

6 Tris Mamone, "I Wish I Had Learned LGBTQ+ History in High School," HuffPost, June 12, 2018, https://www.huffingtonpost.com/entry/opinion-mamone-LGBTQ+-history-school_us_5b1eb078e4b0adfb826c632a.

7 Olivia B. Waxman, "As More States Require Schools to Teach LGBTQ History, Resources for Teachers Expand," *Time*, December 13, 2019, https://time.com/5747670/lgbtq-history-resources/.

8 Arizona repealed its "No Promo Homo" law in 2019. In 2021 the state senate approved a bill that "would prohibit schools from teaching about sexual orientation, gender expression, and LGBTQ history" without parental consent; the governor vetoed it. (Brian Pietsch, "Arizona Governor Vetoes Bill Restricting L.G.B.T.Q. Education," *New York Times*, April 21, 2021, https://www.nytimes.com/2021/04/21/us/doug-ducey-gender-sexual-orientation-aids-lgbtq.html?action=click&module=In%20Other%20News&pgtype=Homepage.)

9 John Paul Brammer, "'No Promo Homo Laws' Affect Millions of Students Across the U.S.," NBC News, February 9, 2018, https://www.nbcnews.com/feature/nbc-out/no-promo-homo-laws-affect-millions-students-across-u-s-n845136.

10 Don Romesburg, interview with the author, August 6, 2020, Ridgefield, CT, tape/notes/transcript in the author's possession.

11 Debra Fowler and Steven LaBounty-McNair, "Contextualizing LGBT+ History within the Social Studies Curriculum," National Council for Social Studies, September 2019, https://www.socialstudies.org/position-statements/contextualizing-lgbt-history-within-social-studies-curriculum.

12 "Executive Order on Guaranteeing an Educational Environment Free from Discrimination on the Basis of Sex, Including Sexual Orientation or Gender Identity," The White House, March 8, 2021, https://www.whitehouse.gov/briefing-room/presidential-actions/2021/03/08/executive-order-on-guaranteeing-an-educational-environment-free-from-discrimination-on-the-basis-of-sex-including-sexual-orientation-or-gender-identity/?emci=ebbc8095-b482-eb11-85aa-00155d43c992&emdi=9d49caa2-4383-eb11-85aa-00155d43c992&ceid=427726.

Bibliography

"2019 Session: House Bill 2023." *The Oregonian*. Accessed October 14, 2020. https://gov.oregonlive.com/bill/2019/HB2023/.

Abrajano, Marisa. "Are Blacks and Latinos Responsible for the Passage of Proposition 8? Analyzing Voter Attitudes on California's Proposal to Ban Same-Sex Marriage in 2008." *Political Research Quarterly* 63, no. 4 (December 2010): 922–32.

ACLU San Diego and Imperial Counties. "New California History-Social Science Framework Approved by State Ed Board: LGBT Advocates and Scholars Applaud the New Standards." Last modified July 14, 2016. https://www.aclusandiego.org/lgbt-framework/.

ACT UP. "ACT UP Accomplishments and Partial Chronology." Accessed March 16, 2018. https://endaids.actupny.com/the-community.

Adely, Hannan. "Can Parents Opt Out of New Jersey's LGBTQ Curriculum Law?" *North Jersey*. June 26, 2019. https://www.northjersey.com/story/news/education/2019/06/26/teaching-lgbtq-in-schools-can-nj-parents-opt-out/1549151001/.

Advocates for Youth. "I Am Who I Am." Last modified December 8, 2017. https://advocatesforyouth.org/wp-content/uploads/3rscurric/documents/7-Lesson-6-3Rs-IAmWhoIAm.pdf.

Advocates for Youth. "Who We Are: About Advocates for Youth." Last modified 2021, accessed May 4, 2021. https://www.advocatesforyouth.org/about/.

Alter, Gloria T. "Discovery, Engagement, and Transformation: Learning about Gender and Sexual Diversity in Social Education." *Social Education* 81, no. 5 (2017): 279–87.

Alter, Gloria T. "LGBTQ+ Issues in Social Education: Understanding, Inclusion, and Advocacy." *Social Education* 81, no. 5 (2017): 277–8.

The American Independent Institute. "Group Fighting California's Gay-Inclusive Education Law Short on Signatures, Accused of Violations." Last modified September 2011. http://www.americanindependent.com/197541/group-trying-to-repeal-cas-lgbt-inclusive-education-law-short-on-signatures-accused-of-violations.

American Social History Project: Center for Media and Learning. "LGBTQ+ Curriculum Project for NYC Department of Education Completed." September 18, 2020. https://ashp.cuny.edu/news/lgbtq-curriculum-project-nyc-department-education-completed.

Anderson, Barbara. "Clips from a Minnesota Child Protection League Presentation." Filmed November 18, 2013 at Southwest Metro Tea Party. Video, 7:22. https://www.youtube.com/watch?v=vFIxKtcaOJA.

Anti-Defamation League. "Caitlyn Jenner and the Power of Coming Out." Accessed July 16, 2015. http://www.adl.org/education-outreach/lesson-plans/c/caitlyn-jenner-and-the-power-of-coming-out.html#.VbBfg4u4n5Y.

Anti-Defamation League. "Matthew Shepard and James Byrd, Jr. Hate Crimes Prevention Act." Accessed July 6, 2015. http://www.adl.org/education-outreach/lesson-plans/c/matthew-shepard-and-james-byrd-jr.html#.VbBU_Yu4n5Y.

Anti-Defamation League. "The History and Impact of Anti-LGBT Slurs." Curriculum Connections. Accessed August 1, 2018. https://www.adl.org/media/6788/download.

Anti-Defamation League. "The Invisibility of LGBT People in History: 'Peculiar Disposition of the Eyes.'" Curriculum Connections. Accessed July 31, 2018. https://www.adl.org/media/6779/download.

Anti-Defamation League. "The Stonewall Uprising." Accessed October 9, 2020. https://www.adl.org/media/12966/download.

Anti-Defamation League. "Transgender Identity and Issues." 2014, accessed October 6, 2020. https://www.adl.org/media/4767/download.

Anti-Defamation League. "Understanding Homophobia/Heterosexism and How to Be an Ally." Accessed July 16, 2015. http://www.adl.org/education-outreach/lesson-plans/c/understanding-homophobia-heterosexism-ally.html#.VbBf1Iu4n5Y.

Anti-Defamation League. "Unheard Voices: Stories of LGBT History." Accessed July 21, 2018. https://www.adl.org/media/4699/download.

Anti-Defamation League. "Wedding Cake, Same-Sex Marriage, and Discrimination." Accessed January 7, 2019. https://www.adl.org/media/10779/download.

Anti-Defamation League. "Who We Are." Accessed July 31, 2018. https://www.adl.org/who-we-are.

Anti-Defamation League. "Winning the Right to Marry: Historic Parallels." Curriculum Connections. Accessed August 1, 2018. https://www.adl.org/media/6790/download.

Anti-Defamation League, GLSEN, and StoryCorps. "In-Group, Out-Group: The Exclusion of LGBT People from Societal Institutions." GLSEN. Accessed August 1, 2018. https://www.glsen.org/sites/default/files/UV%20Lessons.pdf.

Armstrong, Elizabeth A., and Suzanna M. Crage. "Movements and Memory: The Making of the Stonewall Myth." *American Sociological Review* 71, no. 5 (October 2006): 724–51.

Arnold, Lori. "Gov. Schwarzenegger Vows to Veto Gay-Friendly Curriculum Bill." *Christian Examiner*, June 9, 2006. http://www.christianexaminer.com/article/gov.schwarzenegger.vows.to.veto.gay.friendly.curriculum.bill/43205.htm.

Assembly Committee on Education. "Discrimination Based on Sexual Orientation in Instructional Services and Programs." Bill Analysis AB 222—As Amended March 24, 1999. Last modified April 7, 1999. http://www.leginfo.ca.gov/pub/99-00/bill/asm/ab_0201-0250/ab_222_cfa_19990407_112400_asm_comm.html.

Assembly Committee on Education. "Instruction: Prohibition of Discriminatory Content." Bill Analysis. Last modified June 22, 2011. http://www.leginfo.ca.gov/pub/11-12/bill/sen/sb_0001-0050/sb_48_cfa_20110621_104537_asm_comm.html.

Astacaan, Eric. "1999 Legislation." California Legislative Lesbian, Gay, Bisexual, and Transgender Caucus. Accessed March 16, 2016. http://lgbtcaucus.legislature. ca.gov/1999-legislation.

Austrian, J. J. *Worm Loves Worm*. New York: HarperCollins, 2016.

Bajko, Matthew S. "40 Years Ago, San Francisco Adopted Historic Gay Rights Law." *Bay Area Reporter*, April 12, 2018. https://www.ebar.com/news/news//258422.

Bajko, Matthew S. "CA Schools Already Teaching Gay History." *Bay Area Reporter Online*, April 21, 2011. http://www.ebar.com/news/article. php?article=5645&sec=news.

Baldor, Lolita C., and Zeke Miller. "Biden Reverses Trump Ban on Transgender People in Military." *AP News*, January 25, 2021. https://apnews.com/article/ biden-reverse-ban-transgender-military-f0ace4f9866e0ca0df021eba75b3af20.

Barabak, Mark Z. "Gays May Have the Fastest of All Civil Rights Movements." *Los Angeles Times*, May 20, 2012. http://articles.latimes.com/2012/may/20/nation/ la-na-gay-rights-movement-20120521.

Barbanel, Josh. "Under 'Rainbow,' a War: When Politics, Morals and Learning Mix." *New York Times*, December 27, 1992. https://www.nytimes.com/1992/12/27/ nyregion/under-rainbow-a-war-when-politics-morals-and-learning-mix.html.

Barbeauld, Paige Hamby. " 'Don't Say Gay' Bills and the Movement to Keep Discussion of LGBT Issues Out of Schools." *Journal of Law and Education* 43, no. 1 (Winter 2014): 137–46.

Bareilles, Jack. "Women, Gays, and Other Voices of Resistance." In *Voices of a People's History of the United States: Teacher's Guide*, edited by Gayle Olson-Raymer, 235–46. New York: Seven Stores Press, 2005.

Barton, Keith C., and Linda S. Levstik. *Teaching History for the Common Good*. New York: Routledge, 2004.

Berkeley Academic Guide. "About the Program." Lesbian, Gay, Bisexual, and Transgender Studies. Accessed April 21, 2018. http://guide.berkeley.edu/ undergraduate/degree-programs/lesbian-gay-bisexual-transgender-studies/.

Berkeley History-Social Science Project. "The Lavender Scare." Accessed April 23, 2018. http://ucbhssp.berkeley.edu/content/lavender-scare.

Berman, Stacie Brensilver. "Books Have Their Own Stories: LGBTQ History in United States History Textbooks, 1990–2015." In *Comparative Perspectives on School Textbooks: Analyzing Shifting Discourses on Nationhood, Citizenship, Gender, and Religion*, edited by Alexander Wiseman and Dobrochna Hildebrandt-Wypych. London: Palgrave Macmillan, 2021.

Biegel, Stuart. *The Right to Be Out*. Minneapolis: University of Minnesota Press, 2010.

Bink, Adam. "Stop SB 48 Campaign: 'We're Working on an Initiative.' " Equality on Trial. Last modified 2011. http://www.equalityontrial.com/category/ fair-education-act/page/2/.

Boyle-Baise, Marilynne, and Carl A. Grant. "Citizen/Community Participation in Education." In *Critical Issues in Social Studies Teacher Education*, edited by Susan Adler, 145–64. Greenwich, CT: Information Age, 2004.

Brammer, John Paul. "'No Promo Homo Laws' Affect Millions of Students across the U.S." NBC News. February 9, 2018. https://www.nbcnews.com/feature/nbc-out/no-promo-homo-laws-affect-millions-students-across-u-s-n845136.

Brigham, Roger. "Kuehl Waters Down Textbook Bill." *Bay Area Reporter Online*, August 10, 2006. http://www.ebar.com/news/article.php?article=1069&sec=news.

Brinkmann, Susan. "California's 'Pro-Gay Indoctrination' Bill Advances in Same Week That Priest Is Accused of 'Anti-Gay Indoctrination.'" *WOG Blog*. Last modified March 30, 2011. http://www.womenofgrace.com/blog/?p=7547.

Buchanan, Wyatt. "Group Fighting LGBT Teachings Fails Petition Drive." *SF Gate*, October 13, 2011. http://www.sfgate.com/bayarea/article/Group-fighting-LGBT-teachings-fails-petition-drive-2327869.php.

Burney, Melanie. "LGBTQ Education Is Now Mandatory in N.J. Schools. Here's How Teachers Are Preparing." *Philadelphia Inquirer*, January 20, 2020. https://www.inquirer.com/education/nj-lgbtq-education-curriculum-lesson-plans-mandate-20200120.html.

Cain, Patricia A. "Litigating for Lesbian and Gay Rights: A Legal History." *Virginia Law Review* 79, no. 7 (October 1993): 1551–641.

California Department of Education. "2017 History-Social Science Adoption." Last modified October 9, 2018. https://www.cde.ca.gov/ci/hs/im/hssadoptedprograms.asp.

California Department of Education. "Curriculum Frameworks & Instructional Materials." Last modified December 28, 2017. https://www.cde.ca.gov/ci/cr/cf/.

California Department of Education. "History-Social Science Framework for California Public Schools: 2005 Edition with New Criteria for Instructional Materials." Last modified June 5, 2009. https://www.cde.ca.gov/ci/cr/cf/documents/histsocsciframe.pdf.

California Legislative Lesbian, Gay, Bisexual, and Transgender Caucus. "Past Legislation." Accessed March 16, 2016. http://lgbtcaucus.legislature.ca.gov/legislation.

California Legislative Information. "SB-48 Pupil Instruction: Prohibition of Discriminatory Content." Last modified July 14, 2011. http://leginfo.legislature.ca.gov/faces/billNavClient.xhtml?bill_id=201120120SB48.

California State Assembly. "AB 537 Assembly Bill—Chaptered." *Legislative Counsel's Digest*. Last modified February 18, 1999. http://www.leginfo.ca.gov/pub/99-00/bill/asm/ab_0501-0550/ab_537_bill_19991010_chaptered.html.

California State Senate. "FAIR Education Act: Senate Third Reading." Last modified 2011. https://leginfo.legislature.ca.gov/faces/billNavClient.xhtml?bill_id=201120120SB48.

California State Senate. "SB 777 Senate Bill—Chaptered." *Legislative Counsel's Digest.* Last modified February 23, 2007. http://www.leginfo.ca.gov/pub/07-08/bill/sen/sb_0751-0800/sb_777_bill_20071012_chaptered.pdf.

California State Senate. "SB 1437 Amended." *Legislative Counsel's Digest.* Last modified May 1, 2006. http://leginfo.legislature.ca.gov/faces/billTextClient.xhtml?bill_id=200520060SB1437.

"California's Senate Votes Bill Repealing Sexual Prohibitions." *New York Times*, May 2, 1975. https://www.nytimes.com/1975/05/02/archives/californias-senate-votes-bill-repealing-sexual-prohibitions.html.

Campaign for Children and Families. "They're BAACCKK: California 'Gay' Brainwashing Bills (SB 777 and AB 394)." Americans for Truth. Last modified March 26, 2007. https://americansfortruth.com/2007/03/27/theyre-baacckk-california-gay-brainwashing-bills-sb-777/.

Campos, David. "Battling the Bullying of LGBTQ+ Students." *Social Education* 81, no. 5 (2017): 288–95.

Catholics for the Common Good. "Governor Ignores Thousands of Phone Calls; CCG Evaluating Next Step." Last modified July 14, 2011. http://ccgaction.org/node/1084.

Celis, III, William. "Schools Across U.S. Cautiously Adding Lessons on Gay Life." *New York Times*, January 6, 1993. https://www.nytimes.com/1993/01/06/us/schools-across-us-cautiously-adding-lessons-on-gay-life.html.

Chauncey, George. *Why Marriage?: The History Shaping Today's Debate over Gay Equality.* New York: Basic Books, 2004.

Christie, Jim. "California Orders Gay History in School Textbooks." Reuters. July 14, 2011. https://www.reuters.com/article/us-gays-california-history/california-orders-gay-history-in-school-textbooks-idUSTRE76D7QT20110715.

Cillizza, Chris, and Sean Sullivan. "How Proposition 8 Passed in California—and Why It Wouldn't Today." *Washington Post*, March 26, 2013. https://www.washingtonpost.com/news/the-fix/wp/2013/03/26/how-proposition-8-passed-in-california-and-why-it-wouldnt-today/.

City College of San Francisco. "History." Accessed October 1, 2020. https://www.ccsf.edu/academics/ccsf-catalog/courses-by-department/history.

CLAGS Center for LGBTQ+ Studies. "About CLAGS." Center for LGBTQ+ Studies. Accessed April 23, 2018. clags.org/about-clags/.

Clarke, Jay. "Gay Rights Fight Shaping Up in Miami." *Washington Post*, March 27, 1977. https://www.washingtonpost.com/archive/politics/1977/03/27/gay-rights-fight-shaping-up-in-miami/e4f596c1-f8e0-4785-b528-599077a478ba/?utm_term=.04a11f177c6e.

Cohen, Micah. "In California, Growing Diversity First Made Its Mark." *New York Times*, October 8, 2012. https://fivethirtyeight.blogs.nytimes.com/2012/10/08/in-california-growing-diversity-first-made-its-mark/.

Cohen, Robert. "'Two, Four, Six, Eight, We Don't Want to Integrate': White Student Attitudes toward the University of Georgia's Desegregation." *Georgia Historical Quarterly* 80, no. 3 (Fall 1996): 616–45.

Cohen, Robert. *Freedom's Orator: Mario Savio and the Radical Legacy of the 1960s.* New York: Oxford University Press, 2009.

Cohen, Robert, and David J. Snyder, eds. *Rebellion in Black and White: Southern Student Activism in the 1960s.* Baltimore: Johns Hopkins University Press, 2013.

Colorado Education Association. "HB 19–1192: Inclusion of American Minorities in Teaching Civil Government." Accessed October 14, 2020. http://scorecard. coloradoea.org/2019/bills/hb-19-1192/.

Committee on Lesbian, Gay, Bisexual, and Transgender History. "Don Romesburg Prize." Accessed January 5, 2019. http://clgbthistory.org/prizes/ don-romesburg-prize.

Committee on Lesbian, Gay, Bisexual, and Transgender History. "HIST 490:004 Special Topics in American History: U.S. Lesbian, Gay, Bisexual, and Transgender Histories." Accessed June 16, 2014. http://clgbthistory.org/wp-content/uploads/2013/03/HIST-490-U.S.-LGBT-Histories1.pdf.

Committee on Lesbian, Gay, Bisexual, and Transgender History. "Syllabi." Accessed April 23, 2018. http://clgbthistory.org/projects/syllabi.

DefendChristians.org. "Urgent: Help Stop Radical Bill from Manipulating Our Kids." Last modified September 27, 2011. http://defendchristians.org/news/ urgent-help-stop-radical-bill-from-manipulating-our-kids.

D'Emilio, John, and Estelle B. Freedman. *Intimate Matters: A History of Sexuality in America.* Chicago: University of Chicago Press, 2012.

Denegre, Peter. "Is Everyone Protected by the Bill of Rights?" Thirteen Ed online. Accessed August 1, 2018. https://www.thirteen.org/edonline/lessons/billofrights/.

Department of the Interior Bureau of Education. *The Social Studies in Secondary Education.* Washington, DC: Government Printing Office, 1916.

Derose, Jason. "DePaul University to Offer Minor in 'Queer Studies.'" NPR. Accessed April 22, 2018. https://www.npr.org/templates/story/story.php?storyId=5173232.

Dunn, Jalaya Liles. "Our New Name: Learning for Justice." Learning for Justice. February 3, 2021. https://www.learningforjustice.org/magazine/ our-new-name-learning-for-justice.

Ellis, Danika Leigh. "The 38 Best Queer YA Novels." *Vulture,* June 21, 2018. https:// www.vulture.com/2018/06/38-best-lgbtq-ya-novels.html.

England, Karen. "Outrageous Homosexual Bill Passes California Senate–SB 777 a Serious Assault on Religious Freedom and Morality in Schools." *Christian News Wire,* May 24, 2007. http://www.christiannewswire.com/news/933623242.html.

Equality California. "Equality Organizations Launch Coalition to Protect FAIR Education Act." Last modified August 25, 2011. http://www.eqca.org/site/apps/nlnet/ content2.aspx?c=kuLRJ9MRKrH&b=6493233&ct=1119989.

Equality California. "Governor Says He Will Veto Bill Protecting Students and Fostering Tolerance in Schools." Last modified May 25, 2006. http://www.eqca.org/site/apps/nlnet/content2.aspx?c=kuLRJ9MRKrH&b=4025925&ct=5195357.

Equality California. "Governor Signs Six LGBT Bills, Secures Protections for LGBT Youth." Last modified October 12, 2007. http://www.eqca.org/site/apps/nlnet/content2.aspx?c=kuLRJ9MRKrH&b=4026083&ct=5198249.

Equality California. "Hate Groups Backing FAIR Education Act Referendum Must Be Exposed." Last modified August 30, 2011. http://www.eqca.org/site/apps/nlnet/content2.aspx?c=kuLRJ9MRKrH&b=6493233&ct=1120262.

Equality California. "Issues: Non-Discrimination." Accessed June 27, 2015. http://www.eqca.org/site/pp.asp?c=kuLRJ9MRKrH&b=4026611.

Equality California. "Senator Mark Leno Introduces FAIR Education Act." Last modified December 13, 2010. http://www.eqca.org/site/apps/nlnet/content2.aspx?c=kuLRJ9MRKrH&b=4869041&ct=8971441.

Equality Illinois. "LGBTQ Inclusive Curriculum Bill Approved by Illinois Gov. JB Pritzker." Accessed October 14, 2020. https://www.equalityillinois.us/%EF%BB%BFlgbtq-inclusive-curriculum-bill-approved-by-illinois-gov-jb-pritzker/.

Equality Illinois, Illinois Safe Schools Alliance, a program of Public Health Institute of Metropolitan Chicago, and The Legacy Project. "Inclusive Curriculum Implementation Guidance, Condensed Edition." Illinois Inclusive Curriculum Advisory Council. Accessed October 17, 2020. https://www.isbe.net/Documents/Support-Students-Implementation-Guidance.pdf.

Equality on Trial. "We're Working on an Initiative." 2011, accessed June 2, 2015. http://www.equalityontrial.com/category/fair-education-act/page/2/.

Facing History and Ourselves. "LGBTQ History and Why It Matters." Accessed October 8, 2020. https://www.facinghistory.org/educator-resources/current-events/lgbtq-history-and-why-it-matters.

Facing History and Ourselves. "Our Mission." Accessed October 8, 2020. https://www.facinghistory.org/about-us.

Family Policy Alliance. "OREGON: Ask Governor Kate Brown to Veto Legislation Mandating LGBT Content in ALL School History, Geography, Economics and Civics Curriculums." June 5, 2019. https://familypolicyalliance.com/issues/2019/06/05/oregon-ask-governor-kate-brown-veto-legislation-mandating-lgbt-content-school-history-geography-economics-civics-curriculums/.

Fernandez, Joseph A., and John Underwood. *Tales Out of School: Joseph Fernandez's Crusade to Rescue American Education*. Boston: Little, Brown, 1993.

FindLaw. "Alabama Code Title 16. Education § 16-40A-2." Accessed July 31, 2018. https://codes.findlaw.com/al/title-16-education/al-code-sect-16-40a-2.html.

FindLaw. "Texas Health and Safety Code § 85.007. Educational Materials for Minors." Accessed October 8, 2020. https://codes.findlaw.com/tx/health-and-safety-code/health-safety-sect-85-007.html.

FLASH. "Home." Accessed October 19, 2020. https://www.etr.org/FLASH/.

FLASH. "Lesson Selection Tool." Accessed October 19, 2020. https://www.etr.org/
FLASH/.

Focus on the Family. "About." Accessed July 30, 2018. https://www.focusonthefamily.
com/about.

Focus on the Family. "Capturing Children's Minds." True Tolerance—A Project of
Focus on Family. Accessed July 30, 2018. https://www.truetolerance.org/2011/
capturing-childrens-minds/.

Fowler, Debra, and Steven LaBounty-McNair. "Contextualizing LGBT+ History
within the Social Studies Curriculum." National Council for Social Studies.
September 2019. https://www.socialstudies.org/position-statements/
contextualizing-lgbt-history-within-social-studies-curriculum.

Garden State Equality. "Governor Phil Murphy Signs LGBTQ-Inclusive Curriculum
Legislation—Second in the Nation." Accessed October 14, 2020. https://www.
gardenstateequality.org/curriculum_legislation.

Gates Jr., Henry Louis. "What Was the Civil Rights Movement?" PBS. Accessed October
16, 2020. https://www.pbs.org/wnet/african-americans-many-rivers-to-cross/
history/what-was-the-civil-rights-movement/.

Gay, Geneva. "Social Studies Teacher Education for Urban Classrooms." In *Critical
Issues in Social Studies Teacher Education*, edited by Susan Adler, 75–96. Greenwich,
CT: Information Age, 2004.

"Gay Liberation Front: Manifesto." Fordham University. Accessed January 18, 2019.
https://sourcebooks.fordham.edu/pwh/glf-london.asp.

General Assembly of the State of Colorado. "House Bill 19–1192." May 28, 2019. https://
leg.colorado.gov/sites/default/files/2019a_1192_signed.pdf.

GLAAD Media Institute. *Where We Are on TV '19–'20*. New York: GLAAD Media
Institute, 2019. https://www.glaad.org/sites/default/files/GLAAD%20WHERE%20
WE%20ARE%20ON%20TV%202019%202020.pdf, p. 8.

GLSEN. *The 2013 National School Climate Survey: The Experiences of Lesbian, Gay,
Bisexual and Transgender Youth in Our Nation's Schools*. New York: Gay, Lesbian, and
Straight Education Network, 2014.

GLSEN. *The 2017 National School Climate Survey: The Experiences of Lesbian, Gay,
Bisexual and Transgender Youth in Our Nation's Schools*. New York: Gay, Lesbian, and
Straight Education Network, 2018.

GLSEN. *The 2019 National School Climate Survey: The Experiences of Lesbian, Gay,
Bisexual and Transgender Youth in Our Nation's Schools*. New York: Gay, Lesbian, and
Straight Education Network, 2020.

GLSEN. "Alan Turing: True to Himself." Last modified 2015, accessed August 2, 2018.
https://www.glsen.org/sites/default/files/Alan%20Turing%20True%20to%20
Himself-Final_0.pdf.

GLSEN. "LGBTQ History Timeline." Accessed October 7, 2020. https://www.glsen.org/
activity/lgbtq-history-timeline-lesson.

GLSEN. "Love, Simon: Coming Out & Invisible Identities Lesson." Accessed October 19, 2020. https://www.glsen.org/article/love-simon-coming-out-invisible-identities-lesson.

GLSEN. "No Promo Homo Laws." Accessed December 12, 2017. https://www.glsen.org/learn/policy/issues/nopromohomo.

GLSEN. "Policy Maps." Updated August 2020, accessed October 2, 2020. https://www.glsen.org/policy-maps.

GLSEN. "Read, Watch, Collaborate: GLSEN PD for Educators." Accessed April 13, 2018. https://www.glsen.org/educate/professional-development.

GLSEN. "ThinkB4YouSpeak Guide for Educators of Grades 6–12." Accessed July 17, 2015. http://www.glsen.org/sites/default/files/Guide%20to%20ThinkB4YouSpeak.pdf.

GLSEN. "Unheard Voices: Stories and Lessons for Grades 6–12." Accessed July 31, 2018. https://www.glsen.org/unheardvoices.html.

GLSEN. "When Did It Happen: An LGBT History Lesson." Accessed July 1, 2015. http://www.glsen.org/sites/default/files/When%20Did%20it%20Happen%20Lesson%20Plan_0.pdf.

Gross, Jane. "California Governor, in Reversal, Signs a Bill on Gay Rights in Jobs." *New York Times*, September 26, 1992. http://www.nytimes.com/1992/09/26/us/california-governor-in-reversal-signs-a-bill-on-gay-rights-in-jobs.html.

GSA Network. "Governor Signs 3 Gay Rights Bills, Vetoes 2." Last modified October 15, 2009. http://www.gsanetwork.org/news/governor-signs-3-gay-rights-bills-vetoes-2/101509.

GSA Network. "History and Accomplishments." Accessed March 28, 2018. https://gsanetwork.org/about-us/history.

GSA Network. "Our Approach." Accessed March 28, 2018. https://gsanetwork.org/about-us.

Guttmacher Institute. "Sex and HIV Education." October 12, 2020. https://www.guttmacher.org/state-policy/explore/sex-and-hiv-education#.

Hastings, Deborah. "L.A. Law Kiss Hailed by Gay Rights Group." Associated Press. February 9, 1991. https://apnews.com/62a4f9c94e3839eddb95916ee43d54f6.

Hemmelgarn, Seth. "Decline to Sign Campaign Developing." *Bay Area Reporter Online*, August 4, 2011. http://www.ebar.com/news/article.php?sec=news&article=5912.

Hemmelgarn, Seth. "EQCA: No Illusion on Stop SB 48." *Bay Area Reporter Online*, September 1, 2011. http://ebar.com/new/article.php?sec=news&article=6005.

Hess, Diana. "Teaching about Same-Sex Marriage as a Policy and Constitutional Issue." *Social Education* 73, no. 7 (2009): 344–9.

Higgins, Laurie. "Back to School: Teachers Who Exploit Their Position." Illinois Family Institute. Last modified August 13, 2013. https://illinoisfamily.org/education/back-to-school-teachers-who-exploit-their-position/.

Hinds, Stuart. "Anita Bryant: Hate Monger Descends on Kansas City." *Phoenix Newsletter*, October/November 2015. https://library.umkc.edu/content/images/glama/timeline/1977-bryant.pdf.

History Unerased. "Curriculum." Accessed May 5, 2021. https://unerased.org/resource/curriculum.

History UnErased. "History Unerased." Accessed May 5, 2021. https://unerased.org/.

Hobart and William Smith Colleges. "History." LGBT Studies. Accessed April 24, 2018. http://www.hws.edu/academics/lgbt/history.aspx.

Hobson, Emily, and Felicia T. Perez. "Questions, Not Test Answers." In *Understanding and Teaching U.S. Lesbian, Gay, Bisexual, and Transgender History*, edited by Leila J. Rupp and Susan K. Freeman, 77–91. Madison: University of Wisconsin Press, 2014.

Howard Zinn.org. "Zinn Education Project." Accessed August 2, 2018. https://www.howardzinn.org/related-projects/zinn-education-project/.

Hudnell, Kari. "GLSEN Statement on the Start of LGBT History Month." GLSEN. October 1, 2015. https://www.glsen.org/article/glsen-statement-start-lgbt-history-month.

Human Rights Campaign. "Growing Up LGBT in America: HRC Youth Survey Report Key Findings." Last modified 2012. https://assets2.hrc.org/files/assets/resources/Growing-Up-LGBT-in-America_Report.pdf?_ga=2.144728948.1389147936.1533265876-1406905136.1424747565.

Human Rights Campaign. "HRC Story: HRC Foundation." Accessed March 16, 2018. https://www.hrc.org/hrc-story/hrc-foundation.

Human Rights Campaign. "HRC Story: Mission Statement." Accessed March 16, 2018. http://www.hrc.org/hrc-story/mission-statement.

Human Rights Campaign. "Time to Thrive." Accessed April 20, 2018. timetothrive.org.

Human Rights Resource Center. "I Now Pronounce You … Same-Sex Marriage Legislation." Last modified 2000, accessed July 1, 2015. http://www1.umn.edu/humanrts/edumat/hreduseries/TB3/act6/act6f.html.

Human Rights Resource Center. "Introduction: Understanding Lesbian, Gay, Bisexual, and Transgender Rights as Human Rights." Last modified 2000. http://hrlibrary.umn.edu/edumat/hreduseries/TB3/details.htm.

Human Rights Resource Center. "Words Really Matter." Last modified 2000, accessed August 1, 2018. http://hrlibrary.umn.edu/edumat/hreduseries/TB3/details.htm.

Hurewitz, Daniel, Don Romesburg, and Wendy Rouse. "Words That Shape the World: Historians, Teachers, and Partnerships for LGBT History." Presentation at the American Historical Association Annual Meeting, Washington, DC, January 5, 2018.

Hyde, Sue. "School Doors Open, with Deadly Consequences." National LGBTQ+ Task Force. Accessed April 24, 2018. http://www.thetaskforce.org/school-doors-open-with-deadly-consequences/.

Illinois Family Institute. "About." Accessed July 30, 2018. https://illinoisfamily.org/about/.

Illinois Inclusive Curriculum Advisory Council. "How to Use the Search Portal." Last modified 2021, accessed May 6, 2021. https://icl.legacyprojectchicago.org/search.

Illinois Safe Schools Alliance. "Virtual Professional Development Sessions." Last modified 2020, accessed May 6, 2021. https://www.ilsafeschools.org/virtual-pd-sessions?emci=b1d2deb2-33f7-ea11-99c3-00155d039e74&emdi=4df6b9d4-cb12-eb11-96f5-00155d03affc&ceid=2304351.

It Gets Better Project. "Our Misson/Vision/People." Accessed January 29, 2019. https://itgetsbetter.org/initiatives/mission-vision-people/.

Jacobs, Rick. "Letter to the Editor: Courage Campaign Asks for Truth in Dialogue about SB 48." *San Diego Gay & Lesbian News*, August 24, 2011. http://sdgln.com/tags/courage-campaign?page=1#sthash.aMzVtPzP.dpbs.

Jenkins, Richard. *Social Identity*. New York: Routledge, 2008.

Kaczorowski, Craig. "Mattachine Society." GLBTQ Archive. Accessed March 19, 2018. http://www.glbtqarchive.com/ssh/mattachine_society_S.pdf.

Kellogg, Carolyn. "Once Controversial, 'Heather Has Two Mommies' Is Now Collectible." *Los Angeles Times*, May 11, 2017. http://www.latimes.com/books/jacketcopy/la-ca-jc-heather-has-two-mommies-20170511-story.html.

Kobrin, David. *Beyond the Textbook: Teaching History Using Documents and Primary Sources*. Portsmouth, NH: Heinemann, 1996.

Kopan, Tal, and Eugene Scott. "North Carolina Governor Signs Controversial Transgender Bill." CNN. March 24, 2016. https://www.cnn.com/2016/03/23/politics/north-carolina-gender-bathrooms-bill/index.html.

KQED News. "Governor Signs FAIR Education Act—LGBT History Bill." Accessed July 16, 2018. https://www.kqed.org/news/33986/governor-signs-fair-education-act-lgbt-history-bill.

Kuehl, Sheila. "Letter to School Superintendents." GSA Network. Last modified December 18, 2002. https://www.gsanetwork.org/files/resources/SKLetter.pdf

Ladson-Billings, Gloria. "Crafting a Culturally Relevant Social Studies Approach." In *The Social Studies Curriculum: Purposes, Problems, and Possibilities*, edited by E. Ross, Chapter 10. Albany, NY: SUNY Press, 2001.

Laird, Cynthia. "EQCA to Fight SB 48 Referendum." Edge Media Network. Last modified July 30, 2011. http://www.edgemedianetwork.com/news/local/news//122766/eqca_to_fight_sb_48_referendum.

Lambda Legal. "Lambda Legal History." Accessed March 16, 2018. https://www.lambdalegal.org/about-us/history.

Laub, Carolyn. "FAIR Education Act's 1st Victory!" GSA Network Blog. Last modified March 23, 2011. https://www.gsanetwork.org/news/blog/fair-education-act's-1st-victory/03/23/11.

Laub, Carolyn. "It Doesn't Inevitably Get Better: Implement the FAIR Education Act." GSA Network. Last modified January 17, 2013. https://www.gsanetwork.org/news/it-doesn't-inevitably-get-better-implement-fair-education-act/011713.

Learning for Justice. "Bayard Rustin: The Fight for Civil and Gay Rights." Accessed
    March 3, 2021. https://www.learningforjustice.org/classroom-resources/lessons/
    bayard-rustin-the-fight-for-civil-and-gay-rights.
Learning for Justice. "Challenging Gender Stereotyping and
    Homophobia in Sports." Lessons. Accessed March 3, 2021. https://
    www.learningforjustice.org/classroom-resources/lessons/
    challenging-gender-stereotyping-and-homophobia-in-sports.
Learning for Justice. "Critiquing Hate Crimes Legislation." Accessed March
    3, 2021. https://www.learningforjustice.org/classroom-resources/lessons/
    critiquing-hate-crimes-legislation.
Learning for Justice. "James Baldwin: Art, Sexuality, and Civil Rights." Accessed
    March 3, 2021. https://www.learningforjustice.org/classroom-resources/lessons/
    james-baldwin-art-sexuality-and-civil-rights.
Learning for Justice. "Lessons." Accessed March 3, 2021. https://www.
    learningforjustice.org/classroom-resources/lessons?keyword=&field_
    grade_level%5B38%5D=38&field_subject%5B13%5D=13&field_
    subject%5B11%5D=11&field_subject%5B19%5D=19&field_topic%5B6%5D=6.
Learning for Justice. "Lorraine Hansberry: LGBT Politics and Civil Rights." Accessed
    March 3, 2021. https://www.learningforjustice.org/classroom-resources/lessons/
    lorraine-hansberry-lgbt-politics-and-civil-rights.
Learning for Justice. "Marriage Equality: Different Strategies for Attaining Equal Rights."
    Accessed March 3, 2021. https://www.learningforjustice.org/classroom-resources/
    lessons/marriage-equality-different-strategies-for-attaining-equal-rights.
Learning for Justice. "Pauli Murray: Fighting Jane and Jim Crow." Accessed March
    3, 2021. https://www.learningforjustice.org/classroom-resources/lessons/
    pauli-murray-fighting-jane-and-jim-crow.
Learning for Justice. "What's So Bad about That's So Gay?" Lessons. Accessed
    March 3, 2021. https://www.learningforjustice.org/classroom-resources/lessons/
    whats-so-bad-about-thats-so-gay.
Ledbetter, Les. "Bill on Homosexual Rights Advances in San Francisco." *New York
    Times*, March 22, 1978. https://www.nytimes.com/1978/03/22/archives/bill-on-
    homosexual-rights-advances-in-san-francisco.html.
Leff, Lisa. "Calif. Gay History Referendum Faces Uphill Battle." Associated Press.
    September 3, 2011. http://news.yahoo.com/calif-gay-history-referendum-faces-
    uphill-battle-220939816.html.
Leno, Mark. "California's FAIR Education Act: Addressing the Bullying Epidemic
    by Ending the Exclusion of LGBT People and Historical Events in Textbooks
    and Classrooms." *QED: A Journal in GLBTQ Worldmaking*, inaugural issue (Fall
    2013): 105–10.
Lesbian, Gay, Bisexual and Transgender Studies. "Lesbian, Gay, Bisexual and
    Transgender Studies AA Major—Active." City College of San Francisco. Accessed
    April 24, 2108. http://www.ccsf.edu/dam/ccsf/documents/OfficeOfInstruction/

Catalog/Programs/LesbianGayBisexualandTransgenderStudies/LesbianGayBisexual andTransgenderStudiesMajor.pdf.

Lesbian, Gay, Bisexual and Transgender Studies. "Lesbian, Gay, Bisexual and Transgender Studies AA Major—Active." City College of San Francisco. Accessed October 1, 2020. https://ccsf.curricunet.com/Report/GetReport?entityId=1137&enti tyType=Program&reportId=29

Lesbian, Gay, Bisexual, & Transgender Studies Program. "The History of LGBT Studies at Maryland." University of Maryland. Accessed June 16, 2014. http://www.lgbts. umd.edu/lgbthistory.html.

Levstik, Linda S., and Keith C. Barton. *Doing History: Investigating with Children in Elementary and Middle Schools.* Mahwah, NJ: Lawrence Erlbaum Associates, 1997.

Lewis, Gregory B. "Black-White Differences in Attitudes towards Homosexuality and Gay Rights." *Public Opinion Quarterly* 67, no. 1 (Spring 2003): 59–78.

Lewis, Maria M., Allison Fetter-Harrot, Jeffrey C. Sun, and Suzanne E. Eckes. "Legal Issues Related to Sexual Orientation, Gender Identity, and Public Schools." *Social Education* 81, no. 5 (2017), 322.

LGBT History Month. "About LGBT History Month." Accessed November 30, 2018. https://lgbthistorymonth.com/background.

LGBTQ Studies. "About." DePaul College of Liberal Arts and Social Sciences. Accessed April 23, 2018, https://las.depaul.edu/academics/LGBTQ+-studies/about/Pages/ default.aspx.

LGBTQ Studies. "Lesbian, Gay, Bisexual, Transgender, and Queer Studies." University of Colorado Boulder. Accessed May 12, 2014. http://lgbt.colorado.edu.

Library of Congress. "Lesbian, Gay, Bisexual, Transgender Pride Month: About." Accessed July 30, 2018. https://www.loc.gov/lgbt-pride-month/about/.

Liptak, Adam. "In Narrow Decision, Supreme Court Sides with Baker Who Turned Away Gay Couple." *New York Times*, June 4, 2018. https://www.nytimes. com/2018/06/04/us/politics/supreme-court-sides-with-baker-who-turned-away- gay-couple.html.

Lo, Malinda. "A Decade of LGBTQ YA since Ash." Malinda Lo. May 14, 2019. https:// www.malindalo.com/blog/2019/3/18/a-decade-of-lgbtq-ya-since-ash.

Lo, Malinda. "LGBTQ+ YA by the Numbers: 2015–2016." Malinda Lo. Accessed April 23, 2018. https://www.malindalo.com/blog/2017/10/12/ LGBTQ+-ya-by-the-numbers-2015–16.

Los Angeles Times Editorial Board. "Gays in Textbooks: Best Told by Historians, Not by Politicians." *Los Angeles Times*, April 8, 2011. http://articles.latimes.com/2011/ apr/08/opinion/la-ed-textbook-20110408.

Machlin, Sherri. "Banned Books Week: And Tango Makes Three." New York Public Library. Last modified September 23, 2013, accessed April 23, 2018. https://www. nypl.org/blog/2013/09/23/banned-books-week-and-tango-makes-three.

Mamone, Tris. "I Wish I Had Learned LGBTQ+ History in High School."
    HuffPost. Last modified June 12, 2018. https://www.huffingtonpost.com/entry/
    opinion-mamone-LGBTQ+-history-school_us_5b1eb078e4b0adfb826c632a.

Mannie, Sierra. "Why Students Are Ignorant about the Civil Rights Movement."
    The Hechinger Report. October 1, 2017. https://hechingerreport.org/
    students-ignorant-civil-rights-movement/.

Massachusetts Department of Elementary and Secondary Education. *2018 History and
    Social Science Framework, Grades Pre Kindergarten to 12.* Malden: Massachusetts
    Department of Elementary and Secondary Education, 2018.

Massachusetts Department of Elementary and Secondary Education. "Safe Schools
    Program for LGBTQ Students." Accessed October 17, 2020. https://www.doe.mass.
    edu/sfs/lgbtq/.

Mass.gov. "Safe Schools Program for LGBTQ Students." Accessed
    October 19, 2020. https://www.mass.gov/info-details/
    safe-schools-program-for-lgbtq-students#inclusive-curriculum-materials-.

McCarthy, Justin. "Record High 60% of Americans Support Same-Sex Marriage."
    Gallup. May 19, 2015. https://news.gallup.com/poll/183272/record-high-americans-
    support-sex-marriage.aspx.

McDonald, Patrick Range. "Stop SB 48 Campaign Seeks to Repeal California's
    Gay History Law." *LA Weekly*, July 25, 2011. http://www.laweekly.com/news/
    stop-sb-48-campaign-seeks-to-repeal-californias-gay-history-law-2390481.

McKinley, Jesse, and Kirk Johnson. "Mormons Tipped Scale in Ban on Gay Marriage."
    New York Times, November 14, 2008. https://www.nytimes.com/2008/11/15/us/
    politics/15marriage.html.

McNaron, Toni. *Poisoned Ivy: Lesbian and Gay Academics Confronting Homophobia.*
    Philadelphia: Temple University Press, 1996.

Minsberg, Talya. "'Boys Are Boys and Girls Are Girls': Idaho Is First State to Bar
    Some Transgender Athletes." *New York Times*, April 1, 2020. https://www.nytimes.
    com/2020/04/01/sports/transgender-idaho-ban-sports.html.

Myers, Steven Lee. "Ideas & Trends; How a 'Rainbow Curriculum' Turned into Fighting
    Words." *New York Times*, December 13, 1992. https://www.nytimes.com/1992/12/13/
    weekinreview/ideas-trends-how-a-rainbow-curriculum-turned-into-fighting-words.
    html.

National Center for Lesbian Rights. "Mission and History." Accessed March 16, 2018.
    http://www.nclrights.org/about-us/mission-history/.

National Center for Lesbian Rights. "NCLR Annual Report 2016–2017." Accessed
    March 16, 2018. http://www.nclrights.org/wp-content/uploads/2017/12/NCL17CA-
    AR-Web-Version-No-Donors.pdf.

National Council of Teachers of English. "About." Accessed October 19, 2020. https://
    ncte.org/about/.

National Council of Teachers of English. "Diverse Gender Expression and Gender Non-Conformity Curriculum in English Grades 7–12." July 1, 2014. https://ncte.org/statement/gender-curriculum-7-12/.

National Council for Teachers of English. "Why Class Size Matters Today." Last modified April 1, 2014, accessed January 21, 2018. http://www2.ncte.org/statement/why-class-size-matters/.

National LGBTQ+ Task Force. "About: Mission and History." Accessed March 16, 2018. http://www.thetaskforce.org/about/mission-history.html.

National Public Radio. "After Rutgers Suicide Columnist Promises 'It Gets Better.'" October 5, 2010. https://www.npr.org/templates/story/story.php?storyId=130349924.

New York City Department of Education. "Health Education." Accessed October 19, 2020. https://www.schools.nyc.gov/learning/learn-at-home/activities-and-supports/health-education.

New Jersey State Legislature. "An Act Concerning Instruction and Instructional Materials in Public Schools and Supplementing Chapter 35 of Title 18A of the New Jersey Statutes." January 31, 2019. https://www.njleg.state.nj.us/2018/Bills/PL19/6_.HTM.

Newman, Leslea. "Kids Books." Leslea Kids. Accessed April 23, 2018. http://www.lesleakids.com/mommy.html.

Newman, Leslea, GLSEN, The Matthew Shepard Foundation, and Candlewick Press. "He Continues to Make a Difference: Commemorating the Life of Matthew Shepard." GLSEN. Accessed July 6, 2015. http://www.glsen.org/matthewshepard.

Newman, Maria. "Board Adopts a Curriculum about AIDS." *New York Times*, January 19, 1995. https://www.nytimes.com/1995/01/19/nyregion/board-adopts-a-curriculum-about-aids.html.

NYC Department of Education. "Hidden Voices: LGBTQ+ Stories in United States History." WeTeachNYC. Accessed March 11, 2021. https://www.weteachnyc.org/media2016/filer_public/e4/6e/e46e71d1-f2ca-4ce3-89d2-6ce2db1decda/hv_lgbtq_v13_ada.pdf.

O'Brien, Anne. "Inclusive Anti-Bullying Policies Create a Safer Environment for LGBT Students." George Lucas Educational Foundation. Last modified October 27, 2015, accessed April 24, 2018. https://www.edutopia.org/blog/inclusive-anti-bullying-policies-create-safer-environment-lgbt-students-anne-obrien.

Office of Superintendent of Public Instruction. "Eleventh Grade Unit Outlines." Last modified October 8, 2018. http://www.k12.wa.us/SocialStudies/Outlines/UnitOutlinesEleventhGrade.pdf, p. 7.

ONE Archives. "AIDS and HIV Activism." Accessed October 8, 2020. https://www.onearchives.org/wp-content/uploads/2019/02/one-archives-foundation-los-angeles-aids-crisis.pdf.

ONE Archives. "LGBTQ Civil Rights." Accessed October 9, 2020. https://www.onearchives.org/wp-content/uploads/2019/02/one-archives-foundation-civil-rights.pdf.

ONE Archives. "LGBTQ Equality, 1950–1970." Accessed October 9, 2020. https://www. onearchives.org/wp-content/uploads/2019/02/one-archives-foundation-coming-out. pdf.

"Oregon Law Now Requires Schools Teach LGBTQ Curriculum to All Ages." *Pulpit and Pen*, July 23, 2019. https://pulpitandpen.org/2019/07/23/ oregon-law-now-requires-schools-teach-lgbtq-curriculum-to-all-ages/.

Oregon Legislative Assembly. "House Bill 2023." May 23, 2019. https://olis.leg.state. or.us/liz/2019R1/Downloads/MeasureDocument/HB2023/Enrolled.

Original LGBT History Month Committee Members. "Op-ed: The Story behind the First LGBT History Month." *The Advocate*, September 2, 2015. https://www.advocate. com/commentary/2015/09/02/op-ed-story-behind-first-lgbt-history-month.

Our Family Coalition. "Staff." Accessed April 20, 2018. http://www.ourfamily.org/about/ our-staff.

Our Family Coalition. "Welcoming and Inclusive Schools Program." Accessed April 18, 2018. www.ourfamily.org/schools/wisp.

Pacific Justice Institute. "Stop SB 48 Petitions Now Available." Last modified July 28, 2011. http://www.pacificjustice.org/press-releases/ stop-sb-48-petitions-now-available.

Palencia, Roland. "Letter to Fair Political Practices Commission." Equality California. Last modified September 28, 2011. http://www.eqca.org/atf/cf/{34f258b3-8482- 4943-91cb-08c4b0246a88}/SB%2048%20COMPLAINT%20TO%20FPPC%2009-28- 2011.PDF.

Palencia, Roland. "Letter to Governor Jerry Brown: EQCA Urges Your Signature Re: SB 48- F.A.I.R. Education Act (Leno)." Equality California. Last modified July 7, 2011. http://www.eqca.org/atf/cf/%7B34F258B3-8482-4943-91CB-08C4B0246A88%7D/ SB%2048%20EQCA%20Governor%20Letter.pdf.

Pannoni, Alexandra. "Don't Overlook LGBTQ+ History in High School." *U.S. News and World Report*, October 16, 2017. www.usnews. com/high-schools/blogs/high-school-notes/articles/2017-10-16/ dont-overlook-LGBTQ+-history-in-high-school.

PBS Learning Media. "Activism: Marsha P. Johnson." Accessed October 9, 2020. https://www.pbslearningmedia.org/resource/fp18.lgbtq.marsha.p.johnson/ activism-marsha-p-johnson/support-materials/.

PBS Learning Media. "Alain Locke." Accessed October 8, 2020. https://www.pbslearningmedia.org/resource/fp20-alain-locke/ alain-locke-first-person-classroom-understanding-lgbtq-identity-educators-toolkit/.

PBS Learning Media. "Audre Lorde." Accessed October 8, 2020. https://www. pbslearningmedia.org/resource/fp19.lgbtq.lorde/audre-lorde/.

PBS Learning Media. "James Baldwin." Accessed October 8, 2020. https://www. pbslearningmedia.org/resource/fp18-lgbtq-baldwin/james-baldwin/.

PBS Learning Media. "The LGBTQ Movement and the Stonewall Riots." Accessed October 9, 2020. https://www.pbslearningmedia.org/resource/fp18-socst-lgbtq-stonewall/the-lgbtq-movement-and-stonewall-riot/.

PBS Learning Media. "Lorraine Hansberry." Accessed October 8, 2020. https://www.pbslearningmedia.org/resource/fp19.lgbtq.hansberry/lorraine-hansberry/.

PBS Learning Media. "Pauli Murray." Accessed October 8, 2020. https://www.pbslearningmedia.org/resource/fp20-vid-pauli-murray/pauli-murray/.

PBS Learning Media. "We'Wha." Accessed October 8, 2020. https://www.pbslearningmedia.org/resource/fp20-we-wha/wewha-first-person-classroom/.

Penan, Hayley. "Fair Education Act." *The Notice*, June 3, 2013. http://thenoticeca.com/2013/06/03/fair-education-act/.

Pew Research Center. "Attitudes on Same-Sex Marriage." May 14, 2019. https://www.pewforum.org/fact-sheet/changing-attitudes-on-gay-marriage/.

Pew Research Center. "Changing Faiths: Latinos and the Transformation of American Religion." April 25, 2007. https://www.pewresearch.org/hispanic/2007/04/25/changing-faiths-latinos-and-the-transformation-of-american-religion/.

Pew Research Center. *A Survey of LGBT Americans: Attitudes, Experiences and Values in Changing Times*. Washington, DC: Pew Research Center, 2013. https://www.pewresearch.org/social-trends/2013/06/13/a-survey-of-lgbt-americans/.

PFLAG. "Cultivating Respect: Safe Schools for All." Accessed March 16, 2018. https://www.pflag.org/cultivating-respect-safe-schools-all.

PFLAG. "Our People." Accessed April 20, 2018. https://www.pflag.org/about/our-people.

PFLAG. "Our Story." Accessed March 16, 2018. https://www.pflag.org/our-story.

PFLAG. "PFLAG Policy Statements." March 18, 2017, accessed March 7, 2018. https://www.pflag.org/policystatements.

Philipps, Dave. "New Rule for Transgender Troops: Stick to Your Birth Sex, or Leave." *New York Times*, March 13, 2019. https://www.nytimes.com/2019/03/13/us/transgender-troops-ban.html.

Pietsch, Brian. "Arizona Governor Vetoes Bill Restricting L.G.B.T.Q. Education." *New York Times*, April 21, 2021. https://www.nytimes.com/2021/04/21/us/doug-ducey-gender-sexual-orientation-aids-lgbtq.html?action=click&module=In%20Other%20News&pgtype=Homepage.

Presgraves, Daryl. "Schools across the Country Celebrate 10th Anniversary of GLSEN's No Name-Calling Week." GLSEN. Last modified January 20, 2014. https://www.glsen.org/article/10th-anniversary-glsens-no-name-calling-week.

Pride Center of Vermont. "LGBT History Month: Rodney Wilson." October 31, 2017. http://www.pridecentervt.org/news/item/lgbt-history-month-rodney-wilson.

Proctor & Gamble and GLAAD. *LGBTQ Inclusion in Advertising and Media: Executive Summary*. New York: GLAAD, 2020. https://www.glaad.org/sites/default/files/P%26G_AdvertisingResearch.pdf.

Project Look Sharp. "About Project Look Sharp." Last modified April 2018. https://www.projectlooksharp.org/?action=about_pls.

Project Look Sharp. "Media Construction of Social Justice: Case Study: Gay Affirmative or Gay Negative?" Accessed July 17, 2015. http://www.projectlooksharp.org/?action=justice.

Protect Kids Foundation. "Help Stop Passage of California Bill (SB 48) Requiring Promotion of Homosexuality in Grades K–12." Last modified February 28, 2011. http://www.protectkidsfoudnation.org/?page_id=1356.

Public Policy Institute of California. "Just the Facts: California's Population." April 2020. https://www.ppic.org/publication/californias-population/#:~:text=No%20race%20or%20ethnic%20group,the%202018%20American%20Community%20Survey.

"The Rainbow, Revised." *New York Times*, January 30, 1993. https://www.nytimes.com/1993/01/30/opinion/the-rainbow-revised.html.

ReCAPP. "Toward Understanding … Some of Us Are Lesbian or Gay." Last modified 2007, accessed August 1, 2018. http://recapp.etr.org/recapp/index.cfm?fuseaction=pages.LearningActivitiesDetail&PageID=170.

Ring, Trudy. "Morehouse to Offer Course in Black LGBT History, Culture." *The Advocate*, December 20, 2012. https://www.advocate.com/society/education/2012/12/20/morehouse-offer-course-black-lgbt-history-and-culture.

Romesburg, Don. "Words That Shape the World: Historians, Teachers, and Partnerships for LGBT History." Presentation at the American Historical Association Annual Meeting, Washington, DC, January 5, 2018.

Romesburg, Don, Leila J. Rupp, and D. M. Donahue. *Making the Framework FAIR: California History-Social Science Framework Proposed LGBT Revisions Related to the FAIR Education Act*. San Francisco, CA: Committee on Lesbian, Gay, Bisexual, and Transgender History, 2014.

Romesburg, Don, Stacie Brensilver Berman, David Duffield, Daniel Hurewitz, Rachel Reinhard, and Wendy Rouse. "Words That Shape the World: Historians, Teachers, and Partnerships for LGBT History." Presentation at the American Historical Association Annual Meeting, Washington, DC, January 5, 2018.

Rosky, Clifford. "Anti Gay Curriculum Laws." *Columbia Law Review* 117, no. 6 (October 2017): 1461–541.

Safe Schools Coalition. "Our Mission." About Us. Last modified April 7, 2015. http://www.safeschoolscoalition.org/about_us.html#OurMission.

San Diego State University. "Lesbian, Gay, Bisexual and Transgender Studies | What Can I Do with This Major?" Career Services. Accessed April 24, 2018. https://go.sdsu.edu/student_affairs/career/lesbiangaybisexualtransgender.aspx.

SaveCalifornia.org. "Pro-Family Response to Jerry Brown's Signing of SB 48." Last modified July 14, 2011. http://savecalifornia.com/7-14-11-pro-family-response-to-jerry-brown-signing-lgbt-role-models-bill.html.

Schmidt, Peter. "N.Y.C. Debate over 'Rainbow' Curriculum Still Raging in Many Board Races." *Education Week*, March 24, 1993. https://www.edweek.org/ew/articles/1993/03/24/26board.h12.html.

Senate Committee on Education. "Instruction and Instructional Materials: Sexual Orientation." Bill Analysis. Last modified March 23, 2011. http://www.leginfo.ca.gov/pub/11-12/bill/sen/sb_0001-0050/sb_48_cfa_20110322_113330_sen_comm.html.

Senate Judiciary Committee. "Discrimination: The California Student Civil Rights Act." SB 777 Senate Bill—Bill Analysis. Last modified April 9, 2007. ftp://leginfo.ca.gov/pub/07-08/bill/sen/sb_0751-0800/sb_777_cfa_20070418_124057_sen_comm.html.

Senate Judiciary Committee. "Instruction: Prohibition of Discriminatory Content." Bill Analysis. Last modified April 5, 2011. http://www.leginfo.ca.gov/pub/11-12/bill/sen/sb_0001-0050/sb_48_cfa_20110404_134404_sen_comm.html.

Senate Rules Committee. "Instruction: Prohibition of Discriminatory Content." Bill Analysis. Last modified March 29, 2011. http://leginfo.ca.gov/pub/11-12/bill/sen/sb_0001-0050/sb_48_cfa_20110408_105410_sen_floor.html.

Sex, etc. "Stories." Accessed August 1, 2018. https://sexetc.org/sex-ed/info-center/stories/.

Snider, Kevin T. "Request to Prepare Circulating Title and Summary Using the Amended Language." State of California Department of Justice: Office of the Attorney General. Last modified December 21, 2011. http://oag.ca.gov/system/files/initiatives/pdfs/11-0093%20(i1038_11-0093_ais_(stop_sb_48)).pdf.

Southern Poverty Law Center. "Know Your Rights: Students and LGBTQ+ Rights at School." Accessed April 18, 2018. https://www.splcenter.org/know-your-rights-students-LGBTQ+-rights-school.

Sprigg, Peter. "Homosexuality in Your Child's School." Family Research Council. Last modified 2006. https://downloads.frc.org/EF/EF06K26.pdf.

Stanford History Education Group. "Stonewall Riots." Accessed October 9, 2020. https://sheg.stanford.edu/history-lessons/stonewall-riots.

State of Illinois. "HB0246." 101st General Assembly. August 9, 2019. https://www.ilga.gov/legislation/fulltext.asp?DocName=10100HB0246&GA=101&SessionId=108&DocTypeId=HB&LegID=114183&DocNum=0246&GAID=15&Session=.

Stein, Marc. *Rethinking the Gay and Lesbian Movement (American Social and Political Movements of the 20th Century)*. New York: Routledge, 2012.

Stewart-Winter, Timothy. "Queer Law and Order: Sex, Criminality, and Policing in the Late Twentieth-Century United States." *Journal of American History* 102, no. 1 (June 2015): 61–72.

Stop SB 48. "SB 48 and the Churches." Last modified 2011, accessed June 20, 2015. http://archive.constantcontact.com/fs078/1100422530046/archive/1107189511593.html.

Stopbullying.gov. "Laws & Policies." Last modified September 2017, accessed April 25, 2018. https://www.stopbullying.gov/laws/index.html.

Stopbullying.gov. "LGBTQ+ Youth." Last modified September 24, 2017, accessed April 24, 2018. https://www.stopbullying.gov/at-risk/groups/lgbt/index.html.

Supreme Court of the United States. "*Lawrence v. Texas* (02-102)." Legal Information Institute. Last modified June 26, 2003. https://www.law.cornell.edu/supct/html/02-102.ZO.html.

Taylor, Kathe. *Comprehensive Sexual Health Education Data Survey*. Olympia, WA: Office of Superintendent of Public Instruction, 2019. https://www.k12.wa.us/sites/default/files/public/communications/2019-12-Sexual-Health-Education-Data-Survey.pdf.

Teaching LGBTQ History. "Home." Accessed October 24, 2020. http://www.lgbtqhistory.org/.

Teaching Tolerance. "Creating an LGBT-Inclusive School Climate." Accessed August 1, 2018. https://www.tolerance.org/magazine/publications/creating-an-lgbtinclusive-school-climate.

Teaching Tolerance. *Teaching the Movement: The State of Civil Rights Education in the United States in 2011*. Montgomery, AL: Southern Poverty Law Center, 2011.

The Learning Network. "Teaching and Learning about Gay History and Issues." *New York Times*. Last modified June 2016. https://learning.blogs.nytimes.com/2011/11/22/teaching-and-learning-about-gay-history-and-issues/.

The State Education Department and The University of the State of New York. "New York State Grades 9–12 Social Studies Framework." New York State Education Department. Last modified February 2017, accessed April 25, 2018. http://www.nysed.gov/common/nysed/files/9-12FrameworkRevFebruary2017.docx.

Thornton, Stephen. "Silence on Gays and Lesbians in Social Studies Curriculum." *Social Education* 67, no. 4 (2003): 226–30.

Thornton, Stephen. *Teaching Social Studies that Matters: Curriculum for Active Learning*. New York: Teachers College, 2005.

"Timeline: Proposition 8." *Los Angeles Times*, November 30, 2012. https://www.latimes.com/local/la-prop8-timeline-story.html.

Tran, Mark. "Arnold Schwarzenegger Signs Law Establishing Harvey Milk Day." *The Guardian*, October 13, 2009. http://www.theguardian.com/world/2009/oct/13/schwarzenneger-law-harvey-milk-day.

Trecker, Janice Law. "Women in U.S. History High-School Textbooks." In *Sex Bias in the Schools: The Research Evidence*, edited by Janice Pottker and Andrew Fishel, 146–61. Madison, NJ: Fairleigh Dickinson University Press, 1977.

Tyack, David, and Larry Cuban. *Tinkering toward Utopia: A Century of Public School Reform*. Cambridge: Harvard University Press, 1995.

UC Berkeley History-Social Science Project. "LGBTQ History." Accessed October 23, 2020. https://ucbhssp.berkeley.edu/teacher-resources/lgbtq.

UCLA Lesbian, Gay, Bisexual, Transgender, and Queer Studies. "History." UCLA. Accessed April 15, 2018. https://lgbtqstudies.ucla.edu/about/history/.

United States Department of Education. "U.S Education Department Releases
    Analysis of State Bullying Laws and Policies." Last modified December 6,
    2011, accessed April 26, 2018. https://www.ed.gov/news/press-releases/
    us-education-department-releases-analysis-state-bullying-laws-and-policies.

United States Congress. "S.311—Safe Schools Improvement Act of 2015." Accessed
    April 13, 2018. https://www.congress.gov/bill/114th-congress/senate-bill/311.

University of Maryland. "Department of Women's Studies." Accessed October 1, 2020.
    http://wmst.umd.edu/academics/courses.

University of Maryland. "Fall 2020 WMST, LGBT, & Black WMST Undergraduate
    Courses, Department of Women's Studies." Accessed October 1, 2020. http://wmst.
    umd.edu/academics/courses.

University of Maryland. "The History of LGBT Studies at Maryland." Accessed June 16,
    2014. http://www.lgbts.umd/edu/lgbthistory.html.

Van Slooten, Phillip. "LGBTQ-Inclusive Curriculum Laws Take Effect in N.J.,
    Ill." *Washington Blade*, September 9, 2020. https://www.washingtonblade.
    com/2020/09/09llo/lgbtq-inclusive-curriculum-laws-take-effect-in-n-j-ill/.

"Vote: Assembly Floor: Third Reading—Final Passage." LegiScan. Accessed October 14,
    2020. https://legiscan.com/NJ/rollcall/S1569/id/780779.

"Vote: Senate Floor: Third Reading—Final Passage." LegiScan. Accessed October 14,
    2020. https://legiscan.com/NJ/rollcall/S1569/id/768662.

"Vote: Third Reading in the House." LegiScan. Accessed October 14, 2020. https://
    legiscan.com/IL/rollcall/HB0246/id/820403.

"Vote: Third Reading in the Senate." LegiScan. Accessed October 14, 2020. https://
    legiscan.com/IL/rollcall/HB0246/id/870676.

Washington State Department of Health. "Sexual Health Education." Accessed
    October 19, 2020. https://www.doh.wa.gov/CommunityandEnvironment/Schools/
    SexualHealthEducation.

Waxman, Olivia B. "As More States Require Schools to Teach LGBTQ History,
    Resources for Teachers Expand." *Time*, December 13, 2019. https://time.
    com/5747670/lgbtq-history-resources/.

Webb, Jo Ann. "U.S. Department of Education Continues Work after First-Ever
    Federal Summit on Bullying." U.S. Department of Education. Last modified
    August 16, 2010, accessed April 26, 2018. https://www.ed.gov/news/press-releases/
    us-department-education-continues-work-after-first-ever-federal-summit-bullying.

Weingarten, Elizabeth. "Is This the End of the Crusade for Gender-Equal Curricula?"
    The Atlantic, June 15, 2017. https://www.theatlantic.com/education/archive/2017/06/
    is-this-the-end-of-the-crusade-for-gender-equal-curricula/530493/.

Weiser, Scott. "Legislation Expands Mandatory Civics and History Education to Include
    Asians and LGBTQ Minority Groups." *Complete Colorado*, April 12, 2019. https://
    pagetwo.completecolorado.com/2019/04/12/legislation-expands-mandatory-civics-
    and-history-education-to-include-asians-and-lgbtq-minority-groups/.

Welcoming Schools. "Creating Safe and Welcoming Schools for All Children & Families." Accessed March 16, 2018. http://www.welcomingschools.org.

Welcoming Schools. "Great LGBTQ+ Inclusive Picture and Middle Grade Books." Accessed April 15, 2018. http://www.welcomingschools.org/pages/books-inclusive-of-LGBTQ+-family-members-and-characters/.

Welcoming Schools. "Program History." Accessed April 18, 2018. http://www.welcomingschools.org/our-program/history/.

Weymouth, Lally. "Mrs. Cummins's Triumph." *Washington Post*, January 8, 1993. https://www.washingtonpost.com/archive/opinions/1993/01/08/mrs-cumminss-triumph/4b23129f-a0e3-49ed-a11c-64e473b45d09/?utm_term=.1f338993de2e.

The White House. "Executive Order on Guaranteeing an Educational Environment Free from Discrimination on the Basis of Sex, Including Sexual Orientation or Gender Identity." March 8, 2021. https://www.whitehouse.gov/briefing-room/presidential-actions/2021/03/08/executive-order-on-guaranteeing-an-educational-environment-free-from-discrimination-on-the-basis-of-sex-including-sexual-orientation-or-gender-identity/?emci=ebbc8095-b482-eb11-85aa-00155d43c992&emdi=9d49caa2-4383-eb11-85aa-00155d43c992&ceid=427726.

The White House. "Inaugural Address by President Barack Obama." Last modified January 21, 2013. https://obamawhitehouse.archives.gov/the-press-office/2013/01/21/inaugural-address-president-barack-obama.

Will, George. "Just Another Kind of Love." *Washington Post*, December 6, 1992. https://www.washingtonpost.com/archive/opinions/1992/12/06/just-another-kind-of-love/42ef9eca-5f3b-4bf2-9a6c-780b8bb14ecc/?utm_term=.80b0e305c59b.

Wilson, Rodney. "Knowing LGBT History Is Knowing Yourself." *The Advocate*, October 1, 2015. https://www.advocate.com/commentary/2015/10/01/knowing-lgbt-history-knowing-yourself.

Yale University Lesbian, Gay, Bisexual, and Transgender Studies. "The History of LGBTS at Yale." Yale University. Accessed April 15, 2018. https://lgbts.yale.edu/history-lgbts-yale.

Youth in Motion. "Brother Outsider: The Life of Bayard Rustin Curriculum Guide." Frameline. Accessed July 15, 2015. http://rustin.org/wp-content/uploads/Discussion%20Guide%20-%20Brother%20Outsider.pdf.

Zimmerman, Jonathan. "Where the Customer Is King: The Textbook in American Culture." In *A History of the Book in America, Volume 5: The Enduring Book: Print Culture in Postwar America*, edited by David Paul Nord, Joan Shelley Rubin, and Michael Schudson, 304–24. Chapel Hill: University of North Carolina Press, 2009.

Zimmerman, Jonathan. *Whose America? Culture Wars in the Public Schools*. Cambridge: Harvard University Press, 2002.

Index

www.ingramcontent.com/pod-product-compliance
Lightning Source LLC
Chambersburg PA
CBHW060153280326
41932CB00012B/1744